Irish Gothic

Edinburgh Companions to the Gothic

Series Editors
Andrew Smith, University of Sheffield
William Hughes, Bath Spa University

This series provides a comprehensive overview of the Gothic from the eighteenth century to the present day. Each volume takes either a period, place, or theme and explores their diverse attributes, contexts and texts via completely original essays. The volumes provide an authoritative critical tool for both scholars and students of the Gothic.

Volumes in the series are edited by leading scholars in their field and make a cutting-edge contribution to the field of Gothic studies.

Each volume:
- Presents an innovative and critically challenging exploration of the historical, thematic and theoretical understandings of the Gothic from the eighteenth century to the present day
- Provides a critical forum in which ideas about Gothic history and established Gothic themes are challenged
- Supports the teaching of the Gothic at an advanced undergraduate level and at masters level
- Helps readers to rethink ideas concerning periodisation and to question the critical approaches which have been taken to the Gothic

Published Titles
The Victorian Gothic: An Edinburgh Companion
  Andrew Smith and William Hughes
Romantic Gothic: An Edinburgh Companion
  Angela Wright and Dale Townshend
American Gothic Culture: An Edinburgh Companion
  Joel Faflak and Jason Haslam
Women and the Gothic: An Edinburgh Companion
  Avril Horner and Sue Zlosnik
Scottish Gothic: An Edinburgh Companion
  Carol Margaret Davison and Monica Germanà
The Gothic and Theory: An Edinburgh Companion
  Jerrold E. Hogle and Robert Miles
Twenty-First-Century Gothic: An Edinburgh Companion
  Maisha Wester and Xavier Aldana Reyes
Gothic Film: An Edinburgh Companion
  Richard J. Hand and Jay McRoy
Twentieth-Century Gothic: An Edinburgh Companion
  Sorcha Ní Fhlainn and Bernice M. Murphy
Italian Gothic: An Edinburgh Companion
  Marco Malvestio and Stefano Serafini
Irish Gothic: An Edinburgh Companion
  Jarlath Killeen and Christina Morin

Visit the Edinburgh Companions to the Gothic website at:
www.edinburghuniversitypress.com/series/EDCG

Irish Gothic

An Edinburgh Companion

Edited by
Jarlath Killeen and
Christina Morin

EDINBURGH
University Press

Edinburgh University Press is one of the leading university presses in the UK. We publish academic books and journals in our selected subject areas across the humanities and social sciences, combining cutting-edge scholarship with high editorial and production values to produce academic works of lasting importance. For more information visit our website: edinburghuniversitypress.com

© editorial matter and organisation Jarlath Killeen and Christina Morin, 2023
© the chapters their several authors, 2023

Edinburgh University Press Ltd
The Tun – Holyrood Road
12(2f) Jackson's Entry
Edinburgh EH8 8PJ

Typeset in 10.5/13pt Sabon LT Pro
by Cheshire Typesetting Ltd, Cuddington, Cheshire, and
printed and bound in Great Britain

A CIP record for this book is available from the British Library

ISBN 978 1 3995 0055 5 (hardback)
ISBN 978 1 3995 0057 9 (webready PDF)
ISBN 978 1 3995 0058 6 (epub)

The right of Jarlath Killeen and Christina Morin to be identified as the editors of this work has been asserted in accordance with the Copyright, Designs and Patents Act 1988, and the Copyright and Related Rights Regulations 2003 (SI No. 2498).

Contents

List of Figures	vii
Acknowledgements	viii
Introduction: Exorcising the Dead, Summoning the Living *Jarlath Killeen and Christina Morin*	1

PART I: IRISH GOTHIC IN THE EIGHTEENTH AND NINETEENTH CENTURIES

1.	'Quitting the Plain and Useful Path of History and Fact': Early Irish Gothic and the Literary Marketplace *Christina Morin*	29
2.	'How Mute their Tongues': Irish Gothic Poetry in the Nineteenth Century *Julia M. Wright*	46

PART II: IRISH GOTHIC GENRES AND FORMS

3.	'A Dead, Living, Murdered Man': Staging the Irish Gothic *Christopher Morash*	65
4.	Gothic Forms in Irish Cinema *Michael Patrick Gillespie*	83
5.	Gothic Fiction and Irish Children's Literature *Anne Markey*	98
6.	Irish Ecogothic *Eóin Flannery*	114
7.	Gothic Fiction in the Irish Language *Jack Fennell*	135

PART III: IRISH GOTHIC, THEOLOGY, AND CONFESSIONAL IDENTITIES

8. Protestant Gothic 153
   Alison Milbank

9. Bram Stoker, *Dracula* and the Irish Dimension 174
   Jarlath Killeen

10. Irish Catholic Writers and the Gothic: Situating Thomas Furlong's *The Doom of Derenzie* (1829) 194
    Sinéad Sturgeon

PART IV: IRISH GOTHIC WRITERS: GENDER AND SEXUALITY

11. Irish Women Writers and the Supernatural 213
    Melissa Edmundson

12. Reflection, Anxiety and the Feminised Body: Contemporary Irish Gothic 232
    Ellen Scheible

13. Foreign Bodies, Irish Voices: Gothic Masculinities in Irish Literature, Film and Radio Drama 252
    Sorcha de Brún

Notes on Contributors 272
Index 276

Figures

1 Settlement V, 2011, © Anthony Haughey. Courtesy of the artist. 6
2 This contemporary etching of an impressively-muscled Edmund Kean in the title role of Maturin's *Bertram* (Drury Lane, London; 1816) suggests the opposite of the 'wasted frame' mentioned in the script; instead, we have the returned past as full bodily presence.
The print is in the collection of the Billy Rose Theatre Division, The New York Public Library. *The New York Public Library Digital Collections*. 1816. digitalcollections.nypl.org/items/510d47dd-ecdd-a3d9-e040-e00a18064a99. 70
3 The stage minimalism of Yeats's *Purgatory* starkly frames the juxtaposition of the living and the dead. In this 2004 production, the 'dead, living, murdered man', is played by a third actor, Ned Dennehy, while Eamon Morrissey and Matthew Dunphy play the Old Man and the Boy, respectively. *Purgatory* by W.B. Yeats, Abbey Theatre, Peacock stage, 2004. 72
Photo: Kip Carroll; Courtesy of the Abbey Theatre Archive.
4 In her notes for the play, Marina Carr refers to the Catwoman character as 'gothic'; however, the play deploys many Gothic conventions. This photo shows Joan O'Hara as Catwoman and Olwen Fouéré as Hester Swane in a scene from the world premiere of *By The Bog of Cats …* by Marina Carr, Abbey Theatre, 1998. 73
Photo: Amelia Stein; Courtesy of the Abbey Theatre Archive.
5 'The Irish "Vampire"', *Punch*, 24 October 1885, 199. Courtesy of the British Library. 179

Acknowledgements

This collection was initially conceived of and proposed in the early days of the COVID-19 pandemic, shortly before Ireland and much of the rest of the world went into national lockdowns. We are grateful to our contributors for their dedication to the volume despite the very trying circumstances of the Coronavirus crisis. Thanks also to series editors Bill Hughes and Andy Smith, and to Edinburgh University Press more widely, for their patience and flexibility throughout the compilation of this *Companion*.

Introduction: Exorcising the Dead, Summoning the Living
Jarlath Killeen and Christina Morin

Then she did something I wished she had not. Reaching into her cloak she pulled out a copy of that accursed book that I wish I had never seen or begun to contrive. When I bring to mind the thousands of wasted hours it represents, the mausoleum made of paper, the hundreds of miles I walked in its wretched company, I hate myself for ever having been born with the storytelling disease and having squandered, in its service, whatever life I was intended to live.

'This work is your country,' she said. 'Is it no consolation?'

It took every famished fibre of the little manliness I have remaining not to seize the book from her hands and hurl it out the window. Followed by her. And me.

'No,' I said. 'It is not'.

— Joseph O'Connor, *Shadowplay*

An evocative retelling of the haunted and haunting composition process of Bram Stoker's now most famous work, *Dracula* (1897), Joseph O'Connor's award-winning novel, *Shadowplay* (2019), provides a suggestive reflection on the contemporary reception and more modern afterlife of what has become both the ur-vampire tale and the quintessential Irish Gothic.[1] In the exchange quoted above, an imagined conversation between Stoker and famed British actress Ellen Terry (1847–1928), O'Connor's work poignantly highlights the discrepancy between its reasonable, but by no means remarkable, success upon first publication and its current status as vampire text to end them all. Destined never to know or benefit from the extraordinary cultural footprint his novel began to make in the years following his death, Stoker feels himself brought low by a creativity that serves only to sicken and starve him. Entombed within the pages of his own book, Stoker here suggests, he has wasted his time, his effort, his very life for nothing, an idea that recurs in several recent fictions featuring Stoker, including Dacre Stoker's sequel to *Dracula, The Undead* (2009), Elizabeth Kostova's *The Historian* (2005), Neil Jordan's *Mistaken* (2011) and Kim Newman's Anno Dracula novels (1992–2014). Yet, as is suggested by the legacy of Stoker's novel in the twentieth and twenty-first centuries – demonstrated in the countless adaptations, translations, new media treatments and material culture derivations, of which O'Connor's atmospheric fiction is but one example – *Dracula* and, by extension, its creator, continues vitally to live on and inform both popular culture and its academic study. Indeed, so prominent has *Dracula* become, particularly in our understanding of Gothic and Irish Gothic literature, that it stands almost alone, functioning, as O'Connor's Ellen Terry puts it, as a 'country' in itself while also near monolithically representing the Gothic literary production of its author's native country, Ireland.

While O'Connor's novel draws attention to the single-mindedness with which we view *Dracula* when it comes to discussions of Irish Gothic – an issue to which we will return later in this volume, with Jarlath Killeen's consideration of *Dracula*'s 'Irish dimension' – it also highlights the persistent appeal of the body of literature we now refer to as 'Irish Gothic' or 'the Irish Gothic'.[2] *Shadowplay* is just one recent indication of the ways in which Irish Gothic has become enduringly lodged in a transnational cultural consciousness. It is now possible, for instance, to spend a lazy Saturday evening binge-watching the Canadian YouTube web series *Carmilla* (2014–2016), as you sit beneath your artistic word-art poster of *The Picture of Dorian Gray* and sip on Melmoth the Wanderer IPA from your *Dracula*-themed mug.[3] If you would prefer to expand your horizons beyond the 'holy trinity' of Irish Gothic – Le Fanu, Maturin and Stoker – you might easily turn elsewhere for your Irish Gothic fix. Settle down instead with the award-winning Irish Film Board-funded horror flick *The Lodgers* (2017), one of Tramp Press's recent editions of the ghost stories of Dorothy Macardle (1889–1958), or the 2019 Starz/RTÉ adaptation of Tana French's Gothic noir tale *In the Woods* (2007). Suggestive of the uptick in Gothic production following the decline of the Celtic Tiger (Killeen), these works attest to the vibrancy of contemporary Gothic in Ireland. At the same time, they remind us of the continued debates surrounding this body of work. What exactly constitutes this phenomenon of 'Irish Gothic' or 'the Irish Gothic'? Is it the literary expression of a peculiarly national form of divided subjectivity, exploring – as many early Irish Gothic scholars argued – the repressed fears, anxieties and desires of the Anglo-Irish population? Is it a canon, a mode, a form, a tradition, a genre, a feeling or all of these at the same time? What relationship, if any, does it maintain with alternative forms of cultural expression in Ireland, or with Gothic elsewhere? Why has so much of it been forgotten or overlooked in the historiographies of Irish cultural production, on the one hand, and of the Gothic, on the other?

These are questions that have informed a number of scholarly considerations in recent years, with few definitive answers reached.[4] Not wishing unnecessarily to re-visit this very well-trodden terrain or to provide reductive resolutions, it is nevertheless worth briefly summarising conventional scholarly conceptualisations of Irish Gothic literature before moving on in more detail to recent re-appraisals. Long conceived of as a derivative literary production comprised of servile imitations of a more established English literary tradition, Irish Gothic has been pushed to the peripheries of what Pasquale Casanova compellingly terms 'the world republic of letters' (xii). Only a select few authors and texts have managed to secure for themselves the 'literary capital' necessary to move, in Casanova's terms, 'from literary inexistence to existence, from invisibility to the condition of literature' (17, 126). Those that have successfully negotiated this transition – in large part thanks to translation and adaptation – have naturally tended to form the focal point of scholarly analysis. For much of the twentieth century, psychoanalytically informed readings of a handful of works, including *Carmilla*, *Dracula* and *The Picture of Dorian Gray*, dominated the field. These helped produce the stubbornly durable idea of the Gothic in Ireland as defined by its expression of the fears and desires of a minority ruling class worried about annihilation at the hands of an unruly native population.[5] Despite the popularity of 'the Gothic novel' in Britain and Ireland in the latter half of the eighteenth century, particularly in the 1790s, Irish Gothic has traditionally been seen to begin with the publication in 1820 of Maturin's *Melmoth the Wanderer*. The Irish Big House setting of that novel's frame narrative, combined with its attention to questions of inheritance and dispossession, as well as its striking exploration of psychological terrors, signalled a new Irish chapter in the history of Anglophone Gothic, which was, by then, falling out of favour. However, according to traditional accounts, the Irish Gothic as a fully-fledged genre would only come into its own in the latter half of the nineteenth century, with the works of Le Fanu, Wilde and Stoker, each of whom displace their concern with Ireland onto English settings, thus encouraging an understanding of their engagement with Ireland as allegorical.

Scholarship in the late twentieth and early twenty-first centuries has sought to move away from strictly psychoanalytic or allegorical readings of Irish Gothic, in part through the recovery of a much larger and more varied body of texts than hitherto recognised. On the one hand, this comprises the fleshing out of the oeuvres of writers like Le Fanu and Stoker, nuancing their engagement with the Gothic by way of a consideration of their lesser-known works.[6] Such work is the matter of both academic and public interest, as is clear in projects such as Katie Mishler's 'Mapping Gothic Dublin' at the Museum of Literature Ireland,[7] the inaugural Le Fanu Festival hosted in Abington, Co. Limerick in October 2021,[8] and the 'Ragged, Livid & on Fire: The Wanderings of Melmoth at 200' celebration at Marsh's Library that same month.[9] On the other hand, it involves recovering to view the scores of works, in particular those from the late eighteenth and early nineteenth centuries, that might be classified as Irish Gothic but which have been neglected or overlooked in both Irish and Gothic literary historiography.[10] A hitherto unthinkable bibliographic expanse of Gothic and Irish Gothic literature has been opened in recent years, in part through the digitisation of key archives, including the Castle Corvey collection of popular fiction gathered by bibliophile Victor Amadeus. This new material accessibility and discoverability has fundamentally enabled a shift in our thinking about the range and breadth of Irish Gothic literature, even as it has presented challenges of its own.[11] One such challenge, as Claire Connolly observes, is to bring scholarship in line with currently available data: 'critical analyses of the fictions [must] keep pace with the new findings: at present, we are richer in data than in the means to deal with it' (18).

Irish Gothic Today: Post-Celtic Tiger Ireland and its (Ir)realities

The present volume is an attempt to do just that: to integrate more completely into Irish literary and cultural history the new bibliographic (re)discoveries of the past ten to twenty years and to square them with existing scholarship. The need to update scholarly perspectives, to reflect more accurately current cultural realities, evokes the common stereotype of Ireland as firmly situated in the past. In the 1970s, an endlessly repeated joke was that as planes arrived into Belfast's airport, the pilots would warn their passengers to reset their watches to local time: 1690 (or, in some iterations, 1689). This joke has some scholarly traction: in his magisterial *States of Mind* (1985), Oliver MacDonagh, too, argues that in Ireland, the past is always the present, complaining that 'while the English do not remember any history, the Irish forget none' (1). This 'Irish habit of historical thought', which allows (forces?) the living and the dead to live always cheek by jowl, can help explain the importance of the Gothic to much Irish culture, given the extent to which the mode depends so much on not just the 'return of the repressed', but also the refusal of the dead to accept their posthumous state and move on.[12] As Declan Kiberd puts it in an analysis of Máirtín Ó Cadhain's comic-Gothic novel *Cré na Cille* (*Graveyard Clay*) (1949), Ireland is a country in which the divisions between the living and the dead are so completely broken down that 'the dead may not even know that they are dead, but go on talking anyway' (*Irish Classics* 574).[13] In the late 1990s, though, it seemed that the Irish attitude to time had been completely updated. With the cultural impact of the 'Celtic Tiger' (1998–2008), in which the Irish economy went through a period of enormous economic growth, there was a sense in which, as the historian Roy Foster put it, the past suddenly disappeared 'bewilderingly', and Ireland became 'determined to live aggressively in the present' (*Luck and the Irish* 189). Even events of the recent past were recast as if they had taken place in the Dark Ages. The journalist Eamonn Sweeney has perceptively pointed out that, ever since the economic boom, even 'the years from 1973–1994 … are sometimes treated like an impossibly distant era, one barely relevant to today's Ireland' (1).

This Ireland appeared to be left behind with the arrival of the Celtic Tiger, the Irish public undergoing what has been described as a kind of ontological 'motion sickness' (Kiberd, 'The Celtic Tiger' 280), as it was jolted from one age (dominated by the past) to another set very firmly in the perpetual present with its face to the future. Ireland had experienced, by way of an 'economic miracle', an identity makeover, transformed from a financial basket-case into a postmodern state with one of the fastest growing economies on the planet in the flash of an eye (Sweeney, *Irish Economic Miracle*, passim.). In many ways, during the period of prosperity, Irish identity seemed to have been fused fully with the economy. So integral to national naval gazing had economic success become that Fintan O'Toole argued in 2010 that the Celtic Tiger had become a 'substitute identity' for the nation (3). Unsurprisingly, then, the collapse of the Irish economy in 2008 caused an existential as well as an economic shock, the implications of which are still being dealt with at the time of writing. While the Irish economy had finally begun to sprout some very delicate 'green shoots' of recovery in the course of the last government (2017–2019), the economic and cultural impact of the Coronavirus pandemic and the series of lockdowns imposed by the Irish state from March 2020, make it likely that the period of unrelenting uncertainty in which the population has been living since 2008 will continue.

The end of the Celtic Tiger did not mean a return to a 'traditional' Ireland. Indeed, according to some influential critics and commentators, since the late 1990s the Irish have been living 'after Ireland' (Kiberd, *After Ireland*; Lloyd). Exactly what version of Ireland is supposed to have been left behind, though, is not all that clear. After all, one of those traditional versions of the country that was supposed to have been banished by the presentism of the Celtic Tiger was that of Ireland as a 'Gothic lost world', Ireland as a rather weird, unsettling site of the bizarre, a mythic-Gothic land of fairies, ghosts and demons (Fennell 38–39). It turns out, though, that far from really banishing this Gothic Ireland, the Celtic Tiger and its disastrous aftermath merely provided new, glossier uniforms for the one-dimensional characters that populated that otherworld. The housing boom, upon which so many Irish fortunes were based, soon produced 'ghost estates'; the financial wizardry admired all over the world magicked up 'zombie banks'. Property developers, who had for a decade been lauded as engineers of a cosmopolitan future, were reviled as Frankensteins, vampires and ghouls. Haunted houses, malevolent fathers and clerics, abused innocence ... none of it had really gone away.[14] In other words, in the economic downturn we re-entered Gothic Ireland (or, more credibly, we never really left it).

Figure 1 Settlement V, 2011, © Anthony Haughey. Courtesy of the artist.

Popular cultural forms or modes like the Gothic are often useful, if counter-intuitive, guides to widespread ideas and beliefs. As Elizabeth Butler Cullingford argues, 'those who live by the pen or the box office are necessarily closer to their audience than most academics are' (4), and it is interesting that in the last decade 'Irish' horror films have been produced with startling frequency,[15] often ironically commenting on the *persistence* of Gothic Ireland despite its rumoured demise. The effective and quite nasty *In Fear* (2013; dir. Jeremy Lovering), involves a young English couple who make the mistake of assuming that a romantic weekend in Ireland will be no more dangerous than one in any other destination in the British Isles.[16] The failure of the satellite navigation system in their rented car as they drive around in circles, bumping their way down narrow, pot-holed, neglected roads, searching in vain for a hotel that does not seem to exist, is an indication that they have entered a kind of Celtic twilight zone. When, towards the end of the film, the 'Kilairney House Hotel' is finally located, it is derelict, perhaps as a consequence of the economic downturn which converted many Irish hotels, recklessly constructed in the middle of nowhere to capitalise on the growth of the tourism industry, into 'ghosts', completely priced out of existence (O'Carroll; Baxter). The hotel is surrounded by discarded, broken-down cars as if it is not just the end of the road, but the end of the world – this is where capitalism has come to die, appropriately, perhaps, since for a time in 2008 it looked like the collapse of Anglo-Irish Bank might have created a black hole into which the entire world economy would be absorbed.

In Fear warns its audience that the Irish countryside, despite (or because of) the impact of the Celtic Tiger, is as weird and as threatening as it has ever been. 'After Ireland', in other words, is not necessarily 'after Gothic Ireland'. However, it is true that other, long-standing iterations of Irish identity may have been, temporarily at least, relegated to the sidelines. Given the centrality of both the institutional Catholic Church and Catholicism as a cultural force to Irish identity in the nineteenth and twentieth centuries, and the importance of Catholicism to the Gothic more generally, it is interesting that in many contemporary horror films, Catholicism hardly makes an appearance at all. This absence may reflect the displacement of the Catholic Church from its historical position at the centre of Irish society. Debates about the relative secularity of the developed world are complicated (Taylor), but however secularism is understood, Ireland's exceptionalism has, until recently, been a persistent factor in analyses of the place of religion in 'developed' societies (Whyte). Right through the 1970s and 1980s, for example, weekly Mass attendance by those identifying as Catholic was as much as 91 per cent, an extraordinarily high level compared to Ireland's European neighbours. In the last three decades, this number has dropped precipitously, and, in the European Values Survey in 2016, reached a low of 36 per cent (Ganiel 34). As the historian Oliver P. Rafferty puts it, 'Now, Catholicism as an institutional influence on Irish life appears to be at an end' (260; see also Foster *Luck and the Irish*, 37–66). The collapse in Irish Catholic enthusiasm is usually traced to a series of scandals, beginning in 1992 with the revelation that the very popular Bishop of Galway, Eamon Casey, had been in a sexual relationship with a woman in the early 1970s and had secretly fathered a child. Subsequently, further scandals were unearthed, most recently in 2014, when the findings by local historian, Catherine Corless, that human remains of those who had died at a Bon Secours Mother and Baby Home in County Galway, including those of children, had been deposited in an unmarked grave – a grave later revealed to have been the site of a septic tank (Smith 143–48). These scandals exposed the ways in which the Catholic Church in Ireland had been guilty not only of extraordinary levels of moral hypocrisy, but also of being a facilitator of, and a party to, a subculture of physical and sexual abuse and cover-up throughout the twentieth century (Fuller; Nic Ghiolla Phádraig). Most of these scandals were revealed to the public during the Celtic Tiger years, and this contributed to the sense that Ireland (like the heroine of an eighteenth-century Gothic novel) was leaving behind its dark, nightmarish (Catholic) past and emerging into the shiny, new (secular) future. This Gothic reading of recent Irish history is articulated by film historian Kevin Rockett who vividly describes how 'the rupture into society of issues such as institutional abuse and migration indicated that the repressed had returned at the moment of celebratory capitalism in Celtic Tiger Ireland' (553).

While these scandals certainly damaged the Catholic Church's reputation in Ireland, it is likely that they merely speeded up a more general drift away from institutional expressions of belief and spirituality.[17] It is, then, unsurprising that the theological centre of gravity in many of the Irish-set horror films that were produced after the economic collapse is not these Catholic institutions or their official representatives, but traditions and rituals that (supposedly) predate the arrival of Christianity on the island (Davie). In Irish horror circles, at least, 'Catholic Ireland' has been displaced by its earlier pagan alter ego.

Irish Folk Horror

In many ways, the contemporary interest in the pagan is not new at all in terms of Irish Gothic. As Jack Fennell sets out in his chapter for this collection, the mining of folk material, including that gathered by the Folklore Commission, has been a major feature of both English and Irish language Gothic writing from the nineteenth century onwards.[18] In *My Ireland* (1937), Lord Dunsany, arguably the greatest Irish writer of weird fiction, describes the country as a kind of Oriental paradise:

> I was alluding just now to eastern philosophy, while speaking of the Irish point of view; and this touch of the East that there is in Irish thought, and which with Æ [George Russell (1867–1935)] was far more than a touch, is something not to be lost sight of when thinking of Ireland […] one can see clearly enough in the minds of the Irish people a certain lore, a wise way of looking at things, which in greater or lesser degree all peasantries have, but which seems to me to come from the East and which shines now and then in their talk, like flashes from gold that has come from a far country. (46–47)

The 'lore' of the peasantry that Dunsany references here is the folklore and legendary stories that had fascinated a previous generation of Irish Protestant writers and collectors, and which had sometimes been treated as an articulation of an ancient occult wisdom and an alternative to the vitiated Christianity of the contemporary world.

In Dunsany's Gothic novel, *The Curse of the Wise Woman* (1933), the protagonist Charles, the son of a landlord, has his Christian faith disrupted by the 'old beliefs' revealed to him by Mrs Marlin, the titular Wise Woman who lives on the edge of a bog where the power of the ancient spiritual past can still be felt. Charles describes himself as vacillating between Christianity and the ancient spiritual beliefs and practices, 'hovering between two worlds, that both claimed the same area of Ireland', with the bog representing a pathway to *Tír na nÓg*, the mythological land of youth (57). Dunsany's sense that Ireland is essentially a pagan place with a Christian veneer echoed the views of W. B. Yeats a generation earlier.[19] Yeats explored his fascination with a bewildering variety of occult beliefs and practices in his Gothic fiction, *The Secret Rose* (1897), as well as his collections of fairy and folk tales. His occult interests had a political edge in that, like many Irish Protestants in this period, he believed that the sectarian divisions of the country could be bridged by accessing this pagan wisdom which was still to be found in Ireland in an isolated and remote folkloric bastion: 'I have not yet lost the belief that some day, in some village lost among the hills or in some island among the western seas, in some place that remembers old ways and has not learned new ways, I will come to understand how this pagan mystery hides and reveals some half-forgotten memory of an ancient knowledge' (Yeats, 'Away' 317).[20] Yeats's hope that somewhere there is an Irish village in which the old ways have retained their power and resonance has, in one sense, been vindicated by the recent focus on the rural outposts of contemporary Ireland in the 'folk horror' films that have been such a feature of twenty-first century Irish cinema, films in which the nominal Catholicism of the country is hardly even a residual theological presence.

Given that film is best considered in terms of industrial practice and collaboration, it is difficult to know how much this series of folk horrors is responding even indirectly to the recent collapse in the explanatory credibility of Irish Catholicism by locating spiritual possibilities elsewhere, in the pagan, in folklore. Before suggesting the ways in which these films can be understood as, partly, an investigation of the possibilities of alternative, non-Christian (or even anti-Christian) sources of meaning and significance in an Irish context, it is important to contextualise Irish folk horror in relation to a much broader British tradition that has two distinct 'waves'. The 'first wave' of British folk horror encompasses material from the 1960s to the end of the 1980s, including the young adult novels of Alan Garner, especially *The Weirdstone of Brisingamen* (1960) and *The Owl Service* (1967), television adaptations of the work of M. R. James (and one by Charles Dickens) broadcast as *A Ghost Story for Christmas* (1971–1978), and, probably most importantly, a range of films including *Witchfinder General* (1968; dir. Michael Reeves), *The Blood on Satan's Claw* (1971; dir. Piers Haggard) and *The Wicker Man* (1973; dir. Robert Hardy). These texts drew attention to what Robert MacFarlane has called the 'eeriness of the English countryside', and the distinctly pre-Christian folk beliefs and practices that could supposedly be located in the 'nooks and crannies of the woodlands' (Haggard), moors, fields and villages scattered throughout the land.

The reasons for the explosion of interest in Britain's pagan traditions in this period have been much debated, and critics and historians have pointed to the influence of 1960s counterculture (which drew deeply on paganism and the occult), as well as the folk revival in skiffle, jazz and progressive rock (see Scovell). These aspects of British culture seem likely to have arisen following what the historian Callum Brown has identified as the real beginnings of British disengagement from Christianity in the 1960s. Brown argues that, unlike traditional versions of British 'secularisation' which traced the slow demise of God to the Victorian period, as he succumbed to death by a thousand cuts (the knives wielded by the likes of Charles Lyell, A. G. Swinburne, George Eliot, Charles Darwin, Matthew Arnold and so on),[21] Christianity in Britain actually went through a long century of relative institutional and cultural health from the 1850s–1950s, only to suffer a credibility crisis and go into (terminal?) decline 'quite suddenly' in the 1960s (Brown). In the aftermath of this precipitous collapse of Christian epistemological authority, alternative sources of meaning and identity – including ones rooted in the pre-Christian past – became increasingly attractive, or at least available as intellectually viable sources of belief.

Folk horror has recently experienced a 'second wave' of popularity, associated with the films of Ben Wheatley, especially *Kill List* (2011), *Sightseers* (2012), *A Field in England* (2013), and *In the Earth* (2021), a revival which may be tracked in relation to the debate in British politics between what David Goodhart has called the 'somewheres' and the 'anywheres' – an argument which culminated to some extent in the referendum on British membership of the European Union (*The Road to Somewhere*). A number of the folk horror films released in this 'second wave' are set in, contain significant reference to, or have been filmed in Ireland, and many partly financed by *Bord Scannán na hÉireann*/the Irish Film Board. These films include: *Wake Wood* (2009; dir. David Keating), *Grabbers* (2012; dir. Jon Wright), *From the Dark* (2014; dir. Conor McMahon), *The Devil's Woods* (2015; dir. Anthony White), *The Hallow* (2015; dir. Colin Hardy), *A Dark Song* (2016; dir. Liam Gavin), *Without Name* (2016; dir. Lorcan Finnegan), *Crone Wood* (2016; dir. Mark Sheridan), *The Lodgers* (2017; dir. Brian O'Malley), *Don't Leave Home* (2018; dir. Michael Tully), *The Hole in the Ground* (2019; dir. Lee Cronin), *You Are Not My Mother* (2021; dir. Kate Dolan). Given the degree to which these films come out of the folk horror second wave, it is important not to exaggerate the significance of Ireland in determining their meaning.[22] Indeed, as Michael Patrick Gillespie details in his chapter on Irish Gothic cinema for this collection, while filmmakers in the 1950s and 1960s 'sought to contextualise their narratives in environments that evolved out of characteristics generally perceived as Irish', this has not often been the case for the 'last half-century' where 'both filmmakers and viewers have shown an increasing lack of interest in what the conception Irish entails' (96). In many ways, Ireland is simply part of a much more extensive British folk economy, one of the outlandish, fringe locations on the margins of the British Isles, and takes a place with almost anywhere outside the urban centres for filmmakers and contemporary audiences who homogenise all rural locations.

Indeed, the lack of geographical specificity in many of these films is particularly telling. While it is usually possible to deduce where exactly in Ireland the events are supposed to be taking place, these places are rarely directly referenced within the diegetic structure of the film itself. As Ruth Barton has pointed out, Irish horror films are 'amongst the most globalised of Irish productions' (79). However, in some cases the filmmakers *do* directly engage with aspects of contemporary Irish culture, which suggests that while it is crucial to contextualise these films in relation to the British folk horror genre, at times they speak to specific Irish issues and contemporary Irish debates, and have resonance for an Ireland whose religious landscape is now in considerable flux, and in which folk beliefs and pagan rituals now have a validity that was absent prior to the 'post-Catholic' phase of Irish history.

As Catholicism became increasingly seen as morally bankrupt, and therefore unable to provide an adequate response to the dislocations of the collapse of the Celtic Tiger, other forms of spirituality, often associated with popular or mythic versions of 'native' spiritual traditions, gained traction, such as John O'Donoghue's bestselling *Anam Cara* (1996), a mixture of pop psychology, self-help and 'Celtic' spirituality, and the series of books by the Kerry mystic, John Moriarty. The growth of alternative spiritualities and interest in Irish folklore, too, has offered different ways to confront contemporary existential anxiety.[23] If Irish Protestants like Yeats and Lord Dunsany found an answer to the dislocation of an increasingly Catholic Ireland in occult organisations, rituals and folklore in the late nineteenth and early twentieth centuries, pagan and folkloric spirituality has filled in the gap once again in postmodern Ireland.[24] In the remainder of this section, we will look briefly at the use of folklore in 'Irish' horror, to explore the ways in which the relationships between 'traditional' and 'contemporary' Ireland is negotiated. What is significant in these films is that, while the Irish Protestant writers of the occult revival did find satisfactory alternative modes of being through their encounters with pagan spirituality and rituals, the protagonists of these folk horror films find only horror and destruction.

One thing that connects many of the films is that their protagonists come from outside the rural community in which the action takes place. Many of these outsider characters are recovering from traumatic events and seek solace in the out-of-the-way and off-the-beaten-track. In *The Hole in the Ground*, to escape from a possibly violent broken marriage, Sarah O'Neil and her young son, Christopher, move to a rented house on the edge of a forest in County Wicklow; the protagonist of *Without Name* is a Dublin land surveyor engaged in an affair with his assistant who thinks that time alone in the Wicklow woods will provide him with respite from his dysfunctional family; the friends travelling to a music event in the *The Devil's Woods* are attempting to salvage their fractured relationships through a trip into the forests in Summerhill, County Meath. In each case, what they encounter is an aspect of Irish folklore that threatens their lives: a changeling in *The Hole in the Ground*, sentient trees in *Without Name* and a pagan community in *The Devil's Woods*. These films are marked by an urbanoia[25] that considers rural locations as the source of horror, and this suggests that the spiritual possibilities opened up by the alien beliefs, practices, environment and inhabitants of the Irish countryside are illusory and that the protagonists would have been better off staying put in the metropolis. The representation of the rural folkways here owes a great deal to the backwoods horror tradition in which going remote is always a mistake for its cosmopolitan heroes (Murphy). However, in the backwoods horror, what the protagonists encounter is usually an incestuous, buck-toothed collection of stereotypes from the American South, rather than either a coherent alternative set of beliefs and rituals, or monsters that have literally emerged from folklore.

It is striking that the villages and rural outposts depicted in these films are not completely 'cut off' from the contemporary world – the trappings of modernity are usually on display and fully integrated into the everyday lives of the inhabitants of these folk communities. These are not films that dramatise a simplistic encounter between an Irish rural folklorism and the forces of contemporary modernity, but are set in communities where the past and the present comingle and cross-fertilise each other. In 'Village Ghosts' (1889), Yeats described the Irish village as an occult presence itself: 'The ancient map-makers wrote across unexplored regions, "Here are lions". Across the villages of fishermen and turners of the earth, so different are these from us, we can write but one line that is certain, "Here are ghosts"' (34). The residents of the Donegal village of Wake Wood, however, are not actually all that 'different', except in one crucial respect.[26] The plot of *Wake Wood* concerns the discovery of blow-in veterinarian, Patrick Daley, and his pharmacist wife, Louise, that the village locals practice an ancient pagan ritual that brings the dead back to life for a brief period, to allow grieving families to come to terms with their loss. Patrick and Louise have moved to Donegal from Dublin[27] following the tragic death of their daughter, who was mauled by a German Shepherd being treated in her father's practice. While Wake Wood is indeed an insular rural retreat, it is not isolated from the contemporary world. Even though this is 'Gothic Ireland', it is far more integrated into modernity than previous incarnations – and indeed, the post-Celtic Tiger period in which the film is set is indicated by the boarded-up shops on the main street. While Adam Scovell argues that in folk horror, the landscape must 'isolate a key body of characters' who are then 'cut off from some established social progress of the diegetic world' (17–18), in fact these villagers are only cut off from Christianity, and they have taken everything useful from the modern world with them into their pagan retreat. These 'folk' supplement rationalised, bureaucratic funeral practices with vernacular folk ceremonies, and use the implements and techniques of modern veterinary medicine in their pagan rituals. One of the oddest moments in the film takes place when a mother brings her resurrected child to the local pharmacy to pick up a prescription for anti-inflammatory medication to manage her dead daughter's asthma.

Wake Wood itself (unlike, for example, the township in M. Night Shyamalan's *The Village* [2004]), is a staging post for what the sociologists Kieran Keohane and Carmen Kuhling call Ireland's 'collision culture', as the protagonists negotiate their way 'between pre-modern and modern social forms, an enchanted world of fairies and pishogues and a disenchanted world of medical science and legal-rational authority' (4). While initially sceptical of, and terrified by, the rituals that they stumble upon accidently, Patrick and Louise quickly realise that such pagan practices could provide a way for them to recover from the trauma of their child's death.[28] These slightly strange villagers seem to have understood something about the way the spiritual universe operates that bureaucratic death culture simply does not appreciate. The community to which Patrick and Louise have fled has reactivated a submerged and occluded culture, one that does not exist outside the village boundaries marked by enormous wind turbines. One of the attractions of Wake Wood is that it is a genuine community. The central couple appear to be completely alone in their grief, and do not mention any other family or friends – they are the stereotypical 'buffered' nuclear family described by Charles Taylor as cut off from spiritual renewal (300–4). Wake Wood provides them not just with the chance to be briefly reunited with their daughter, but also to be embraced by a community bound by shared folkloric beliefs, traditions, rituals and relationships, the kind of community that Mary Douglas has called an 'enclave' (12). Patrick agrees that, if they permit him to partake in a ritual resurrection, he will commit to remaining in the village and become part of Wake Wood itself. The folk rituals, however, fail to bring solace and healing to Patrick and Louise. In the second movement of the film, the influence of Stephen King's American folk Gothic *Pet Sematary* (1983), with its psychopathic child-back-from-the-dead, is evident. The resurrected Alice has been down the rabbit hole of Wonderland too long, and goes on a murderous spree, killing some villagers and eventually dragging her mother back into the afterlife with her.

Wake Wood's focus on reviving the dead child is a reminder (as if anyone needed reminding) of one of the reasons why twentieth-century Ireland had, by the time of the Celtic Tiger, come to be seen as a kind of Dantean hell – because of the sheer scale of the abuse and neglect of children in the institutions of church and state, in mother and baby homes, Magdalene Laundries and industrial schools. With twentieth-century Catholic Ireland now considered a crucible of child abuse, an escape back to the pagan or folkloric past may seem superficially attractive. However, far from offering a genuine escape from the paedophobia of recent history, Irish folklore is itself full of child-abusing, child-snatching, pedicidal entities who have been very much part of Irish Gothic writing. Joseph Sheridan Le Fanu's 'The Child that went with the Fairies' (1869–1870), in which the beautiful son of an Irish Catholic peasant is kidnapped by the 'good people', the fairy folk who live in the hills around Limerick, is matched by W. B. Yeats's eerie evocation of the seduction and abduction of children in 'The Stolen Child' (1889), where the 'human child' is enticed from the comfort of the hob and hearth to 'the waters and the wild / With a fairy hand in hand' (3). The Irish fairies were, after all, never the kind that populated Disney films of the twentieth century, or which could be encountered in the images of the Cottingley Fairies in 1917, laughing and playing with their human child companions; they were, instead, malevolent and vicious child snatchers who had to be constantly appeased by their human neighbours, and who felt envious and desirous of beautiful human children (Silver).

If the heroes of *Wake Wood* should learn to leave pagan rituals well enough alone, the characters in *The Hallow* learn the same about the creatures of folklore. The protagonist is Adam, an English conservationist who has moved to the west of Ireland with his wife, Claire, and infant son to survey a forest that is being sold off by the Irish state. Despite warnings that he needs to keep away from the forest, and retain the iron bars that cover all the windows of his house (as the fairies have an aversion to the metal), Adam carries on with his scientific work, believing, as much as any character in an M. R. James story, that 'fairy tales' (or, more accurately, folk tales) have no relevance in the modern world. While it would be possible to construct a reading of the film in which Adam is punished for his refusal to believe in the ancient supernatural beings that surround his home, and for his work aiding and abetting the destruction of the ancient forests (which belong, not to the Irish state at all, but to the *Tuatha Dé Dannan*, the gods of pre-Christian Ireland), the focus of the fairies is not really on Adam at all, but on his son who is, appropriately enough, named Finn (most probably a reference to the Celtic mythological warrior Fionn MacCumhaill), whom they capture and replace with a changeling monster.[29]

These fairies are not out to get Adam because of his enlightened disbelief or his complicity in the despoilation of the Irish forests, but because he has a child that they wish to make a member of their tribe.

In Lady Wilde's folklore collection, *Ancient Legends, Mystic Charms, and Superstitions of Ireland* (1887), she records that 'the Sidhe often strive to carry off the handsome children, who are then reared in the beautiful fairy palaces under the earth, and wedded to fairy mates when they grow up' (39). The film opens with a 'quotation' from the eleventh century *Lebor Gabála Érenn (The Book of Invasions)*, invoking a group of entities called 'the hallow'. *The Book of Invasions* is a mythologised history of Ireland, describing a series of six invasions of the country in which each set of newcomers displaces the previous inhabitants. The last invaders, the Milesians, supplant the Tuatha Dé Dannan, who had ruled for 150 years, and banish them to the underworld, from where, *The Hallow* suggests, they carry out raids and attacks on the conquering Gaels. However, the fact that this revenge is enacted through child abduction indicates, rather, that child envy rather than territorial protection is the main motivation here.

In a similar way, the child-catching creatures of *The Hole in the Ground* are not targeting blow-in Sarah because she is a representative of modernity or cosmopolitanism, and therefore a threat to their continued existence, but, once again, just because she happens to reside close to the forest where they live, and happens to have a child that they want to possess. While folk horror has often been read as a critique of the modern world, and an attempt to reenergise aspects of indigenous rural culture 'that are not governed and controlled by an increasingly global, glossy, homogenous, superficial culture industry', the Irish iterations suggest that these are forces that are best left alone and which cannot be trusted (Newland 163, 176). The characters in these films are vulnerable because they are unfortunate enough to live right on the edge of the paranormal zone and so are relatively easy pickings. There is an arbitrariness here that is doubly disconcerting as it suggests that the hosts of pagan darkness are not ideologically motivated at all, at least not in the way they are in an M. R. James story, and therefore they cannot be appeased by human sacrifices and are completely out of control.

The folk beliefs are not presented as genuinely attractive replacements for the demythologised and now abandoned Catholicism of post-Celtic Tiger Ireland. They are an altogether even more malevolent and child-abusing substitute. In this way, these folk horror films suggest a very different theological response to the pressures of modernity than the early Limerick stories of Sheridan Le Fanu, gathered together into *The Purcell Papers* (1880) after his death. As Alison Milbank notes in her essay for this collection, in these stories Le Fanu explores folk beliefs and practices as a form of 'muted' ecumenism, a way in which the sectarianism of 1830s Ireland can be overcome through an appeal to a shared folkloric past. In twenty-first century Irish folk horror, in contrast, folk belief is an alternative not to interdenominational tensions but to a denuded secular realism. However, while folk horror does indeed 're-enchant' a world whose sacredness has been drained away by rational modernity, the alternative to this rational modernity is nightmarish rather than liberating. Unlike the treatment of folk belief in the female writers examined in Melissa Edmundson's chapter, like Rosa Mulholland, Charlotte Riddell and Katharine Tynan, where 'folk magic and ancestral knowledge' provide 'a form of power for an otherwise powerless community' (218), power is not so democratically distributed in these films, and is retained by the terrifying supernatural creatures causing havoc. The folk community may seem superficially alluring to the anomic individuals and stressed nuclear families who have wandered in from outside, offering a form of solidarity and identity sorely lacking in the disenchanted world beyond the village or forest boundaries, but really all that is offered is an induction into a different form of horror. The entities of Irish folklore are far more likely to kill or maim visitors than offer a hundred thousand welcomes, and are therefore not genuine replacements of either the angels and demons of a traditional Christian cosmology, or the emptiness of urban postmodernity.

New Directions: The Essays in this Collection

The overview of recent Irish cinematic engagements with Gothic themes, modes and tropes within the context of a post-Celtic Tiger Ireland suggests the continued relevance of Irish Gothic to contemporary creative production. It also demonstrates the importance of considering the Gothic's role in exploring Irish cultural and historical legacies as well as the everyday realities of life in Ireland. The essays in this collection seek to expand on these introductory remarks, probing the elisions in our conventional scholarly accounts of Irish Gothic and re-centring the Gothic as a key, transhistorical cultural resource for Irish writers and creators from all walks of life. The essays begin broadly chronologically with discussions of early Irish Gothic fiction in the 1790s and nineteenth-century Irish Gothic verse, by Christina Morin and Julia M. Wright respectively. In these chapters, Morin and Wright tangle with factors that have effected the omission of significant bodies of Irish Gothic from both Irish and Gothic Studies, namely processes of canonisation and the scholarly reification of particular genres or modes as truly 'Irish'. Morin, for her part, considers Irish-authored Gothic romances published between 1790 and 1799, the period associated with the peak of 'the Gothic novel' in Romantic-era Britain. The sixteen works that Morin identifies have generally been seen as one of two things: imitations of more canonical Gothic novels or reactive responses to them. Morin argues instead that they 'engage in a lively and sophisticated exchange of ideas by way of a serious and knowing, if sometimes playful, literary conversation' (32). In so doing, these works undercut 'the conventional divides of nation, gender and genre' that have both shaped our conventional ideas of Gothic in this period and resulted in these authors' marginalisation (ibid.). Wright, in turn, contends that the current lack of a canon of Irish Gothic poetry is due both to our prose-centred conceptualisation of 'the Irish Gothic' and our tendency to associate nineteenth-century Irish verse with nationalist themes, modes and writers. Tracing the Irish history of Thomas Gray's 'Elegy Written in a Country Churchyard' (1751) and its influence on several major Irish Romantic poets, Wright outlines a significant body of Irish Graveyard verse and demonstrates its particular aptness for exploring 'the fundamental antipathy between the Gothic and the nationalist, between colonial terror and political hope' (52). Other examples of nineteenth-century Irish Gothic verse analysed by Wright use folkloric otherworlds and prison settings to dramatise and problematise the nationalist desire for an idyllic, pre-colonial Ireland and to chart the realities of political dissension.

Part II of the collection considers some of the diverse literary and cultural genres and forms that might be seen to draw on Irish Gothic modes or lay claim to an Irish Gothic identity, including cinema, theatre, children's literature, Irish language fiction and eco-literature. Christopher Morash's essay offers a thought-provoking consideration of three seemingly disconnected Irish plays: Charles Maturin's *Bertram; or the Castle of St. Aldobrand* (1816), W. B. Yeats's *Purgatory* (1938) and Marina Carr's *By the Bog of Cats ...* (1998). Acknowledging the very different contexts in which these works were produced, Morash nevertheless suggests that they share a 'kinship' that provides useful insights into the transhistorical nature of the Gothic in Irish drama (66). Michael Patrick Gillespie traces the evolution of Irish Gothic film from early works such as *Return to Glennascaul* (1951) and *From Time to Time* (1953) through *The Kinkisha* (1977), *Words upon the Window Pane* (1994) and *The Butcher Boy* (1997) to contemporary works such as *Tin Can Man* (2007) and *Daisy Chain* (2008). These latter films, Gillespie argues, highlight 'oscillating perspectives of an evolving post-national Ireland' and use the Gothic to explore a postmodern sensibility that is inherently anational (91). Anne Markey's essay adopts a similarly broad chronological scope, examining a selection of Irish children's literature from the eighteenth- to twenty-first centuries to complicate the idea that the didactic aims of children's literature more often than not precludes a recourse to the Gothic. In fact, Markey argues, 'authors with Irish backgrounds pioneered the use of Gothic tropes in children's fiction to add piquancy to the lessons they wished to teach', a practice that continues in fruitful and interesting ways today (101). The works on which Markey focuses – Mary Wollstonecraft's *Original Stories from Real Life* (1791), Lady Mount Cashell's *Stories of Old Daniel* (1808), Father Peter O'Leary's *Séadna* (1904) and Claire Hennessy's *Nothing Tastes as Good* (2016) – combine the 'enculturation impulse' of children's literature with 'an anarchic embrace of the Gothic in both English and Irish that acknowledges children's fascination with wrongdoing and the macabre' (ibid.).

Moving from the broader genres of theatre, cinema and children's literature, Eoin Flannery's essay turns attention to Irish authors working within the Gothic subgenre of ecogothic. Flannery's consideration of a wide range of works, including the poetry of James Clarence Mangan, short fiction by Eugene McCabe, W. B. Yeats's 'The Stolen Child', the big house novels of Elizabeth Bowen and J. G. Farrell and Claire Kilroy's *The Devil I Know* (2012), plots the consistent but varied engagement with the '"othered" topography of Ireland' in Irish works that harness the Gothic to dramatise and explore the troubled relationship between people and land, human bodies and the natural worlds they inhabit (116). Jack Fennell, meanwhile, offers a richly detailed account of Gothic and Gothic-inflected works *as Gaeilge* from the late nineteenth century to today. Tracing the gradual evolution of Irish language Gothic storytelling in this period, Fennell compellingly highlights the varied political and cultural tensions at play in Irish-language writers' adoption and production of Gothic modes.

In Part III of the collection, writers tackle a topic that has long exercised scholars of Irish Gothic: the role of religion and confessional identity in its production. Alison Milbank deals with the traditional view of Gothic literature in Ireland as a specifically Protestant endeavour, and, while not seeking to dispel this idea, productively problematises it. Arguing that, for Irish Protestant writers, 'the employment of tropes of terror can be a way of doing creative theological work', Milbank demonstrates the 'ecumenical impulse' of Irish Gothic works by Protestant authors including Thomas Leland, Regina Maria Roche and Charlotte Riddell, as well as now more well-known writers, Maturin, Le Fanu and Stoker (157). In a similar act of revisiting common assumptions about Irish Gothic, Jarlath Killeen turns attention to that quintessential Irish Gothic novel with which this introduction began: Stoker's *Dracula*.

Beginning with an instructive overview of Irish readings of *Dracula* that have, perhaps too zealously, interpreted a novel without any mention of Ireland as being intrinsically about Ireland, Killeen explores what he considers the more pertinent contexts for the novel's production at its particular moment. Indeed, Killeen approaches the novel as a profoundly religious text invested in questions of theodicy and argues that a focus on the novel as part of 'a general British reaction to events such as the cholera pandemics and the Irish Famine' both provides for richly rewarding readings and also 'places less strain on the critical conversation [than readings of the novel as specifically or allegorically concerning Ireland], while still drawing out potential Irish dimensions of *Dracula*' (187). Finally, Sinéad Sturgeon highlights the often minimised work of Irish Catholic writers in the Gothic mode by way of attention to Thomas Furlong (1794–1827) and his posthumously published poem *The Doom of Derenzie* (1829). This work, Sturgeon argues, 'exemplifies the disparate and innovative ways Irish Catholic writers engaged with the Gothic in the 1820s, both adapting existing modalities of the genre and resituating elements of Irish folklore and superstition in a distinctively Gothic mode' (196).

Sturgeon's eye to folkloric belief provides a neat segue into the final Part of the collection, which begins with an essay by Melissa Edmundson on Irish women writers and the supernatural. Considering a broad range of literary texts by Charlotte Riddell, Katharine Tynan, Dorothy Macardle, Rosa Mulholland and Clotilde Graves, amongst others, Edmundson charts the ways in which Irish women writers harnessed the supernatural and the ghost story to document and explore evolving gender norms and roles as well as the social and political struggles of the nation from the late nineteenth to mid-twentieth century. Moving to the twenty-first century, then, Ellen Scheible looks to two key concepts often linked to the Gothic – the Freudian uncanny and the Burkean sublime – to assess contemporary Irish women writers' provocative depiction of female bodies as sites of Gothic trauma. Analysing fictions by Emma Donoghue, Tana French and Sally Rooney, Scheible argues that these writers create female characters who embody the many social, cultural, political and economic realities of post-Celtic Tiger Ireland by which Irish women have habitually been oppressed. Rather than merely reflecting or attesting to this victimisation, however, these characters actively resist and defy it in subtle – sometimes fleeting – ways, using 'the Gothic to challenge the systemic oppression inflicted by systems of power' (248). The collection closes with a compelling discussion by Sorcha de Brún of Gothic masculinities in literature, film and radio drama in both Irish and English.

Notes

1. *Shadowplay* won the An Post Irish Book of the Year Award in 2019 and was shortlisted for a number of other awards, including the Costa Novel Award.
2. We have used the capitalised form of the word 'Gothic' throughout, as this is the house style of the *Edinburgh Companions*, but would note here the totalising tendencies of this usage and its propensity to suggest uniformity where there is none.
3. For the poster and mug, see, for example, www.theliterarygiftcompany.com/products/the-picture-of-dorian-grey-novelposter and www.teepublic.com/fr/tasse/8570245-bram-stokers-dracula-1992. (Accessed 1 December 2022.) Melmoth the Wanderer IPA is brewed by Four Stacks Brewing Company in Apollo Beach, Florida.
4. See, in particular, Morin and Gillespie.
5. These include, but are not limited to, Backus, Day, Eagleton and Foster.
6. See, for instance, Galiné; Gladwin; Hopkins; Killeen and Cavalli; Reyes.
7. 'Mapping Gothic Dublin: Historical and Literary Hauntings 1820–1900' is funded by the Irish Research Council Enterprise Partnership scheme, in conjunction with the Museum of Literature Ireland (MoLI). It seeks to recover the influence of Dublin as an urban space in the works of Le Fanu, Maturin, Mangan, Wilde and Stoker while also bringing to attention some of the less familiar texts by these writers.
8. The festival aimed, among other things, 'to highlight the work of the Le Fanu family and their connection with Abington, County Limerick'; Le Fanu Festival Proposal, April 2021, shared by email on 6 May 2021.
9. An Irish Research Council funded project, 'Ragged, Livid & on Fire: The Wanderings of Melmoth at 200' sought to celebrate (belatedly due to the COVID-19 pandemic) the 200th anniversary of the publication of *Melmoth the Wanderer*. It did so by exploring the novel's long-lasting cultural impact as well as by identifying and tracing the intertextual references in *Melmoth* and Maturin's other works that might be linked to Marsh's Library. The project culminated in a one-day academic symposium, public reading of excerpts of *Melmoth* and the launch of a virtual and in-person exhibition of materials in Marsh's. See www.marshlibrary.ie/digi/exhibits/show/melmoth. (Accessed 1 December 2022.)
10. Among works that address this issue are Hansen; Killeen, *The Emergence of Irish Gothic Fiction*; Morin, *The Gothic Novel in Ireland*; Sturgeon.
11. This challenge is ably encapsulated by the discovery that *The Adventures of Miss Sophia Berkley* (1760), identified in the early 2000s as a key text in the early history of Irish Gothic, is actually an Irish reprint of an English publication, *The History of Amanda* (1758). Its contribution to the development of Irish Gothic literature is thus more complex than originally understood. See Morin, 'The Adventures of Miss Sophia Berkley'.
12. Indeed, W. J. McCormack, in his seminal essay on Irish Gothic fiction in the *Field Day Anthology*, explained its appeal as, in part, resulting from the inseparability of past and present in Irish history (831).

13. Kiberd is reworking a comment by W. B. Yeats.
14. On the Celtic Tiger and the Gothic, see Carleton; Flannery; Keohane and Kuhling.
15. 'Irish' here is placed in inverted commas because the vast majority are international co-productions. The debate about what exactly is an 'Irish film' is expertly covered by Barton.
16. Though set in Northern Ireland – as the road signs suggest – this film was shot entirely in Cornwall.
17. See Davie.
18. For folklore and Gothic in Ireland, see Fahey.
19. For a perceptive examination of the Irish occult scene at the end of the nineteenth century, see Moore, *A Modern Panarion* and Moore, 'Utopian Occultism'.
20. It is important to point out that, as much as Catholicism has been a persistent interest in Irish Gothic fiction, so too has folklore, and a fascination with both the 'folk' and their beliefs can be seen running through Irish Gothic fiction – almost as powerful as the obsession with Catholicism. For a powerful compendium of 'folk Gothic' stories, see for example, Joseph Sheridan Le Fanu's *The Purcell Papers* (1880), containing stories 'collected' by the fictional proto-folklorist Catholic priest, Francis Purcell.
21. See Wilson.
22. The most extensive analysis of Irish horror cinema is Barton (67–89). See also Radley.
23. For contemporary Irish paganism, see Butler, 'Entering the Magic Mists'; Butler, 'Irish Neo-Paganism'; Butler, 'Paganism in Ireland'.
24. In looking at a much earlier period of fracture and disruption, the Great Famine, S. J. Connolly points out that there was a revival of interest by the ordinary Irish in 'popular supernaturalism in all its forms – not calendar custom alone, but also belief in fairies, in witchcraft and magical healing, in charms, omens and protective rites', which 'provided an explanation for what would otherwise have appeared a meaningless pattern of good and bad fortune, while at the same time enabling people to feel that they exercised some control over the pattern' (119).
25. We are taking this term from Clover (115).
26. *Wake Wood* is an international co-production, led by Hammer Film Productions, and funded by the Irish Film Board and RTÉ in Ireland, Hammer in the UK, and from Film I Sköne and the Swedish Film Institute in Sweden. It was filmed in Pettigo, County Donegal, Ireland, and in Sweden.
27. Patrick's practice is most likely set in Dublin, given that the couple live in a Georgian terrace.
28. The film draws on a number of key horror texts, including *Don't Look Now* (1973; dir. Nicolas Roeg) and *It* (1990; dir. Tommy Lee Wallace).
29. A particularly ineffective one, it must be said since, unlike other changelings, this replacement shrivels and burns up in sunlight.

Works Cited

Backus, Margot Gayle. *The Gothic Family Romance: Heterosexuality, Child Sacrifice, and the Anglo-Irish Colonial Order*. Duke University Press, 1999.

Barton, Ruth. *Irish Cinema in the 21st Century*. Manchester University Press, 2019.

Baxter, Patrick. *Ghost Developments on Film: an Experimental, Ethnographic Exploration of Place and Space in Post-Celtic Tiger Ireland*. 2017. Manchester Metropolitan University, PhD dissertation.

Brown, Callum G. *The Death of Christian Britain: Understanding Secularisation 1800–2000*. Routledge, 2009.

Butler, Jenny. 'Entering the Magic Mists: Irish Contemporary Paganism, Celticity and Indigeneity', *International Journal for the Study of New Religions*, vol. 9, no. 2, 2018, pp. 177–94.

———. 'Irish Neo-Paganism: Worldview and Identity'. *Ireland's New Religious Movements*, edited by Olivia Cosgrove, Laurence Cox, Carmen Kuhling and Peter Mulholland, Cambridge Scholars Publishing, 2011, pp. 111–30.

———. 'Paganism in Ireland: Syncretic Processes, Identity and a Sense of Place'. *Modern Pagan and Native Faith Movements in Europe: Colonial and Nationalist Impulses*, edited by Kathryn Rountree. Berghahn Books, 2015, pp. 196–215.

Carleton, Stephen. 'Contemporary Irish Gothic Drama: The Return of the Hibernian Repressed During the Rise and Fall of the Celtic Tiger', *Gothic Studies*, vol. 19, no. 1, 2017, pp. 1–21.

Casanova, Pasquale. *The World Republic of Letters*. 1999. Translated by M. D. DeBevoise, Harvard University Press, 2004.

Clover, Carol J. *Men, Women, and Chain Saws: Gender in the Modern Horror Film*. Princeton University Press, 1992.

Connolly, Claire. *A Cultural History of the Irish Novel, 1790–1829*. Cambridge University Press, 2012.

Connolly, S. J. *Priests and People in Pre-Famine Ireland, 1780–1845*. Gill and Macmillan, 1982.

Cullingford, Elizabeth. *Ireland's Others: Ethnicity and Gender in Irish Literature and Popular Culture*. Cork University Press, 2001.

Davie, Grace. *Religion in Britain since 1945: Believing without Belonging*. Wiley and Sons, 1994.

Day, William Patrick. *In the Circles of Fear and Desire*. Chicago University Press, 1985.

Douglas, Mary. *In the Wilderness: The Doctrine of Defilement in the Book of Numbers*. Sheffield University Press, 1993.

Dunsany, Lord. *The Curse of the Wise Woman*. Heinemann, 1933.

———. *My Ireland*. Jerrolds, 1937.

Eagleton, Terry. *Heathcliff and the Great Hunger: Studies in Irish Culture*. Verso, 1995.

Fahey, Tracy. 'A Dark Domesticity: Echoes of Folklore in Irish Contemporary Gothic'. *The Gothic and the Everyday: Living Gothic*, edited by Lorna Piatti-Farnell and Maria Belville. Palgrave, 2014, pp. 152–69.

Fennell, Jack. *Irish Science Fiction*. Liverpool University Press, 2014.
Flannery, Eoin. '"Ill fares the land": Ecology, Capitalism and Literature in (post-)Celtic Tiger Ireland'. *The Postcolonial World*, edited by Jyotsna G. Singh and David D. Kim, Routledge, 2016, pp. 395–411.
Foster, Roy. *Luck and the Irish: A Brief History of Change, 1970–2000*. Penguin, 2008.
———. *Paddy and Mr. Punch: Connections in Irish and English History*. Penguin, 1995.
———. 'Protestant Magic: W. B. Yeats and the Spell of Irish History'. *Paddy and Mr. Punch: Connections in Irish and English History*. Penguin, 1995, pp. 212–32.
Fuller, Louise. *Irish Catholicism Since 1950: The Undoing of a Culture*. Gill and Macmillan, 2002.
Galiné, Marine. *Les Représentations de la Femme et du Féminin dans un Corpus Gothique Irlandais du Dix-Neuvième Siècle*. 2019. University of Reims Champagne-Ardenne, PhD dissertation.
Ganiel, Gladys. *Transforming Post-Catholic Ireland: Religious Practice in Late Modernity*. Oxford University Press, 2016.
Gladwin, Derek. *Contentious Terrains: Boglands, Ireland, Postcolonial Gothic*. Cork University Press, 2016.
Goodhart, David. *The Road to Somewhere: The Populist Revolt and the Future of Politics*. Penguin, 2017.
Haggard, Piers. Interviewed by Mark Gatiss, *A History of Horror* (2010), BBC4.
Hansen, Jim. *Terror and Irish Modernism: the Gothic Tradition from Burke to Beckett*. SUNY Press, 2009.
Hopkins, Lisa. 'Bram Stoker's *The Lady of the Shroud*: Supernatural Fantasy, Politics, Montenegro and its Double'. *English Literature in Transition, 1880–1920*, vol. 57, no. 4, 2014, pp. 519–34.
Kiberd, Declan, *After Ireland: Writing the Nation from Beckett to the* Present. Harvard University Press, 2018.
———. 'The Celtic Tiger: A Cultural History'. *The Irish Writer and the World*. Cambridge University Press, 2005, pp. 269–88.
———. *Irish Classics*. Granta, 2000.
Killeen, Jarlath and Valeria Cavalli, editors. *'Inspiring a Mysterious Terror': 200 Years of Joseph Sheridan Le Fanu*. Peter Lang, 2016.
Killeen, Jarlath. *The Emergence of Irish Gothic Fiction: History, Origins, Theories*. Edinburgh University Press, 2014.
———. 'How Celtic Tiger's Death Led to a Gothic Revival,' *Irish Times* (28 April 2017). www.irishtimes.com/culture/books/how-celtic-tiger-s-death-led-to-a-gothic-revival-1.3065069. Accessed 1 December 2022.
Keohane, Kieran and Carmen Kuhling. *Collision Culture: Transformations in Everyday Life in Ireland*. The Liffey Press, 2004.
———. 'What Rough Beasts? Monsters of Post-Celtic Tiger Ireland'. *From Prosperity to Austerity: A Socio-Cultural Critique of the Celtic Tiger and its Aftermath*, edited by Eamon Maher and Eugene O'Brien, Manchester University Press, 2014, pp. 133–147.
Lloyd, David. *Ireland after History*. Cork University Press, in association with Field Day, 1999.

MacDonagh, Oliver. *States of Mind: Two Centuries of Anglo-Irish Conflict, 1780–1980*. 1983. Pimlico, 1992.

Macfarlane, Robert. 'The eeriness of the English countryside', *The Guardian*, 10 April, 2015. www.theguardian.com/books/2015/apr/10/eeriness-english-countryside-robert-macfarlane Accessed 1 December 2022.

McCormack, W. J. 'Irish Gothic and After (1820–1945)'. *The Field Day Anthology of Irish Writing*, volume 2, edited by Seamus Deane, Field Day Publications, 1991, pp. 831–949.

Moore, Pádraic E., editor. *A Modern Panarion: Glimpses of Occultism in Dublin*, exhibition catalogue, Dublin City Gallery The Hugh Lane, 2014.

———. 'Utopian Occultism in fin de siècle Dublin', unpublished lecture, at 'The Occult in Popular Fiction and Entertainments' workshop, Friday 25 November 2016. University College Dublin. www.youtube.com/watch?v=SdeDLvQrvZc&t=1117s.

Morin, Christina and Niall Gillespie, editors. *Irish Gothics: Genres, Forms, Modes, and Traditions*. Palgrave Macmillan, 2014.

Morin, Christina. 'The Adventures of Miss Sophia Berkley: Piracy, Print Culture, and Irish Gothic Fiction'. *Irish University Review*, vol. 49, no. 2, 2019, pp. 229–44.

———. *The Gothic Novel in Ireland, c. 1760–1829*. Manchester University Press, 2018.

Murphy, Bernice M. *The Rural Gothic in American Popular Culture: Backwoods Horror and Terror in the Wilderness*. Palgrave, 2013.

Newland, Paul. 'Folk Horror and the Contemporary Cult of British Rural Landscape: the Case of *Blood on Satan's Claw*'. *British Rural Landscapes on Film*, edited by Paul Newland, Manchester University Press, 2016, pp. 162–79.

Nic Ghiolla Phádraig, Máire. *Religion in Ireland: No longer an exception?* ARK update No. 64, 2009.

O'Carroll, Lisa. 'Ireland's "ghost hotels" to be boarded up', *The Guardian*, 1 February, 2011. www.theguardian.com/business/ireland-business-blog-with-lisa-ocarroll/2011/feb/01/ireland-ghost-hotels-closure-nama Accessed 1 December 2022.

O'Connor, Joseph. *Shadowplay*. Harvill Secker, 2019.

O'Toole, Fintan. *Enough is Enough: How to Build a New Republic*. Faber and Faber, 2010.

Radley, Emma. 'Violent Transpositions: The Disturbing "Appearance" of the Irish Horror Film'. *Viewpoints, Theoretical Perspectives on Irish Visual Texts*, edited by Claire Bracken and Emma Radley, Cork University Press, 2013, pp. 109–23.

Rafferty, Oliver P. 'The Catholic Church in Irish Studies'. *Routledge International Handbook of Irish Studies*, edited by Renée Fox, Mike Cronin and Brian Ó Conchubhair, Routledge, 2021, pp. 260–70.

Reyes, Xavier Aldana, editor. *The Gothic Tales of Sheridan Le Fanu*. British Library Publishing, 2020.

Rockett, Kevin. 'Cinema and Irish Literature'. *The Cambridge History of Irish Literature*, vol. 2, edited by Margaret Kelleher and Philip O'Leary, Cambridge University Press, 2011, pp. 531–61.

Scovell, Adam. *Folk Horror: Hours Dreadful and Things Strange*. Auteur, 2017.

Silver, Carole. *Strange and Secret Peoples: Fairies and Victorian Consciousness*. Oxford University Press, 1999.

Smith, James M. 'Knowing and Unknowing Tuam: State Practice, the Archive, and Transitional Justice'. *Éire-Ireland*, vol. 55, nos. 1 and 2, 2020, pp. 142–80.

Sturgeon, Sinead. '"Seven Devils": Gerald Griffin's "The Brown Man" and the Making of Irish Gothic'. *The Irish Journal of Gothic and Horror Studies*, vol. 11, 2012, pp. 18–31.

Sweeney, Eamonn. *Down Down Deeper and Down: Ireland in the 70s and 80s*. Gill and Macmillan, 2010.

Sweeney, Paul. *The Irish Economic Miracle Explained*. Oak Tree Press, 1998.

Taylor, Charles. *A Secular Age*. The Belknap Press of Harvard University Press, 2007.

Whyte, J. H. *Church and State in Modern Ireland, 1923–1979*. Gill and Macmillan, 1980.

Wilde, Lady. *Ancient Legends, Mystic Charms, and Superstitions of Ireland*. Ward and Downey, 1888.

Wilson, A. N. *God's Funeral: The Decline of Faith in Western Civilisation*. John Murray, 1998.

Yeats, W. B. 'Away'. 1902. *Writings on Irish Folklore, Legend and Myth*, edited by Robert Welch, Penguin, 1993, pp. 308–26.

———. 'The Stolen Child'. *Selected Poems and Four Plays*, edited by M. L. Rosenthal, Scribner Paperback Poetry, 1996, pp. 2–4.

———. 'Village Ghosts'. 1889. *Writings on Irish Folklore, Legend and Myth*, edited by Robert Welch, Penguin, 1993, pp. 34–8.

Part I

Irish Gothic in the Eighteenth and Nineteenth Centuries

Chapter 1

'Quitting the Plain and Useful Path of History and Fact': Early Irish Gothic and the Literary Marketplace
Christina Morin

> This tale reminds us, without any great pleasure, of Mrs Radcliffe's romances. In *Clermont*, mystery is heaped upon mystery, and murder upon murder, with little art, and great improbability. This writer, indeed, claims murders as her *forte*; for, not content with such as are connected with the story, she details three instances at considerable length as episodes. We have also the usual apparatus of dungeons, long galleries, clanking chains and ghosts, and a profusion of picturesque description which, though it displays some merit, serves only to interrupt the narrative.
> — *Critical Review*, 1798 (review of *Clermont*)

> *More Ghosts* would have been superfluous in the present state of novel-writing, had not the author of this work conjured up *her* ghosts with a view of dissipating the horrors, lately excited in the tender breast of many a boarding-school miss, by the more artful and terrific dealers in the article. The ghosts in this piece are rather cunning than terrible; and they add considerably to our entertainment.
> — *Critical Review*, 1798 (review of *More Ghosts!*)

Appearing just a month apart in the *Critical Review*, the assessments of Irish-authored Gothic romances quoted above aptly summarise the general critical view of 1790s 'terror fiction'. Either it imitates the works of others, namely Ann Radcliffe (1764–1823) or Matthew Lewis (1775–1818), or it combats the pernicious tendencies of their works and popular romance more generally. Such evaluations reflect what Lucy Newlyn terms 'the anxiety of reception' inspired by the Romantic period's newly emergent, newly democratised print sphere and the associated drive, particularly within the male critical establishment, to institute categories of 'high' and 'low' literature that effectively marginalised largely female-authored forms of popular fiction, including the Gothic romance (1). In the discourse surrounding authorship, its professionalisation and the quality of material produced by a rapidly expanding body of writers, critics stridently proclaimed their opinions in the pages of 'the Reviews', which, as Megan Peiser notes, swiftly 'emerged as authoritative judges of literary merit' (125).[1] That both of the novels referenced above – Regina Maria Roche's *Clermont* (1798) and Mrs F. C. Patrick's *More Ghosts!* (1798) – were published by the Minerva Press is significant, as William Lane's industrious firm was a particular source of concern for critics. '[T]he greatest manufacturer and distributor of Gothic novels of [the] age', in Frederick S. Frank's terms (qtd. in McLeod 60), Minerva published one-third of all new novels in the period between 1790 and 1820 (Peiser 124). Its particular association with Gothic romance was crystallised in the 1790s, as the press began to focus more exclusively on the popular fiction for which it very quickly became infamous.[2] Its dominant status in the publication of Irish Gothic fiction is clear: of the sixteen Gothics published by Irish authors in the period from 1790–1799, half were originally published by Minerva. The other eight were published by seven different presses: J. J. Robinson, T. J. Evans, J. Haly, J. Connor, H. Long, J. Bell (two) and R. Crutwell. At least one of these latter novels – Roche's *The Maid of the Hamlet* (London: H. Long, 1793) – was also later re-printed by the Minerva Press (1800).[3]

The prominence of the Minerva Press in the publication of 1790s Irish-authored Gothic romance invites further consideration. In fact, Minerva acts as a synecdoche for Gothic literary production across the British Isles in the Romantic period. This is particularly the case in the 1790s, a period that, as Robert Miles has persuasively argued, marks both the 'effulgence' of Gothic and its rapid evolution as writers across the four nations responded to social, political and cultural developments (41–62). Sneering assessments of Minerva fictions provide an accurate sense of the general critical view of Gothic literature, an opinion that has tended to be perpetuated in contemporary literary criticism. The original genre fiction, Gothic romances of the period are still marked by their late-eighteenth and early-nineteenth century positioning as sub-literary. Although Gothic Studies is, and has been for several decades, a vibrant and respected field of intellectual inquiry, challenges associated with the perceived deficiencies of Gothic fiction remain, functioning as what Chris Baldick and Robert Mighall wryly term the 'curse' of Gothic scholarship:

> The derisive laughter with which William Wordsworth greeted the romances of Ann Radcliffe has echoed down the ages, to the discomfort of most scholars of Gothic studies, who have been obliged either to accept the scornful verdict of criticism upon the deficiencies of Walpole, Radcliffe, Lewis, Maturin and their followers, or to devise special strategies to annul its malediction. Until the 1930s, most accounts of Gothic fiction were modestly content to admit that the Gothic was an undistinguished curiosity of literary evolution, which nonetheless merited some scholarly treatment of its sources, influences, biographical contexts and generic features. (209)

The academic 'defiance' of modern Gothic scholarship has produced a dizzying array of re-evaluations of Romantic-era Gothic (Baldick and Mighall 209). However, as is suggested by Franz Potter's study of Gothic publishing, 'trade gothic' such as that associated with Minerva continues to suffer from processes of canonisation both within and outside the field of Gothic Studies that maintain its marginalisation. Judged as different in kind from 'art' or 'canonical' Gothic, Potter indicates, these works are seen to lack the 'high-reaching artistic achievemen[t]' of fiction by Walpole, Radcliffe, Shelley, and Maturin (*Gothic Publishing* 1). They therefore remain comparatively overlooked in the literary historiography of Romantic-era Gothic production, emphasising the critical tendency, already outlined in the introduction to this collection, to take exceptions as the rule, thus leading to a myopic view of both Gothic and Irish Gothic literature.

In Irish literary history, the problem of scholarly neglect of Romantic Gothic fiction has been compounded by conventional views of Irish Romanticism as typified by the national tale and its 'allied genres' (Burgess). Attention to these forms has worked further to sideline Gothic in late eighteenth- and early nineteenth-century Ireland, as indicated by the still common tendency to identify Irish Gothic almost exclusively with Sheridan Le Fanu, Bram Stoker and Oscar Wilde.[4] Recent scholarship has begun to overturn such views, facilitated by the increasing accessibility of archival material, which has enabled a growing recognition of the rich variety of eighteenth-century Irish Gothic literature. As a corollary, we now have available a lengthy – and lengthening – bibliography of forgotten texts to re-integrate into our histories of Irish 'first-wave' Gothic. Rather than chase further examples of overlooked Irish Gothic – as there almost certainly are – this chapter recovers to view Irish Gothic literary production of the final decade of the eighteenth century. Considering the ways in which these fictions – several of them Minervas – adapt, re-shape and complicate the literary models now traditionally associated with Radcliffe, Lewis, Godwin and other now-canonical Gothicists, it subjects to scrutiny the critical tendency to dismiss Irish Gothicists as mere imitators. It seeks to demonstrate that writers such as Roche, Patrick, James White, Anna Milliken and Stephen Cullen never simply attempted to cash in on the popular and critical successes of more respected contemporaries while supplying the undiscriminating reading masses with the 'cheap thrills' they demanded. Instead, their works engage in a lively and sophisticated exchange of ideas by way of a serious and knowing, if sometimes playful, literary conversation that undermines the conventional divides of nation, gender and genre. They thus help break down the distinctions between 'high' and 'low' literature that continue to shape our understanding of this period. Furthermore, the works discussed here demonstrate that Irish writers were central to the development of a vivid Anglophone Gothic culture in the 1790s, even if they failed to achieve the 'literary capital' that Radcliffe, Lewis and other prominent Gothicists now enjoy (Casanova 17).

'Addicted to Gothic Romance': History, Politics and the Meaning of 'Gothic'

The earliest Irish Gothics in the period are examples of what Montague Summers called 'historical gothic' (153–201), including James White's *The Adventures of John of Gaunt* (1790) and *The Adventures of King Richard Coeur-de-Lion* (1791), and Anna Milliken's *Corfe Castle* (1793) and *Eva; an Old Irish Story* (1795). Taking their cue from earlier Gothic-historical works such as Thomas Leland's *Longsword* (1762), these novels adopt English or Irish historical figures and settings in order to explore the politics of the past and their bearing on present-day England and Ireland. They also reveal a keen awareness of the contemporary marketplace and their need to position themselves within it. In the preface to *Corfe Castle*, for instance, Milliken emphasises the historical nature of her tale, already hinted at by her subtitle 'Historic Tracts':

> To the critic I beg leave to declare that I am conscious it has many faults, some of which were committed through the timidity attendant on a first essay, and others in avoiding that too general fault of novels, the insipid tedium of love scenes; and yet endeavouring to enliven by invention the cold historic facts which form its basis, and which can alone recommend it to the notice of the world, now so improved as to look with contempt on those light compositions which were formerly read by the younger part of both sexes with eagerness and pleasure. (1: xii)

Victoria Ravenwood highlights the deliberate nature of this deferential authorial stance. Writers such as Milliken and Anna Maria Mackenzie, whose 1791 novel, *Danish Massacre: an Historic Fact*, bears a similar subtitle as *Corfe Castle* and focuses, like it, on the reign of Ethelred the Unready (r. 978–1013, 1014–1016), Ravenwood argues, 'were aware of the transgressive plot content of their works and therefore use the term "historic" as a form of defence and/or a disguise' (63). Unlike Sophia Lee, who had proposed in the preface to *The Recess* (1783–1785) that history required the addition of romance to humanise cold fact,[5] Milliken purposely distanced herself from romance and its association with the 'light' and ephemeral fictions of the popular press, perhaps in response to the mixed reviews Lee had received.[6] The strategy seemed to pay off for Milliken. Despite the repeated intrusion of romance in the form of the supernatural, including 'the shade' of Edward – King Ethelred's half-brother – demanding revenge for his assassination (Milliken 2: 98), *Corfe Castle* was praised for being unlike contemporary 'fashionable' novels, which were seen to stir up unseemly passions and encourage indecorous behaviour (review of *Corfe Castle* 366). 'We congratulate the county of Cork on the production of a novelist, whose good sense and ingenuity reflect credit on her natal soil', wrote the reviewer for *Anthologia Hibernica* (ibid.). Particularly notable about *Corfe Castle* was the 'refined and cultivated understanding, and a style correct and nervous' evident throughout (ibid.).

Several years later, Mrs F. C. Patrick similarly rejected an association with romance in her preface to *The Jesuit* (1799):

> To those who look upon this as a romance, and the characters (particularly such as are not mentioned in the common histories of the times) as fictitious, I protest that I have with great diligence searched records, read old leases, and perused old chronicles, by which means I am enabled to declare that there is not one name or character in the book that did not really exist. (1: xvii)

The narrative that Patrick delivers is presented as a found manuscript recounting the first person confession of the novel's anti-hero, Anthony Babington. In this, it plays on Walpole's ruse in *The Castle of Otranto* (1764). Where, however, the second edition of that novel revealed the spuriousness of its claims to actual 'Gothic' story – that is, a genuinely old tale – *The Jesuit* insists on its authenticity. 'I acknowledge that there are a few circumstances related different from what are found in Hume, Rapin, Echard, &c.', the 'editor' remarks, 'but I appeal to any person of common understanding, whether that is not rather a proof of my veracity; since were I the contriver of this story, (which I have not talents for) I should have crawled serviley after those who have gone before me' (Patrick, *The Jesuit* 1: x). Patrick's comments simultaneously construct her tale as historically accurate and signal an attentiveness to the accusations of imitation levelled at writers of Gothic romance. At the same time, they exploit romance to maintain readers' interest and indict historiography, not prose fiction, as unoriginal.

In contrast to both Patrick and Milliken, Dublin-born James White unashamedly professed himself a writer of Gothic romance, distinguishing himself from his peers both by his perfect ease with the genre and by a complete lack of interest in enforcing distinctions between fact and fiction, historiography and romance. In his introductory remarks to *The Adventures of King Richard Coeur-de-Lion* (1791), for example, White emphatically underscores contemporary understandings of the term Gothic and its connection to chivalric romance, justifying to his readers his decision to '[treat] of the achievements of ancient chivalry' and describe 'marvellous occurrences … characters and callings … unknown to [the] modern day' (1: iv). Noting that 'the task of delineating the follies of the present times … [is] already in better hands' – those of Frances Burney – he has chosen 'to explore the remote doings of antiquity to show life, as life was, in those heroic days, and evince that our forefathers were as foolish as we are ourselves' (ibid. 1: xiv). 'To this end', he writes, 'I have addicted myself to Gothic romances' (ibid.). Here, White demonstrates very clearly an understanding of 'Gothic' that asserts both a specific literary affiliation – romance versus realism – and an investment in examining the past as a method of reviving it and implicitly comparing it to the present. These things are unknown in the eighteenth century, White argues, because they have 'been swept from the face of the round world, and consigned to a deplorable oblivion' (ibid.). White's Gothic narrative, then, presents itself as a source of historical information and a documentation of the continuities between past and present. People 'in those heroic days', he repeats, were 'as foolish as we are ourselves' (ibid.).

White's observations recall the criticism of the second edition of *Otranto*, the negative reception of which contrasted markedly with reviews of the first edition, which was lauded as a genuinely 'Gothic fiction' that revealed much about an intriguing, albeit barbaric, past (review of *The Castle of Otranto*, *Monthly Review* 97–9). The second edition presented an affront both because it subjected the critics themselves to ridicule and because it suggested that the present was just as bad as the past (Clery 54–5). In contrast to the indignation expressed over Walpole's merging of romance and history, past and present, reviews of *King Richard* gave voice to benign amusement, if also bemusement. Praising the novel as 'pleasing and entertaining', in part because of its rejection of 'the thread-bare story of old manuscripts', the *Critical Review* nevertheless corrected White for factual errors: 'the author seems not to have been aware, that Richard did not return through Germany to Antwerp' (116). The *Monthly Review* more pointedly remarked on White's 'heterogeneous plan, of combining *History* with *Romance*, *Chivalry*, and burlesque *Ridicule*: by which last ingredient, the Dignity of Heroism is oddly caricatured' (231). The review nonetheless concluded by commending White's 'wild and Gothic Romance' as 'hav[ing] afforded us a good deal of amusement: so that, after much laughing *with* the writer, and *at* him, we, on the whole, grew sorry to part with him' (ibid.).[7]

Both reviews dwell on the comedic side of *King Richard*, and that part of the narrative where the historical figure of the English sovereign acts as a largely passive cipher through which to showcase a series of marvellous tales. One of these concerns 'the Man of the Face', who, incidentally, bears no small resemblance to Sheridan Le Fanu's later spectral monkey-seeing curate in 'Green Tea' (1872). One of the first people that Richard meets as he journeys from his former prison in Austria to England, the man of the face describes having suddenly seen a disembodied 'face, the eyes of which seemed steadfastly fixed on me, as if they would have penetrated my most secret cogitations' (White 1: 32). The ghostly countenance is invisible to all but himself, appearing to him every day at a certain hour. He discovers, however, that he can evade the visage by constantly being on the move. He has thus left his home and become a perpetual wanderer, fleeing each location after only a day or two of rest. Resolution occurs when the man of the face seeks the assistance of a priest, who performs an exorcism that causes the spectre to speak and reveal the reason for his haunting presence: the ghost's ancestors had been dispossessed by those of the man of the face. The apparition disappears altogether when the man of the face returns his estates and belongings to their rightful owners, becoming a modest cottager in the process but also releasing himself from his enforced peripatetic lifestyle.

Other tales in the first two volumes of *King Richard* concern more comedic characters than 'the Man of the Face'. These include 'the Knight of the Pitcher', so named for having gotten his head stuck in a large jug of candied fruit, and the Abbess of Heidelberg, who temporarily loses all forty-seven nuns in her charge when, en route to their new abbey, they tie up the sacristan with a lengthy rosary and abscond. Conversely, the third volume of the novel registers a much more serious note, as Richard returns to England – 'disorder[ed] and wound[ed]' owing to the mismanagement of those officials Richard has trusted in his absence, Longchamp, Bishop of Ely in particular (ibid. 3: 98) – and begins to right the wrongs that have occurred while he was away. Much of the third volume consists of a lengthy account of Longchamp's iniquities, his feeble defence of his actions, and the subsequent decision to lay his crimes before Richard, rather than allow the matter to be brought to an impeachment trial. Having heard the charges against Longchamp, Richard promises to 'banish from his presence the author of their late calamities' (ibid. 3: 164), allowing the novel to conclude with an image of peace, prosperity and rightful rule returned to England.

The tonal and narratological shift between the second and third volumes of *The Adventures of King Richard* speaks to White's real political interests. These are minimised, to an extent, by the levity of the narrative as a whole, and are more clearly evident in White's non-fiction, including his 1788 treatise on slavery, *Hints for a Specific Plan for an Abolition of the Slave Trade, and for Relief of the Negroes in the British West Indies*. Through the extended description of the near impeachment of Longchamp, however, as well as the juxtaposition of a poem on the death of Lord Falkland at the end of volume two, White asks his readers to extrapolate the political lessons of the narrative to real life. Indeed, Longchamp's examination and defence undoubtedly recalled for readers the trial of Warren Hastings, with which White was involved. The novel thus invites a consideration of the similarities between past and present, Gothic romance and real life. As James Watt argues, 'The pseudo-historical setting of White's work … allowed explicit criticisms of the present by way of an idealizing appeal' to the past (43). White's political aim, however, seems not to have registered with critics in the same way as Walpole's did, arguably because of its overt playfulness and lack of authorial subterfuge, permitting *King Richard* to elide the objections raised against *Otranto*. In this, White's novel emphasises, as Watt writes, 'the range of possibilities afforded by romance in the final quarter of the eighteenth century', and suggests White's centrality to ongoing experimentation with literary form and mode that marks the development of Gothic in this period (ibid.).

'Frigid, though Romantic'? Imitation, Parody and the Redefinition of Authorship

As the examples of *Corfe Castle*, *The Jesuit* and *The Adventures of King Richard Coeur-de-Lion* suggest, Irish Gothicists in the 1790s entered enthusiastically into the conversation set in train by Walpole and his stated desire to re-introduce 'fancy' to modern literature (9). Their texts interrogate how authors might balance fact and fiction, history and romance within the pages of imaginative literature in a way that does not offend but still manages to excite. They thus contribute to a dialogic exchange that takes place within the pages of their novels themselves, which subtly respond to each other and to the Reviews. Contemporary reviews, in turn, pass judgment, often quite severely, on authors who fail to achieve the correct blend, with the parameters of success established and negotiated in those same reviews. Much of this understated but no less knowing and notable interchange goes unnoticed, both by contemporary reviewers and more recent scholarship alike, as does the experimentation with form and style evident in the examples discussed above. The primary reason for this, I suggest, is the continued understanding of the majority of 1790s Gothic fiction – Irish or otherwise – as straightforward imitations or, indeed, plagiarisms of the works of now more canonical writers such as Radcliffe and Lewis. Regina Maria Roche provides an excellent case study here. Although recognised in the nineteenth century as one of the foremost female novelists of the period,[8] she nevertheless features in twentieth- and twenty-first century scholarship as little better than a Radcliffe-imitator. Modern disregard for Roche reflects the perspective of Romantic-era critics, as indicated by the assessment of *Clermont* (1798) cited in the epigraph of this chapter. Dismissed by late-eighteenth century reviewers as hack fiction, Minerva Press publications have earned an enduring reputation as unremarkable, except, perhaps, for their poor quality. Yet, as Elizabeth Neiman argues, the imitation evident in Minerva fictions such as *Clermont* is purposeful: 'Minerva's derivative themes are an accidental inheritance that furnishes writers with the language to respond to Romantic-era debates, most importantly ... Romantic redefinitions of authorship and literature' (633–34).

Certainly, in Roche's Minerva novels, there is a marked 'literary self-consciousness', as Aileen Douglas describes it: 'intertextuality, self-reflective commentary, the underscoring of fictional tropes, and explicit concern with general issues of representation' (183). This is perhaps most obvious in her later works, including *The Tradition of the Castle: or, Scene in the Emerald Isle* (1824) and *The Castle Chapel; A Romantic Tale* (1825) (Douglas; Morin 154–95). It is also evident in her works of the 1790s, however, where Roche clearly seeks to position her novels amongst those of her contemporaries and contribute her own voice to ongoing debates about authorship, popular fiction and literary value. In both *The Children of the Abbey* (1796) and *Clermont*, references to French educational and sentimental literature allow Roche subtly to engage with questions of female education and reading material. In *The Children of the Abbey*, for example, the heroine reads Jane Dalton's English translation of Bernardin St Pierre's sentimental novel *Paul et*

Virginie (1788; trans. 1789), reflecting the wider influence of Rousseau and his ideas in the novel, evident from the start with Amanda's paternal education and a childhood spent in '[d]omestic bliss and rural felicity' (5). In *Clermont*, meanwhile, Madeline is described as a Rousseavian child of nature. Placing her in the care of his friend, the Countess de Merville, Madeline's father, Clermont, expresses his hope that she might 'continue the unaffected child of nature', to whose education he has committed himself for the past seventeen years (33). 'The culture of his daughter's mind' has not only taken place in complete isolation from society but has also involved a well-rounded course of reading. Madeline is said to have both a 'perfect knowledge of the historian's record, and [a] just conception of the poet's beauty' (ibid. 4, 5). This education, moreover, 'render[s] her a companion well qualified to diversify [Clermont's] lonely hours' (ibid. 5), recalling Wollstonecraft's call in *A Vindication of the Rights of Woman* (1792) for a female education that produces, if not equality between men and women, at least a sense of shared intellectual acumen.

Roche's intertextuality in both *The Children of the Abbey* and *Clermont* largely evades direct questions of popular literature or Gothic romance. It nevertheless cleverly positions these novels alongside contemporary writings about female education in order to emphasise the importance of well-considered reading for women. It is arguably for this reason – the serious but subtle reflection upon female reading and education – rather than their publication by Minerva, that Roche's novels find their way into Austen's oeuvre. As has often been discussed, *The Children of the Abbey* is one of the 'horrid novels' in *Northanger Abbey* (1818), and *Clermont* is Harriet Smith's favourite novel in *Emma* (1817). These references have more often than not been read pejoratively, an indication of Austen's desire to discount and parody popular Gothic romance. However, Austen's allusions to Roche's works function as a sign of the necessity for cultivating a practice of discerning reading, though not necessarily to the detriment of Minerva and other popular fictions, as is often believed (Butler 172–81). As Michael Sadleir suggestively put it, Austen derived considerable 'pleasure and even profit from the Gothic romance … However ready she may have been publicly to make fun of the excesses of a prevailing *chic* – [she] would in her heart have given to that *chic* as much credit for its qualities as mockery for its absurdities' (qtd. in Nowak 185).[9]

The complexities of parody evident in *Northanger Abbey* are also at work in several 1790s Irish Gothic fictions that embrace the mode as a method of responding to and subtly resisting critical objections to popular romance and the associated construction of its authors as mere hack-writers. Mrs F. C. Patrick's *More Ghosts!* purposely evokes earlier Gothic fictions with its found manuscript but subjects the trope to ridicule by the comical nature of its discovery. Unlike the serious and scholarly trappings of the manuscript in *Otranto* – 'found in the library of an ancient catholic family in the north of England' (5) – the manuscript in *More Ghosts!* is discovered while the editor is on holiday in the country and rescues 'a bundle of written papers' from its intended fate as butter wrappings (1: i–ii). The narrative that follows is both a cautionary tale against 'credulity' that sends up the supernatural occurrences of previous Gothic fictions, and a serious investigation of the power of education for both men and women (ibid. 2: 123). Tom Grey, for instance, is presented as 'the feminized dupe of gothic storytelling', who must be sent to university to correct his childhood mis-education, the most notable effect of which is his susceptibility to irrational and overly sensible behaviour (Cannon 586). As Mercy Cannon cogently observes, by making Tom into the kind of (female) reader feared by critics, Patrick 'revers[es] gender roles' in order to '[mock] not only the established relationship between women and romance but also the pervasive association of women's reading with sexual vulnerability' (ibid.). Elsewhere in the novel, Patrick explicitly explores questions of female reading through the heroine, Mary Morney, who very nearly becomes a 'female philosopher' after being introduced to the works of 'Voltaire, Rousseau, Hume, and Gibbon' (*More Ghosts!* 3: 40). Significantly, these works are 'presented as much more dangerous than any gothic romance', suggesting the ways in which, for Patrick and later Gothic parodists such as her fellow Minerva novelist Sarah Green, 'parody provides a means of deflecting criticism surrounding women's reading and the romance genre, while enabling them to encode cultural critiques that escape accusations of radicalism' (Cannon 591, 581).

The title of Stephen Cullen's second novel – *The Castle of Inchvally: a tale – Alas! Too true* (1796) – points to a deployment of parodic humour akin to that found in *More Ghosts!* With supernatural elements that turn on the spectral appearance of exaggerated and oversized body parts accompanied by demonic laughter, *The Castle of Inchvally* both references *Otranto* and harnesses its latent 'comic turn', or, in other words, 'the excess that induces laughter' (Horner and Zlosnik 325). These over-the-top supernatural effects, culminating in the appearance of 'a complete human skeleton … composed of fire of various tints', hover between the terrific and the burlesque, underlining both the intensity and the absurdity of feelings surrounding that which they warn against: the mixed marriage of the novel's hero and heroine, Charles Wilmot and Arabella Howard (Cullen, *The Castle of Inchvally* 2: 56). In fact, the central concern of *The Castle of Inchvally* is religious intolerance and bigotry amongst Catholic and Protestant populations in Ireland, the country in which the majority of the narrative action is set. The concluding revelation of the trickery behind all the apparent ghostly appearances coincides with a reconciliation between the major Catholic and Protestant characters in the novel, a parental approval of the proposed marriage and a prophetic wish that such religious tolerance would soon be a reality in Ireland:

> That time, I trust and foresee, will soon arrive ... when a true Christian preacher, a bigot to no sect, a friend to all, and a scourge to the preachers of dissension, shall arise, and, with the splendour of his talents and the purity of his doctrines, crush that system of disunion that has made Irishmen slaves – make them unite in one body for the mutual support and vindication of their rights, and shew the crooked politician, who divides but to trample on them, that they are but one people, and will have but one fate. (ibid. 3: 284)

Combined with explanatory footnotes on Irish customs that anticipate those of Edgeworth's *Castle Rackrent* (1800), *The Castle of Inchvally*'s attentiveness to religious divisions in Ireland and its attempt to resolve that strife, if only narratologically, anticipates the antiquarian discourse and 'Glorvina solutions' of later national tales.[10] In this, it suggests the ways in which Irish writers could and did manipulate the Gothic to explore national themes that would become more familiar with the fiction of the early 1800s and writers such as Edgeworth, Owenson and Maturin.

Cullen's first novel, *The Haunted Priory: or, the Fortunes of the House of Rayo* (1794), equally looks to *Otranto* with its use of ghostly armour that leads to the novel's concluding revelations and resolution, though in less obviously comedic ways than *The Castle of Inchvally*. Early in the novel, for instance, the Baron sees 'a golden helmet in which was laid my child, my Alphonso: I suddenly grasped the helmet, and snatched the child to my bosom, when looking down, I perceived that the helmet falling had killed his father, who lay bleeding in agony on the ground' (Cullen, *The Haunted Priory* 52–3). Later, Alphonso, the son of the Baron's ward, Don Isidor de Haro, is frightened by the appearance of 'a figure ... far above the common size' wearing 'an enormous warlike plume that nodded on its helmet' (ibid. 130). A similar vision, the approach of which is heralded by 'a violent rattling of armour', appears shortly after to both the Baron de Rayo and Don Isidor (ibid. 161). On each of these occasions, the spectre conjures the characters to follow where it leads, allowing key discoveries to be made that effect the novel's eventual resolution.

Cullen's use of the device of over-sized ghostly armour undoubtedly recalls *Otranto*, but it does so purposely, asking readers to think about the relationship between the two texts. If the 'warlike plume' and murderous 'golden helmet' in *The Haunted Priory* evoke 'the enormous helmet, an hundred times more large than any casque … shaded with a proportionable quantity of black feathers' that kills Conrad (Walpole 18), they do so as a manner of calling attention to the differences, as much as the similarities, between the texts. In particular, Cullen's armour plays a much more central role in the narrative, with its spectral appearance both signalling that something is awry and crucially assisting in righting the wrongs of which it complains. In so doing, it redirects the avenging anger that targets an innocent child in *Otranto* – Conrad – more immediately toward the grown man responsible for the current rottenness in the state of Spain: the novel's villain, Punalada. With evidence gathered through the help of the ghost in armour, in fact, Don Isidor and the Baron de Rayo convince the king to initiate an investigation of Punalada, prompting a confession that reveals his treachery, including the murder of the Baron de Rayo's son, Gonsalvo, and the indictment of the Baron on false accusations of treason. Due to royal involvement, Punalada's defeat is considerably more public than Manfred's in *Otranto*: his fortunes are confiscated and re-distributed, and his title extinguished. Meanwhile, the Baron de Rayo is re-invested with his estates, rank and title.

Despite the recognisable, if implicit, intertextual references to *Otranto*, then, Cullen's novel is far from a servile imitation of Walpole's. Indeed, aside from the nuances discussed briefly above, *The Haunted Priory* is also remarkable as the first Gothic novel set in medieval Spain, anticipating the more familiar Spanish scenes in *The Monk* (1796) and *Melmoth the Wanderer* (1820). Moreover, while *The Haunted Priory* is all but forgotten today, it was undeniably successful in the Romantic period, going through several editions in the final years of the eighteenth century and the first three decades of the nineteenth. It was also redacted as *The Wandering Spirit, or Memoirs of the House of Morno* (1802), included in William Hazlitt's *The Romanticist and Novelists Library* (1839), and adapted for stage as *De Rayo; or, the Haunted Priory: A Dramatic Romance* (1833) (Potter, 'Chapbooks, Pamphlets, and Forgotten Horrors' 30). Even contemporary critics found it appealing, at least to a degree. For its part, the *Critical Review* dismissed it as a 'frigid, though romantic' tale that failed to 'make amends by the graces of fiction for quitting the plain and useful path of history and fact' (468). However, the *British Critic* found much to admire, particularly in *The Haunted Priory*'s difference from most other novels of the period: 'The language of this novel is equally free from vulgarity and affectation, its sentiments from perversion and immorality. Thus far, more may be said in its favour than will be found true of many novels' (299).

Conclusion

With these reviews of *The Haunted Priory*, we return to the issue with which this essay began: contemporary reception of 1790s Gothics as, essentially, one of two things: imitations unworthy of notice, or original fictions that interest precisely because they combat the pernicious tendencies of most other popular romances. Such assessments rely on a homogenising view of popular literary production in the period, one that classes all fiction – regardless of individual particularities of narrative, theme or tone – as one thing or another and go hand in hand with Romantic-era attempts to police imaginative literature. Recent research has underlined the pervasiveness of these views across time. Indeed, one of the principal reasons we no longer read texts such as *The Haunted Priory, The Children of the Abbey* and *More Ghosts!*, despite the notable evidence of their deep and wide-ranging cultural footprint, is because we replicate Romantic-era views of these novels, often without the benefit of a close reading. Although by no means exhaustive, this overview of 1790s Irish Gothic fiction showcases the real variety and richness of the works produced in this period. Far from mere imitations, or, on the other hand, reactive responses to popular fiction, the works discussed here evidence a lively culture of debate and exchange in which Irish writers engaged with contemporary discourse about authorship and literary value while also reflecting on issues such as the relationship between history and fiction, female education and national identity. With access to these texts now made more convenient than ever via digitisation, it is to be hoped that the diversity and fullness of 1790s Irish Gothic fiction might inspire attentive analyses that re-centre them within our historiographies of Romantic-era literary production.

Notes

1. 'The Reviews' collectively refers to the *Monthly Review* and the *Critical Review*.
2. Before 1790 and the adoption of the branding of 'Minerva Press', Lane's lists were generically diverse and included 'song-books, jest-books, annuals, pamphlets, and books of travel' as well as romances and novels (Blakey 39).

This is what Dorothy Blakey refers to as 'the experimental stage' of Lane's publishing endeavours (39). It is worth remembering, however, that Lane's lists remained much more varied than contemporary critics allowed, as Deborah Anne McLeod reminds us (13).
3. For an enumeration of these novels, see Morin 201–11. See also individual author entries in Loeber.
4. On this critical tendency, see Morin 97–105.
5. 'History, like painting only perpetuates the striking features of the mind; whereas the best and worst actions of princes often proceed from partialities and prejudices, which live in their hearts, and are buried with them' (Lee 1: unpaginated preface).
6. See Review of *The Recess*, *Monthly Review* and Review of *The Recess*, *Critical Review*. The reviews specifically noted Lee's mixture of history and romance, with the *Monthly Review* expressing disappointment in the combination, preferring the romantic side of the tale, and the *Critical Review* lauding Lee's innovation in merging the two.
7. Comparison of the largely positive account of White's fiction in the Reviews with the much more negative reviews of female-authored fictions cited elsewhere in this essay emphasises the often gendered nature of critical assessments of Romantic-era popular fiction. While female authorship was sometimes seen by both authors and reviewers to demand gentler treatment than male-authored works, the Gothic romance's particular association with women, coupled with its domination of the marketplace in the 1790s, invited condemnation frequently guided by the author's gender. See, for instance, McLeod 116–43.
8. In the mid-nineteenth century, Roche was named 'a once famous novelist', who, alongside Radcliffe and Isabella Kelly, counted as 'the rival female novelists of the latter part of the eighteenth and the commencement of the nineteenth century' (Allibone 2: 1844).
9. Several scholars, including Butler, Mandal and Nowak, have expanded upon and otherwise developed Sadleir's point, investigating the nuanced reading of popular fiction – including novels produced by the Minerva Press – in Austen's oeuvre.
10. The 'Glorvina solution' refers to the national tale's allegorical marriage between native Irish and English/Anglo-Irish characters and is named after the heroine of Owenson's *The Wild Irish Girl* (Tracy 1–22).

Works Cited

Allibone, S. Austin. *A Critical Dictionary of English Literature and British and American Authors*. 3 vols. Philadelphia, J. B. Lippincott Company, 1902.

Baldick, Chris and Robert Mighall. 'Gothic Criticism'. *A Companion to the Gothic*, edited by David Punter, Blackwell, 2000, pp. 209–28.

Blakey, Dorothy. *The Minerva Press, 1790–1820*. The Bibliographical Society at the University Press, Oxford, 1937.

Burgess, Miranda. 'The National Tale and Allied Genres, 1770s–1840s'. *The Cambridge Companion to the Irish Novel*, edited by John Wilson Foster, Cambridge University Press, 2006, pp. 39–59.

Butler, Marilyn. *Jane Austen and the War of Ideas*. 1975. Clarendon Press, 2002.
Cannon, Mercy. 'On the Edges of Gothic Parody: The Neglected Work of Mrs F. C. Patrick and Sarah Green'. *Eighteenth-Century Fiction*, vol. 32, no. 4, 2020, pp. 579–98.
Casanova, Pascale. *The World Republic of Letters*. Translated by M. D. DeBevoise, Harvard University Press, 2004.
Clery, E. J. The *Rise of Supernatural Fiction, 1762–1800*. Cambridge University Press, 1995.
Cullen, Stephen. *The Castle of Inchvally: a tale – Alas! Too true*. 3 vols. London, J. Bell, 1796.
———. *The Haunted Priory; or, the Fortunes of the House of Rayo*. London, J. Bell, 1794.
Douglas, Aileen. '"Whom gentler stars unite": Fiction and Union in the Irish Novel'. *Irish University Review*, vol. 41, no. 1, 2011, pp. 183–95.
Frank, Frederick S. *The First Gothics: A Critical Guide to the English Gothic Novel*. Garland Publishing, 1987.
Horner, Avril and Sue Zlosnik, 'Comic Gothic'. *A New Companion to the Gothic*, edited by David Punter, Blackwell, 2012, pp. 321–35.
Lee, Sophia. *The Recess; or, a Tale of Other Times*. 3 vols, T. Cadell, 1783–1785.
Le Fanu, Joseph Sheridan. *In a Glass Darkly*. 1872. Edited by Robert Tracy, Oxford University Press, 2008.
Loeber, Rolf and Magda. *A Guide to Irish Fiction, 1650–1900*. Four Courts Press, 2006.
Mandal, Anthony. *Jane Austen and the Popular Novel*. Palgrave, 2007.
McLeod, Deborah Anne. *The Minerva Press*. 1997. University of Alberta, PhD dissertation.
Miles, Robert. 'The 1790s: The Effulgence of Gothic'. *The Cambridge Companion to Gothic Fiction*, edited by Jerrold E. Hogle, Cambridge University Press, 2002, pp. 41–62.
Milliken, Anna. *Corfe Castle; or, Historic Tracts*. 2 vols. Cork: James Haly, 1793.
Morin, Christina. *The Gothic Novel in Ireland, c. 1760–1829*. Manchester University Press, 2018.
Neiman, Elizabeth. 'A New Perspective on the Minerva Press's "Derivative" Novels: Authorizing Borrowed Material'. *European Romantic Review*, vol. 26, no. 5, 2015, pp. 633–58.
Newlyn, Lucy. *Reading, Writing, and Romanticism: The Anxiety of Reception*. Oxford University Press, 2000.
Nowak, Tenille. 'Regina Maria Roche's "Horrid" Novel: Echoes of *Clermont* in Jane Austen's *Northanger Abbey*'. *Persuasions*, vol. 29, 2007, pp. 184–93.
Patrick, Mrs F. C. *The Jesuit; or, the History of Anthony Babington, Esq., an Historical Novel*. 3 vols. Bath, R. Cruttwell, 1799.
———. *More Ghosts!* 3 vols. London, William Lane, 1798.
Peiser, Megan. 'William Lane and the Minerva Press in the Review Periodical, 1790–1820'. *Romantic Textualities: Literature and Print Culture, 1780–1840*, special issue on 'The Minerva Press and the Romantic-era Literary Marketplace', vol. 23, 2020, pp. 124–48.
Potter, Franz J. 'Chapbooks, Pamphlets, and Forgotten Horrors'. *The Palgrave Handbook of Steam Age Gothic*, edited by Clive Bloom, Palgrave, 2021, pp. 27–38.

———. *The History of Gothic Publishing, 1800–1835: Exhuming the Trade.* Palgrave, 2005.

Ravenwood, Victoria. '"Historical Anecdotes are the Most Proper Vehicles for the Elucidation of Mysteries": The "Historical Gothic" and the Minerva Press, 1790–99', *Romantic Textualities: Literature and Print Culture, 1780–1840*, special Issue on 'The Minerva Press and the Romantic-era Literary Marketplace', vol. 23, 2020, pp. 60–74.

Review of *The Adventures of King Richard Coeur-de-Lion. Critical Review*, new series, vol. 2, May 1791, p. 116.

Review of *The Adventures of King Richard Coeur-de-Lion. Monthly Review*, new series, vol. 6, October 1791, pp. 230–31.

Review of *Clermont. A Tale, Critical Review*, new series, vol. 24, November 1798, p. 356.

Review of *Corfe Castle. Anthologia Hibernica*, vol. 2, 1793, p. 366.

Review of *More Ghosts! Critical Review*, new series, vol. 24, October 1798, p. 236.

Review of *The Castle of Otranto. Monthly Review*, vol. 32, February 1765, pp. 97–99.

Review of *The Haunted Priory. The British Critic*, March 1795, p. 299.

Review of *The Haunted Priory. Critical Review*, August 1794, p. 468.

Review of *The Recess. Critical Review*, vol. 55, March 1783, pp. 233–34.

Review of *The Recess. Monthly* Review, vol. 68, May 1783, pp. 455–56.

Roche, Regina Maria. *The Children of the Abbey.* 1796. New York: Thomas Y. Crowell & Co., n.d.

———. *Clermont.* 1798. Edited by Natalie Schroeder, Valancourt Books, 2006.

Summers, Montague. *The Gothic Quest: A History of the Gothic Novel.* 1938. Russell & Russell, 1964.

Tracy, Robert. 'Maria Edgeworth and Lady Morgan: Legality versus Legitimacy'. *Nineteenth-Century Fiction*, vol. 40, 1985, pp. 1–22.

Walpole, Horace. *The Castle of Otranto*, 1764, edited by Nick Groom, Oxford University Press, 2014.

Watt, James. *Contesting the Gothic: Fiction, Genre and Cultural Conflict, 1764–1832.* Cambridge University Press, 1999.

White, James. *The Adventures of King Richard Coeur-de-Lion.* 3 vols. London, T. & J. Evans, 1791.

Chapter 2

'How Mute Their Tongues': Irish Gothic Poetry in the Nineteenth Century
Julia M. Wright

> We made no sign, we said no word.
> — Oscar Wilde, 'The Ballad of Reading Gaol'

This essay must enter uncharted woods: there is no canon of Irish Gothic poetry. There is not even much of a canon of nineteenth-century Irish poetry, though we have a general outline of one that begins with Thomas Moore, followed by James Clarence Mangan and the Young Ireland poets at mid-century, and then W. B. Yeats and his circle, perhaps with a footnote for Oscar Wilde for being Irish but not Irish enough. This organisation of nineteenth-century verse, including Oscar Wilde's marginality, relies on a fairly narrow nationalist rubric, not least in its near-exclusion of women poets except for the most prominent nationalist ones, such as Oscar's mother, Jane 'Speranza' Elgee Wilde. Discussions of the Gothic have been similarly circumscribed: early statements about Irish Gothic have followed British Gothic studies' emphasis on prose fiction, and generally viewed Irish Gothic as derivative of British Gothic or, if not, of British colonial violence.[1] Mangan has emerged as a crucial figure for discussions of a Catholic Irish Gothic that answers a predominantly Protestant canon of Irish Gothic fiction, but such discussions have stressed Mangan's prose, not his verse.[2] Gothic poetry in Ireland thus tends to stand apart from discussions of the Gothic, recognised neither as part of an Irish Gothic centred on prose forms, nor as part of nineteenth-century Irish verse, where nationalist themes rather than genres or modes predominate as organising rubrics.[3]

Moreover, Gothic poetry, on either side of the Irish Sea, is a fraught, and freighted, category. Mixing the 'low' Gothic mode with the 'high' culture of published poetry, the very category of Gothic verse destabilises conventional notions of value that are tied up with assumptions about literary difficulty and the capabilities of classed and gendered readerships. The British canon of nineteenth-century Gothic poetry is dominated by poems written by authors who largely made their reputations in the era through other kinds of writing: 'Christabel' (1816) and 'Rime of the Ancient Mariner' (1798, 1817) by Samuel Taylor Coleridge, lyric poet, theorist and creator of the conversation poem; *Manfred* (1817) by the prolific satirist, Byron; 'The Eve of St Agnes' (1820) by John Keats, praised primarily for his odes; 'The Lady of Shalott' (1833, 1842) and *Maud* (1855) by the poet laureate Alfred, Lord Tennyson; 'Porphyria's Lover' (1836) and 'My Last Duchess' (1842) by Robert Browning, originator of the dramatic monologue.[4] Even Percy Bysshe Shelley, author of Gothic works across multiple forms, including novels, a play and poems, is not generally considered a Gothic author but a lyric one. In broad terms, post-1850 Gothic poetry was otherwise classified, as 'pre-Raphaelite', like Christina Rossetti's 'Goblin Market' (1862), or tied to French symbolism, including verse by writers from Algernon Swinburne to Oscar Wilde, even though it is well established that the Symbolistes were themselves influenced by Edgar Allan Poe, that *rara avis* – an author known for Gothic literature in both prose and verse, including the widely referenced poem, 'The Raven' (1845). In broad terms, British Gothic verse was typically absorbed into other canons, concealing its discomfiting entanglement with a mode associated with the popular, coarse and obvious.

We may lack a general canon of Irish Gothic verse in part, then, because there are so few Irish poets in the nineteenth century with the status to slip 'low' poetry past the gate-keepers of 'serious' literature. The examples of Irish Gothic verse on which I shall focus here can be understood as responses to this legitimacy gap, attaching the Gothic to other forms of authority, including other national literatures, but not in the parasitical way that has been invoked in discussions of Irish Gothic fiction. Irish echoes of Thomas Gray's famous 'Elegy Written in a Country Churchyard' (1751), a founding work of English Gothic, appropriate and reshape the graveyard tradition for Irish purposes, while Irish, Germanic and Nordic folkloric traditions intermix in a more cosmopolitan supernatural Gothic that also centres on graveyard imagery. After sketching these two groups of Gothic poems, I will turn to prison Gothic as another reframing of graveyard verse. Overall, I shall suggest, early responses to Gray's 'Elegy' contribute to an Irish Gothic verse tradition dominated not by supernatural tropes but by dehumanising gestures such as unmarked graves, unburied bodies and oppressive silencing. If 'The [English] Gothic … constitutes significant textual evidence for the writing of the history of the subject' (Miles, *Gothic* 2), then the body of Irish Gothic verse considered here constitutes significant textual evidence for the unravelling of the history of that subject.

The Haunting of Gray's 'Elegy'

There has been important work on ruin discourse in relation to colonial loss in Irish writing, but less attention to the major poem of ruin that undergirds the English Gothic: Gray's 'Elegy'.[5] Gray's 'Elegy' was the last in a cluster of poems that led to the term 'The Graveyard School'; one of the earliest works sometimes associated with the group is 'A Night-Piece on Death' by the Irish poet Thomas Parnell, published shortly after his death in 1718. Parnell's poem invokes the *memento mori* tradition to which these poems contribute: '*Think, Mortal, what it is to dye*' (52). These poems not only participated in what Robert Miles has termed 'fashionable gloomth' ('Eighteenth-Century Gothic' 13) but also contributed to the lexicon of Gothic imagery: night-time darkness and shadows, decomposing bodies, collapsing stone structures (arches, churches, tombs) and hooting owls.

Gray's 'Elegy' has a peculiar Irish history, however. The 'Preliminary Advertisement' for *A Collection of Poems, on Various Subjects* (c. 1794), gathering works by the famous Dublin schoolmaster Samuel Whyte, offers an extensive overview of various English authors' plagiarisms that focuses on Gray's 'Elegy'. According to the Advertisement, around 1780 a 'Mr Giffard' was in a Dublin bookshop and 'dipped into an old Collection of Poems, and, to his great surprise, popped upon one, in an obsolete style, from which Gray had copied almost the whole of his Elegy' (xiv; see also Wright 249, 294). In 'August 1787', Giffard's opinion was confirmed by Peter Pindar who 'related an incident [...] exactly parallel to Mr Giffard's account' (xiv–xv). They cannot prove the plagiarism, however, because neither Giffard nor Pindar can remember the author or volume that included the original poem (xv), and another two witnesses, a couple, owned the book but can no longer find it (xvi–xvii). The charge appears to remain uncorroborated. But this account is important for registering the prominence of Gray's 'Elegy' in late eighteenth-century Irish literary discourse and for outlining what would become a conventional plot-device in Irish Gothic fiction – a tale of questionable (English) title to valuable property that cannot be fully exposed because of a partial documentary record. This plot appears in Maturin's *Melmoth the Wanderer* (1820), various texts by Maria Edgeworth (see Maurer), Lady Morgan's *The O'Briens and the O'Flahertys* (1827), on through to Le Fanu's Gothic works, especially the story that he rewrote a number of times and eventually extended into the novel *Uncle Silas* (1864).

Three major Irish poets at the turn of the century drew substantially on Gray's 'Elegy': Thomas Dermody, James Orr and William Drennan.

Dermody, part of Whyte's circle, echoes Gray in a number of works (Dornan 413, 416). Gray's 'Elegy' begins,

> The Curfew tolls the knell of parting day,
> The lowing herd wind slowly o'er the lea,
> The plowman homeward plods his weary way,
> And leaves the world to darkness and to me.
>
> Now fades the glimmering landscape on the sight,
> And all the air a solemn stillness holds,
> Save where the beetle wheels his droning flight,
> And drowsy tinklings lull the distant folds;
>
> Save that from yonder ivy-mantled tow'r
> The mopeing owl does to the moon complain. (1–10)

In his 'Contemplative Verses on the Tombs in Drumcondra Church-Yard, in the Manner of Gray' (1789), Dermody not only flags his debts in the title but also echoes Gray's 'Elegy' in the time of day, the motion of the first verse, the quietness broken by an owl's lament, and so on, as well as the alternating couplets of iambic pentameter and the sounds of Gray's opening rhymes ('ay' and 'ight'):

> Now sober Ev'ning, clad in mantlet grey,
>   In solemn pomp steals on to shadowy Night,
> The twinkling Stars begin their lucid way,
>   And bashful Cynthia shews her silver light.
>
> No noise is heard, save yonder hooting Owl,
>   That shrieks his mournful dirge in scream of woe.[6] (1–6)

But Dermody's poem transforms Gray's in important ways. Gray locates his deserted churchyard in a powerful nation, where there are 'Hands, that the rod of empire might have sway'd' but instead stayed out of the fray: 'Some village-Hampden, that […] The little Tyrant of his fields withstood; / Some mute inglorious Milton here may rest, / Some Cromwell guiltless of his country's blood' (47, 57–60). Irish literary theorist Robert Burrowes discusses these lines in Gray's 'Elegy' in a 1793/94 essay for the Royal Irish Academy: 'Political opinions take so strong an hold on the minds of English authors that they almost always bring themselves into notice. Gray has, in his Elegy, shewn us that Hampden, Milton and Cromwell were, in his mind, the greatest personages in English history' (90). This critique of Gray reverberates through Irish graveyard verse. Dermody thus echoes Gray's line about Milton with the lament for an Irish 'Poet', 'mute, alas! too mute his tuneful tongue' (51), but in life Milton's Irish counterpart 'could jocund mirth diffuse' (54) and fulfills a rural role that is more consonant with the pre-fallen world of Oliver Goldsmith's 'Deserted Village' than Gray's 'neglected spot' (45).

James Orr's 'Elegy, Written in the Church-yard of Templecorran' (1804) bears close comparison to Dermody's revision of Gray. Like Dermody, Orr announces his poem's relationship to Gray's 'Elegy' in his title, relocates the elegy to a specific Irish graveyard and begins by echoing the familiar features of Gray's early stanzas (though Orr switches to iambic tetrameter). But, as with Dermody, the emphasis is on horror, ruin and muteness, from the first verse: 'The falling fragment, heard with fear, / To silence awes the Owls that scream' (5–6). Orr's church is falling into ruin before the speaker's eyes:

> Hail, hoary structure! wrapt I trace
> The grass-crown'd wall, the weedy pew,
> And arches tott'ring to their base,
> And doors on high, that none pass thro'. (9–12)

Orr locates his poem in an early Christian church, rebuilt in the early 1600s and home of the first Presbyterian preacher in Ireland, Edward Brice.[7] Carol Baraniuk has read the poem biographically, as a reference to the death of Orr's father (59), but the poem reaches across centuries, like the church-yard itself, as 'Ruin yawns where Rapture glow'd' (20). Orr builds on the specific history of this church to shift Gray's trope of muteness to post-sectarianism:

> How still their hands! how mute their tongues!
>   Nor hearts embrace, nor heads invent,
> With party toasts, and party songs,
>   These trampled roofs are never rent [...]
> In vest of Green the breast is pent,
>   Who once the badge of Orange chose. (33–36, 39–40)

Orr and Dermody thus displace the English politics of Gray's 'Elegy' to comment on a colonised and fragmented Ireland in which muteness is almost endemic.

They also intensify its Gothic resonances. A few years after Gray's 'Elegy' was published, Edmund Burke published his *Philosophical Enquiry Into the Origins of our Ideas of the Sublime and Beautiful* (1757), a work also considered crucial to the development of the Gothic. For Burke, 'DARKNESS is terrible' and can 'cause pain' (132), and the 'loudness' of 'raging storms' can 'fill [us] with terror' (75). Burke, in short, provides the theoretical basis for the cliché of the 'dark and stormy night'. Orr's speaker wails, 'Yes, drench me, rain! and pierce me, wind! / And doleful darkness shade me o'er / Ye can't to me be more unkind' (97–99). Dermody's speaker also echoes Burke's key point that 'obscurity' intensifies fear (54–55): 'the herse in solemn grandeur comes, / The torches flashing thro' the dusk of night, / Each chequer'd gleam reflects the murky tombs, / And horror is encreas'd' (81–84).

Drennan's 'Glendalloch' also has 'close echoes' of Gray's 'Elegy', but shifts the focus from 'forefathers' to 'Princes and [...] prelates' in lamenting the death of 'sovereignty itself' (Wright 68), extending the colonial reframing of Gray's 'Elegy' by poets such as Orr and Dermody. The trope of the national graveyard, and the nation as graveyard, reaches its limit in Jane Wilde's Famine poem, 'The Stricken Land'. It appeared in *The Nation* on 23 January 1847 and was later republished in 1864 as 'The Famine Year': 'We've no strength left to dig them graves—there let them lie [...] Without a tear, a prayer, a shroud, a coffin, or a grave' (34, 38), until 'our whitening bones against ye will arise as witnesses, / From the cabins and the ditches, in their charred uncoffin'd masses [...] A ghastly, spectral army' to 'arraign ye as our murderers' (44–45, 47, 48). In this Gothic vision, the horror of unburied bodies gives way to the terror of resurrected skeletons and ghosts, shifting from the colonial abject to the national sublime in what Christopher Morash has termed 'the massed voices of the army of dry bones' in Famine verse (183). This attention to bodies that horrify because they are not properly buried predates the Famine, however, in such works as the Banims' 'Chaunt of the Cholera' (1831), where 'serfs, in tens of thousands, / Do blacken on the ground' (27–28), and Thomas Davis's 'My Grave' (1842): 'Shall they fling my corpse in the battle mound, / Where coffinless thousands lie under the ground'? (15–16). And, again, silence is another symptom of inhumane treatment: 'Die! Rot! And leave behind ye / Nothing! not even names!' (Banims 183–84); 'no tombstone there' (Davis 23).

In this context, it is worth considering a work by Moore, a student of both Whyte and Burrowes. In 'Shall the Harp Then Be Silent' (1821), an elegiac song on the death of the Irish parliamentarian Henry Grattan, Moore reverses Dermody's and Orr's appropriation of Gray's 'mute, inglorious Milton'. While Dermody's speaker laments, 'mute, alas! too mute his tuneful tongue' (51) and Orr's complains, 'how mute their tongues!' (33), Moore's speaker asks, 'Shall a Minstrel of Erin stand mute by the grave?' (3), and responds, 'No – faint tho' the death-song may fall from his lips [...] yet it shall sound' (5, 7). As if in answer to Gray's query, 'Can storied urn or animated bust / Back to its mansion call the fleeting breath?' Moore's speaker also insists, 'O'er a monument Fame will preserve, 'mong the urns / Of the wisest, the bravest, the best of mankind' (47–48). In Moore's poem, the patriot's fame endures, in part because Erin's poet cannot 'stand mute'. In this pointed transformation of Irish Gothic graveyard verse, nationalism animates the grave-side scene and, so to speak, unmutes the national poet. Moore thus invokes the fundamental antipathy between the Gothic and the nationalist, between colonial terror and political hope, that informs the sorts of canonical trends with which this chapter began.

Folkloric Otherworlds

Richard Haslam suggests that a 'distinctive feature of Irish Gothic', and especially Irish Catholic Gothic, is 'its recurrent incorporation of folklore' ('Irish Gothic' 5). Haslam follows Seamus Deane who introduced the term 'Catholic-nationalist Gothic' in a discussion of a prose work by Mangan (126). But Irish poetry predates this 'recurrent incorporation'. The trope of Irish folklore appears, for instance, in Moore's 'By that Lake Whose Gloomy Shore' (1811), where the ascetic Kevin is pursued by Kathleen 'And with rude, repulsive shock, / Hurls her from the beetling rock' (31–32). This incident is detailed in Fisher's 'Description of the Valley of Glendalough' in *Scenery of Ireland* (1795), but Fisher's Kathleen survives her fall and Moore's is transformed into a ghost in a passage that echoes the apotheosis of a prince in John Leslie's *Killarney* (Wright 90–91). More to my point here, Moore's footnote ties his text to folklore, indicating 'This Ballad is founded upon one of the many stories related of St. Kevin' (247n).

Moore was not the first to build a Gothic poem on rural folklore from this particular region. Drennan's 'Glendalloch' repeats a better-documented tale of St Kevin, in which a blackbird lays her eggs on St Kevin's hand, which he kindly keeps outstretched 'till she had hatch'd her brood' (184). In 'Glendalloch', the gentle Kevin that protects the eggs, for instance, is a 'living skeleton' and his hand is 'stiff' and 'wither'd' (176, 180), and he 'leads the black procession' of Catholic monasticism and the incident with the blackbird is followed by a possible suicide (190–94). Immediately before the passage with the legend of St Kevin, Drennan associates folklore with Gothic excitement that owes much to Burke's ideas of terror (see Wright 72–73):

> The ragged minstrel of the glade,
> With an uncouth, and visage pale,
> Pours forth the legendary tale [...]
> We listen – then a pleasing thrill
> Creeps thro' our frame, and charms our will,
> Till, fill'd with forms fantastic, wild,
> We feign – and then become the child. (158–60, 163–66)

Drennan and Moore find in rural Ireland folkloric resources that would shortly be catalogued by Thomas Crofton Croker's *Researches in the South of Ireland* (1824) and then the Ordnance Survey. While much Irish supernatural verse stays on the frothy side of things – William Allingham's fairy poems for instance – in these poems the rural repository of 'the legendary tale' offers the Gothic frisson of 'a pleasing thrill' (Drennan 160, 163).

Moore, however, also turned to Continental Europe. In 'The Ring: A Tale', purportedly a German medieval story that Moore's fictional editor traces through a footnote, a bridegroom slips his bride's wedding ring onto a statue's finger and the statue then clenches its fist to hold onto it; three nights he awakes with a spectre between him and his bride, and then he finally gets the spectre to release the ring. It is clearly Gothic, as H. P. Lovecraft recognised: 'Thomas Moore adapted from such sources the legend of the ghoulish statue-bride […] which echoes so shiveringly in his ballad of *The Ring*' (23). One of Moore's early biographers was less impressed, but equally aware the poem was Gothic even if he was reluctant to use that term:

> in two other poems, *Reuben and Rose* and *The Ring*, we find Moore wandering off after the fashion of the German spectral ballad:–
> 'Twas Reuben, but ah! he was deathly and cold,
> And fleeted away like the spell of a dream.'
> And so on, with cold carcases and other properties of this form of composition, to which the poet never returned – wisely recognising that it was not for him to make readers' flesh creep. (Gwynn 26)

Both poems mentioned by Gwynn appeared in Moore's *Poetical Works of Thomas Little* (1801). Moore also wrote a poem about a ghost ship, 'Written on Passing Dead-Man's Island', for *Epistles, Odes, and Other Poems* (1806), and 'returned' again to 'mak[ing] readers' flesh creep' in 'By that Lake Whose Gloomy Shore' for the *Irish Melodies* (1811).

Mid-century Irish poets followed Moore's 1801 poems into medieval Continental Europe, including through key translations. In 1834 and then again in 1846, Mangan translated G. A. Bürger's 'Lenore' (1774), a German poem foundational to the very idea of the 'spectral ballad' and the era's strong identification of the Gothic with the Germanic. In 1849, Jane Wilde translated another German text, William Meinhold's *Sidonia the Sorceress* (1848), a Gothic work about a woman prosecuted as a witch in the Renaissance that is well-established as an influence on the Pre-Raphaelites. In verse, Jane Wilde translated 'Thekla, a Swedish Saga', which appeared in her 1864 *Poems*. In her *Driftwood from*

Scandanavia (1884), Wilde describes 'Thekla', 'an ancient tale of sin, sorrow, and temptation, of repentance and expiation, as all life-dreams are, but which had an additional interest for me just then, for the surroundings of sea and shore and shadowy pines happened to be the very framework in which the poem was set' (203).

'Thekla' is a Faustian fiction,[8] with a gendered twist: Thekla makes a pact with a witch to preserve her beauty through reproductive sterility. While most of the poem is in ballad stanzas, the first part of 'Thekla' adapts the meter of Tennyson's 'Lady of Shalott':

> With her wand the magic Mother
>   Draws a circle on the floor.
>
> Grains of yellow corn, seven,
>   Takes she from a sack beside,
> Draws the gold ring of her lover
>   From the finger of the bride.–
>
> 'Seven children would have stolen
>   Light and beauty from thine eyes –
> But as I cast the yellow corn
>   Through thy gold ring, each one dies.[']
>
> Slowly creaked the mill, then faster
>   Whirled the giant arms on high;
> Shuddering, hears the trembling maiden
>   Crushing bones and infant's cry. (*Poems* 152)

Thekla is haunted by sounds for most of the poem, such as those of the last verse above, until she repents and is forgiven. After she confesses her sin, her husband calls her 'A devil – not a woman fair / Like coiling snakes I seem to see / Each twisted tress of golden hair. / I hate thee, as I hate God's foe' (159). Isobel Murray has connected the poem to the novel by Wilde's son, *The Picture of Dorian Gray* (1891), but the link largely rests on the protagonists' shared desire to preserve their beauty (3). 'Thekla' also resonates with the *Picture* in its debts to the myth of Narcissus: 'In that mirror idly gazing / She beholds, with inward praising, / Her own beauty in amaze' (148). In 'Thekla', however, the representation of children draining life from their mother is more vampiric than the simple aging that frightens Dorian Gray: 'For the beauty of the mother / Is the children's – sister, brother, / As she fades away, will bloom' (150). Thekla's refusal to submit to this transfer of life, in which 'Mother's woe is children's weal' (149), makes her a Gothic monster. She is not only a 'devil' with Medusa-like hair, but also anticipates some of the specifics of Bram Stoker's vampires. She cannot touch 'A child just blessed by holy rood' (156) and she does not cast a shadow: 'Woman or fiend! Look, if you dare, / The palfrey casts a shadow plain, / But yours – O horror! – is not there!' (157).

While British Gothic medievalism was largely set tacitly in England, from Coleridge's 'Christabel' to Keats's 'Eve of St. Agnes', Irish Gothic medievalism thus often turned to Continental Europe. The nationalist project of representing pre-colonial Ireland as well-governed, culturally rich and populated by idealised characters pulls against the transfer of the medievalist tropes that informed – and to a significant extent even defined – British Gothic verse. Mangan's 'A Vision of Connaught in the Thirteenth Century' (1846) is illustrative on this point: in the distant past, Connaught (largely untouched by Norman colonisation in the early 1200s) is 'a land of Morn' with 'seas of corn' (2, 5), when 'a change / From light to darkness' leads to a 'terror […] None seemed to understand' (38–39, 45). The speaker then sees a 'sky […] fleckt with blood', 'an alien sun' and a 'skeleton' (50–51, 54), but notes, 'in the Teuton's land, […] I dreamed this dream' (57–58). Mangan's footnote ties these 'portent[s]' to the death of the Connaught king and the thirteenth-century *Annals of the Four Masters*, authenticating its medievalism. But the poem roots the 'dream' not in ancient Ireland or its *Annals* but in Germany. In medieval Ireland, 'terror' is even beyond their 'understand[ing]'. It can only emerge for an idealised pre-colonial Ireland retrospectively via a German frame.

Prison Gothic

'Thekla' appeared in 1864, just as the Irish Republican Brotherhood was on the rise. By the late 1860s, the IRB and 'Fenianism' more broadly constituted a transatlantic movement associated with violence, known particularly for a series of raids on Canada starting in 1866 and the Clerkenwell explosion on 13 December 1867 in London, in which twelve people were killed and dozens injured in an effort to break Fenians out of the Clerkenwell prison. Fenians were also blamed for the 1868 assassination of Young Ireland poet and Canadian politician, Thomas D'Arcy McGee. Jane Wilde, like Davis, McGee and Mangan, contributed poetry to *The Nation* in the middle of the century. She also continued to publish verse long after the end of Young Ireland and through the Fenian period. In January 1870 in the Boston *Pilot*, and later in the expanded 1871 edition of her *Poems*, Wilde published 'The Prisoners', dated 'Christmas, 1869' in both versions, setting it almost exactly two years after the Clerkenwell explosion. Wilde's poem centres on 'young lives […] wept out in dungeons' outside of Ireland

(*Poems* 173). The prison is a Gothic setting, far from 'loved mountain scenes': it is the site of 'torture and sorrow', 'the gloom of the desolate cell' and the apocalyptic 'wrath of the sevenfold vials / Seem poured to turn Earth to a Hell' (invoking Revelations 15) (173). In this darkness,

>   a night where no Angel appears,
> The wasted limbs heavy with fetters,
>   The weary heart heavy with tears;
> With the ghost of dead youth crushing on them
>   And the gloom of the years yet to be,
> With a blackness of darkness upon them. (175)

This goes far beyond Burkean 'obscurity' to shift the meaning of weight from 'fetters' on the weak to 'tears' to 'the ghost of dead youth'.[9] While the first verse contrasts the prisoners' exilic dungeon with the fresh air and scenes of Ireland, the final verse juxtaposes Christmas celebrations with the details of burial: 'Through our wassail the wail from their prison, / With sorrow wrapped round like a garment [...] With bonds tight'ning close as a cerement' (175). No Easter hope of resurrection here—no Christmas of birth and renewal. This is Christmas as midwinter, a time of death and of the end of the year that awaits only 'the gloom of the years yet to be'.

Imprisonment, then, intersects with exile, as it had so often before in Irish verse, including J. J. Callanan's 'Convict of Clonmel' (1823). But while such early nineteenth-century poems ring with nostalgia and regret for an idealised, but lost, Ireland, like the Irish medievalism noted in the previous section, later poems such as Wilde's 'Prisoners' delineate the horrors of the charnel house. This continues to the 1890s. For instance, in 1891, Dora Sigerson published 'Lady Kathleen' in the *Irish Monthly*. The 1891 publication places the poem before the major 'Cathleen' works of the modernists, and instead puts it in a genealogy that goes back at least to Mangan's contribution to the *Irish Penny Journal* in 1841, 'Kathaleen Ny-Houlahan':

> Think her not a ghastly hag, too hideous to be seen,
> Call her not unseemly names, our matchless Kathaleen;
> Young she is, and fair she is, and would be crowned a queen,
> Were the king's son at home here with Kathaleen Ny-Houlahan!
>
> Sweet and mild would look her face, O none so sweet and mild,
> Could she crush the foes by whom her beauty is reviled. (5–10)

Sigerson's Kathleen, also echoing Tennyson's 'Lady of Shalott', is in a tower weaving 'a cloak for th[e] rescue' of her beloved, who she calls

'Sweet', weaving so long that she grows old and her beloved, at the end of the poem, can no longer recognise her. The imagery of her travel from one prison to the other, from her tower to the fairy fort where her lover is kept, is insistently Gothic:

> A ghostly moon in a steel cold sky,
> A dance of leaves by the wind swept by,
> Like the mirthless rushing of phantom feet [...]
> She sped without fear in the awe of night,
> Though the shuddering shadows would stay her flight
> With the thought of a horror unknown. (*Verses* 510–11)

In the world of the fairies, she appears as a phantom herself:

> To the white thorn tree on the fairy rath
> The Lady Kathleen quick took her path,
> Till she stood in the midst of the elfin host,
> Like a lily pale or a fair white ghost. (511)

As in a number of Sigerson's poems, including the powerful 'Man's Discontent' that appeared in *Verses* (1893) along with 'Lady Kathleen', the male beloved's failure to recognise and value a woman's love and ageing beauty leads to her death. Sigerson's 'Lady Kathleen', then, is not the 'mother Ireland' of so many Kathleen works. The 'ghastly hag' of the myth becomes the faded beauty of 'a heart denied' (511): 'My hands grew hard as they wove for thee / The magic cloak that hath set thee free. / My face grew sad, and my hair grew white / In the silent horror of many a night' (511). As in Jane Wilde's 'Thekla' and Oscar Wilde's *Picture of Dorian Gray*, the inevitability of ageing and thus death lies at the core of the Gothic machinery – the focus of what David B. Morris has termed the 'vertiginous and plunging – not a soaring – sublime' of the Gothic (306). But in the work of these women poets, the focus is specifically on the body of the non-fecund woman as the site of monstrosity and death.

Oscar Wilde's poetry also connects to this Irish Gothic tradition, including 'Requiescat': 'Coffin-board, heavy stone, / Lie on her breast' (13–14). His most famous Gothic poem is, like 'Lady Kathleen', centred on a tale of thwarted love and imprisonment: 'The Ballad of Reading Gaol'. Like his mother in her prison poem, Oscar Wilde stresses the weight of 'fetters', separation from the natural world ('that little tent of blue / Which prisoners call the sky' [15–16]) and the relentless reminder of death:

> Yet though the hideous prison-wall
>   Still hems him round and round,
> And a spirit may not walk by night
>   That is with fetters bound. (499–502)

'The Ballad of Reading Gaol' is also, in substantial ways, a graveyard poem, returning again and again to the executed prisoner's grave in the final third of the poem. In an Irish context, one passage is particularly resonant:

> There is a pit of shame
> And in it lies a wretched man
>   Eaten by teeth of flame,
> In a burning winding-sheet he lies,
>   And his grave has got no name.
>
> And there, till Christ call forth the dead,
>   In silence let him lie. (638–44)

Moore's 'O Breathe Not His Name' in the *Irish Melodies* famously refers to Robert Emmet's request that his grave be unmarked, a request also echoed in Davis's 'My Grave'. In the 'Ballad', the prison itself is represented as a graveyard without the marking of names: 'each man trembled as he crept / Into his numbered tomb' (245–46). As in other Irish Gothic poems, erasure and silence rather than decaying commemoration is the subject to which Wilde returns: 'we made no sign, we said no word' (165). Once again, muteness is the mark of oppression:

> We did not dare to breathe a prayer,
>   Or to give our anguish scope:
> Something was dead in each of us,
>   And what was dead was Hope. [...]
> So, like things of stone in a valley lone,
>   Quiet we sat and dumb. (357–60, 375–76)

And, as in the various poems that deplore the unburied dead, the failure to recognise humanity through rituals of commemoration is part of the Gothic horror: 'They hanged him as a beast is hanged: / They did not even toll / A requiem that might have brought / Rest to his startled soul' (511–14).

Conclusion

It is conventional to note the influence of the Graveyard School on English Gothic, but Irish responses to Gray's 'Elegy' are differently threaded through Gothic verse. The rural graveyard of the Patriot's hopes in Dermody became the graveyard of national sovereignty in Drennan, and then the Famine made everywhere a graveyard and finally prisons created graveyards for the living as well as the dead. If there is a dominant thematic thread in the canonical English Gothic poems that I mention above, it is domestic marriage plots gone awry. In the selection of Irish Gothic poems considered here, the focus is on death, not marriage, as the site of social failure. Unmarked graves, unburied bodies, unfecund women, prisons – all erase and 'mute' the subject, locating it outside of genealogy and beyond commemoration.

Notes

1. For some important early statements, see McCormack, Moynahan and Kilfeather. Recent Irish Gothic studies are expanding our range of vision considerably.
2. See Deane (126) and Haslam ('Irish Gothic' and 'Broad Farce'). The elision of Mangan's Gothic poetry predates Deane's introduction of Catholic Irish Gothic as a category: Andrews suggested in 1989 that it was 'only in prose [that Mangan] explored the Gothic genre' (241).
3. For early key statements on verse and nationalism, see, e.g., David Lloyd's *Nationalism and Minor Literature* (1987) and Mary Helen Thuente's *Harp Re-Strung* (1994); the importance of the national tale in early studies of Irish Romantic-era fiction also supported an emphasis on genre and nationalism.
4. A number of these poems are prominent in Miles's book as well as anthologies by Wagner and Franklin; for a valuable discussion of Victorian Gothic poetry, see Ackerman.
5. For a brief overview of influential work on ruin discourse, see Wright (57); on the Graveyard School and the Gothic, see, for instance, Botting (32–35).
6. Except for quotations from Sigerson, the Banims, and Jane Wilde's 'Thekla' and 'The Prisoners', all Irish poetry is quoted from Wright, *Irish Literature, 1750–1900*.
7. For more, see Baraniuk.
8. The text is Faustian in drawing on the plot of selling one's soul for immediate, worldly gain, as in Johann Wolfgang von Goethe's *Faust*, a work with a complicated publication history that runs from 1790 to 1831.
9. See Howes on the importance of 'tears' in Wilde's writing.

Works Cited

Ackerman, Michael. *Phantoms of Old Forms: The Gothic Mode in the Dramatic Verse of Tennyson and Browning*. 2009. Wilfrid Laurier University, PhD dissertation.

Andrews, Jean. 'James Clarence Mangan and Romantic Stereotypes: "Old and Hoary at Thirty-Nine"'. *Irish University Review*, vol. 19, no. 2, 1989, pp. 240–63.

Banim, John and Michael Banim. 'Chaunt of the Cholera'. 'Writing Ireland Into Europe: An Edition of Three Nineteenth-Century Poems', edited by Julia M. Wright, *Canadian Journal of Irish Studies*, vol. 30, no. 1, 2004, pp. 58–61.

Baraniuk, Carol. *James Orr, Poet and Irish Radical*. Routledge, 2014.

Botting, Fred. *Gothic*. Routledge, 1996.

Burke, Edmund. *A Philosophical Enquiry into the Origin of our Ideas of the Sublime and Beautiful*, edited by Adam Phillips, Oxford University Press, 2008.

Burrowes, Robert. 'Essay on the Following Subject, Proposed by the Academy, viz. "On Style in Writing".' *Transactions of the Royal Irish Academy*, vol. 5, 1793/1794, pp. 39–92.

Deane, Seamus. *Strange Country: Modernity and Nationhood in Irish Writing Since 1790*. Clarendon, 1997.

Dornan, R. Stephen. 'Thomas Dermody's Archipelagic Poetry'. *European Romantic Review*, vol. 21, 2010, pp. 409–23.

Dunne, Tom. 'Haunted by History: Irish Romantic Writing, 1800–1850'. *Romanticism in National Context*, edited by Roy Porter and Mikuláš Teich, Cambridge University Press, 1988, pp. 68–91.

Franklin, Caroline, editor. *The Longman Anthology of Gothic Verse*. Routledge, 2010.

Gray, Thomas. 'Elegy Written in a Country Churchyard'. *The Complete Poems of Thomas Gray*, edited by H. W. Starr and J. R. Hendrickson, Clarendon, 1966, pp. 37–43.

Gwynn, Stephen. *Thomas Moore*. Macmillan, 1905.

Haslam, Richard. '"Broad Farce and Thrilling Tragedy": Mangan's Fiction and Irish Gothic'. *Éire-Ireland*, vol. 41, no. 3–4, 2006, pp. 215–44. doi:10.1353/eir.2007.0005.

———. 'Irish Gothic: A Rhetorical Hermeneutics Approach'. *Irish Journal of Gothic and Horror Studies*, no. 2, 2007, irishgothichorror.files.wordpress.com/2018/03/richard-haslam.pdf.

Howes, Marjorie. 'Tears and Blood: Lady Wilde and the Emergence of Irish Cultural Nationalism'. *Ideology and Ireland in the Nineteenth Century*, edited by Tadhg Foley and Seán Ryder, Dublin, Four Courts Press, 1998, pp. 151–72.

Kilfeather, Siobhán. 'Gothic Novel'. *The Cambridge Companion to the Irish Novel*, edited by J. W. Foster, Cambridge University Press, 2006, pp. 78–96.

Kilfeather, Siobhán Marie. 'Terrific Register: The Gothicization of Atrocity in Irish Romanticism', *boundary 2*, vol. 31, 2004, pp. 49–71.

Lloyd, David, *Nationalism and Minor Literature: James Clarence Mangan and the Emergence of Irish Cultural Nationalism*. University of California Press, 1987.

Lovecraft, Howard Phillips. *Supernatural Horror in Literature* (1927), 'Introduction' by August Derleth. Ben Abramson, 1945.

Maurer, Sara L. 'Disowning to Own: Maria Edgeworth and the Illegitimacy of National Ownership'. *Criticism,* vol. 44, no. 4 (Fall 2002), pp. 363–88.

McCormack, W. J. 'Irish Gothic and After (1820–1945)'. *Field Day Anthology of Irish Writing*, gen. ed. Seamus Deane, Derry, Field Day, 1991, II: 831–54.

Miles, Robert. 'Eighteenth-Century Gothic'. *The Routledge Companion to Gothic*, edited by Catherine Spooner and Emma McEvoy, Routledge, 2007, pp. 10–18.

———. *Gothic Writing, 1750–1820: A Genealogy*. 2nd ed. Manchester University Press, 2002.

Morash, Christopher. *Writing the Irish Famine*. Clarendon, 1995.

Morris, David B. 'Gothic Sublimity'. *New Literary History*, vol. 16, no. 2, 1985, pp. 299–319.

Moynahan, Julian. *Anglo-Irish: The Literary Imagination in a Hyphenated Culture*. Princeton University Press, 1995.

Murray, Isobel. 'Introduction'. *The Complete Shorter Fiction of Oscar Wilde*. Oxford University Press, 1979, pp. 1–18.

Parnell, Thomas. 'A Night-Piece on Death'. *Collected Poems of Thomas Parnell*, edited by Claude Rawson and F. P. Lock, University of Delaware Press, 1989, pp. 168–71.

Sigerson, Dora. *Verses*. Elliot Stock, 1893.

Thuente, Mary Helen, *The Harp Re-Strung: The United Irishmen and the Rise of Irish Literary Nationalism*. University of Syracuse Press, 1994.

Wagner, Corinna, ed. *Gothic Evolutions: Poetry, Tales, Context, Theory*. Broadview P, 2014.

Whyte, Samuel. *Collection of Poems, On Various Subjects*, edited by Edward Athenry Whyte. 2nd ed. Dublin, 1792, pp. xi–xxvii. *Eighteenth Century Collections Online*.

Wilde, Jane. *Driftwood from Scandinavia*. Richard Bentley, 1884.

———. *Poems by Speranza*. 1871. Dublin, M. H. Gill & Sons, 1907.

Wright, Julia M., editor. *Irish Literature, 1750–1900: An Anthology*. Wiley-Blackwell, 2008.

———. *Representing the National Landscape in Irish Romanticism*. Syracuse University Press, 2014.

Part II

Irish Gothic Genres and Forms

Chapter 3

'A Dead, Living, Murdered Man': Staging the Irish Gothic
Christopher Morash

A Mercurial Mode

'What hath been with thee?', the character of Clotilda asks Imogine, the doomed heroine in Charles Robert Maturin's *Bertram*, from 1816. 'Something dark that hovered', Imogine replies (*'deliriously'*):

> Upon the confines of unmingling worlds,
> In dread for life – for death too sternly definite,
> Something the thought doth try in vain to follow –
> Through mist and twilight – (50)

More than a century later, in W. B. Yeats's *Purgatory* (1938), a boy and an old man stand before their ancestral house on a moonlit night, when a figure appears in the window – the old man's father – even though the house is a ruin and 'the floorboards are all burned away'. In horror, the boy cries out at the sight of 'A dead, living, murdered man! […] A body that was a bundle of old bones/ Before I was born. Horrible! Horrible!" (Yeats, *The Variorum Edition of the Plays of W. B. Yeats* 1048). Almost exactly sixty years later, once again on the stage of Dublin's Abbey Theatre,[1] the character of Hester Swane in Marina Carr's *By the Bog of Cats …* (1998) enters 'a bleak white landscape of ice and snow', trailing the corpse of a black swan, where she encounters the Ghost Fancier. 'Mr Ghost Fancier', she asks him, 'what ghost are you ghoulin' for around here?', 'I'm ghoulin' for a woman be the name of Hester Swane'. When Hester says that she is, in fact, Hester Swane, the Ghost Fancier apologises, asking whether it is dawn or dusk. If she is in fact Hester Swane, he explains, and she is still alive, then 'I must be too previous. I mistook this hour for the dusk' (Carr 13–14).

In any conventional history of theatre, these three plays – *Bertram*, *Purgatory*, and *By the Bog of Cats …* – belong to three quite distinct periods. *Bertram* belongs to the flourishing of Irish Romantic drama in the early decades of the nineteenth century. Largely played out on the London stage, (even after the opening of the major Irish theatre of the period, on Dublin's Hawkins Street in 1821), it sits alongside Richard Lalor Shiels's *The Apostate* (1817), John Banim's *Damon and Pythias* (1821), or the work of James Sheridan Knowles, whose *Virginius* (1820), provided a staple role for William Charles Macready for many years (Connolly 185–214). Yeats's *Purgatory*, by contrast, is an exemplary work of late modernist theatre. The performance space is almost empty, consciously a stage, with only the shell of a ruined house and 'a bare tree in the background' (*The Variorum Edition of the Plays of W. B. Yeats* 1041). The resonances with Samuel Beckett's *Waiting for Godot* – Beckett was in the audience when *Purgatory* first opened in August of 1938 – have been noted by more than one commentator, with Michael McAteer arguing that the similarities between *Purgatory* and Beckett's later work extend well beyond bare trees to an abiding concern with 'the combination of stasis and slow decay'(191). If *Purgatory* is thus a prime example of the Irish modernism of the 1930s, Marina Carr's *By the Bog of Cats …* is equally one of the defining Irish plays of the 1990s. When it was first staged in 1998, following the success of two of Carr's previous plays, *The Mai* (1994) and *Portia Coughlan* (1996), *By the Bog of Cats …* seemed to audiences to belong to a growing body of work by a new generation of Irish playwrights, including Conor McPherson, Martin McDonagh and Enda Walsh. Indeed, even the play's supernatural elements were not out of place in this context. One of the most successful plays of the decade, Conor McPherson's *The Weir* (1997) is based around a series of ghost stories, and his later play, *The Seafarer*, concerns a Faustian pact with a character who may (or may not) be the devil. Indeed, Emilie Pine has pointed out that plays like *The Weir*, *By the Bog of Cats …*, and Stewart Parker's 1987 play, *Pentecost* (set in a Belfast house in which the past inhabitants are an active presence) collectively demonstrate that 'ghostly liminality has been a notable feature of Irish drama over the past thirty years', arguing that these plays constitute part of a wider engagement of recent Irish theatre with memory, and 'that ghosts are best understood as fragments of memory' (154).

So, from a theatre history perspective, *Bertram*, *Purgatory*, and *By the Bog of Cats …* belong in three very different theatrical contexts. At the same time, it is difficult to shake the sense that there is a kind of kinship among the three plays, something not as definite as influence, tradition or even generic convention, but something palpable, nonetheless. To put it simply, when Imogine raves about 'something dark that hovered', or the Boy looks in horror at the figure in the window, or ghosts appear among the living on the Bog of Cats, even at the most basic level of imagery, we recognise something we can call the Gothic, particularly if we accept that the literary Gothic, as Dale Townshend puts it (paraphrasing Julian Wolfreys), 'loses much of its formal and generic stability' once we move beyond the first wave of Gothic novels and plays in the late eighteenth century, 'fragmenting and dissolving instead into a mercurial mode that stealthily works its way into the most unsuspecting and unlikely of cultural forms' (16). Or, as Francesca Saggini puts it in her structuralist-inflected study of Gothic fiction and drama, 'although the Gothic had no generic consistency, the presence of ubiquitous signifiers and recurrent structures of feeling provided a unifying frame, confirming the similarities that existed between related artistic forms' (137).

The related concepts of a 'mercurial mode' and 'recurrent structures of feeling' are useful here, if only because they allow us to identify those markers – images, narrative tropes, certain formations of affect – that operate across literary historical periods, and across generic forms. Not only do these three plays – *Bertram*, *Purgatory*, and *By the Bog of Cats ...* – each belong to three distinct periods of theatre history; they also belong to three distinct iterations of the Gothic. For instance, Claire Connolly has argued that *Bertram* belongs to 'a post-1641 Anglican tradition' in Irish Romanticism 'that associated Catholicism with horror, violence, and fear', and which was to bear as its fruit an important genre of Gothic writing (188). Although this association between horror and Catholicism is by no means confined to this period, it had a particular resonance in the over-heated sectarian climate of nineteenth-century Ireland, and this in turn has helped to shape a dominant reading of nineteenth-century Irish Gothic writing more generally. In this regard, we can refer back to the work of W. J. McCormack in the 1980s, later developed in the work of scholars likes Jarlath Killeen, Richard Haslam, Christina Morin, and others, all of whom make cogent, historically-grounded arguments for reading nineteenth-century Irish Gothic (primarily fiction) in the context of religious anxieties of various hues. In the case of Maturin, the fact that he was an Anglican clergyman gives further substance to the case. Equally, there is an extensive critical literature on Yeats's *Purgatory*, much of which reads it in the context of political anxieties of dispossession and decadence in relation to post-Independence Ireland and European fascism. '*Purgatory*', asserts Marjorie Howes, 'which was first published in *On the Boiler*, represents the culmination of Yeats's eugenic theory of nationality' (176). Indeed, it was McCormack who first made the link from Yeats's play to the Gothic of the nineteenth century, arguing that as well as being a 'self-regulating modernist art-work', the play, 'establishes real relations with the world it comes from [...] in the disturbed soil of nineteenth (and early twentieth) century social change' (McCormack, 'Yeats's "Purgatory"' 37). In the case of *By the Bog of Cats ...*, this is a play that is seen as a part of a wider set of challenges to gender roles in Irish culture in the 1990s, not least in an Irish theatre culture that had long been male-dominated. In this regard, Carr's work has emerged as one of the defining works of the decade, and it is in this context that its Gothic elements have been read: as the return of a repressed element in Irish culture. For instance, we find Melissa Sihra arguing that the unseen character of Josie Swane (Hester's mother, and one of the play's ghosts), is in fact 'a spectre of womanhood on the Irish stage whose unexplained disappearance has simply been accepted' (122).

There is something curious at work here, however. On one hand, we have the testimony of several decades of scholarly work, demonstrating that all three plays are capable of producing rich, revealing historical readings. At the same time, the elements that allow us to identify them as Gothic in the first instance appear to function trans-historically. As a way of thinking through this situation, we take an imaginative excursion, and think of *Bertram, Purgatory*, and *By the Bog of Cats ...* as if they constituted one long, strange play, beginning with Imogine in her room in the castle, a single lamp burning, as if she were the figure in the window in Yeats's ruined house, while the desolate landscape around, with its single bare tree, is the Bog of Cats, where an Old Man kills his son, and a woman kills her daughter. Thinking of the plays in this way serves to remind us that, as historically specific as they have been shown to be, they share a coherent set of images and narrative tropes. As Carr noted to herself about the character of the Catwoman in one of her manuscript notebooks kept while writing *By the Bog of Cats ...*: 'There is something Gothic about her appearance'.[2] The same could be said about all three plays, and not only the one – *Bertram* – that belongs to what Jeffrey N. Cox calls 'Gothic drama proper', which 'arose in England between 1789 and 1832' (125).

The stage Gothic, (no less than any other form of the Gothic), endures around an immediately recognisable set of images, which even in the nineteenth century were recognised as conventional: 'the sheeted ghost gliding from the churchyard – the midnight bell struck by airy hands – [...] the damp vault, and the bloody shroud'.[3] The key point here is not only what Jerrold E. Hogle defines as the Gothic's 'insistent artificiality' (15) – a point to which we will return – but the trans-historical quality of these conventions, which are simultaneously capable of speaking to individual historically specific concerns, whether in 1816, 1938 or 1998, and, at the same time, functioning across those specific moments. One possibility, of course, is that they are purely empty signifiers, which can be filled with whatever content happens to press itself upon the moment – an argument familiar from Eve Kosofsky Sedgwick's *Coherence of Gothic Conventions* (1986). The other possibility – which will ghost my argument here – is that the Gothic's concerns are those revealed to us by psychoanalytic reading telling us something about universal human behaviour. However, there is a third option here, one that does not mutually exclude the other two: that the theatrical Gothic also functions trans-historically in reference to the one thing that *Bertram*, *Purgatory* and *By the Bog of Cats …* all share: theatricality itself.

Death, Time and Excess

If there is a single, over-riding concern that dominates the Gothic, no matter how narrowly or loosely defined, it is arguably death, as Andrew Smith has shown in his literary history of Gothic death; or, more precisely, the representational problem posed by death. On the most obvious level, the familiar palette of images that populate every manifestation of the Gothic from *The Castle of Otranto* to a Hallowe'en lawn display are almost all indices of death: from the skeletons, crypts, vampires, corpses, shrouds and cemeteries that make up its signature set of images, to the narrative tropes of murder, suicide and haunting, to the obsession with religion and questions of eschatology, the sign of the skull acts as Gothic's immediately recognisable signature. In the three plays considered here, we have not only the shared set of images and tropes, there is equally a shared problematisation of the representation of death, which recognises that it is not simply a matter of making visible something that would otherwise be unseen. We grasp the problem immediately by turning to an early print of the actor Edmund Kean playing Bertram from the Drury Lane production in 1816 (see Figure 2); what strikes us most forcibly is the way in which the costume displays his physique: he is undeniably an embodied presence on the stage.

For instance, in *Bertram*, when Imogine is asked what she has seen, she describes 'something dark that hovered / Upon the confines of unmingling worlds'. The phrase 'unmingling worlds' here could mean a number of things, but the next line makes it clear that the worlds in question are the worlds of life and death: 'In dread for life – for death too sternly definite'. There is something complex taking place here. What does it mean to hover 'upon the confines' of two otherwise distinct states of being, two 'unmingling worlds'? Whatever it means, it is clearly not the same as being within the confines of those worlds; and, if that is the case, then

Figure 2 This contemporary etching of an impressively-muscled Edmund Kean in the title role of Maturin's *Bertram* (Drury Lane, London; 1816) suggests the opposite of the 'wasted frame' mentioned in the script; instead, we have the returned past as full bodily presence.

The print is in the collection of the Billy Rose Theatre Division, The New York Public Library. *The New York Public Library Digital Collections.* 1816. https://digitalcollections.nypl.org/items/510d47dd-ecdd-a3d9-e040-e00a18064a99.

'hovering upon the confines' means that the 'confines' are not confining at all, and therefore the 'unmingling' worlds are, in fact, mingling. As to the nature of those worlds – 'confined' and yet porous, 'unmingling' and yet, somehow, mingled – when spoken on stage, 'dread' and 'dead' are almost homonyms, so we get the conjunction of 'dead' and 'life' in the same phrase, a suggestion that is confirmed in the next phrase: 'for death too sternly definite'. However, this phrase in turn begs a question: if the dark thing hovering offstage is 'too sternly definite' for death, what is its nature: what could be more 'sternly definite' than death? When the broken syntax is factored in, it becomes apparent that if we try to follow through the logical or grammatical sense of this sentence, we are caught up in a meditation on the life and death that 'the thought doth try in vain to follow'.

The place of death in Yeats's *Purgatory* could equally be said to be something which 'the thought doth try in vain to follow', but in a different way. Much has been written about Yeats's beliefs regarding the afterlife, but the basic outline – garnered from his reading of Swedenborg, Plotinus, Hindu mysticism, and a lifetime of involvement with magical societies and psychical investigations – can be stated simply enough. In the 1920 essay (written in 1914), 'Swedenborg, Mediums and the Desolate Places', Yeats tells us that the soul after death is at first confused, after which it moves into 'a period which may last but a short time or many years, while the soul lives a life so like that of the world that it may not even believe that it has died' (*The Collected Works of W. B. Yeats* 50). Yeats wrote this essay just before he and his wife George Hyde-Lees embarked upon automatic writing, taking page after page of dictation from the spirits of the dead, which fed in turn into all of his writing, not least of all his theatre. Yeats's spirit interlocuters had much to say about plays such as *The Only Jealousy of Emer* (1919), in which the mythological character of the hero Cuchulain (who features throughout Yeats's work) appears after death, played (in masks) by two actors, one of whom is The Figure of Cuchulain, the other The Ghost of Cuchulain (Morash, *Yeats on Theatre* 9–12). Eventually, like so much else in those years, this would feed into Yeats's great unclassifiable work, *A Vision*, 'The Gates of Pluto' section of which is almost wholly concerned with the soul after death; the first edition of *A Vision* appeared in 1925, the second in 1937, just before *Purgatory*. 'I have put nothing in my play because it seemed picturesque', he told a correspondent. 'I have put there my own conviction about this world and the next' (*The Letters of W. B. Yeats* 913). Without going any further into the dark corners of Yeatsian eschatology, we can say that *Purgatory* is, at one level, the staging of an eschatology that sees death not as the end, but as a change in the condition of being. And here the kinship with Maturin's *Bertram* comes into focus, in that in both the distinction between life and death has suddenly become fluid. In Yeats's case, he is able to express the idea that Imogine's thought 'doth try in vain to follow' into the hard, spare vernacular of Boy's exclamation at the sight of 'a dead, living, murdered man'. The theatrical effect required to have living actors share the stage with a figure that is both living and dead may not be complex; however, it must be effective, for the entire play hinges upon it (see Figure 3).

In much the same way, the dead are everywhere in *By the Bog of Cats* … . 'Ah Christ, not another ghost', complains the Catwoman, when the ghost of Joseph Swane appears to her. 'Go 'way and lave me alone. I'm on me day off' (Carr 44). If *Bertram* is predicated on anguished belief in received religion, and *Purgatory* on the equally anguished assertion of

Figure 3 The stage minimalism of Yeats's *Purgatory* starkly frames the juxtaposition of the living and the dead. In this 2004 production, the 'dead, living, murdered man', is played by a third actor, Ned Dennehy, while Eamon Morrissey and Matthew Dunphy play the Old Man and the Boy, respectively. *Purgatory* by W.B. Yeats, Abbey Theatre, Peacock stage, 2004.

Photo: Kip Carroll; Courtesy of the Abbey Theatre Archive

Yeats's own devised 'system' (as he called it), the ghosts in *By the Bog of Cats* … have a slightly more ironic disposition, and a figure such as the Catwoman contains a self-conscious nod towards the tradition of which she is a part (see Figure 4).

In the 2015 revival of the play at the Abbey Theatre, for instance, the actor David Shannon played the Ghost Fancier as a down-at-heel country singer, clearly not belonging to any recognisable doctrine of the afterlife other than the play's own. Even in the moments in which the play attempts to confront death more directly, there is a slightly tongue-in-cheek element present, as when the ghost of Joseph Swane complains that he wants 'to

Figure 4 In her notes for the play, Marina Carr refers to the Catwoman character as 'gothic'; however, the play deploys many Gothic conventions. This photo shows Joan O'Hara as Catwoman and Olwen Fouéré as Hester Swane in a scene from the world premiere of *By The Bog of Cats...* by Marina Carr, Abbey Theatre, 1998.

Photo: Amelia Stein; Courtesy of the Abbey Theatre Archive.

live again. I want to stop walkin'. I want to rest, ate a steak, meet a girl, I want to fish for wild salmon [...] It's fierce hard to knock the best out of nothin', fierce hard to enjoy darkness the whole time' (ibid. 44–45). In *By the Bog of Cats* ..., the collapse of the distinction between the living and the dead is so complete that the dead are as common (and as much an annoyance) as the living. In the end, however, this is as much a play in which the dead and the living are far from 'unmingled' as those of Maturin or Yeats. 'The fact that we are dying probably *is* the only significant thing for all of us', Carr once told an interviewer. 'And *how* we live, and *how* we die. I think that is so important – *how* one dies' (Carr and Sihra 56).

If the most basic of binary oppositions – life and death – is deconstructed at the levels of syntax and of imagery in the Irish stage Gothic, then this opens the way for other fundamental conceptual frameworks to come unravelled as well. Among the most basic of these is an understanding of time as linear. As Sidney Shoemaker observes, from Aristotle's *Physics* onwards, it is 'universally admitted', (to use the words of J. M. E. McTaggart), that 'there would be no time if nothing changed' (63). If our perception of time, then, is predicated on change, it will also be predicated to some extent on the most profound change that human consciousness can imagine (or, indeed, struggle to imagine): its own non-being, or death. 'Death', writes Heidegger in *Being and Time* (1927), 'reveals itself as that *possibility which is one's ownmost, which is non-relational, and which is not be outstripped* [unüberholbare]. As such, death is something distinctively *impending*' (II. 1, p. 50: 294). Or, to put an extremely complex set of arguments simply, one of the most necessary experiential underpinnings for the concept of linear temporality is death; we are alive in the present, but at some point in the future, we will be dead; by the same logic, those who are dead now once lived in the past. As McTaggart put it in his influential essay in *Mind* in 1908, 'The Unreality of Time':

> We perceive events in time as being present, and those are the only events we perceive directly. And all other events which, by memory or inference, we believe to be real, are regarded as past or future – those earlier than the present being past, and those later than the present being future (458).

The epitome of 'events' which we can only 'believe to be real' because they exist only 'by memory or inference' are the lives of those who are dead, or (by inference) the 'impending' (to use Heidegger's word) prospect of our own death.

The figure that returns from the dead (the word 'revenant' is richly suggestive here) therefore not only disrupts any clear distinction between 'unmingled' life and death; it also disrupts the linearity of time. When the dead return, they do so as an eruption of the past in the present. Again, this is one of the most characteristic tropes in Gothic literary narratives of all types, and one to which much political and cultural significance has been attached in an Irish context. As Jarlath Killeen comments early in *The Emergence of Irish Gothic Fiction*, 'if the Gothic is often seen as the return of the repressed, the past that will not stay past, Ireland has usually been constructed as a place where the past had never in fact disappeared, a place where the past is in fact the always present' (10). This feature of Irish Gothic was once described, in structuralist terms, as 'anachrony at the level of the fabula' (Morash, '"The Time is Out of Joint"' 133). Likewise, Terry Eagleton once argued that 'Protestant Gothic is a kind of ontological crisis, in which the past – a country less real than the present – comes to imbue actual experience with a kind of spectral insubstantiality' (194). In this respect, Maturin's *Melmoth the Wanderer* has become a kind of exemplary document, in which, as David Punter succinctly puts it, 'there is no linear, coherent history' (114). While this feature of the Irish Gothic has been related to the disrupted colonial history of Ireland (and more recently to uneven modernisation), it is not unique to the Irish Gothic. As Christina Morin reminds us, 'early Irish Gothic adheres closely to contemporary understandings of the term Gothic as a signifier of the past and its relationship to the present' (362). The point is well made, for histories of the Gothic in literature more generally remind us that the word enters the vocabulary of culture during the long eighteenth century as term of historical periodisation, initially referring to the post-classical period of antiquity later rechristened as 'medieval' (Townshend 4).

In narrative terms in Gothic theatre, as Francesca Saggini explains it, typically the Gothic narrative includes both a 'narrativized past', in which the audience are told of the events in the past that have shaped the present circumstances (conforming to the familiar structuralist distinction between *fabula* and *szujet*) (Todorov 29–32), to which it adds what she calls 'an ostensive past', where objects from the past appear on the stage. 'These symbolic articles may be a blood-stained weapon, an heirloom, a tell-tale miniature, or, more importantly, a highly spectacular on-stage ghost' (146). And, turning back to *Bertram, Purgatory* and *By the Bog of Cats* …, this combination of narrativised and ostensive past is present in all three, disrupting any sense of a linear temporality. In *Bertram*, the entire unnatural disruption that constitutes the play's action is the return of the title character, washed up on the shore after he was believed to be long dead. In *Purgatory*, the disruption of time is refined even further, both in the appearance of the figure in the window of the house – a dead man who was, as the Boy says, 'a bundle of old bones/Before I was born' – and in the play's final moments, where there is an evocation of time as endless repetition, in which the past recurs, 'not once but many times'. Finally, the opening scene in *By the Bog of Cats* …, in which the Ghost Fancier mistakes sunrise for sunset, is only one of a series of temporal confusions and repetitions in that play, extending from the naming of Hester Swane's mother and daughter (both called 'Josie') to the constant appearance of the dead, to a setting in which landscape and costuming defy easy historical identification, where the Catwoman, dressed in 'a coat of cat fur that reaches to the ground, studded with cat's eyes and cat paws' (Carr 19), mingles with characters dressed for a wedding in gowns and evening coats that could as easily be from 1898 as from 1998.

Finally, both of these features of the Gothic – the mingling of 'unmingled' life and death, and the disruption of linear time – are dependent upon a third element that goes beyond the level either of content or of narrative: excess. Fred Botting opens his influential account of the Gothic with an unequivocal statement: 'Gothic signifies a writing of excess', taking as his opening epigraph Foucault's observation that 'the novels of terror introduce an essential imbalance within works of language: they force them of necessity to be always excessive and deficient' (1). As with the other definitional concerns of the Gothic – death and the disruption of temporal linearity – excess in the Gothic is not so much a set of conventions, as an aesthetic or affect. In *Bertram*, the entire atmosphere of the play – from the crashes of thunder and flashes of lightning that fill the stage before a word has been spoken, into which two monks 'enter in terror' (Maturin 5), to the scale of the stage spaces – is produced by a visual aesthetic of excess. 'The dramas that emerged in the late eighteenth century and into the nineteenth' argues Kelly Jones, 'were able physically to heighten the already excessive renderings of spaces, bodies and liveness to be found in the literary Gothic mode' (164). Moreover, in *Bertram*, as throughout Gothic theatre, excess is always the product of desire, which creates the narrative situation, and drives it forward.

In this regard, Yeats's *Purgatory* might seem to be a very different matter, with its almost empty stage, cast of two, and its almost meditative opening, with the Old Man's injunction to 'study that house' (*The Variorum Edition of the Plays of W. B. Yeats* 1041). And yet, *Purgatory*'s central shocking event is a moment of pure excess: the Old Man's murder of his son. It is a moment of excess both in the sense that it is an effect that seems to exceed any causality, but also in being a repetition. The Old Man has already admitted to the murder of his own father, the groom from the stable who seduced the lady of the manor, who now haunts its abandoned rooms. In such narrative, the murder of his son may seem superfluous, in the way that the sadism in Jacobean tragedy exceeds the logic of revenge. 'I killed that lad because had he grown up', the Old Man tells us, 'He would have struck a woman's fancy, / Begot, and passed pollution on' (ibid. 1049). If this moment – which never ceases to horrify an audience – seems in its own right excessive, it is immediately followed by another, in which the ghostly figure reappears in the window, so that repeated event – the killing of both father and son – is swallowed up within an even more powerfully determining pattern of repetition, in which the mother must live out her life over and over again, without remission. 'Twice a murderer and for nothing', cries out the Old Man at the play's end. 'And she [his mother's ghost] must animate that dead night / Not once but many times!' (ibid. 1049).

If killing of the son in *Purgatory* is a moment of pure excess, it is a moment that is repeated in *By the Bog of Cats* … . For all of its slightly uneasy comedy with the Ghost Fancier in the opening scene, the play's tone changes completely in the final scene, when Hester stabs her young daughter Josie to death, screaming at the people around her, 'she's mine and I wouldn't have her waste her life dreamin' about me and yees thwartin' her with black stories against me' (Carr 80), before turning the knife on herself, cutting out her own heart. While the conscious echoes of *Medea* have been established here (O'Brien 20–36; Sihra, 2018, 119–121), it has also been pointed out that the play's filicide also carries echoes of Yeats's play (Russell 160–163), and it is in this context that there has been more than one critic who has seen in Carr's theatre what Mária Kurdi describes (and praises) as its 'Gothic excess' (285). Michael McAteer develops this point in his recent study, *Excess in Modern Irish Writing* (2020), arguing that 'the singularity of the murders that conclude both plays is ruptured by the fact that, in repeating earlier crimes, they introduce multiplicity. […] The killings stand in excess, not only in view of their nature as filial murders, but equally in consideration of the fact that they provide no unifying order to the total action of both plays' (86). The Gothic's repetitions rob death of its singularity; in the regime of repetition, it is no longer 'unmingled', no longer the endpoint in linear time.

Theatre's Gothic Double

If we were to ask if these three inter-related elements – death, time and excess – are unique to Irish Gothic theatre (as opposed to Irish Gothic fiction, or even to Gothic fiction more generally), the answer would clearly be that they are not. At the same time, we could reverse the emphasis in the question, and ask if they function in a particular way in theatre that differs from fiction (which they do), and whether they are unique to Gothic theatre, as opposed to theatre more widely. Again, the answer would be a qualified 'no'. The well-documented echoes of classical Greek tragedy in *By the Bog of Cats* … should remind us that Gothic theatre has no monopoly on death, disrupted time or excess, and we could trace a lineage that extends from the ghost of Clytemnestra in Aeschylus's *Eumenides* through to the hauntings, tortures and buckets of blood of the Jacobean stage that would provide ample examples of all three. Indeed, Jeffrey N. Cox has suggested that the first Gothic dramas seemed to many contemporaries to be 'an attempt to revive the conventions and motifs of great Elizabethan and Jacobean plays' (125). Nor would our evidence look exclusively backwards; the year in which Marina Carr's *By the Bog of Cats* … was first staged – 1998 – was also the year of Sarah Kane's *Cleansed* and Peter Rose's *Snatch*, and was the year after Martin McDonagh's *The Cripple of Inishmaan*, all instances of a violent theatre of excess of the 1990s that Aleks Sierz memorably called 'in-yer-face theatre' in his book of that name.

One possible avenue forward here would be to trace some of the ways that Gothic theatre (and Irish Gothic theatre in particular) resembles theatrical forms, by way of borrowing or influence. However, there is another (and by no means mutually exclusive) way in which to frame the question. Could it be that Irish Gothic theatre is not unique, but that it activates the constitutive elements of the theatrical *per se* in a distinctive way? If this becomes the question, one way of cutting quickly to that irreducible core is to turn to Jerzy Grotowski, who as a theorist and as a theatre-maker with The Theatre Laboratory in the 1950s and 1960s made one of the most concerted attempts in modern theatre to refine the theatre event to its foundational elements. At one point, Grotowski attempts to strip away the non-essential, to arrive at the core of theatricality itself:

> We discover that the essence of the theatre is found neither in the narration of an event, nor in the discussion of a hypothesis with the audience, nor in the representation of life as it appears from the outside, nor even in a vision – but that the theatre is an act carried out *here* and *now* in the actor's organisms, in front of other men, when we discover that the theatrical reality is instantaneous, not an illustration of life something linked to life only by analogy. (86)

As Bert O. States remarks of this passage, this is 'what we might loosely call a *phenomenological theater* (as opposed to semiological)' (109), concerned with producing something to be experienced or perceived, rather than something that produces meaning. Stripping away non-essential elements such as narrative, exposition, explanation, and even the concept of representation itself, Grotowski defines the core of the theatre event in terms that all relate to the idea of presence. Here, then, is an irreducible core of the theatre event: it must take place in the present ('*here* and *now*'). There is no such thing as a theatrical past tense. An actor cannot *walked* across a stage; everything that happens on the stage exists in the present (and in the presence of) the audience. Even when past events are narrated, they are narrated in the present moment. This also means that the living body of the actor ('the actor's organisms') is an equally irreducible element of live performance (even when, as in the case of Beckett's *Breath* (1969) or *Not I* (1972) the body is reduced to its individual organs). This presence – the living body in the present moment – is, for Grotowski, the core of the theatrical event.

Stripping back (or perhaps 'reducing') theatre to its phenomenological core may sound like the very antithesis of the Gothic's theatre of excess. But it may be that this is precisely the point; that what Grotowski achieved by paring away, the Gothic achieves by piling high. Paradoxically, the Gothic theatre compels us to acknowledge the living presence of the actor by loading every element of the stage – from the language to narrative to design – with reminders of death. In some respects, the ultimate assertion of the liveness of the actor is to make the dead live. In the same way, much of the fascination of the Gothic comes from its fixation on a present moment with such an intensity that it is capable of absorbing even the past, and singularity is presented as repetition. To put it simply, even if Gothic theatre approaches theatricality by the road of excess rather than by the path of ascetic discipline, its dominant concerns are those of theatricality *per se*. In this respect, then, the Gothic theatre is actually a kind of anti-theatre in the sense in which Martin Puchner uses the term to signal 'a variety of attitudes through which the theatre is being kept at arm's length and, in the process of resistance, utterly transformed' (2). And here is where what Jerrold E. Hogle defines as the Gothic's 'insistent artificiality' comes into play (15): on the Gothic stage, liveness, presentness, and singularity appear to be negated as life-in-death, past-in-present, and repetition; but – and this is the key point – that negation occurs under the sign of an artificiality signalled by the very excessiveness of the spectacle, or of the narrative, so that the negation is negated. We are made all the more aware of the actor's living body when they play a character returned from the dead; their very sinews seem to deny the figure of death. Likewise, the recurrence of the past in the present does not set aside the intrinsically present-tense nature of performance. Instead, it as if the present moment has become thick enough to absorb not only itself, but the past as well. It is perhaps this that constitutes the persistent trans-historical core of Gothic theatre – not least of Irish Gothic theatre.

Notes

The author would like to thank Mairead Delaney, Barry Houlihan, and the Abbey Theatre Archive for their help; and a special thanks to Kip Carroll and Amelia Stein for their generosity.

1. In a different building, however; the original Abbey burnt in 1951 and was replaced.
2. Marina Carr, *By the Bog of Cats* ..., Handwritten Draft 1 Act 1/Scene 2, p. 9. 30 Nov., 1995; NLI Ms 4892/5/1; cited in Sihra 134.
3. George Stillman Hillard, *Six Months in Italy*, 2 vols (Boston: Tiknor, Reed, and Fields, 1853), vol. 2, p. 233; cited in Townshend 6.

Works Cited

Botting, Fred. *Gothic*. Methuen, 1995.
Carr, Marina. *By the Bog of Cats* ... Dublin, The Gallery Press, 1998.
Carr, Marina and Melissa Sihra, 'Marina Carr in Conversation with Mellissa Sihra'. *Theatre Talk: Voices of Irish Theatre Practitioners*, edited by Lillian Chambers et al., Dublin, Carysfort Press, 2001, pp. 55–63.
Connolly, Claire. 'Theatre and Nation in Irish Romanticism: The Tragic Dramas of Charles Robert Maturin and Richard Lalor Sheil.' *Éire-Ireland*, vol. 43, nos. 3 and 4, Fall/Winter 2006, pp. 185–214.
Cox, Jeffrey N. 'English Gothic Drama.' *The Cambridge Companion to Gothic Fiction*, edited by Jerrold E. Hogle, Cambridge University Press, 2002, pp. 125–144.
Eagleton, Terry. *Heathcliff and the Great Hunger: Studies in Irish Culture*. Verso, 1995.
Grotowski, Jerzy. *Towards a Poor Theatre*. Bloomsbury, 2013.
Haslam, Richard. 'Maturin's Catholic Heirs: Expanding the Limits of Irish Gothic.' *Irish Gothic: Genres, Forms, Modes, and Traditions, 1760–1890*, edited by Christina Morin and Niall Gillespie, Palgrave Macmillan, 2014, pp. 112–129.
Heidegger, Martin. *Being and Time*. Translated by John Macquarrie and Edward Robinson, Blackwell, 1962.
Hogle, Jerrold E. 'Introduction: The Gothic in Western Culture.' *The Cambridge Companion to Gothic Fiction*, edited by Jerrold E. Hogle, Cambridge University Press, 2002, pp. 1–20.
Howes, Marjorie. *Yeats's Nations: Gender, Class and Irishness*. Cambridge University Press, 1998.
Jones, Kelly. 'The Theatrical Gothic in the Nineteenth Century.' *The Cambridge History of The Gothic: Vol. II*. Edited by Dale Townshend and Angela Wright, Cambridge University Press, 2020, pp. 162–181.
Killeen, Jarlath. *The Emergence of Irish Gothic Fiction: History, Origins, Theories*. Edinburgh University Press, 2014.
———. *Gothic Ireland: Horror and the Irish Anglican Imagination in the Long Eighteenth Century*. Dublin, Four Courts, 2005.
Kurdi, Mária. 'Contesting and Reversing Gender Stereotypes in Three Plays by Contemporary Irish Women Writers.' *Subversions: Trans-National Readings of Modern Irish Literature*, edited by Ciaran Ross. Rodopi, 2010, pp. 265–86.
Maturin, Charles Robert. *Bertram: Or, The Castle of St. Aldobrand. A Tragedy in Five Acts*. Thomas H. Palmer, 1822.

McAteer, Michael. *Excess in Modern Irish Writing: Spirit and Surplus*. Palgrave Macmillan, 2020.

———. *Yeats and European Drama*. Cambridge University Press, 2010.

McCormack, W. J. *Sheridan Le Fanu and Victorian Ireland*. 1980. Dublin, Lilliput, 1991.

———. 'Yeats's "Purgatory": A Play and a Tradition.' *The Crane Bag*, vol. 3, no. 2, 1979, pp. 33–44.

McTaggart, J. M. E. 'The Unreality of Time.' *Mind*, vol. 17, no. 4, 1908, pp. 457–475.

Morash, Christopher. '"The Time is Out of Joint (O Cursèd Spite!)": Towards a Definition of Supernatural Narrative.' *That Other World: The Supernatural and the Fantastic in Irish Literature and Its Contexts*, edited by Bruce Stewart. Colin Smythe, 1998, pp. 123–142.

———. *Yeats on Theatre*. Cambridge University Press, 2021.

Morin, Christina. 'The Gothic in Nineteenth-Century Ireland.' *The Cambridge History of The Gothic: Vol. II.*, edited by Dale Townshend and Angela Wright, Cambridge University Press, 2020, pp. 359–375.

Morin, Christina. *The Gothic Novel in Ireland, c. 1760–1829*. Manchester University Press, 2018.

Neil. Mann. *A Reader's Guide to Yeats's* A Vision. Clemson University Press, 2019.

O'Brien, Karen. 'Re-envisioning "Woman": Medea as Heroine in Versions by Brendan Kennelly and Marina Carr., *Études littéraires*, vol. 37, no. 1, 2012, pp. 1–37. doi.org/10.4000/etudesirlandaises.3051.

Pine, Emilie. *The Politics of Memory: Performing Remembrance in Contemporary Irish Culture*. Palgrave Macmillan, 2017.

Puchner, Martin. *Stage Fright: Modernism, Anti-Theatricality, and Drama*. Johns Hopkins University Press, 2002.

Punter, David. 'Scottish and Irish Gothic.' *The Cambridge Companion to Gothic Fiction*, edited by Jerrold E. Hogle, Cambridge University Press, 2002, pp. 105–124.

Russell, Richard. 'Talking with the Ghosts of Irish Playwrights Past: Marina Carr's *By the Bog of Cats...* .' *Comparative Drama*, vol. 40, no. 2, Summer, 2006, pp. 149–168.

Saggini, Francesca. *The Gothic Novel and the Stage: Romantic Appropriations*. Routledge, 2015.

Sedgwick, Eve Kosofsky. *The Coherence of Gothic Conventions*. Methuen, 1986.

Shoemaker, Sidney. 'Time Without Change.' *The Philosophy of Time*, edited by Robin le Poidevin and Murray MacBeath, Oxford University Press, 1993, pp. 63–79.

Sierz, Aleks. *In-Yer-Face Theatre: British Drama Today*. Faber and Faber, 2000.

Sihra, Melissa. *Marina Carr: Pastures of the Unknown*. Palgrave Macmillan, 2018.

Smith, Andrew. *Gothic Death: A Literary History 1740–1914*. Manchester University Press, 2016.

States, Bert O. *Great Reckonings in Little Rooms: On the Phenomenology of Theater*. University of California Press, 1985.

Todorov, Tzvetan. *Introduction to Poetics*, translated by Richard Howard, University of Minnesota Press, 1981.

Townshend, Dale. 'Introduction: Gothic in the Nineteenth Century, 1800–1900.' *The Cambridge History of The Gothic: Vol. II.* edited by Dale Townshend and Angela Wright, Cambridge University Press, 2020, pp. 1–28.

Yeats, W. B. *The Collected Works of W. B. Yeats: Vol. V: Later Essays*, edited by William H. O'Donnell, Charles Scribner's Sons, 1994.

———. *The Letters of W. B. Yeats*, edited by Allan Wade, Rupert Hart-Davis, 1954.

———. *The Variorum Edition of the Plays of W. B. Yeats*, edited by Russell K. Alspach, Macmillan, 1965.

Chapter 4

Gothic Forms in Irish Cinema
Michael Patrick Gillespie

Like pornography, patriotism or piety, the terms Irish and Gothic initially seem to conform to obvious, widely accepted meanings. However, encountering them in literature, painting, film or any other medium almost always elicits individual, and sometimes even contradictory, responses. With that in mind, let me begin by touching on my approach to the use of each term.

Irishness remains a vexed issue, and exploring its fragmentation and mutability stands as a topic outside the scope of this essay. In reference to it, I simply acknowledge my awareness of the provisionality of any application, and I offer a sampling of citations that present a range of points of view that have been adopted as ways of engaging the concept.[1] One finds the same dispersion of perspectives on nationality in studies of the Irish cinema, and there, too, I will simply reference a sampling of such views rather than take up the debate over the clearest conception.[2] Suffice it to say that I understand Irish to be a provisional term more convenient than precise.

Gothic is an equally perplexing concept, but one that because of the argument that I am making requires a bit more discussion.[3] From its emergence in the eighteenth century, the Gothic impulse has always been to challenge perceptions of the status quo and to frustrate individual efforts to apply familiar Cartesian models to explain unique and unnerving behaviour. Despite the variety of forms these disruptions can take, two fundamental characteristics distinguish any manifestation of the Gothic: the presence of the uncanny and the immanence of menace. Further, in contrast to the Horror genre, which often evokes the supernatural in one form or another, Gothic cultivates postmodern assertions that deny the efficacy of abstract values and the existence of a metaphysical world.

Gothic cinematic manifestations always emphasise their baffling and unnerving effect upon viewers in a way that runs parallel to broader postmodern tendencies particularly as they lead to the corrosion of conventional concepts – like nationality – that influence the formation of an individual's nature. In such films, characters quickly discover that conventional, linear, cause and effect reasoning proves insufficient to explain the abrupt, chaotic and alarming intrusions that have disrupted their lives. As these motion pictures unfold ambiguity and anxiety work in tandem to increase the Gothic impact. They chronicle the panic that arises when one is confounded by events and cut off from the supposed support and protection of society.

From this perspective, the Gothic presence corrodes confidence in the status quo by enforcing a relentless, subversive power, manifest through jarring and insistent contradictions of traditional, conventional conceptions. Individuals experience an escalating sense of disorientation, loss of control, and fear. In such a world, communal values and societal traditions seem to crumble and leave nothing in their place. Gothic privileges indeterminacy, and in the process it puts nationality under erasure and even undermines the integrity of individual identities. Thus, although I will examine a number of films that integrate Gothic features into their narratives, I will show in the three films examined in the final portion of this essay that, in its purest form, Gothic cinema moves to embrace entropy to become anational.

* * *

The Gothic form did not come to prominence in Irish motion pictures until the 1990s, but the forces shaping the genre appeared in pioneering Continental works during the early decades of the last century. In particular, a number of films made by now well-known German Expressionist directors from the 1920s highlighted elements that would become paradigmatic for the Gothic cinema that followed. I offer below a brief summary of three major works to illustrate key elements that continue to have a profound impact on filmmakers who work in that genre and whose achievements in that form are clearly manifest in the works of the three Irish Gothic directors highlighted in the final portion of this essay.

Robert Wiene's *The Cabinet of Dr. Caligari* (1920) relies heavily on the uncanny to convey its representations of an abnormal reality. It is a striking example of how a filmmaker employs the Gothic form to enhance an already *avant garde* narrative disposition. Characters are costumed with flamboyant eccentricity and made up to exaggerate select facial features to give them a garish look. They adopt distracted, otherworldly expressions, and they often move in a jerky, stilted fashion.

The lighting imposes sharp contrasts on the self-consciously outlandish settings, suggesting distorted views of reality much like the representations found in an Edvard Munch painting. The strangeness of the movie's atmosphere, characters and events heightens the distorted perceptions of Francis, the central character, suggesting these elements reflect the norm, at least within the context of the film. This creates in viewers a sense of disorientation so powerful that the apparent resolution of the narrative upheavals, revealing that Francis is an inmate in an insane asylum who has been creating hallucinations that incorporate the staff and other inmates into fantastic expressions, leaves an uneasy sense of the inadequacy of the conclusion.

Another German Expressionist motion picture, F. W. Murnau's *Nosferatu* (1922), also emphasises abnormality in characterisations, action, settings and lighting. Its use of a preternatural figure, the vampire who physically threatens inhabitants of the natural world, gives a specific source to the menace and the uncanny that runs through its narrative. The eponymous creature's powers undeniably mark a viewer's sense of the motion picture, as the title character fascinates and then dominates a series of otherwise normal individuals who populate the motion picture. Further, despite the film's concluding with the seeming destruction of Count Orlock, the 'undead' element of vampirism leaves the restoration of order as, at best, provisional.

Even when a director eschews overt evocations of Gothic sensibilities, a film can powerfully convey attitudes directly tied to the genre. Fritz Lang's *Metropolis* (1927) presents a dystopian society where dehumanising authoritarianism has been normalised. In *Metropolis*, menace and the uncanny have assumed normative roles in society embodied through the contrasted extravagant architecture and the lavish lifestyle enjoyed by the elite and the oppressive, subterranean world of the impoverished workers. As a consequence, the immediacy of materialism and the absence of anything beyond situational scruples touch on the dissociative impulse that runs throughout the Gothic. Milieu self-consciously dominates the action of the film in a way that is markedly different from the other movies cited. Lang uses gargantuan, fantastic settings to introduce a malevolent neo-realism that overwhelms individuality. Although *Metropolis* has central figures – Joh Federson, Feder Federson and Maria – to advance the narrative, the emphasis is on the inversion of normalcy across society. The film foregrounds a dominant post-modern disposition at the heart of contemporary Gothic works.

* * *

The earliest examples of integrating Gothic features into Irish films were admittedly tentative efforts. Nonetheless, they reflect how the fragmented nature of Irishness complements the chaotic world of the Gothic. *Daughter of Darkness* (dir. Lance Comfort; 1948) is a Paramount-British production filmed in the UK with a predominantly English cast. It uses the otherness of its central character Emmy Baudine (Irish actress Siobhan McKenna in only her second film role) playing upon notions of insularity and religion to give the film a Gothic tone, perhaps unconsciously heightened by a broad association with another menacing outsider, the Irish author Bram Stoker's Dracula.

Daughter of Darkness echoes the transnational features of Stoker's novel, though albeit with a less panoramic sweep. It begins in a small Irish village where Emmy is the housekeeper of the local parish priest (Liam Redmond). Her attractiveness makes the women jealous, and they pressure Father Corcoran to send her away to England. There, Emmy finds employment with the Tallents, a family friendly with Father Corcoran, but the same sexual friction experienced in Ireland recurs.

Beyond the instinctual suspicions that emerge from the clannish dispositions found in any small community, as a Catholic from an insular country, Emmy is viewed with intensified suspicion by the Church of England villagers, particularly by women. The film cultivates her role as the other to underscore the resentment and bafflement that many feel towards her. In the most blatant threat, she stands as a sexual force exuding an energy that disrupts the regular course of village life. However, that force seems to go beyond simple physical attraction to suggest a power that renders the men whom she encounters helpless and vulnerable.

Over the course of the film, several of those who have shown an interest in Emmy are found murdered. The narrative indirectly connects her to these deaths, but concrete links are never revealed. That does not stop Bess Stanforth (Anne Crawford), daughter of the owner of the farm, from feeling increasing hostility to Emmy, in part because her husband Robert (Barry Morse) is drawn to the young woman. After suspicions grow about Emmy's influence over the men of the village, Bess orders her out of the local Anglican Church and the motion picture ends with Emmy – the Catholic and the other – being attacked by the dog of one of the murdered men.

The film, though artistically undistinguished, provides useful examples of how imaginative directors enhanced otherwise prosaic narratives by playing elements of ambivalent Irishness off against the features of Gothic cinema. It foregrounds the centrality of superstition, parochialism, clannishness and disenfranchisement. In the narrow world of the rural Catholic parish, Irish women cannot tolerate or even understand Emmy, whose origins the narrative never fully explains. After her displacement to Britain, the close community bonds in an English farming town again automatically isolate Emmy, and her second-class status as a citizen of a former colony enhances her vulnerability to the bullying and exploitation of her English employers. Nonetheless, her otherness enforces an uncanny aura and produces an undefined though very visible menace that shields and sustains her through most of the film.

The contemporaneous short film *Return to Glennascaul* (1951) was directed and produced by Hilton Edwards and Micheál MacLiammóir who are perhaps best known as the co-founders of Dublin's Gate Theatre. This motion picture counterpoints creative elements in *Daughter of Darkness* with examples of how a production can enhance the conventional features of a Gothic film through aspects of Irishness. Orson Welles, playing himself, picks up a hitchhiker on lonely Irish road. The man tells Welles of similarly picking up two women, a mother and daughter, in the same location. The man drove the women to their home and went in for a drink. While conversing, he learns that the daughter is the long-lost love of his dead uncle. After leaving, he remembers that he had left his cigarette case at the house. When he returns for it, he finds the house in ruins and later learns that the mother and daughter had been dead for years.

Though *Return to Glennascaul* seems more a traditional ghost story than anything else, it, too, reflects a Gothic tendency in Irish films. The narrative plays upon ambivalence and disorientation, and the cinematography draws upon *film noir* techniques to produce a sense of menace and uncanniness. The invocation of the dead uncle simultaneously brings out a sense of the communal ties to the past and a feeling of isolation heightened by the ambiance of the decrepit Big House, reminding viewers of the Anglo-Irish colonialism still on the edge of their lives.

Edwards and MacLimmoir repeated their efforts, though with less success and without the inclusion of Welles, in another short made two years later in which a patronising view of rural quaintness threatens to diminish its impact. *From Time to Time* (1953) is set in the Dublin Mountains. A young woman (Maureen Cusack), cycling with her boyfriend (Patrick Bedford), has an accident that knocks her unconscious. When she awakens, she tells of being at the same spot where an informer was killed by the IRA and of reliving that incident. To support her story, the farmer (Colm O'Grady) who found her shows the girl and her boyfriend the memorial stone erected by the IRA who had not meant to kill the woman. The duration of the film and its limited production values blunt the impact, but the invocation of the innocent dead woman underscores a moment when identity in Ireland was both evolving and ambiguous.

These mid-twentieth century films provide examples of tentative and generally unselfconscious attempts at Irish Gothic cinema, and they did not spur others to immediate imitation. In fact, as critics have noted, filmmaking in Ireland remained a sporadic endeavour until the late 1970s.[4] Thus, for the next twenty-five years, there are no Irish directed motion pictures made in the Gothic form, though a few films by non-indigenous filmmakers took a colonising approach by imposing their own impressions of the Gothic on artificial constructions of Irish settings.

Francis Ford Coppola's *Dementia 13* (1963) though putatively set in Ireland is little more than a cut rate version of one of Roger Corman's motion pictures. It came about because of a small budget surplus in his film *The Young Racers* (1963) allowed Corman to underwrite the efforts of his protégé, Coppola, in his directorial debut. Unsurprisingly, *Dementia 13* follows the artistically dubious but commercially rewarding Corman model of using sex and violence for titillation while giving little concern for acting or script. It is a slasher film set in an old castle with an insane relative successively murdering members of the family, with a series of gruesome events held together by sensationalism and resolved with a programmatic use of violence to end violence.

Robert Altman's *Images* (1973), filmed in County Wicklow, is also putatively set in the Irish countryside. However, with its American director, its international cast, and its generic Gothic plot, only the loosest definition of the term would qualify the film as an Irish motion picture. It centres on a woman who, with her husband, comes to rural Ireland from London to relieve the stress that seems to be bringing on paranoia and hallucinations. The woman has a series of visions involving men she had loved and whom now she seems to kill. Unlike *Dementia 13*, this film seems to take itself seriously, trying to evoke a Bergman-like angst to cover its plodding self-referentiality.

The first real attempt in twenty-five years to reintegrate the Gothic into an Irish film came with Tommy McCardle's *The Kinkisha* (1977). At sixty minutes running time, it goes well beyond the Edwards-MacLimmoir efforts of the early 1950s, though it too develops its Gothic atmosphere in a muted fashion. Set in the Irish countryside, it plays on superstition, and, as is often the case in Gothic forms, amalgamates those attitudes with religious beliefs. The action turns on the belief that a baby born on Pentecost will kill or be killed unless a robin is crushed in the child's hand within a few weeks after it has been born. (According to Kevin Rockett, '"Kinkisha" is an anglicisation of "Cincise", the Irish word for "Whit" [Pentecost]' [28]). After a great deal of stress and uncertainty, the family performs the ritual and life seems to return to normal. Though the narrative is much more understated than most Gothic films, its reworking of folk Catholic ritual reminds viewers of the mutability of religious sense in Irish consciousnesses.

For the next decade and a half, there were no Gothic films to speak of. The effort closest to the term, *Rawhead Rex* (dir. George Pavlou; 1986), is little more than an English slasher film with a superimposed Irish setting. Much like *Dementia* 13, it relies on sex and violence, more graphically presented than its predecessor, to hold the audience's attention. The excruciating experience of participating in this film may or may not have shaped Donal McCann's performance in *The Dead*, but the memory of it doubtlessly embarrassed him for the rest of his all too short life.

Then, in 1994, in the midst of a strong cinematic revival that was envigorating the Irish film industry, a motion picture appeared to suggest that directors were again taking interest in the artistic possibilities of the uncanny, though in a fashion that aggressively anglicises the Irish context. Mary McGuckian's *Words upon the Window Pane* uses a medium and séances to tell of the struggle of Jonathan Swift (Jim Sheridan) and his lovers Stella (Brid Brennan) and Vanessa (Orla Brady), though, despite drawing on spiritualism, it follows a highly conventional approach. It flirts with the Gothic but in the end produces a ghost story more like Yeats than Swift.

Other directors showed far greater imaginative facility in their reworkings of the genre. Neil Jordan's *The Butcher Boy*, released in 1997, is adapted from Patrick McCabe's rural noir novel of the same name. It moves much closer to a postmodern and, paradoxically, anational interpretation of the Irish Gothic than any of its predecessors. Its relentlessly agonizing treatment of a dysfunctional Irish family gives a more contextualised and contemporary sense of the menace. It is particularly powerful in that, despite its setting in rural Ireland in the early 1960s and its invocation of many of that era's iconic images, it shows a fully alienated world in which Catholicism provides at best a superficial connection to the community, and tribalism has deteriorated into random pairs of symbiotic relationships and at worst a thin screen hiding brutality and sexual abuse. (Whether Patrick McCabe's novel or Neil Jordan's adaptation treat these subjects with sufficient gravity and concern are topics that merit another study.)

The film focuses on Francie (Eamonn Owens), an only child who has learned to cope with the mood swings of both his alcoholic and abusive father (Stephen Rea) and his psychotically delusional mother (Aisling

O'Sullivan). From the beginning of the film, Francie's own behaviour reflects deep-seated neuroses. It increases exponentially, after his mother's suicide and his father's death from drinking. Living a demented, hermit-like existence means that Francie will have no one to rein in his compulsion to follow his appetites and urges, shaped by fears and insecurities.

Isolation heightens Francie's anti-social, anarchic impulses. Inevitably, he begins to act on these urges, and his consequent behaviour violates all the norms of the small town in which he lives and shows him capable of the most extreme violence. He persecutes his neighbor, Mrs Nugent (Fiona Shaw), while imagining that he has visions of the Blessed Virgin Mary (Sinéad O'Connor), who offers him guidance. Francie exists on the edge of society, moving from one form of isolation to another—runaway, industrial school, mental institution and prison after he murders Mrs Nugent. In an ironic touch Stephen Rea plays both Francie's father and the adult Francie who narrates the film, subtly suggesting a cyclical, arbitrary rhythm to the world it depicts.

Over the last ten years, abundant examples have accrued in which Irish directors have embraced a more overtly conventional approach to the genre and produced programmatic imitations of American Gothics with a conscious emphasis on the Irish context. One of the most striking instances of this conformity appears in Rebecca Daly's *The Other Side of Sleep* (2011). Her film uses a claustrophobic representation of Ireland to rejuvenate the familiar formula of a young woman struggling to form an identity in a world of conflicting attitudes and ambiguous markers. Filmed in Offaly, it opens with Arlene (Antonia Campbell-Hughes), a deeply disturbed young woman, waking up outdoors next to the body of another woman. The scene shifts abruptly to the routine of her daily life, working at a factory, talking with her mother, or going to a party. An air of menace runs through her experiences with no clear indication as to its source. There are several references to Arlene's sleepwalking, and it is never clear to what degree she may be hallucinating. The film ends with no resolution or even clarification of Arlene's experiences.

Following another time-tested cinematic pattern Lee Cronin's *The Hole in the Ground* (2019) shifts from small town paranoia to rural terror in a narrative arc like many Gothic-horror films produced in Hollywood. Sarah (Seána Kirslake) moves to the Irish countryside with her son Chris (James Quinn Markey). When Chris runs into the forest after an argument with his mother about whether his father will join them, Sarah searches for him and discovers the large hole of the film's title. She finds Chris next to it apparently unharmed, yet in the ensuing days she notices changes in his behaviour. She has an unpleasant encounter with an old woman, Noreen (Kati Outinen), who tells her that Chris is not her son. After the old woman's violent death, Sarah learns that the woman also believed that her own son was not really hers. Sarah eventually comes to believe that Chris has been replaced by a doppelgänger. She goes to the woods and rescues the boy she thinks is Chris from the hole in the ground. Then, she confines one Chris to the basement, burns down her house, and takes the other Chris to a new life in the city. However, as the film ends, Sarah is growing increasingly unsure that the boy whom she saved is actually her son Chris.

* * *

The motion pictures I have touched on trace the struggle to integrate Gothic features into an Irish cinema by following the paradigm of Classic Hollywood Cinema.[5] Though often technically well-constructed, they have a template quality in their structures that suggests a striving to meet conventional expectations rather than a conscious effort to extend the limits of the genre. In the first decade of the twenty-first century, however, a number of directors rejected the predictable, invoking the Gothic form to articulate their own oscillating perspectives of an evolving post-national Ireland: the safe has become malevolent; the dependable has become devious; the coherent has become incomprehensible; and Ireland as a viable imaginative construct has lost all its existential integrity. For these filmmakers Irish settings do not equal Irish culture, and their most innovative efforts to represent the Gothic are the least concerned with enforcing an Irish context.

This new approach to the Gothic in Irish films does not simply highlight an individual encountering isolated, aberrant behaviour patterns. Instead, it represents all of society as suffering from an erosion of conventional values and drifting in a near incomprehensible malaise. These motion pictures incorporate the arbitrariness of postmodern sensibilities with a feeling of dread for the unexplained menace that punctuates the experiences of the central characters. It is these films that make the greatest contributions to the form, and in the remainder of this essay I will present a more extended examination of three early twenty-first-century examples of such approaches.

Ivan Kavanagh has been making provocative films for two decades. He has achieved a measure of critical acclaim and some commercial success with two recent Hollywood-style motion pictures, *The Canal* (2014) and *Never Grow Old* (2019). Both films reflect the Gothic flavour that colours the atmosphere of all of Kavanagh's work, but they emphasise the broad Gothic-horror convention prevalent in many traditional movies in this genre. However, his earlier work was much more idiosyncratic.

In particular, Kavanagh's first feature-length film stands out as an example of how a deft use of the uncanny and of menace can produce terrifying sequences with little reliance on traditional Horror conventions or, for that matter, without the budget that provides the option for enhanced special effects that are the hallmark of Hollywood. That is not to say that Kavanagh steps completely away from popular conventions, for in its opening scenes *Tin Can Man* (2007) seems to fit the mode of a traditional thriller. The film opens in the apartment of Peter (Patrick O'Donnell), an isolated young man who has recently been dumped by his girlfriend. He answers a knock on the door and finds Dave (Michael Parle), who asks to use the phone. After talking his way into the apartment, Dave begins to dominate and terrorise Peter through a series of scenes that culminate in Peter becoming the new Tin Can Man, a figure with his tongue cut out, imprisoned in a basement, entertaining others as tin cans tied to his body clank cacophonously.

The action begins in a deceptively straightforward and easy to follow fashion. Nonetheless, it quickly becomes profoundly unnerving. Almost immediately, Dave's intensity and Peter's passiveness make it apparent that the latter will have no recourse but to allow himself to be caught up in whatever scenario that the stranger chooses to play out. From the moment he appears at Peter's door, Dave takes control and unwaveringly moves the action forward in a series of alternately arbitrary and sadistic gestures that demand compliance. Peter lacks the will to defy Dave's bullying commands, and there seems no individual or institution to which Peter can turn for aid. A visit to Peter's father's house, for example, provides the young man with no solace or support, but it does give Dave the knowledge to employ additional ways to intimidate Peter. Random encounters with other characters show either people who are incapable of helping Peter or who are colluding with Dave in tormenting the young man. It is an extraordinarily painful film to watch, yet it rivets one's attention from the beginning to the end.

Unlike the plotline of the silent film classic, *Nosferatu*, Kavanagh's film never provides an explanation for the motivation behind anything that Dave does. However, Dave pursues his quarry with the same single-minded relentlessness and a similar strength of personality as that of the Transylvanian vampire. Of course, some variations obtain. While Dracula fascinates individuals with his magnetic presence, Dave dominates the discourse with nonstop talking punctuated by ominous threats of violence. Further, instead of Nosferatu's seductive assaults on his victims, actual brutality follows quickly from Dave's threats.

His sudden, unpredictable, and yet calculated behaviour combined with randomness and the uninhibited force of Dave's cruelty gives a disorienting, insistent sense of menace to the film.

Kavanagh's direction plays on the uncanny in a masterful way. While to some degree, the behaviour of Dave and Peter is predictable, the context in which it unfolds makes the action unnervingly strange. The world they inhabit has a generic stark, post-industrial setting strikingly unlike that the Dublin environment familiar to viewers of contemporaneous adaptations of Roddy Doyle's novels – recently constructed apartment buildings of dubious quality, landmarks that identify the city, and gloomy suburban terraces. The characters do behave in self-absorbed yet often disoriented fashion that one expects from that milieu. The ending, which thrusts Peter into the role of the new Tin Can Man, voiceless and a figure of derision, uses the Gothic to make a broader comment on the erasure of Irishness in a post-national, postmodern milieu.

As the preceding paragraphs detail, *Tin Can Man* combines graphic physical violence with relentless psychological abuse. Kavanagh's decision to shoot his film in black and white, contrasting bright moments with dark surroundings, evokes a strong noir quality to viewing. In the noir tradition, the film employs shadows to cover sparse sets while allowing the viewers' imaginations to fill in the details. At the same time, as if to underscore the artificiality of the technique, for a number of sequences the actors unselfconsciously hold flashlights to illuminate their faces from below and to give a sense of scattered lighting. This aggressive cinematography suppresses context, not to produce a generic Gothic but to highlight the loss of conventional identity.

In 2008 Aisling Walsh made *The Daisy Chain*, a film with a tone as ominous as that found in *Tin Can Man* but without the latter's determination to confront its viewers with instances of graphic violence. A couple moves from London to a small Irish town, birthplace of the husband, Tomas (Steven Mackintosh), who has been hired to teach at the local school. Martha (Samantha Morton), his wife, is pregnant. Viewers learn later in the film that the couple had lost a child to sudden infant death syndrome.

The villagers regard the couple as outsiders. Nonetheless, they become involved with a local girl, Daisy (Mhairi Anderson), whom they take in after Daisy's brother drowns and her parents are killed shortly thereafter in a fire. In short order, Daisy comes to dominate their lives, though the film is careful not to offer any clear reason for her ability to assert such control. As the narrative evolves, the locals come to blame Daisy for a series of problems including an outbreak of meningitis. With events seemingly spiralling out of control after the death of a neighbour who was particularly hostile to Daisy, the young girl is scheduled to be put into care. However, before she can be taken from Tomas and his wife, Martha gives birth and collapses. It is not clear if Martha has died or simply passed out. In any case, the film ends with Daisy singing 'Rock-a-bye, Baby' in a fashion that punctuates the final image with a general sense of dread.

In playing with rural superstition, in a manner analogous to Kavanagh's emphasis on urban alienation, the Gothic again creates menace through a movement from the socially familiar into the alienated unknown. The generic hometown ambience, like a Potemkin village, serves initially to misdirect perceptions. Conventional roles are no more than superficial distractions masking a loss of identity. Traditional patterns of behaviour provide a false and unsustainable sense of purpose. Though its dystopian features emerge more slowly than they do in *Metropolis*, perhaps because the rural ambiance has created very different expectations, by the end of the movie the same sense of general disfunction and particular hopelessness obtains.

In another instance of contemporary Irish Gothic Cinema, with a narrative deftness every bit as subtle and unnerving as Henry James' novella *The Turn of the Screw*, Margaret Corkery's film, *Eamon* (2009), follows the vibrant work of Kavanagh and Walsh and reflects the same powerful vision with a compelling but understated presentation. In a post-nationalist gesture common to a great deal of Irish cinema in the twenty-first century, it moves away from a grounding in familiar cultural institutions. Its narrative arc resembles to some degree the claustrophobia of earlier films. However, it goes beyond those that bring a few Gothic elements dominating individuals in a conventional milieu to suggest instead that the Gothic consciousness has evolved into the disruption of institutions and is broadly eroding the larger society.

To this end, *Eamon* posits a nihilistic world in a matter-of-fact way without relying upon the extreme brutality of *Tin Can Man* or the sporadic violence of *Daisy Chain* to underscore its point. The film initially seems to conform to a conventional comedic plot of a hapless family on vacation. However, as the action unfolds, it becomes increasingly less comedic and far more menacing. Characters exist in a world without any real sense of boundaries underscored by a deft infusion of Gothic sensibilities through the title character's perspective. Indeed, it follows the pattern of *The Cabinet of Dr. Caligari* in initially presenting an only slightly aberrant or erratic environment, then relentlessly eroding any feeling of regularity and predictability, and finally like *Caligari* concludes with a chilling sense of the superficiality of normalcy.

When Eamon's mother, Grace (Amy Kirwan), realises that her young son (Robert Donnelly) will be on school vacation for a week, she balks at the idea of caring for him at home. Instead, she bullies Eamon's father, Daniel (Darren Healy), into taking time off from his job as a bus driver to bring them to a cottage owned by her aunt in County Wicklow for a seaside holiday. Early on, Corkery seems to be aiming at a heavy-handed Freudian representation of familial misersy. Grace will not have sex with Daniel, and her relationship with Eamon swings wildly between doting affection, indifference and open hostility. Daniel resents Eamon and aches for sexual gratification. Grace fantasises about a body builder whom she sees on the beach. She invents an excuse to enter his caravan, and finds he has a wife and child. When Daniel out of jealousy confronts the body builder in a men's toilet, the man begins to give him oral sex. Grace sees this, and this leads to her and Daniel having intercourse on the beach, which Eamon observes.

In fact, sex and sexual appetites are little more than emblems of much deeper traumas. Grace emerges as a deeply angry and deeply confused individual, someone with an unstable identity who can only see the world around her in antagonistic terms. Daniel is equally alienated, but his overwhelming passivity deprives him of the agency he would need to act to counter the environment that oppresses him. Eamon is the most opaque of the three. It would be simplistic to explain his behaviour as autistic and go no further. He is rather completely self-absorbed and dextrously inventive of ways to impose himself on the world that he inhabits.

Although all of the characters manifest anti-social behaviour to the point of seeming feral, it is Eamon who provides the fullest, most desolate sense of their milieu. He moves about with indifference to much of the world around him but also shows flashes of cruelty and hostility in a random almost careless fashion. He bullies his mother, but he is timid around other children. He practices unprovoked viciousness, and he shows no real sense of affection. He unquestioningly embraces pointlessness as the defining, irrevocable feature of the world he inhabits.

Gradually, events in the narrative increasingly demonstrate that characters in the film take only glancing notice of the larger environment and that they operate on a purely material level with no concern for communal strictures. After running out of money, the family leaves to return to Dublin. As they are driving home, Grace and Daniel's bickering escalates to the point that leads to a car accident. With his parents pinned in their overturned car, the film seems to have reached a gruesome resolution. Instead, the narrative teases viewers with the vague promise of a more or less conventional ending. Grace sees that her son has not been injured by the crash, and so she sends Eamon to get help.

Instead, Eamon walks aimlessly down the road until he is picked up by a baffled French couple, presumably on holiday as well. The film ends as he sits in the back seat of the car laconically responding to the couple's questions while seemingly settling into a new environment without any vestige of Irishness: Catholicism had disappeared long before the narrative began. Eamon's symbiotic relations with his parents, with other children on holiday, and finally with the French couple is the new form of colonialism, and the tribalism that he barely tolerated has succumbed to aggressive isolation.

The construction of the Gothic films touched on in this essay, particularly the last three, underscore the evolving vision of filmmakers working in that genre. Initially, such projects sought to contextualise their narratives in environments that evolved out of characteristics generally perceived as Irish. However, over the last half-century both filmmakers and viewers have shown an increasing lack of interest in what the conception Irish entails.

In the twenty-first century, Irish cinema, like all of Irish society, has struggled to discern the usefulness of a cultural identity. The Celtic Tiger did much to make Ireland more European, and even after the economic bubble burst that inclination towards the erosion of a collective identity remains strong. With this in mind, it seems most likely that future Irish Gothic films will increasingly put their national character in brackets and move towards a more postmodern sensibility.

Notes

1. For a sampling of perspectives, see Arensberg and Kimbal; Caherty; Donoghue; Gibbons; McWilliams.
2. A number of critics have addressed the nature of Irish filmmaking from a range of perspectives, and in some cases have been quick to presume a conceptual unity that is not fully sustained from one motion picture to another. For a cross-section of various approaches to film in Ireland, see McLoone; Pettit; Barton; Gillespie, *The Myth of an Irish Cinema*.
3. The editors of this collection present in their Introduction a very useful overview of the term. Nonetheless, to clarify the central concern of the argument of my essay, I think it important to elaborate on the elements of the term to which I give specific emphasis in fairly particular ways.
4. For further details, see Gillespie 'Irish Film under Erasure'.
5. For a more detailed explanation of the elements of Classic Hollywood Cinema, see Gillespie, *Film Appreciation through Genres*, especially the 'Introduction: Do the Right Thing', 4–22.

Works Cited

Arensberg, Conrad M. and Solon T. Kimbal. *Family and Community in Ireland*. 1940. Harvard University Press, 1968.

Barton, Ruth. *Irish National Cinema*. Routledge, 2004.

———. *Irish Cinema in the Twenty-First Century*. Manchester: Manchester University Press, 2019.

The Butcher Boy. Directed by Neil Jordan, 1997

Caherty, Thérèse, editor. *Is Ireland a Third World Country?* Belfast, Beyond the Pale Publications, 1992.

The Canal. Directed by Ivan Kavanagh, 2014.

The Daisy Chain. Directed by Aisling Walsh, 2008.

Donoghue, Denis. *We Irish*. University of California Press, 1988.

Eamon. Directed by Margaret Corkery, 2009.

Gibbons, Luke. *Transformations in Irish Culture*. Cork University Press, 1996.

Gillespie, Michael Patrick, *Film Appreciation through Genres*. McFarland & Co., 2019.

———. 'Irish Film under Erasure'. *New Hibernia Review*, vol. 23, no. 4, Winter 2019, pp. 30–43.

———. *The Myth of an Irish Cinema*. Syracuse University Press, 2009.

The Hole in the Ground. Directed by Lee Cronin, 2019.

McLoone, Martin. *Irish Film: The Emergence of a Contemporary Cinema*. British Film Institute, 2000.

McWilliams, David. *The Pope's Children: Ireland's New Elite*. Dublin, Gill and Macmillan, 2005.

The Other Side of Sleep. Directed by Rebecca Daly, 2011.

Pettit, Lance. *Screening Ireland: Film and Television Representation*. Manchester University Press, 2000.

Rawhead Rex. Directed by George Pavlou, 1986.

Rockett, Kevin. *Irish Filmography: Fiction Films, 1896–1996*. Dublin, Red Mountain Media, 1996.

Tin Can Man. Directed by Ivan Kavanagh, 2007.

Chapter 5

Gothic Fiction and Irish Children's Literature
Anne Markey

Twenty-first-century critical discussion of Irish Gothic has been enriched by debates that re-chart the territory to be explored and so complicate definitions of what constitutes the field of study. Christina Morin and Niall Gillespie, for example, trace the emergence of the influential critical association of this type of writing with the diminishing fortunes of the Anglo-Irish ascendancy over the eighteenth and nineteenth centuries only to undermine and complicate any easy linkage between 'genre and religious affiliation' (29). Richard Haslam, meanwhile, asks these questions about Irish Gothic: 'is it a genre, mode, tradition, or illusion? Which formal and thematic properties do Irish Gothic texts possess? When did these texts emerge, flourish, languish and revive and why?' (29). These questions await definitive responses, which seem unlikely to be offered in the short term, but towards which this current collection knowledgeably gestures.

Since the adoption of children's literature as a division of the Modern Language Association in 1980, experts in the area have likewise differed on what exactly constitutes their field of study. Here, disagreement arises at least partly because of the elasticity of the words that are combined to form the compound 'children's literature', a term of debatable denotation and confusing connotation. At what age do people become or end being children, and does literature refer only to written texts? The *Oxford English Dictionary* offers sixteen definitions of 'child' and five of 'literature', so it is hardly surprising that disagreement arises when the possessive plural of the first word is used as an adjective qualifying the second. In the late twentieth century, Peter Hunt argued that the term 'children's literature' refers to prose narratives 'written expressly for children who are recognisably children, with a childhood recognisable today'; on that basis, Hunt distinguished between 'live' books for today's children and 'dead' books that entertained previous generations of young readers but that now 'concern no-one else except historians' (67, 61). This view has been disputed by other critics, including Perry Nodelman, who argues for the value of historical children's literature in illuminating not just changes in literary taste but also in adult constructions of childhood (156). Acknowledging that children 'have consumed, and still consume, a huge variety of material', M. O. Grenby describes children's literature as 'a distinct part of print culture' that emerged 'in Britain and America [around] 1700' and confines this description to texts written by adults and intended primarily for young readers that appear in book form and aim 'to entertain children as much as to instruct them' (*Children's Literature* 2, 4).[1] Prefixing the contested term 'children's literature' with the qualifier 'Irish' leads to further complications; as Jarlath Killeen notes: 'Which authors and what texts count as "Irish" in Irish literary history has been continually debated' ('Irish Gothic Tradition'). Critical debates about 'Irish Gothic' and 'children's literature' suggests that these concepts and their constituent terms are complex and unstable. Consequently, this essay aims to contribute to ongoing critical discussions by examining the relationship between 'Gothic' fiction and 'Irish' children's literature over a period of more than two centuries, paying attention to both 'live' and 'dead' books for children.

It is generally agreed that Gothic fiction emerged as a recognisable form of print culture during the second half of the eighteenth century, with more recent critics producing checklists of the most common tropes to be found in this new type of story (Gamer 215; DeLamotte 4). In the same period, children's books became an established and profitable product in the English literary marketplace. While a number of Irish-born authors, including Oliver Goldsmith (1728–1774) and later Maria Edgeworth (1768–1849), published successful books for children in England, the trade in children's books in Ireland was slower to take off.[2] Nevertheless, by 1810 approximately twenty Irish booksellers were importing or reprinting books for juveniles originally published in England (Markey, 'Irish Children's Books' 35). Expanding demand for improving and educational texts for young readers on both sides of the Irish Sea generally reflects Enlightenment support for rational thought and action; it more specifically echoes and reflects the influence of John Locke's disapproval in *Some Thoughts Concerning Education* (1693) of subjecting the minds of children 'to Frights, fearful Apprehensions, Weakness, and Superstition' and of allowing maids or other servants to tell them stories about 'Goblins, Spectres, and Apparitions' (227). Locke's treatise is concerned with the education of the sons of gentlemen and his comments about servants are indicative of upper- and middle-class distrust of social inferiors. That distrust is readily discernible in early children's fiction, which, as Andrew O'Malley points out, also warns 'middle-class readers against emulation of the elite', reflecting 'a growing discontent with the inherited privilege enjoyed by the upper classes' (3). Given that early Gothic fiction shared that 'anti-aristocratic sentiment' (Ellis 92), both it and children's literature can be usefully situated within the changing social contexts in which they first appeared.

Nonetheless, there are significant differences between early Gothic novels and most early children's literature. Noting that both *The Castle of Otranto* and *The History of Little Goody Two-Shoes* were first published in 1764, Dale Townshend argues that the tame delights of the former, with its overarching didactic impulse along with its eschewal of old wives' tales and the unexplained supernatural, became popular largely because it deliberately excluded the type of terror associated with the latter; in support, and not acknowledging that some early Gothic fiction allows for the explanation or even dismissal of allegedly supernatural phenomena, Townshend discusses an episode in *Little Goody Two-Shoes*, which may have been at least partly written by Goldsmith, in which the apparent appearance of a ghost is rationally explained and so proved to be an illusion (16).[3] M. O. Grenby claims that 'the Gothic, with its extolment of excess and exaggeration and its challenge to order, moderation and decency ... was naturally anathema to those who produced the new children's literature' and points out that Maria Edgeworth warned in *Practical Education* (1798) of the dangers of fanning 'any "early propensity to supernatural terrors"' (Grenby, 'Gothic and the Child Reader' 245–6). Nonetheless, Grenby claims that the gulf between early children's literature and the Gothic was 'not so large as has been thought' (ibid. 247). Given that 'the primary impulse of Gothic tales is the arousal of fear' (Clemens 1), and that fear has long been associated with the discipline and raising of children, even by Locke, who advised: 'Fear and Awe ought to give you the first Power over their Minds' (43), the two apparently diverging literary forms can indeed be usefully aligned. As will become apparent, texts containing Gothic elements have been and continue to be used to teach children how to think and behave in ways considered appropriate by their elders.

Irish children's fiction is here defined as stories read by young people that were written by authors either born in Ireland or of Irish origin or those who spent some time in Ireland, which is reflected in the text. A survey of such fiction published between the 1780s and 1980s reveals that only a handful of them can be described as Gothic if that description requires more than the inclusion of one or two relevant elements or tropes. Since the 1990s, the inclusion of multiple Gothic tropes in Irish children's fiction, as in children's fiction more generally, has become commonplace. However reductive an inventory approach may be, it nonetheless can be useful in distinguishing between Gothic and other types of text, and here 'Gothic' fiction is defined as stories that contain more than one or two features associated with that type of writing, such as madness, unjust persecution, imprisonment, claustrophobic or labyrinthine caves, ruined buildings, anti-Catholicism, doubling and the appearance of ghosts and spectres.[4] This essay will show that authors with Irish backgrounds pioneered the use of Gothic tropes in children's fiction to add piquancy to the lessons they wished to teach, and that later Irish authors followed that lead. To that end, the focus will be on four texts addressed to young readers that contain elements characteristic of Gothic fiction: Mary Wollstonecraft's *Original Stories from Real Life* (1791), Lady Mount Cashell's *Stories of Old Daniel* (1808), Father Peter O'Leary's *Séadna* (1904) and Claire Hennessy's *Nothing Tastes as Good* (2016). The analysis of various Gothic elements in these disparate texts written over the course of more than two hundred years, from the late eighteenth to the early twenty-first century, highlights the enculturation impulse common in books written by adults for young readers. It also suggests that while didacticism is the defining feature of children's literature, philosophical, social and political ideas about which boundaries should not be transgressed vary across time and place. Nevertheless, within these texts, didactic enculturation is tempered by an anarchic embrace of the Gothic in both English and Irish that acknowledges children's fascination with wrongdoing and the macabre.

Born in Spitalfields in London, Mary Wollstonecraft (1759–1797) is not generally regarded as an Irish writer and is not mentioned by Rolf and Magda Loeber in *A Guide to Irish Fiction 1650–1900*, which nonetheless includes 'authors of Irish descent who were born elsewhere … [or] who wrote works dealing with Ireland or the Irish' (lxxiv). Wollstonecraft's maternal grandfather, Henry Dickson, was a Protestant wine merchant based in Ballyshannon, County Donegal, where his daughter, Elizabeth, who later married Edward John Wollstonecraft, was born and raised (Taylor; Carlson 22). From 1786 to 1787, Mary Wollstonecraft was in Ireland herself, mostly in Mitchelstown Castle, County Cork, the country seat of Lord and Lady Kingsborough, as governess to their daughters; describing her dejection on arrival at the Castle, she reported: 'I entered the great gates with the same kind of feeling as I should have had if I was going into the Bastille' (Todd 84). Wollstonecraft, who had completed *Thoughts on the Education of Daughters* (1787) prior to her departure for Ireland, was initially appalled by her charges: 'The children are, literally speaking, wild Irish, unformed and not very pleasing' (ibid. 85–86). Nevertheless, she soon developed a close bond with the eldest, Margaret, to the chagrin of Lady Kingsborough, who dismissed the governess when the opportunity presented itself. Back in London, Wollstonecraft published *Original Stories from Real Life,* a didactic story for children that features two young girls, Mary and Caroline, based on Margaret and Mary King, for whom she had cared in Ireland. Indeed, Margaret King's biographer claims that the book is effectively set in 'the Kingsborough household' (McAleer 47). Consequently, *Original Stories* has some considerable claim to be regarded as an Irish work with what the Loebers describe as a disguised Irish setting (ciii). It recounts the re-education of the two girls, following the death of their mother, by a widowed, distant relative, Mrs Mason. By means of stories, her example and their own experiences, Mrs Mason teaches the girls to renounce vanity, indolence and selfishness and instead to embrace rationality, compassion and industry, virtues associated with the rising middle classes. The tales Mrs Mason tells her charges frequently employ Gothic tropes, often to critique inherited privilege and aristocratic idleness or to promote a realisation of one's duty towards social inferiors. 'The story of crazy Robin', for example, is about a poor but honest and industrious man whose family is evicted from their home by the avaricious heir of their late landlord; Robin eventually loses his wits having witnessed the untimely deaths of his wife and children and dies alone in a small cave after his faithful dog is shot by an angry squire. 'The History of Charles Townley', a story that teaches the dangers of procrastination and is sparked by the sight of a ruined castle in a shadowy forest, features a wealthy old rake married to Townley's young true love whose husband has her 'confined to a madhouse' (89); when eventually rescued by Townley she is a gibbering wreck who dies soon after. Perhaps even more chillingly, 'The Man Confined in the Bastille' – the French prison acting as a *locus classicus* of tyranny in the eighteenth century and recalling Wollstonecraft's first impression of Mitchelstown Castle – tells of the complete desolation of an isolated captive whose pet spider, his only source of companionship, is killed by his jailers. Although Dale Townshend argues the Gothic was soundly suppressed in early children's literature, he nonetheless acknowledges that *Original Stories from Real Life,* with its 'scenes of absent maternity, crumbling battlements, ruined dwellings, and horrid descriptions of French modes of imprisonment' can be said to 'qualify as Gothic' (21–22). Like Mary and Caroline, child readers of *Original Stories* are encouraged to abhor idleness and to behave rationally, compassionately and unselfishly. There is little evidence of any emotional affection between Mrs Mason and her charges, who regard her with fear and awe; here, the wise adult is most definitely in charge and the foolish young girls learn under her dispassionate influence how to conduct themselves properly in both domestic and social situations. Intriguingly, it was a work inspired and coloured by Mary Wollstonecraft's sojourn with King family in Mitchelstown that first incorporated elements of adult Gothic fiction into a collection of didactic stories designed to promulgate emergent bourgeois values amongst young readers.

Wollstonescraft's scandalous life and initially disreputable posthumous reputation contrasts starkly with the respect enjoyed by her near contemporary, Maria Edgeworth, also born in England but who spent most of her adult life in Ireland. Described by F. G. Harvey Darton as 'one of the most natural story-tellers who ever wrote in English', Edgeworth has long been acknowledged as a pioneering and influential author of children's fiction (142). Mitzi Myers has argued for the significance in wider literary terms of Edgeworth's writing for children because it introduced subjects and forms that would become central to the novel as genre and also because its didacticism nurtured the writer's realism (55). That realism is apparent in Edgeworth's first collection for children, *The Parent's Assistant* (1796), which uses everyday life as the backdrop to stories that feature credible young characters, mainly from the middle classes. Relationships between adults and children are generally portrayed as affectionate, and Edgeworth stresses the need for children to learn from their own experiences, often under the unobtrusive guidance of their elders. Grenby argues that these stories 'contain much that might be considered Gothic' ('Gothic and the Child Reader' 247). In support, he cites an extract from a paragraph of 'Lazy Lawrence', in which the thieving young protagonist is duped under the full light of the moon by a dastardly stable boy and later sleeps fitfully, 'tormented by that most dreadful of all kinds of fear, that fear which is the constant companion of an evil conscience' (ibid. 247). While Grenby is mistaken in declaring that the action occurs during a black night in which Lawrence is tormented by the 'fear of death', his claim that the extract's focus on 'oppressive guilt' and 'impending doom' is 'enough to make the reader's blood, like Lawrence's, run cold' is arguably credible (ibid.). Nevertheless, this short extract from one story that underscores the dangers of stealing and associating with stable boys is insufficient to support the claim that the respected and respectable Edgeworth knowingly Gothicised the moral tales contained in *The Parent's Assistant*. Apart from this one possible instance, the collection as a whole privileges rational instruction and eschews the Gothic, while promoting domestic and social harmony in situations in which children learn from experiences engineered by adults or through the intervention of their elders.

Margaret King, one of Wollstonecraft's Irish charges, not only went on to emulate her one-time governess's example by leading what was seen as a scandalous life herself but also by intentionally including Gothic elements in her first collection of didactic stories for children. In 1791, she married Stephen Moore, the Earl of Mount Cashell, and the couple had three sons and two daughters in quick succession. In 1801, they set out from Ireland on a continental tour, stopping first in London, where Lady Mount Cashell visited Wollstonecraft's widower, William Godwin. In Paris in June 1802, another son was born and in Rome in 1804 Lady Mount Cashell gave birth to a daughter but also fell in love with an Irish emigré, William Tighe. The following year, she separated from her husband, whom she never saw again and who retained custody of their seven children. Calling herself 'Mrs Mason' and describing herself as 'a vagabond upon the face of the earth' (McAleer 119), the former Lady Mount Cashell subsequently lived openly with Tighe, with whom she visited London in 1807. There, she renewed her friendship with Godwin, who had remarried and established the Juvenile Library with his second wife, Mary Jane. This business specialised in the publication of children's books, and *Stories of Old Daniel* appeared anonymously under its imprint in 1808. The eponymous elderly storyteller is a retired common soldier, said to be based on 'a real man, between ninety and a hundred, in a little village in Ireland', who, it has been argued, sounds 'very much like a resident of Kingston College', established in Mitchelstown by Lady Mount Cashell's great-grandfather to provide homes and shelter for indigent members of the Church of Ireland (ibid. 122, 17). In this disguised Irish setting, Old Daniel entertains a group of village boys with apples, gingerbread and didactic but enthralling tales every Sunday evening, on which they later base exciting games. The boys like and admire Daniel, who is equally fond of them, and this intergenerational affection adds warmth to the tone of this collection of morally instructive stories. This collection resembles other examples of early children's fiction in its commendation of such values as honesty, hard work, sobriety and kindness but its author's desire 'to indulge that love of the wonderful so natural to children of all ages and dispositions' was highly unusual for its time (Moore 79). Old Daniel imaginatively transports his young listeners, and the young readers to whom the volume is addressed, to exotic locations with his stories of adventure. Those stories warn against lying, stealing and 'being afraid of ghosts, fairies and all those sort of things', but nonetheless employ Gothic tropes to create a *frisson* of pleasurable terror that adds to their appeal (ibid. 87).

The opening story, entitled 'The Church-Yard' and loosely based on the international folktale 'Frightened to Death' (ATU Type 1676B), features a group telling ghost stories near a macabre burial site where 'the ground was strewed with skulls which were whitened by the air' (ibid. 85). Daniel recounts the tale of a frightened young man who believes he has been trapped by a ghost in the graveyard to teach his young listeners how foolish it is to be afraid of supernatural occurrences. However, the descriptions of the dark, frosty church-yard, heaps of skulls and the horrified panic of the young man evoke the very dynamic of terror that the story purports to scupper. Terror also permeates 'The Robbers' Cave', as Daniel recalls an occasion when he was captured on mountain patrol and blindfolded by a murderous group of scoundrels who lead him through a labyrinthine maze of 'caves and ruined buildings well adapted to their purpose' (ibid. 88); impressed by his honesty in acknowledging that he is a soldier and his promise never to betray them, the thieves release him. In a later story continued over two chapters, Daniel tells his spellbound young listeners how years later he came across one of his former captors, dressed as a Franciscan friar, leaving an inn in Italy. The two instantly recognise each other but remembering his promise never to betray any of the thieves Daniel says nothing to his commanding officer or anyone else. At the inn, he learns that the man, known as Father Giacomo and revered locally, had recently ministered 'to two murderers who had been executed in that neighbourhood' (ibid. 103). Later, Daniel and his companions are robbed in a dark forest by a group of stiletto wielding banditti and brought to a remote ruin, where they are told to confess their sins to a menacing hermit in preparation for their imminent deaths: 'A single lamp, burning before a picture of the Virgin, threw sufficient light on the surrounding objects to show us all the horror of our situation' (ibid. 107). A few minutes later, Father Giacomo appears and leads them to safety, explaining that this is Daniel's reward for keeping his promise not to betray him. The Italian setting, the denigration of Catholicism and the use of dramatic suspense in this didactic story have much in common with early Gothic fiction by writers such as Horace Walpole and Ann Radcliffe. Here, a Gothic atmosphere is evoked to impart the lesson that one should always keep one's word. Nevertheless, Daniel's decision not to tell tales turns out to be at least as much practical as virtuous so the story raises ethical questions about moral decision-making and one's position in relation to authority and the greater good when in possession of secret knowledge. 'The Man-Hater', another extended story, is equally unsettling. Henry, the central character, begins life as the well-meaning but self-absorbed son of indulgent parents, but over time his inability to take responsibility for his actions or for those in his care leads to the death of his younger brother and his best friend, and to ruin of his fiancée. Echoes of both 'The Story of Charles Townley' and of 'The Man-Hater', not least that their protagonists' personal failings ultimately lead to the deaths of their loved ones, are evident in Mary Shelley's *Frankenstein; or the Modern Prometheus* (1818). Consequently, it can be argued that Mary Wollstonecraft's sojourn in Ireland, which inspired *Original Stories from Real life* with its recourse to Gothic tropes that in turn influenced Lady Mount Cashell's wonderful use of terror in *Stories of Old Daniel*, ultimately fed into her daughter's Gothic masterpiece. From this perspective, it can be plausibly claimed that early Irish children's fiction shaped the development of Gothic fiction.

Be that as it may, Irish children's fiction eschewed recourse to the Gothic for almost one hundred years after the publication of *Stories of Old Daniel* in 1808. Undoubtedly, such celebrated Victorian authors as Bram Stoker and Oscar Wilde incorporated elements of the supernatural into *Under the Sunset* (1881) and *The Happy Prince and Other Tales* (1888), but there is nothing distinctively Gothic as defined above about these collections as a whole.[5] In the same period, popular writers of children's fiction, such as L. T. Meade, produced more realistic work in the Edgeworth tradition. Until the early twentieth century, Irish fiction, whether for children or adults, referred to works written in English by Irish authors or authors associated with Ireland. However, thanks to the Gaelic League's efforts to promote the development of a modern literature in the native language, stories in Irish began to be published in the first decade of the new century. One such work was Father Peter O'Leary's *Séadna* (1904), which began life as a serial in *The Gaelic Journal* in 1894 and was not published in its entirety by the Irish Book Company until ten years later. Commonly regarded as the first major literary work of the Gaelic revival, the book features a young girl, Peig, telling her friends the story of Séadna, a cobbler who accepts money from *An Fear Dubh* [the devil] promising that he will go with him after thirteen years has elapsed (Ua Laoghaire, *Séadna* 2–5). With the help of the Blessed Virgin, Séadna finally outwits the devil but, in the interim, he exists in a Gothic hinterland of guilt, fear and isolation. Peig's group of friends are in thrall to the story but keen to avoid the errors made by the adult protagonist. The framing narrative provides anthropological insights into aspects of early-twentieth-century life amongst a rural, Irish-speaking community while the embedded narrative's unsettling focus on the transgression of boundaries and the antagonistic otherness of the title character, 'his cruelty to his neighbours and his indifference to the woman who loves him', destabilise both the realism of the text and the apparent restoration of order at the end of the story (Titley, 'The Novel in Irish' 172).

On first publication as a full-length work running to some 300 pages, *Séadna* was greeted as a pioneering, if difficult to categorise, work of fiction for adults and has been similarly regarded by most subsequent critics (O'Leary 105). Nevertheless, Fr O'Leary himself later declared that this Gothic mixture of realist fiction and folkloric terror was inspired by the realisation that there were no books in the Irish vernacular available to *children* and his desire to remedy that lack (Ua Laoghaire, *Mo Scéal Féin* 147). Conceived as a children's story, *Séadna* reflects both a nationalist aspiration to foster a love of the Irish language in the rising generation and its clerical author's wish to promote a reverence for the Catholic Church along with respect for the types of traditional family and community structures associated in the early twentieth century with rural Irish life. However, its length was apparently perceived as a deterrent for younger readers. As a result, in 1914 the Irish Book Company produced a 121-page abridged edition in supposedly simplified spelling, retitled *Shiana*, which announced on the inside cover opposite the title page: 'Now used in National Schools with excellent results' (Ó Laeri n.p.) Following the establishment of the Irish Free State in 1922, Irish became a compulsory subject in National Schools and the demand for books in that language which could be used in the classroom increased over the decades. Around 1947, R. A. Breatnach produced *Scéal Shéadna*, an abridged, school edition of Father O'Leary's novel presenting only the embedded Faustian narrative, which adopted official spelling reforms that standardised differences between dialects and adhered to agreed grammatical forms. The removal of the framing narrative, with its focus on a group of girls within a domestic setting, emphasised the masculine, Gothic nature of the central story, which could now escape its realist grounding in a specific time and particular community. This version was used in primary schools until the 1960s, with the result that it became well known to cohorts of Irish children. Novelist and critic, Alan Titley, recalls that it was the first story 'a chuir an cac trasna orm' (that scared the crap out of me) and that its influence was inescapable not only for him but for generations of Irish-language writers (Titley 'Séadna (1901)' 17, 18). That children were the primary intended audience of this innovative, influential prose narrative that employs Gothic elements to teach its readers what it means, or should mean, to be Irish reveals how important the rising generation was to the nationalist project.

Over the course of the twentieth century, authors of Irish children's fiction often looked to the country's history, folklore or mythology for inspiration, but it was not until the 1990s that such writers, in common with their counterparts elsewhere, increasingly began to turn towards the Gothic as a way of exploring the challenges faced by modern-day young readers. This pervasive recourse to the Gothic in young-adult fiction, now recognised as a distinctive branch of children's literature, can be related to 'concerns about what it means to be human in an age when developments in technology problematise previous approaches to that timeless but increasingly pressing ontological issue' (Markey, '"Walking ... into the Night"' 132). Given twenty-first-century attitudes to such previously taboo subjects as single parenthood, abortion and homosexuality, it is unsurprising that teenage readers are now routinely presented with texts that refigure 'traditional monsters as heroes' (Jackson 4). That Darren Shan (creator of the *Cirque du Freak* series) and Derek Landy (creator of the *Skulduggery Pleasant* series) are published both in Britain and the USA and regularly feature in international discussions of the significance of Gothic in contemporary children's literature testifies to the significance of the Irish contribution to this contemporary literary phenomenon (Serrato; Buckley '"Do Panic. They're Coming"'; Buckley, *Twenty-First-Century Children's Gothic*). However, the absence of any specifically Irish markers in Shan's internationally successful *Cirque du Freak* series tellingly reveals how 'all sense of the national and local' has been eradicated from much successful Irish children's fiction (Keenan 201). Indeed, the current era of globalisation can be seen as a form of invidious colonialism that effaces national markers. It is telling that Buckley describes Landy's use of Gothic tropes in *Skulduggery Pleasant* as 'shaped by mass-market forces' ('"Do Panic. They're Coming"' 19) while Serrato concludes that Shan's Gothic *Cirque du Freak* 'series ends up assuming a meaningful place within the post 9/11 world for post 9/11 readers' (64). Based on these readings, there is little distinctively Irish about these Gothic fictions, whose intended readers are generic adolescents confronted by global challenges over which they have little apparent control.

Claire Hennessy's *Nothing Tastes as Good* (2016), a young-adult novel set in a well-to-do Dublin suburb, also deals with universal challenges confronted by twenty-first-century teenagers – for example, suffering from eating disorders, coping with family breakdowns, balancing study with other pursuits, getting on with peers, choosing a career, becoming sexually active and dealing with mental health issues. The title's deliberate evocation of Kate Moss's controversial 'nothing tastes as good as skinny feels' mantra introduces the narrative focus on the contemporary destructive relationship between dieting, body image and self-worth (Wardrop). That Moss's comments received wide coverage in the Irish media and that Hennessy used them in the title reveals the type of international pressure to which Irish teenagers are now routinely exposed. Indeed, this novel joins a growing number of young adult texts that explicitly deal with eating disorders, such as Sarah Dessen's *Just Listen* (2008) and Laurie Halse's *Wintergirls* (2009), both set in American high schools. *Nothing Tastes as Good* follows the attempts of the ghost of Annabel McCormack, an Irish 17-year-old whose heart failed because of anorexia, to act as a spirit guide to Julia, an overweight former schoolfellow. The focus throughout is on a young peer group, and while adult influence is acknowledged it is shown to be either irrelevant or harmful. Eventually, despite Annabel's attempts to control her mind and actions and unaided by the adults around her, Julia comes to terms with her body and becomes a comforting friend to Annabel's bereaved young sister. This Gothic tale of haunting, shadowing and doubling, written from a teenage perspective, explores young people's efforts to negotiate the boundaries between childhood and adulthood, particularly when presented with situations beyond the experience and comprehension of their elders.

However, even though the Irish setting is not specified until page 53, and only occasionally invoked later, other aspects of the story are particularly relevant in the Irish context. For example, the deputy principal's censorship of an article about suicide in the school newspaper that comments on 'a recent report published about youth mental health services in Ireland' underscores the article's opening claim that '[t]he shocking lack of support in schools cannot be glossed over or excused' (Hennessy 53). Hennessy's recourse to the Gothic similarly gestures towards particularly Irish contexts. The first paragraph reveals that the afterlife inhabited by Annabel, the dead, bodiless narrator, involves 'no wings, no heavenly music, no fluffy white clouds here – just me and the Boss (not God, don't go getting any ideas there)' (ibid. 3); this ghostly deviation from Christian teaching deftly underscores the irrelevance of the Catholic Church to most contemporary Irish teenagers. Perhaps even more significantly, the subplot of Julia's sexual exploitation by a trusted family friend who turns out to be a serial predator reverberates with what is known in Ireland as the X case, which led to two amendments relating to abortion being made to the Irish Constitution.

Consequently, *Nothing Tastes as Good*, although published in London and dealing with situations likely to be encountered by first-world teenagers, is particularly relevant to young Irish readers. Rather than teaching explicit lessons, the text encourages young readers to draw their own conclusions about what happens to the principal characters and how that might be relevant to their own situations, which is of course a lesson in itself.

Overall, then, the relationship between Gothic fiction and Irish children's literature is complex and continually evolving, reflecting changes in both specific Irish circumstances and more general literary developments. Two women belonging to, or at the very least associated with, the Protestant Ascendancy in Ireland were the first to draw consistently on Gothic tropes when writing stories for children. Both *Original Stories* and *Stories of Old Daniel* were published anonymously in London and although it can be claimed that they feature disguised Irish settings they are addressed to a putative English child in need of moral instruction from a responsible adult. While Wollstonecraft uses Gothic tropes to inspire fear and awe of adults in children, Lady Mount Cashell employs them to captivate young English readers. By contrast, *Séadna*, published in Dublin as part of the Gaelic Revival, exemplifies the nationalist impulse to keep Irish alive by engaging the hearts and minds of young Irish readers in a terrifying story. More recently, the *Cirque du Freak* and *Skulduggery Pleasant* series, published in Britain and the USA, feature a vampire and a walking, talking skeleton respectively to teach young readers everywhere how best to conduct themselves. By contrast, *Nothing Tastes as Good*, published in London, negotiates the global and more local pressures experienced by contemporary Irish teenagers, who have little to learn from the adults around them and who are encouraged to think for themselves. The four texts that form the focus of this essay present different constructions of childhood and of the ideal relationship between young people and adults across time and place. While their authors' recourse to the Gothic leavens their didacticism, they all have lessons to impart to their readers, highlighting both the ongoing, universal unequal power relationship between adults and children and temporal, cultural shifts in that dynamic.

Notes

1. For an informed perspective on this debate, see Gubar.
2. See for example, *Dr. Goldsmith's Roman History Abridged by Himself for the Use of Schools* (1772) and Edgeworth's *The Parent's Assistant* (1796).
3. For Goldsmith's possible authorship of *Little Goody Two-Shoes*, see for example, 'The History of Little Goody Two-Shoes'. While critical opinion on the matter is divided, informed commentators believe it is unlikely that Goldsmith wrote the book.
4. For a discussion of the inventory and other approaches to the Gothic, see for example, DeLamotte 3–7.

5. See, however, readings of *Under the Sunset* by William Hughes and Carol Senf in Killeen, *Bram Stoker*, which draw attention to what they consider to be Gothic elements within the collection.

Works Cited

Buckley, Chloe. '"Do Panic. They're Coming": Remaking the Weird in Contemporary Children's Literature'. *New Directions in Children's Gothic: Debatable Lands*, edited by Anna Jackson, Routledge, 2017, pp. 16–31.

———. *Twenty-First-Century Children's Gothic: From the Wanderer to Nomadic Subject*. Edinburgh University Press. 2018.

Carlson, Julia. 'Family'. *Mary Wollstonecraft in Context*, edited by Nancy E. Johnson and Paul Keen, Cambridge University Press, 2020, pp. 21–28.

'child, n'. *OED Online*, Oxford University Press, June 2021, www.oed.com/view/Entry/31619. Accessed 12 June 2021.

Clemens, Valdine. *The Return of the Repressed: Gothic Horror from* The Castle of Otranto *to* Alien. State University of New York, 1999.

Darton, F. G. Harvey. *Children's Books in England: Five Centuries of Social Life*, revised by Brian Alderson, Cambridge University Press, 1982.

DeLamotte, Eugenia C. *Perils of the Night: A Feminist Study of Nineteenth-Century Gothic*. Oxford University Press, 1990.

Ellis, Markman. *The History of Gothic Fiction*. Edinburgh University Press, 2003.

Gamer, Michael. 'Gothic Fictions and Romantic Writing in Britain'. *The Cambridge Companion to Gothic Fiction*, edited by Jerrold E. Hogle, Cambridge University Press, 2002, pp. 85–104.

Grenby, M. O. *Children's Literature*. Edinburgh University Press, 2008.

———. 'Gothic and the Child Reader, 1764–1850'. *The Gothic World*, edited by Glennis Byron and Dale Townshend, Routledge, 2014, pp. 243–53.

Gubar, Marah. 'On not Defining Children's Literature'. *PMLA*, vol. 126, no. 1, January 2011, pp. 209–16.

Haslam, Richard. 'Negotiating the Poetics of Irish Gothic Fiction'. *'The Common Darkness where the Dreams Abide': Perspectives on Irish Gothic and Beyond*, edited by Ilaria Natali and Annalisa Volpone, Aquaplano, 2018, pp. 29–53.

Hennessy, Claire. *Nothing Tastes as Good*. Hotkey Books, 2016.

The History of Little Goody Two-Shoes. British Library. www.bl.uk/collection-items/the-history-of-little-goody-two-shoes. Accessed 12 June 2021.

Hunt, Peter. *Criticism, Theory and Children's Literature*. Blackwell, 1991.

Jackson, Anna. 'New Directions in Children's Gothic: Debatable Lands'. *New Directions in Children's Gothic: Debatable Lands*, edited by Anna Jackson, Routledge, 2017, pp. 1–15.

Killeen, Jarlath, editor. *Bram Stoker: Centenary Essays*. Dublin, Four Courts Press, 2014.

———. 'Irish Gothic Tradition'. *Oxford Bibliographies Online*, 11 January 2018, DOI: 10.1093/obo/9780199846719-0134. Accessed 15 June 2021.

'literature, n'. *OED Online*, Oxford University Press, June 2021, www.oed.com/view/Entry/109080. Accessed 12 June 2021.

Locke, John. *Some Thoughts Concerning Education*. A & J Churchill, 1693.

Loeber, Rolf and Magda Loeber [with Anne Mullin Burnham]. *A Guide to Irish Fiction 1650–1900*. Dublin, Four Courts Press, 2006.

Markey, Anne. 'Irish Children's Books 1696–1810: Importation, Exportation and the Beginnings of Irish Children's Literature'. *Children's Literature Collections: Approaches to* Research, edited by Keith O'Sullivan and Pádraic Whyte, Palgrave Macmillan, 2017, pp. 33–52.

———. '"Walking ... into the Night": Growing up with the Gothic'. *Irish Children's Literature and Culture: New Perspectives on Contemporary Writing*, edited by Valerie Coghlan and Keith O'Sullivan, Routledge, 2011, pp. 129–44.

McAleer, Edward C. *The Sensitive Plant: A Life of Lady Mount Cashell*. University of North Carolina Press, 1958.

Moore, Margaret King. *Stories of Old Daniel. Children's Fiction 1765–1808*, edited by Anne Markey, Four Courts Press, 2011, pp. 75–141.

Morin, Christina and Niall Gillespie. 'Introduction: De-Limiting the Irish Gothic'. *Irish Gothics: Genres, Forms, Modes, and Traditions, 1760–1890*, edited by Christina Morin and Niall Gillespie, Palgrave Macmillan, 2014, pp. 1–12.

Myers, Mitzi. 'Socializing Rosamond: Educational Ideology and Fictional Form'. *Children's Literature Association Quarterly*, vol. 14, no. 4, 1989, pp. 52–58.

Nodelman, Perry. *The Hidden Adult: Defining Children's Literature*. John Hopkins University Press, 2008.

Ó Laeri, Peaduir. *Shiàna*. Irish Book Company, 1914.

O'Leary, Philip. *The Prose Literature of the Gaelic Revival: Ideology and Innovation*. Pennsylvania State University Press, 1994.

O'Malley, Andrew. *The Making of the Modern Child*. Routledge, 2003.

Serrato, Phillip. '"These are troubling, confusing times:" Darren Shan's *Cirque du Freak* as Post 9/11 Gothic'. *New Directions in Children's Gothic: Debatable Lands*, edited by Anna Jackson, Routledge, 2017, pp. 51–66.

Taylor, Barbara. 'Wolstonecraft [married name Godwin], Mary (1759–1797). *Oxford Dictionary of National Biography*, Oxford University Press. doi.org/10.1093/ref:odnb/10893. Accessed 15 June 2021.

Titley, Alan. 'The Novel in Irish'. *The Cambridge Companion to the Irish Novel*, edited by John Wilson Foster, Cambridge University Press, 2006, pp. 171–89.

———. 'Séadna (1901)'. *Úrscéalta na Gaeilge*, edited by Ronan Doherty, Brian Ó Conchubhair and Philip O'Leary, Cló Iar-Chonnacht, 2017.

Todd, Janet, editor. *Collected Letters of Mary* Wollstonecraft. Columbia University Press, 2003.

Townshend, Dale. 'The Haunted Nursery'. *The Gothic in Children's Literature: Haunting the Borders*, edited by Anna Jackson, Karen Coats and Roderick McGillis, Routledge, 2008, pp.15–38.

Ua Laoghaire, Peadar. *Séadna*, edited by Liam Mac Mathúna, Carbad, 1995.

———. *Mo Scéal Féin*. Cló Thalbóid, 1999.

Wardrop, Murray. 'Kate Moss: "Nothing tastes as good as skinny feels"'. *Irish Independent*, 19 November 2009. www.independent.ie/regionals/herald/lifestyle/health-beauty/kate-moss-nothing-tastes-as-good-as-skinny-feels-27932555.html. Accessed 16 June 2021.

Wollstonecraft, Mary. *Original Stories from Real Life: With Conversations, Calculated to Regulate the Affections and Form the Mind to Truth and Goodness.* Joseph Johnson, 1788.

Chapter 6

Irish Ecogothic
Eóin Flannery

Ecogothic

One of the most trenchant critiques of Western dualistic thought is provided by the Australian feminist philosopher, Val Plumwood. Though Plumwood's historical perspective provides for a deep lineage, including Platonic thought, she is conscious of the ways in which such structural dualisms have underwritten what she calls 'the logic of modernity. ... [which] has treated the human/nature relation as a dualism' (2–3). Key considerations for Plumwood are the mechanisms through which unequal and exploitative hierarchies of value are sustained by, and sustain, a patriarchal capitalistic macrostructure. These are equally evident in Felix Guattari's earlier, *The Three Ecologies*: '[e]cology in my sense questions the whole of subjectivity and capitalistic power formations' (52). Guattari's point invokes the long-held dyadic conceptualisation of human and non-human relations, a legacy of Cartesian dualism that underwrites the baleful hierarchical nature of a paternalistic Western mind-set. But in suggesting a more holistic and integrated notion of ecological subjectivity, Guattari does not propose a reductive negation of species difference, rather his contention is for a full acknowledgement of common ground – in figurative and literal senses.

The kinds of dyadism noted by Plumwood and Guattari are familiar from the formal patternings and thematic preoccupations of the Gothic genre, a point alluded to by Fred Botting: 'Nature appears hostile, untamed and threatening: darkness, obscurity, and barely contained negative energy reinforce atmospheres of disorientation and fear' (4). Just as 'nature' was frequently conceived of within the Romantic lyric tradition as sublime and salvific, Gothicised topographies served as correlatives of fevered subjectivities and irredeemable otherness. 'Nature', then, 'is consistently constructed in our stories as Other, excessive, unpredictable, disruptive, chaotic, enticing, supernaturally powerful, and, perhaps most disturbingly, alive. It importantly threatens our very definitions of "humanness"' (Parker and Poland 1). The latter point distils Guattari's broader argument on the necessity to reconceive our anthropocentric sense of imperviousness to, and imperiousness over, all non-human life forms. It is in this context that the analytical resources of what is termed the 'ecogothic' prove illuminating. Rather than remaining satisfied with Gothic critiques content to read the non-human as merely a function of human emotion or affect, the ecogothic 'poses a challenge to a familiar Gothic subject (nature) taking a non-anthropocentric position to reconsider the role that the environment, species, and non-humans play in the construction of monstrosity and fear' (Del Principe 1). Ecogothic texts and analyses place a premium on decentring the volition and the security of the anthropogenic perspective, as well as insisting upon the inalienable mutuality of human and non-human ecological actors. As Keetley and Sivils argue, the ecogothic evokes the sense that humanity is 'interpenetrated, and sometimes stalked by a non-human with an agentic force' (7).

In the context of Irish ecogothic, to date, Derek Gladwin's *Contentious Terrains* is the most sustained and enabling intervention. Gladwin's debts to post-colonial studies, feminist critique, theatre studies, Gothic studies are in full view across his analyses of a familiar cast of authors and texts, including: Bram Stoker, Seamus Heaney, Marina Carr and Frank O'Connor. Of pertinence to our suite of analyses below are Gladwin's summative comments on the critical possibilities of the ecogothic, which he details as:

> ecological approaches to Gothic literature and culture where the natural environment can be investigated through fear and anxiety, as well as the sublime and the supernatural. [...] through catastrophic horror narratives of destruction and annihilation, with the concept that fear generates this particular impulse. (235)

Our survey begins with a focus on two literary representations of the kind of environmental catastrophe invoked by Gladwin. Though discrete in historical terms, the poetry of James Clarence Mangan and the short fictions of Eugene McCabe chart topographies of death in the context of the Great Irish Famine. In short, then, we move from the 'common ground' of Guattari's eco-politics to the barren and 'unyielding' grounds of Mangan's and McCabe's Famine landscapes. McCabe's short narratives document the horrors of the famished bodies at the same time as he mines for redemptive agency in the emergent sexualities of his young female protagonists. Meanwhile,

Mangan's allegorical Siberia is presented as indifferent, and therefore threatening, to the needs of humanity.

From landscapes that are replete with the horrors of barrenness, we move to an exemplary instance of William Butler Yeats's poeticisation of the unseen agents of the Irish West. Despite the simplicity of the poem, in terms of form and figuration, 'The Stolen Child' draws attention to how Yeats's early poetry emphasised and exploited the 'otherness' of the Irish landscape for political ends. While immanence constitutes an enlivening facet of the Irish landscape within Yeats's cultural nationalist imaginary, no such consolation is available to the anxious and increasingly alienated residents of Elizabeth Bowen's and J. G. Farrell's 'big house' novels – *The Last September* (1929) and *Troubles* (1970), respectively. In these narratives the edificial scar tissue of anthropogenic agency is not just the legacy of the past, but a premonition of the future. The 'othered' topography of Ireland is seen to reclaim, and to subdue, the architectural assertions of the country's imperial past. If the action of Bowen's and Farrell's narratives differentially engage with the fading embers of British colonialism in Ireland, Claire Kilroy's *The Devil I Know* (2012) partakes of the spirit and form of such 'big house' novels in its reckoning with the destructive transvaluations of the Irish landscape during the Celtic Tiger property 'boom'. Such transvaluations ultimately accrued widespread material dereliction, and ensured that urban and rural corners of the country were pockmarked by the ruins of overleveraged speculation and investment.

Famine – James Clarence Mangan and Eugene McCabe

Without abjuring the politicised complex of commemorative narrations of the Irish Famine, and as warranted by an ecogothic reading, our analysis begins by restating the obvious point that the human devastation endured was entirely bound up with a biological dependence upon a staple food resource. While Irish dependence upon the potato and the specific agricultural practices attendant to its cultivation both assumed cultural significance in terms of the Irish-British colonial relationship, the ecogothic goes beyond such anthropocentrism. Though the dominant historical and mythological processing of the Irish Famine has dilated upon the resulting global dispersal of swathes of the Irish population, the global or planetary nature of the invasive potato blight must also be registered. In true Gothic fashion, the blight – *phytophthora infestans* – was exogenous to Ireland, indeed to Europe, having originated in the Toluca Valley in Mexico. But, by 1844 the contagion was making its presence felt with devastating effects across the European continent. Invisible and incurable, the blight only revealed its presence once the potato crop was uprooted and harvested. From the viewpoint of contemporary political economy, the starving Irish body, then, might well be symptomatic of a rebarbative populous and, as Peter Gray outlines in his work on British government policy in Ireland in the 1840s, an obsolete suite of agricultural practices. But that same hunger-ravaged body reveals its porosity and fragile organicism as part of the mutually sustaining ecology of the human and non-human. Ultimately, the 'common ground' of these historically dichotomised constituencies is revealed through the horror of starvation. As we detail below, Mangan furnishes a contemporary allegorisation of catastrophic human suffering, while, given the date of publication, McCabe engages with the politics of commemoration in contemporary Ireland. Of more significance are the ways in which both authors engage with versions of form — poetic in Mangan's case and bodily in McCabe's stories. Poetic form and bodily form are enlisted in divergent ways but with similar critical intent, as redemptive potentialities are divined in the partial and the fragmentary by Mangan and McCabe.

Glossing Walter Benjamin's assertions on the redemptive valences of allegory, Terry Eagleton offers the following summative comments: 'The mortified landscape of history is redeemed, not by being recuperated into spirit, but by being raised, so to speak, to the second power – converted into a formal repertoire, fashioned into certain enigmatic emblems which then hold the promise of knowledge and possession' (20). Thus, out of the ruins of history, the partial and the discarded are potential repositories of political and ethical redemptive agency. Benjamin's retrieval of allegory from the shadow of symbol rests on the former's problematisation of metaphysical unity, as well as its capacity to reveal the repressed 'otherness' of all semiotic utterances. Equally, just as the fragmentary nature of allegorical representation contradicts the formal integrity of symbolism, it also contradicts the teleological linearity of 'empty, homogeneous time'. And this sense of the elusive and the provisional is appropriate to our reading of Mangan's poetic allegorisation of the Irish Famine in 'Siberia', published in 1846. And, while Mangan's forty-one-line poem gestures to the 'blank and pitiless' topography of its manifest location, it ultimately furnishes a complex allegorical rendering of the 'slow violence' of Famine suffering and starvation in the poet's contemporary Ireland.

Such is its fluidity, allegorical representation harbours the capacity to diffuse singular notions of historical progress, and, consequently, we might speak of the contradictory temporalities of allegory. In other words, the allegorical content is dialectical, shifting and, as Benjamin insists, entirely fungible. 'Siberia' is utterly impersonal in its portrait of that locale's 'wastes … [and] killing snows'. But, the extent to which Mangan spotlights the human body firmly situates humanity within the exposed and sublime physicality of the more-than-human world. The poem ends with the line, 'His last breath was drawn', a resolution that capstones the gradual but unrelenting breakdown of the somatic due to the rigours of physical assault within this landscape. As he attempts to give form and content to the blank sublimity of these polar reaches, Mangan repeatedly returns to the bodily, both in terms of his descriptions of the human and the non-human. And this is apparent in the poem's opening stanza: 'In Siberia's wastes / The Ice-wind's breath / Woundeth like the toothed steel. / Lost Siberia doth reveal / Only blight and death' (Mangan 108). The proximity of anthropomorphism and simile appears consistent with a lyrical reduction of non-humanity to the requirements of the poetic. But, this apparent figurative foreclosure proves less dominant as the poem progresses through a series of dynamic somatic processes and actions. We can trace a hint of the living nature of this, and other desolate landscapes, with Mangan's invocation of 'reveal'. Primary among the carceral sensations experienced in this poetic allegory are those attendant on the endurance of suffering. And, if allegory affords temporal slippage across historical contexts, 'Siberia' draws attention to the temporalities of isolated and intense human suffering. Embedded within such remote locations, in thrall to the extremities of the natural world, the duration of human life is measured out in the endurance of hardship: 'In Siberia's wastes / The blood blackens, the heart pines. / In Siberia's wastes … / Nought is felt but dullest pain, Pain acute, yet dead; / Pain as in a dream, When years go by / Funeral-paced, yet fugitive, / When man lives, and doth not live, / Doth not live – nor die' (ibid. 108).

The formal fecundity of Mangan's poem cannot be gainsaid, and we note the sequenced deployments of alliteration, metaphor, anadiplosis, anaphora, as well as the keen-like insistence of the poem's central refrain. But, the rhetoric of metaphysical cohesion is haunted by the contradictory energies of decay and dying. The crafted composure of the poem's design belies the desolation of the allegorical and 'othered' content of Mangan's authorial vision. And the symmetry offered by the aural patterns of 'Siberia', evident in its use of rhyme and repetitions are, in fact, only discernible because of the silence that prevails in the allegorised Famine spaces of Mangan's Ireland. They are less the aural effects of a strident poetic form than a series of poignant death-knells resounding for ravaged cultural and natural ecologies. Each poetic note is haunted by the absence of an auditor, as 'Siberia' evinces a dialectical relation between the integrative patterns of poetic form and the disintegration of human and non-human forms amid acute food scarcity and agricultural devastation. The troubling temporality of allegory befits the spectrality of the starving human forms that score the Irish landscape. The latter notion – human form – is one of several 'forms' germane to our analysis. 'Siberia' presents a constellation of bodily parts, sensations and conditions, a pattern that sunders the unified corporeality of the human body in contradistinction to the cohesive framing of the poem's figurative architecture. Once more in sequence, we encounter: 'breath', 'toothed', 'blood', 'heart', 'tears', 'the brain', 'pain', 'gaunt', 'tongue', 'hunger-gnawn', 'cold-slain', and, finally, 'corpse' (ibid. 108–9). The disintegration of the human form partakes of a recursive spectrality just as it coheres with the contestatory temporality of the allegorical form.

By means of its plurality of narrative strategies, *Tales from the Poorhouse* is simultaneously a critique of the limits of instrumental liberal political economy, a retrieval of indigenous Irish hope toward the future, and an ecumenical literary account of the lateral destruction wrought by the arrival of the potato blight and the onset of mass hunger and dislocation. There is a focus on form and voice across the collection of four narratives, but McCabe is deeply attentive to the pathologisation of femininity under a battery of repressive moral codes. Equally, the politics of food and human vulnerability to, and implication in, the emergence and transmission of a pathogenic contagion provide the historical and social contexts of McCabe's narratives as they dramatise 'the more disturbing and unsettling aspects of our interactions with non-human ecologies' in the form of the potato blight (Keetley and Sivils 1).

In specific ecogothic ways, with its alignment of animality and femininity in moral terms, McCabe's literary reckoning with the Famine cannot escape the centrality of the bodily as the site of suffering, exploitation and expressiveness even in the throes of societal trauma and ecological collapse. McCabe's short story cycle contains four narratives, each focalised through a first-person narrator. The 'tales' are 'The Orphan' by Roisin Brady; 'The Master' by Reggie Murphy, the master of the local poorhouse; 'The Landlord' by Lord Clonroy; and 'The Mother' by Mary Brady, Roisin's mother. Both female narrators deliver their narratives in standard first-person form, echoing the intimacy of the Irish oral storytelling tradition in the respective tones and themes of their testimonies. Thus, the women's stories, the first and the final in the collection, bracket the textual records of the two male narrators. The master's narrative is presented in the form of a confessional, indeed apologetic, letter to a sister whom he previously abandoned to hunger and death.

Likewise, the landlord's narrative is constructed as intermittent entries in his personal diary. In this way, McCabe demarcates between oral narration – which is here retained by the female protagonists – and the textual record.

In *Tales from the Poorhouse*, female sexuality manifests as an ambivalent yet strident force. On the one hand, consistent with mainstream Gothic representations, it is threatening and voracious. From another perspective, the female sexual excess on display harbours the possibility of living on beyond the prevailing cultural cataclysm, but it is also figured in terms of an array of animalistic or beastly tropes. Yet at the same time the modes employed to repress such bodily agency charted in the fictions, and recorded historically, can equally be understood as McCabe's awareness of historical efforts to deny an interest in the future to strains within native Irish culture. Conceived in this manner, the female sexual assertion of McCabe's tales becomes a mark of native Irish resilience in the face of a social and cultural disaster, a response to the prospect of obliteration. The female body is a dominant figurative referent in the opening story, 'The Orphan', appearing in a range of resonant allusions to menstruation, childbirth, desire, athleticism, sexual prowess and virginity. Margaret Kelleher, in examining the literary representation of the Famine, alludes to the gendered semiotic configurations of these literary narratives. She argues that 'throughout famine representations, female images are chosen to represent famine's worst consequences, in characterisations ranging from heroic self-sacrifice to "monstrous" Perversions of "Nature"' (239). Kelleher's comments signal the reduction of the stigmatised Brady sisters to less-than-human status. Though they are identified as physically and sexually vital, such vitality is wedded to the withered and failed crop yield. The incessant disquiet registered at the twins' behaviour is linked to the Famine conditions themselves. In other words, we are witness to a paranoiac conviction that their immorality is causally linked to the severity of the collective hunger. The excess of sexual energy harboured and displayed by the sisters is of a piece with the excess of suffering and deprivation visited upon the family and community.

Despite the devastating hunger sweeping the landscape, which has brought disease and death to their own household, Roisin – 'The Orphan' – reveals that: 'No matter how hungry we were she'd always have bought soap in the house or if there was no money she'd make it herself … Water costs nothin', she'd say, and by God you girls'll keep your bodies clean and your souls pure as long as you're in my care' (McCabe 15). Roisin describes the protracted and policed ritual purgation that their mother demands. What begins as hygiene is, in the end, a symbolic and penitent cleansing rite under which these sexualised bodies are normalised: 'She smelled of carbolic herself and made sure we did too. It was out to the turfshed every mornin', summer and winter, with the tin jug and basin, teeth first with soot, then strip down while she watched to make sure we'd wash neck, ears, back passage and up between our legs, and there was stuff in that soap went up into you like a bee sting' (ibid.). Not only does this scene reiterate the animalistic figuration of the sisters and their bodies, but the act of washing is also plainly witnessed as a punitive act.

The narrative of the burgeoning sexual lives of the Brady twins is nested within McCabe's broader representation of cultural ruination. McCabe's treatment of the twin sisters as sexually provocative in the face of maternal and institutional censure parallels the Malthusian critique of the sexually active body. For Malthus 'when man degrades himself through promiscuous sexual activity, he degrades woman, her sphere, and those who come in contact with her. Irrational sexual passion is thus the single most dangerous element operating within society' (Davenport 420). The reputed promiscuous actions of the Brady siblings are thus figured as a second blight on the local community. And, these sexually emergent female bodies are framed as infective threats to the moral welfare of a community that is simultaneously being ravaged by the physical punishment of the widespread hunger. When the mother scolds her daughters, she registers her disapproval in terms of animalistic behaviour that is instinctual rather than cognitive or rational: 'What would the priest and the neighbours think of her two daughters were near hoors out dancin' and gallivantin' like mad heifers in heat and half the parish half dead from hunger?' (McCabe 26). Here, the female body is transmuted into that of a sub-human creature, incapable of tempering carnal urges. Similarly, McCabe juxtaposes the animal 'in heat' with the starving nation; on the one hand we have the vibrant sexual potency of the feminine, and on the other, the disintegrating nation and culture under the onslaught of famine. For McCabe, that sense of vibrancy and sexual energy is a force of regeneration, even of cultural resistance. The sisters, in their different ways, represent an interest in the future denied under the mass mortality of the Famine.

Folklore – the Early Poetry of W. B. Yeats

If the socio-cultural anteriority of Ireland's husbandry of its landscape was deemed contributory to its catastrophic endurance of successive years of famine in the 1840s, then towards the latter end of the nineteenth century, writers such as W. B. Yeats mobilised such perceived anteriority for cultural nationalist ends. And, this is, as Joep Leerssen has argued, central to Yeats's early aesthetic and political projects. Leerssen outlines that '[t]he evocation of the Celtic temperament as being curiously otherworldly, shadowy, liminal and remote from the practicalities of the real world and real time ... dovetails geographical peripherality with ahistoricity' (188). Though taking a measure of Yeats's Celticism here, Leerssen's idiom is marbled with the critical lexis of more recent ecogothic analysis. The 'otherness' of Ireland's geography infuses Yeats's early poetry, and this takes on a more explicitly ecogothic form in 'The Stolen Child' (1889). Rather than stage a locational binary, in 'The Stolen Child' the paranormal and the physical co-exist as the geography of the poem alights upon places familiar to Yeats from his childhood. Drawing upon a repertoire of folktales, the poem wears its mystical Blakean Romanticism overtly, and does not showcase a landscape of passive purity. The real locations of Slish Wood, Glencar (Glen Car), and Rosses Point are suffused with the menace, and prey to the volition, of 'otherwordly' forces. But, the presence of transgressive non-human agencies is precisely the point. Yeats stresses the assertiveness of the irrational within the Irish cultural landscape, at the same time as he focuses upon the strange unknowability of these corners of the west of Ireland.

'The Stolen Child' embodies the later symbolism detailed by Yeats when he insists that in poetic composition 'we would seek out those wavering, meditative, organic rhythms, which are the embodiment of the imagination, that neither desires nor hates, because it has done with time, and only wishes to gaze upon some reality, some beauty' (120). Yeats privileges a concentration on 'ahistoricity', which is crucial to an ecogothic reading of the poem. Yeats eschews teleology though not formal poetic integrity, as the latter is pivotal to the invocation of his 'organic rhythms'. If the source material of 'The Stolen Child' is mined from Irish folklore, Yeats couples this with the rhyme scheme of the Italian folk form of 'rispetto'. But while the watermarks of anthropocentric poetic creativity are manifest in the architecture of the poem, the landscape to which it devotes its attention is largely devoid of humanity. Indeed, the consistency of the form belies the extent to which Yeats generates a tone of immanent threat in this series of 'othered' localities. In a gesture that decentres the agency of humanity in this pairing of poetic and geographical contexts, the poetic speaker is not human, we hear the voice of a non-human fairy spirit: 'Where dips the rocky highland / Of Sleuth Wood in the lake, / There lies a leafy island / Where flapping herons wake / The drowsy water rats; / There we've hid our faery vats, / Full of berries / And of reddest stolen cherries' (ibid. 14). There is an alignment of all non-humanity here, the actions and bounties of the natural world co-exist with the unseen presences that are given voice by Yeats. The organic vitality of the landscape is matched by the dynamism of its paranormal inhabitants, and thereby the poem, and the terrain, escape and reject the boundaries of a reductive rationalism. And it is in this capacity that 'The Stolen Child' emerges as an artefact of not just Irish cultural nationalism, but as a poetic expression of the power of the ecogothic. The poem is exemplary of Yeats's fascination with, and poeticisation of, landscapes 'where plain sight is continually menaced by flickerings from other worlds' (Punter and Byron 3).

Though the body of the poem is denuded of human agency, it is in Yeats's use of poetic refrains at the close of each of the poem's four stanzas that human presence is summoned. Each of the first three stanzas ends with the following: 'Come away, O human child! / To the waters and the wild / With a faery, hand in hand. / For the world's more full of weeping than you can understand' (Yeats 14). Significantly, this is not a benign paranormal, and Yeats dramatises the traditional belief that fairies would kidnap young children leaving a 'changeling' child in their place. This may not equate to the horrors of McCabe's or Mangan's famine landscapes, but Yeats attends to the malignant possibilities of the more-than-human that transcend and subvert the 'despotism of fact'. The repeated refrains are incantatory in effect, and their repetitive nature is consistent in no small way with the poem's 'othered' temporal rhythms, which lie athwart the linear teleology of progressive historicism.

The Irish 'Big House' Novel – J. G. Farrell and Elizabeth Bowen

The paranormal presences of the Irish West might have suffused Yeats's early work, but by the later stages of his writing and political careers, there is a recurring attention devoted to the lapsed grandeur of the landed Anglo-Irish constituency in Ireland. If the landed estate was the dominant unit of property in Ireland under British colonialism since the early modern period, within each of these 'units' the presiding seat of local authority 'was the landlord's country residence, traditionally referred to in Ireland as the "Big House" by the wider community' (Dooley 9). The term, 'big house', is legible in both literal and pejorative terms, depending on the context. For Dooley, the nomination quite simply 'captures the essence of the *raison d'etre* behind the building of these houses – to announce the economic and social strength of their owners in their localities and as a class as a whole, to inspire awe in social equals and possibly encourage deference in the lower classes' (9). Yet, *pace* Dooley's closing assertion, such concreted grandeur is equally interpretable as symptomatic of insecurity and expressive of a submerged affective response to historical expropriation, what Roy Foster describes as 'a sense of displacement, [and] a loss of social and psychological integration' (50). And in reckoning with the literary history of the 'big house' and landlordism in Ireland, we disinter some provocative thematic complexes: power and vulnerability; belonging and displacement; loyalty and betrayal; and trust and paranoia. Indeed, the real and imagined threats to this class are most often figured in terms of a minatory 'natural' hinterland. Decay and cultural decline are, then, slow processes of return to the 'natural', and such processes appear in both figurative and literal terms across the texts under consideration here.

Published in 1970, J. G. Farrell's novel *Troubles* is part of his Empire Trilogy, which also includes *The Siege of Krishnapur* (1973) and *The Singapore Grip* (1978). All three narratives explore the decline of British imperial control across Ireland, India and Singapore respectively, in the nineteenth and twentieth centuries. *Troubles* is set during the post-Great War period in Ireland, which also saw the commencement of the Irish War of Independence after a decade of sustained cultural, political and militant nationalist activism. And, though conceived of in the late 1960s, the narrative draws upon the classical 'big house' structure, as it directly confronts the history of British imperial decline in Ireland, but also, by implication, the emerging anti-British terrorist war and civil strife in Northern Ireland during the late 1960s. The novel is set in a hotel, the Majestic, rather than a functioning private domestic space, but the residents are of Anglo-Irish stock, and their relationships with the surrounding Irish population are structured by the same rigid class and religious distinctions we note in other 'big house' texts. The story relates the experiences of Major Brendan Archer, recently demobilised after a traumatic Great War, at the Majestic in the company of its few residents and its proprietors, the Spencer family. In a manner akin to Elizabeth Bowen's *The Last September* (1929), Farrell conveys the increasing obsolescence of the Spencers and their guests within the local and the national communities. The house-hotel is a precarious remnant on the landscape and is thoroughly haunted by its impending ruination. While the main narrative details the eccentricities of life at the Majestic – the defiant delusions of continuing grandeur and relevance – Farrell punctuates the text with extra-diegetic materials that signal the violent and ever-increasing demise of the British Empire in Ireland and across the globe. The insecurity of tenure suggested by

Farrell's importation of the 'big house' mode, then, resonates with the novel's thematic concern for the globality of dispossession endured by the waning British Empire.

The core narrative relates the insularity and the whimsy of the Spencer circle through the eyes of the Major, and Farrell does this in a tone of sympathetic irony. The local imperial geography into which Archer strays in its twilight days is remembered in terms that bespeak of the leisured domestication of this Irish property. The history of the Majestic detailed by the Major expresses the extent to which it was transfused with social and cultural capital, most of which has now bled away as the frayed remains of the hotel, the family, and the empire's Irish holdings are laid bare across the narrative. Tellingly, as the novel opens, we note the omniscient narration is conducted in the past tense: 'In those days the Majestic was still standing in Kilnalough at the very end of a slim peninsula covered with dead pines leaning here and there at odd angles. At that time there were probably yachts there too during the summer since the hotel held a regatta every July' (Farrell 9). The scene is one of both privilege and isolation, and is fitting for the social class, and the Spencer family, at the centre of the narrative. The Majestic 'had once been a fashionable place. It had once even been considered an honour to be granted accommodation there. ... By the time Edward Spencer bought it on his return from India, however, it retained little or nothing of its former glory' (ibid. 10). But there is a third temporal perspective present in the opening pages of the novel, the narrator's present, and from this temporal standpoint, the hotel is now little more than a ruin; ruination and absence are thereby signalled as keynotes of the ensuing tale of late imperial decline.

In one of the recurring figurations of the novel, Farrell describes the grand building as not just under threat from external damage, but as being in danger of structural collapse from the interior. In addition to the unseen but very real threats housed in the surrounding geographies, the 'big house' faces an encroaching non-human agent within its confines: 'The Palm Court proved to be a vast, shadowy cavern in which dusty white chairs stood in silent, empty groups, just visible here and there amid the gloomy foliage. ... The foliage ... was really amazingly thick ... running in profusion over the floor, leaping out to seize any unwary object' (ibid. 20–21). The shadowiness experienced by the Major in space is of the 'insubstantial' nature of the 'big house' and its populace. The absences that might have occupied the rows of dusty seating contrasts sharply with the organic vitality of the plant-life. The latter appears to fill the vacuums left behind by the retreating human occupants of the hotel, shedding the decorative functions of their placement within the 'Palm Court'. There is something 'primitive' to the description of this interior space; the Major seems to be stepping outside the refined geographies of 'civility' as he progresses to this recessed location within the Majestic. In a sense, the mass of unruly vegetation induces a form of interior 'othering' within the erstwhile refinement of the Majestic hotel. From the Major's perspective this dense tangle of vegetation is animated with agency as it gropes for prey from among the static occupants of the Palm Court. In stark contrast to the human population of the Majestic, the vegetation teems with life; its virility is in direct juxtaposition to the sterility and terminal decline of Spencers and the hotel guests. Equally significant is the fact that the plant life flourishing here is typically non-native to Ireland, thus, at one level, we witness a horticultural iteration of reverse colonisation. The scene confronted by the Major in the Palm Court is denuded of any degree of anthropocentric management, and instead his response to the thriving greenery is indexical of an innate trepidation at the prospect of its seemingly inexorable growth.

Bowen's *The Last September* opens with an arrival at the 'big house' at Danielstown, as the Montmorencys, potent symbols of the 'unhousing' of the Anglo-Irish during the early part of the twentieth-century in Ireland, enter the Naylor's estate: 'About six o'clock the sound of a motor, collected out of the wide country and narrowed under the trees of the avenue, brought the household out in excitement on to the steps' (7). Yet this auspicious, celebratory and communal beginning is a distraction from the real force of the novel. There may be a dynamism to the first sentence of the novel, but it belies the thread, and threat, of ruination that suffuses much of the remainder of the narrative. Our protagonist, Lois Farquhar, reveals this sense as she watches the guests arrive: 'The dogs came pattering out of the hall and stood beside her; above, the vast facade of the house stared coldly over its mounting lawns. She wished she could freeze the moment and keep it always. But as the car approached, as it stopped, she stooped down and patted one of the dogs' (ibid.). While Lois's eye to the future is partly conditioned by the difficult choices she faces as a young woman of marriageable age, Bowen's terminology suggests more grave prospects. The insular social and cultural routines of the Naylors and the Montmorencys achieve a 'frozen' quality. In fact, the tea parties, dances, visitations and tennis parties, during a guerrilla war between the British state and Irish militia, have both tragic and comedic effects. Bowen's lexical selection, 'freeze', then, hints at something that is passing, a class, a lifestyle, a set of social mores and habits, that are obsolete, and under threat, from the unseen indigenous terrors that haunt the territories beyond, and within, the demesned estate. And in true terrorist fashion, the unseen violences and threats play upon the imaginations of the landed Anglo-Irish.

In the wake of a nationalist 'outrage', we witness Lois's perspectives of the landscape, and of her situation within the physical and cultural geographies of Ireland:

> She [Lois] wondered they were not smothered; then wondered still more that they were not afraid ... The house seemed to be pressing down low in apprehension, hiding its face, as though it had her vision of where it was. It seemed to gather its trees close in fright and amazement at the wide, light lovely, unloving country, the unwilling bosom whereon it was set ... And the kitchen smoke, lying over the vague trees doubtfully, seemed the very fume of living. (ibid. 67)

There is no explicit mention of human agency in this extended rumination. Bowen anthropomorphises the Naylors' 'big house' to underscore the emotional force of Lois's sense of vulnerability and isolation within these physical and cultural topographies. In addition, Bowen deploys a familiar trope within colonial literature as she contrasts the spaces of 'big house' civility with the encroaching forestlands surrounding the estate. Of course, the forest here forms part of the cosmetic arrangement of the estate, a physical realignment of space that speaks to the prevailing mores of the dominant cultural constituency. But the passage articulates the Gothic ambivalence at the heart of the colonial relationship with occupied territory, a disquieting ambivalence that no amount of horticultural husbandry can quell. The exercises and the legacies of colonial history are pressing hard against the boundaries of the demesne, and they are exerting their force upon the imaginative and figurative faculties of Lois's consciousness. As Lois travels back to the 'big house' at Danielstown, after the news of the terrorist attack, her forward motion could easily be taking her into the past rather than towards any viable future at the estate. And this sense of ghostliness in a landscape punctuated with affective and physical wounds of colonial and anti-colonial conflict takes more overt form on another journey made by Lois outside the confines of the 'big house'.

Together with Hugo Montmorency and Marda Norton, Lois undertakes what begins as a leisurely walk along the local river, the Darra. Just as a maudlin Hugo is about to emote to Marda on the condition of his marriage, she interjects with: 'Oh, what is that? The ghost of a Palace Hotel?' (ibid. 122–23). The walk is interrupted by the prospect of a ruined mill on the banks of the river. Both embedded within the longer history of industrialisation and now exterior to the lineaments of productive historical time, the defunct building looms over the walkers: 'The mill startled them all, staring, light-eyed, ghoulishly, round a bend in the valley ... The river darkened and thundered towards the mill-race, light came full on the high facade of decay. Incredible in its loneliness, roofless, floorless, beams of criss-crossing dank interior daylight, the whole place tottered, fit to crash at a breath' (ibid.). The mouldering ruin's decay and abandonment, its obscurity and its emptiness, are harbingers of the future for the witnesses to its current condition. If the imagined and/or real unseen terrorists occupy the sylvan hinterlands of the Naylors' estate, in this case it is the absence of human agency that has returned the mill to a disturbing scene and site of ruination. But the latter is purely cultural in its reference points; the mill's gradual decline explicitly figures the permeable boundaries between human and non-human ecologies. As the mill crumbles it retreats from anthropocentric functionalism, and Lois's description is an attempt to domesticate its unnerving appearance, and the implications of that appearance, through semiotic and aesthetic closure. Within the symbolic economy of Bowen's Gothic narrative, the sundered mill anticipates the eventual demise through arson of the 'big house' at Danielstown.

The vista at the mill also includes vestiges of indigenous Irish ruination crouching in the shadow of the larger ruin, with the borders between so-called natural history and human history evincing ominous signs of leakage. As the trio progress, tentatively, they note:

> some roofless cottages nestled under the flank of the mill with sinister pathos. A track going up the hill from the gateless gateway perished among the trees from disuse. Banal enough in life to have closed this valley to the imagination, the dead mill now entered the democracy of ghostliness ... was transfigured by some response of the spirit, showing not the decline of its meanness, simply decline. (ibid. 123)

The scene is one of profound Shelley-like levelling; time returns the concreted assertions of hubris, colonial in this case, to fragments. But, in this instance, there is an explicit alignment between the presence of the past and the contemporary conditions of violent uprising by the native Irish populous. Lurking within the frayed structure of the mill, the visitors discover what one can assume is a local Irish 'terrorist'. As Lois investigates the interior of the mill with Marda, they disturb the sleeping vagrant: 'But the man rolled over and sat up, still in the calm of sleep. "Stay there," he said, almost persuasively: a pistol bore the persuasion out ... "It is time," he said, "that yourselves gave up walking. If you have nothing better to do, you had better keep in the house while y'have it"' (ibid.). Thus we have an anonymous voice of indigenous resistance, not a voice that is tinged with fear or anger, but, rather, seems to be assured in how the historical narrative of Irish colonialism will play out.

The mill straddles the anthropocentric measures of economic history and the cyclical patterns of the non-human world, given its dependence upon the resources of the latter. But as the three walkers approach, the disjunctive presence of the mill in the landscape is in the process of being redressed. The decline might well be protracted but the building's absence will endure far longer than its productive presence. In this sense, we are reminded of the spectral temporalities of Mangan and McCabe, wherein the composure of the present is disturbed by the irruptions of 'othered' temporal realities and possibilities. The disused stone cottages that abut the mill were likely to have been manufactured utilising the material deposits of geological deep time. And their abandoned condition marks them as potently synecdochic of the ambivalence of non-human deep historical processes to human endeavour and necessity.

Celtic Tiger Hauntings

Ireland is repeatedly and enduringly cited as a country that is haunted by its social and political histories, yet of more pressing concern in the context of Celtic Tiger Irish culture is the way haunting assumed new forms under the auspices of the global debt economy. Indebtedness is fundamental to the material experiences of everyday living and is structural to conceptions of narrative and temporality under financial capitalism. As Annie McClanahan maintains: 'the temporality of debt … concerns the continued presence of the past, its frightening inescapability' (132). Indebtedness might well facilitate an intensification of consumption in the present, but all indebted presents are haunted by the initial debt arrangement and by the deferred day of repayment. This sense of being out-of-place, of lacking the capacity to apprehend one's immediate context, a feeling that the world is becoming less comprehensible are widely diagnosed as common and necessary effects of financial capitalism.

The uncanniness of life lived in shadow of pervasive indebtedness intersects with the case made by Andrew Smith and William Hughes in their introductory comments on the ecogothic. For Smith and Hughes, 'nature becomes constituted in the Gothic as a space of crisis which conceptually creates a point of contact with the ecological' (3). Furthermore, in terms that speak directly to Claire Kilroy's engagement with the experiences, and the legacies, of the Celtic Tiger debt economy, Smith and Hughes add that 'the process of ecological unconscionization is deliberately reversed through *stagings of uncanny states* that dramatize the traumatic impact of abstract economic systems on local ecologies' (ibid. 13; emphasis added). It is no surprise that the 'local ecology' most commonly in evidence in cultural renderings of the Celtic Tiger's personal and environmental impacts are 'ghost' housing estates. These are physical and cultural terrains that are specific and historical, but whose post-boom conditions cannot be unwedded from the past and present histories of global financial capitalism. Taken in aggregation 'ghost estates' register as an uncanny array of homes in terms of their abandonment and they signal the ambivalence of mortgaged ownership within the global debt economy.

Published in 2012, Claire Kilroy's *The Devil I Know* combines straight literary realism with elements of genre fiction in its retrospective narration of the machinations and the decline of Ireland's property surge. The narrative relays the events surrounding Tristram St Lawrence's immersion in the nether regions of Ireland's credit/debt economy at the outset of the twenty-first century. On returning after a prolonged absence from Ireland, Tristram, whose family are of Anglo-Irish ancestry, encounters an erstwhile acquaintance from his schooldays, Des Hickey, who inveigles Tristram into partnering him in a thoroughly ambitious, and outsized, property investment. But Tristram's decisions, and indeed agency, are guided by his AA 'sponsor', Mr Deauville ['devil'], who is only contactable remotely by phone. And it is through this narrative device that Kilroy transcends the conventions of literary realism, and invests her narrative with Faustian textures. Early in the novel, our protagonist and narrator, Tristram, is being driven on the coast road above Dublin Bay by his future business associate, Hickey, and he provides the following portrait of his environment:

> The truck ascended past ponied meadows and heathered slopes until the road crested and Dublin Bay appeared below, broad and smooth and greyish blue, patrolled by the Baily lighthouse. The whitethorn was in full blossom and the ferns were pushing through. Better to have been born somewhere dismal, I sometimes think. Better to have grown up shielded from striking natural beauty, to have never caught that glimpse of Paradise in the first place only to find yourself sentenced to spending the rest of your life pining for it, a tenderised hole right in the heart of you, a hole so big that it seems at times you're no more than the flesh defining it, I rolled the window up to seal the beauty out. (Kilroy 16)

What commences as a vision redolent of the conventions of Romantic lyricism – with its congregation of alliterative and assonant sound effects – declines into an introspective confrontation with humanity's capacity for destruction and with the transience of human life. Kilroy's opening here evinces a feeling of ill-accommodation within these surroundings, which tallies with the overall thrust of Tristram's retrospective narrative. His entrepreneurial partnership is centred on precisely the looting of the non-human physical resources of his locale, but all that is accomplished is the production of a version of the all-too-familiar 'ghost estate' housing developments. The lyricism of the opening description is bleakly ironic given the orientation of Tristram's, and the country's, priorities. The overtly Romantic apparel of Kilroy's portrait quickly mutates into a more brooding antagonistic relation between the human and the non-human. Kilroy, thereby, solicits the reader to take this as a keynote moment for the narrative that explores how the Irish became beguiled by the potential that lay in disfiguring the open spaces of its natural environment with what became the aforementioned 'ghost estates'.

The crux of the narrative action is that having become embroiled in a gargantuan property investment, Tristram is indebted and culpable for the construction of an incomplete development – a 'ghost' property. And the moments of reckoning are the points at which the Faustian and the 'big house' formal patternings of Kilroy's narrative are rendered most visible, and where the idiom of indebtedness is clearly linked with guilt and punishment. As Tristram returns to his ancestral/family home for the final time, he describes the scene of aftermath that presages his imminent fate. Tristram's home belongs to the architectural and novelistic genealogy of the Irish 'big house', which, as we have noted, was an 'end of empire' literary phenomenon. Kilroy's invocation of the 'big house' literary tradition manifests in such overtly Gothic fashion as dissolving remainders of a once aristocratic family, as well as the persistence, in ghostly, haunting forms, of people and memories from that fading presence on the Irish landscape. In this respect, the anteriority of the big house narrative strand, and the attendant violence and insecurity of the genre, anticipates the imminence of the Faustian plot's denouement.

What was once secure and central to the socio-economic structures of colonial Ireland is perishing in the neoliberal present of the Celtic Tiger:

> I crossed the road to the ribbed columns of the castle entrance … the gatekeeper's cottage was a derelict wreck and so was I … The castle was boarded up like the rest of the county. A carpet of bindweed had smothered the sunken gardens. I paused at the tradesman's entrance but continued around to the vandal's entrance and climbed through that instead, seeing as I was the biggest vandal of them all. They had pulled off the plywood boards and

broken the catch on a sash window. Cider cans littered the parquet floor like autumn leaves. (ibid. 355–6)

In this extended fraction of the narrative colonial and contemporary histories are about to reach points of settlement. This is a quintessential site of dereliction, a fragmented and anachronistic edifice whose original purpose and proprietors have been superseded by the 'Gothic excesses of Celtic Tiger Ireland', and the machinations of Ireland's integration into globalised liberal capitalism and the debt/credit economy (Burke 17). The reference to boarded up properties is an explicit invocation of the blight of 'ghost estates' across Ireland, there is an uncanny resemblance between Tristram's crumbling home and the edificial legacy he has left with his failed investment. The ancestral 'big house' stands in analogous state of disrepair to the legions of newly built houses and estates that litter rural and urban Ireland. Thus, there is a temporal slippage together with a feeling of spatial disorientation characteristic of the uncanny registered as the once familiar is thoroughly defamiliarised under the weight of financial indebtedness. For Tristram there is a visual disturbance of reality as the family seat becomes the uncanny double of the specific wreckage he is complicit in partially constructing. In short, both the ancestral and the Celtic Tiger 'homes' are resolutely estranged.

In an astute appraisal of the ecogothic, Sharae Deckard argues that it 'can be understood as not only figuring the social deformations relating to the economic reorganization of societies, but also the reorganization of social – nature relations around different commodity regimes and the periodic exhaustion of ecologies' (181). While this precis is a fraction of Deckard's broader world-ecological methodology, the attention drawn to formal crisis, economic decline, and resource depletion resonates with the array of texts and contexts surveyed in the foregoing analyses. The ecogothic context underscores the nature and scale of humanity's destructive 'othering' of a host of peripheral topographies under the aegis of colonial and neo-colonial modernities. And the same set of analytical resources also dispels myths of the permeability of species boundaries and of the unassailability of anthropocentric ways of living. Our range of literary interventions is not designed to impress the peculiarity or singularity of the Irish case in terms of ecogothic analysis. Rather, given the protracted nature of the Irish colonial experience, and, latterly, its comprehensive integration into the networks of finance capital, there is ample instructive material that tracks the incremental but relentless discursive objectification and ontological 'othering' of human and non-human ecologies in this context. Given the urgency of the contemporary climate emergency with 'our own environmental monsters inevitably [awaiting] us', the ecogothic could not be timelier as an emerging analytical method (Parker 222).

Works Cited

Benjamin, Walter. *The Origin of German Tragic Drama*, Verso, 1998.
Botting, Fred. *Gothic*, Routledge, 2013.
Bowen, Elizabeth. *The Last September*. 1929. Vintage, 1998.
Burke, Mary. 'Claire Kilroy: An Overview and an Interview'. *LIT: Literature, Interpretation, Theory*, vol. 28, no. 1, 2017, pp. 13–33.
Davenport, Randi. 'Thomas Malthus and Maternal Bodies Politic: Gender, Race, and Empire.' *Women's History Review*, vol. 4, no. 4, 1995, pp. 415–39.
Deckard, Sharae. '"Uncanny states": Global EcoGothic and the World-Ecology in Rana Dasgupta's *Tokyo Cancelled*'. *Ecogothic*, edited by Andrew Smith and William Hughes, Manchester University Press, 2013, pp. 177–94.
Del Principe, David. 'Introduction: The EcoGothic in the Long Nineteenth Century'. *Gothic Studies*, vol. 16, no. 1, pp. 1–8.
Dooley, Terence. *The Big Houses and Landed Estates of Ireland: A Research Guide*. Dublin, Four Courts Press, 2007.
Eagleton, Terry. *Walter Benjamin or Towards a Revolutionary Criticism*. Verso, 1981.
Farrell, J. G. *Troubles*. Jonathan Cape, 1970.
Foster, R. F. *W. B. Yeats, A Life, I: The Apprentice Mage 1865–1914*. Oxford University Press, 1998.
Gladwin, Derek. *Contentious Terrains: Boglands in the Irish Postcolonial Gothic*. Cork University Press, 2016.
Gray, Peter. *Famine, Land and Politics: British Government and Irish Society 1843–1850*. Irish Academic Press, 1999.
Guattari, Felix. *The Three Ecologies*. 1989. The Athlone Press, 2000.
Hughes, William. 'A Singular Invasion: Revisiting the Postcoloniality of Bram Stoker's *Dracula*'. *Empire and the Gothic: The Politics of Genre*, edited by William Hughes and Andrew Smith, Palgrave, 2003, pp. 88–102.
Keetley, Dawn and Matthew Wynn Sivils. 'Introduction: Approaches to the Ecogothic'. *Ecogothic in Nineteenth-Century American Literature*, edited by Dawn Keetley and Matthew Wynn Sivils, Routledge, 2017, pp. 1–20.
Kelleher, Margaret. 'Irish Famine in Literature'. *The Great Irish Famine*, edited by Cathal Póirtéir, Cork, Mercier Press, 1995, pp. 232–47.
Kilroy, Claire. *The Devil I Know*. Faber and Faber, 2012.
Leerssen, Joep. *Remembrance and Imagination: Patterns in the Historical and Literary Representations of Ireland in the Nineteenth Century*. Cork University Press, 1996.
Mangan, James Clarence. *Poems*, edited by David Wheatley, Dublin, The Gallery Press, 2003.
McCabe, Eugene. *Tales from the Poorhouse*. Dublin, The Gallery Press, 1997.
McClanahan, Annie. *Dead Pledges: Debt, Crisis, and Twenty-First-Century Culture*. Stanford University Press, 2016.

Parker, Elizabeth and Michelle Poland. 'Gothic Nature: An Introduction'. *Gothic Nature*, vol. 1, 2019, pp. 1–20.

Parker, Elizabeth. '"Just a Piece of Wood": Jan Švankmajer's *Otesánek* and the EcoGothic'. *Plant Horror: Approaches to the Monstrous Vegetal in Fiction and Film*, edited by Dawn Keetley and Angela Tenga, Palgrave, 2016, pp. 215–25.

Plumwood, Val. *Feminism and the Mastery of Nature*. Routledge, 1993.

Punter, David and Glennis Byron. 'Introduction'. *Spectral Readings: Towards a Gothic Geography*, edited by David Punter and Glennis Byron, Palgrave Macmillan, 1999, pp. 1–8.

Smith, Andrew and William Hughes, 'Introduction: Defining the Ecogothic'. *Ecogothic*, edited by Andrew Smith and William Hughes, Manchester University Press, 2013, pp. 1–14.

Yeats, W. B. *The Collected Poems of W. B. Yeats*. Wordsworth Editions, 2000.

———. *Early Essays – The Collected Works of W. B. Yeats, Vol. 4*, edited by George Bornstein and Richard J. Finneran, Scribner, 2007.

Chapter 7

Gothic Fiction in the Irish Language
Jack Fennell

Incomplete modernisation, under-industrialisation and a deference to history and tradition among its people reinforced the popular perception of Ireland as a place disconnected from time, a 'lost world' of sorts, where things persisted that had been pushed out of Britain and other modernised countries, and where science and magic seemed to have equivalent value in the eyes of the local population (Fennell, *Irish Science Fiction* 38–41). This made it a repository of cultural material for Romanticists and Gothicists, such as the writers who secretly contributed original work to British and American compendiums of Irish folklore (Markey 95–8), and the Irish language was a useful signifier of this inspiring anachronism – not least because, out of reverence for 'the authority of tradition', many mediaeval written sources for *Gaeilge* were composed in an 'archaising' style to make them seem older than they were, resulting in texts that combined Early Modern Irish with older grammar and vocabulary that had fallen out of popular use (Doyle 30–31).

Throughout the nineteenth century, English-language writers tackling Irish topics would often make use of phonetically-rendered Irish words, mostly characters' names and folkloric figures; in many of these works, the language is assumed to be a mark of difference between the characters and the reader, as the texts often include footnotes or glossaries, and their inclusion serves the authenticity of the setting rather than characterisation. The paradox, of course, is that if the intended reader truly has no familiarity with the language or culture, then they have no way of judging the text's authenticity to begin with (Fennell, *Rough Beasts* 35); the precise purpose of its inclusion, therefore, was to meet the reader's expectations of the characters using it – usually a closeness or sensitivity to nature, a superstitious personality, or a lack of intelligence. To take one example, there is Thady Quirk's Irish-inflected vernacular in Maria Edgeworth's *Castle Rackrent* (1800), explained in a glossary that, as Kathryn J. Kirkpatrick argues, portrays the Irish as a people 'in need of governing restraint' (xxvii). Another is Sheridan Le Fanu's *Ghost Stories of Chapelizod* (1851), in which the frequency of phonetically-spelled Irish words and accents increases in tandem with the ignorance and/or revolutionary sympathies of the main characters (Fennell, *Rough Beasts* 108–10).

Beginning with the Revival period at the end of the nineteenth century and carrying through to the early twenty-first, this chapter will consider Gothic and Gothic-inflected works written in Irish (*as Gaeilge*). It is beyond the scope of this chapter to re-tread the various arguments over how 'Gothic' should be defined, but for the sake of setting usable parameters, some material must be excluded: barring a few references to particularly macabre images, Irish-language science fiction will not be taken into consideration here; nor will I discuss children's literature in depth, though it seems obvious that child-friendly works such as Orna Ní Choileáin's *Vaimpír* series (2012–2017) may cultivate an appreciation for 'harder' Gothic texts in adulthood. The category of 'Gothic' also somewhat excludes the slimy, cosmic horrors of the Weird, though there is considerable overlap between the two. This means that works like Panu Petteri Höglund's Lovecraftian collection *An Leabhar Nimhe* ('The Book of Poison/The Poison Book') (2014) and Peadar Ó Guilín's *The Call* (2016) fall outside the remit of this chapter, though they are noteworthy for incorporating Gaelic tradition and linguistics into Weird stories in innovative ways. The former makes use of traditional storytelling and the work of the Folklore Commission to 'localise' Lovecraft's Cthulhu Mythos, while the latter positions Primitive Irish as the language of a resurgent Sidhe host, and depicts an alternative Ireland where this primeval dialect is becoming the dominant language, even displacing English. This fictional resurgence is all the more noteworthy for being a complete inversion of the actual history of the language from the seventeenth century to the twentieth.

The Long Road Out of Oblivion

Jarlath Killeen notes that 'Many Irish-language Gothic texts speak of the power of the living dead and the inability to kill that which is most frightening' (55). This is not surprising when one considers the centrality of death and decline to the discourse that surrounded the language for centuries. Declan Kiberd argues that since the 1650s, Irish had 'largely ceased to be a medium in which an intellectual life was possible, becoming the language of the poor and, in truth, a decisive mark of their poverty' (*Inventing Ireland* 133). The prior Irish-speaking intelligentsia were largely made up of the old bardic order of the *filí*, who resented the collapse of the system of patronage that had supported them under the Gaelic aristocracy. Obliged to compete in an emerging literary marketplace subject to public taste, they mourned their loss of status as the death of Ireland itself, to the extent that 'Gaelic Ireland always seemed to be dying ... if not in the loss of native speakers to death or emigration, then in the sheer impoverishment of the words in the spoken language' (Kiberd, *Irish Classics* 21). Siobhán Kilfeather shows how this attitude was reflected in the private diary of Kilkenny schoolmaster Amhlaoibh Ó Súilleabháin. Written in school exercise books and accounting ledgers during the 1820s, Ó Súilleabháin's diary contains detailed records of sundry natural and economic topics, alongside his worries for his own family and his fears for the Irish language; while none of these is 'an overtly Gothic concern', Kilfeather sees certain Gothic tropes and themes woven into this 'elegiac' collection of minutiae and personal reflections, such as 'pathetic fallacy, pervasive melancholy, associative poetics, dislocation, the unspeakable, and the thematics of revenge and disinterment' (66). As Lesa Ní Mhunghaile points out, Ó Súilleabháin's writings begin in English and switch to Irish, and this switch can be correlated both to the decline of the 'literary caste,' and to the 'retreat' of the language generally at the beginning of the nineteenth century, as it was spoken in fewer and fewer areas even as the total number of speakers continued to grow (37–40).

Meanwhile, the Irish language was seen to be part and parcel of Gaelic villainy by virtue of the fact that it was considered impenetrable, a view articulated by Samuel Taylor Coleridge, who warned of the 'Erse' language's 'facilities of concealment' (quoted in Gibbons 67). Others found 'scientific' reasons for disdaining Irish in the nineteenth century: as Killeen summarises, Celtic languages were imagined to contain traces of 'a European ur-language', thus marking the people who spoke them as throwbacks of a sort (10); Luke Gibbons argues that, furthermore, language was one of the factors (the others being craniology and empire) that separated the Celts from 'true Caucasians' in the racialist discourse of the 1830s (39). It is hardly surprising in this context that Daniel O'Connell himself saw the abandonment of the language as inevitable and of little concern. In terms of economic and political utility, Irish was outclassed by English, regardless of its sentimental value to Irish patriots. When the Great Famine ravaged the countryside in the 1840s, roughly halving the remaining number of native speakers left in the country (in areas that, at the time, had limited literacy), the extinction of the language did indeed seem to be a foregone conclusion – and the fact that it was primarily spoken in areas where the Famine death toll was highest only strengthened its Gothic connotations.

In spite of the seeming inevitability of the disappearance of *Gaeilge*, however, efforts were soon underway to preserve what remained. The Society for the Preservation of the Irish Language was established in 1876, and in 1878 the Commissioners for National Education placed the language on the curriculum as an optional subject of study. According to Colmán Ó hUallacháin, the accepted form of nineteenth-century 'high Irish' was adapted from the formal, bardic style of the seventeenth century and did not reflect the commonly spoken dialects that had emerged since that time. When Irish was added to the curriculum in 1878, the texts written by these poets were adopted as classroom reading material. At this time, the vast majority of the native Irish speakers left in the country still came from impoverished rural areas and were unable to read or write the language (Ó hUallacháin 111–12). This gap between oral tradition and the 'official' written version of Irish foreshadowed problems that would emerge in the twentieth century with the advent of language standardisation.

One notable work from the end of the nineteenth century, re-worked and re-issued in the early twentieth, was Father Peadar Ua Laoghaire's *Séadna*, originally serialised in various Irish-language literary journals from 1898 and published as a complete novel in 1904. *Séadna* is an Irish-set composite of the archetypal Faust story and the folktale of the Smith and the Devil, refracted through the author's Catholic worldview, in which the eponymous shoemaker inadvertently sells his soul to the Devil in exchange for enough money to buy sufficient leather to keep him in business for thirteen years. As the deadline approaches, the Virgin Mary herself intervenes to save Séadna from damnation, which rather undermines the narrative, but Ua Laoghaire's version of the Devil is memorably monstrous. He first appears as a 'long, thin, dark man' (fear fada caol dubh), with 'sparks coming from his eyes in poisonous flashes' (teine chreasa ag teacht as a dhá shúil 'na spréachaibh nimhe); he has two goat-like horns, a long blue-grey goatee, a fox's tail and hooves like those of a bull (9). There is an extra claw or barb on the tip of his tail, which he warns Séadna not to touch (24), and he has claws on his hands similar to the talons of an eagle (260). Remarkably, Séadna does not realise that there is anything untoward about this chimerical monster: in fact, he does not realise that this 'Dark Man' is the Devil at all until the climax of the story (273) and even then briefly falls for his tricks a second time (285–86). It was perhaps this combination of flamboyant monstrosity and orthodox Roman Catholic morality that earned

Séadna its place as a core text on the Intermediate Certificate Irish curriculum, alongside Peig Sayers' autobiography.

Neither the alphabet *Séadna* was printed in, nor its spelling of Irish words, were straightforward considerations, and both would become the subjects of strenuous disagreement among Irish speakers generally in years to come. The uncial alphabet, being the closest approximate typeset to the Gaelic manuscript style, was the preferred choice for many language purists, and it had been the default typeset for schoolbooks and Irish-language journals for decades; however, it came with the drawback of limiting the printing of Irish material to a handful of places that were equipped to do it (Ó hUallacháin 112). Meanwhile, demand for simplified spellings of Irish words continued to grow, culminating in An Cumann um Litriú Shimplí (The Society for Simple Spelling) proposing a national standard for the spelling of Irish words, based on the Munster dialect. From the inception of the Free State, this exact kind of standardisation became the guiding principle of the government's engagement with the Irish language.

From the beginning of the twentieth century, a growing number of fluent writers and commentators had been bemoaning the paucity of contemporary subjects in Irish-language literature and criticising the overwhelming focus on rural tropes and the lack of attention paid to city life. Even Pádraig Pearse, with his notoriously Romantic attachment to ancient myth, advocated for a fully modern Irish literature, stating 'We want no Gothic revival' (O'Leary, *Prose Literature* 404). Following the establishment of the Free State, this sentiment seems to have become unofficial policy, particularly where fiction published in newspapers was concerned. As Philip O'Leary summarises, in Irish-language stories of the 1920s and 1930s, supposedly supernatural occurrences are revealed to have mundane causes, 'usually to the comic discomfiture of those gullible enough to be amazed or terrified by what they have seen' (*Gaelic Prose* 157). This pattern persisted into the 1940s and 1950s, with 'ghosts' usually revealed to be pranksters, animals, and less commonly, the products of random happenstance – one notable instance of the latter being the two-part story 'Taibhse an Chaisleán' (The Ghost of the Castle) by 'Tadhg Tostach', published in *The Irish Press* in September 1950, in which the reader learns that the 'ghost' is nothing more than the wind blowing across the neck of a discarded glass bottle. These stories attempted to separate the language from its prior associations with anachronism and cultural extinction – associations that had once prompted its inclusion in Irish Gothic texts and now cast doubt on its relevance to the modern world.

As Christina Morin points out, the literal depiction of supernatural events is not necessarily a key feature of Gothic literature, despite present-day genre expectations (15), and these stories could be placed in the same general constellation as the Radcliffean 'explained supernatural'. However, an interesting aspect to these stories is the aforementioned comic tone, because the humour is derived from the embarrassment of those who tempt fate by scorning storytelling tradition: almost every tale of this type begins with a recitation of an old ghost story, which is ridiculed by another character who is depicted either as a curmudgeon or an obnoxious know-it-all; this character then gets a bad fright which briefly causes them to 'relapse' into believing in the supernatural, before the non-supernatural cause of their fear is revealed, to the amusement of all. For example, in M. I. Ní Fhlannagáin's 'Taidhbhse Dhún Aonghusa' (The Ghost of Dún Aengus), a girl disguises herself as a ghost and enters a reputedly haunted fort, in order to humiliate a pompous boy who begins the story by asking, 'Who would believe in [*púcas*/spirits/demons] but an idiot or a baby?' (Cé chreidfeadh I bpúcaí ach amadán, nó páiste?); an encounter with a horned creature in the dark (obviously a goat) sends them both running for home (1946). In P. Ó Bríain's 1947 story 'Taibhse sa Comhrann' (A Ghost in the Chest/Trunk), a sceptic earns the nickname 'It moved!' (Do bhog sé!) from his panicked reaction to a 'spirit' that turns out to be a cat. As was the case with Gaelic poets, the price for antagonising a *seanchaí* (storyteller) is humiliation: if you cross a storyteller, you will end up as the subject of a story yourself. The contradiction between the rejection of folk material and the insistence upon respect for traditional storytelling speaks to the ambiguities of early twentieth-century Irish cultural production, with tradition simultaneously a source of pride and embarrassment.

In those early decades, however, the predominant mood of the Free State was one of paranoia and suspicion, particularly regarding foreign art forms, cultural influences and scientific discoveries: the castigation of jazz as a sinful and degrading foreign import during these decades is well-documented, as is the suspicion of quantum physics (Fennell, *Irish Science Fiction* 105–6). This mood also manifested in fiction of the time, in pieces such as Seán Ó Cuirrín's 1922 novella 'Beirt Dhéiseach' (Two Waterford Men), in which a young man escapes from a cult named 'The Society for the Exploration of the Hereafter' (Cumann Sírthe na Síorruidheachta), who worship the old god Crom and trick their new recruits into ritual suicide, and Tomás Bairéad's 1930 short story 'An Tríomhadh Bean' (The Third Woman), which tells of two friends, Tríona and Máirdhia, who get lost in the midlands and ask to stay the night at an isolated farmhouse, only to realise that they have interrupted an occult ritual of some kind.

The atmosphere of the Ó Cuirrín story is enhanced by gruesome imagery – such as Tadhg's memory of a slaughtered cow's death throes on his father's farm (3–4) – and there is a humorous touch to the depiction of the senior cultists, who clearly do not believe in their own teachings: while congratulating Tadhg on being chosen by Crom for release from the 'tight prison of the body' (carcar chumang na gcinneamhan) to travel to 'the Land of the Young and the Glorious' (Tír na h-Óige is na Glóire), they are visibly relieved not to have been chosen themselves (1–3). Bairéad's piece is much more unsettling, however, for its use of unelaborated detail to build atmosphere and its lack of concern for safely restoring an agreeable status quo. When the two heroines approach the house first, they hear muttering and whispering inside, hinting at the presence of two or more people (88), but when they return half an hour later as directed, the house is empty; the woman of the house appears to be wearing a hooded robe, as only her nose and chin are visible, and the protagonists notice stacks of candles all over the house's interior – 'Were those left over from Christmastime, they wondered?' (Ar éigin annsin iad ó aimsir na Nodlag, cheapadar?) (90). Despite their misgivings, Tríona and Máirdhia take the room that is grudgingly offered to them; Máirdhia scolds Tríona for complaining about the strange smell, though the cause of the odour is soon revealed. During the night, when she hears men's voices approaching from the direction of the kitchen, Tríona uses a wardrobe in the room to barricade the door:

> She struggled so much with the wardrobe that she woke Máirdhia. Just as she had almost succeeded, the wardrobe's own door opened. What was standing inside it but the corpse of a woman, with her hands and her feet joined with nails. Tríona screamed and shut the door in the same instant.[1]

The story ends with Tríona and Máirdhia climbing out the window and running for their car (92); there is no coda to reassure the reader that the police and the parish priest were called to the scene, nor any explanation for who these people are, or what they were trying to accomplish – we are not even told if Tríona and Máirdhia managed to escape. Other notable tales of the occult include Micheál Mac Liammóir's 'Aonghus Ó Cruadhlaoich' (1923), in which a young man's mystical experiments invite demonic possession – 'Ó Cruadhlaoich', the Irish form of 'Crowley', is an obvious nod to the infamous English occultist of the same name – and Gearóid Ó Nualláin's 'An Sprid' (The Spirit) (1923), which name-checks Helena Blavatsky in depicting an academic's search for mystical enlightenment.

Translation was a charged issue in the early years of the Free State. The pro-translation camp, according to Philip O'Leary, were of the opinion that translating classic works from English to Irish would expand the perceived intellectual capacities of the language and inspire the creation of innovative original work (*Gaelic Prose* 376–79); those who thought this approach misguided believed that it was pointless to produce Irish versions of 'trivial' texts that were already widely available in English (ibid. 387) and that too much translation would have the opposite effect to what was intended, stifling originality rather than inspiring it by implying that native literature was not worth reading (ibid. 384). Whatever the merits of either side of the argument, the state-owned publishing company An Gúm, founded in 1925 under the auspices of the Department of Education, expended great effort to ensure a massive supply of Irish reading material. Among the translations produced during this time were a fair number of Gothic texts: *An Dr. Jekyll agus Mr. Hyde* appeared in 1929, translated by Frederick William O'Connell, who also wrote a number of macabre stories in English under the penname Conall Cearnach; *Wuthering Heights* was translated as *Árda Wuthering* by Seán Ó Ciosáin in 1933 and the aforementioned Seán Ó Cuirrín translated *Dracula* in the same year, taking liberties with the original to produce a 'localised' version that, in Sorcha de Brún's words, replaces intertextuality with 'a masterly display of prose techniques, drawing ... on amplification, alliteration, simile, proverb and metaphor' (80); Ó Cuirrín's translations of 'Rip Van Winkle' by Washington Irving, 'The Long Exile' by Leo Tolstoy, and 'The Indian's Hand' by Lorimer Stoddard were also included in the collection *Beirt Dhéiseach* eleven years earlier.

Harking back to Pearse's implied opposition between a Gaelic Revival and a Gothic Revival, however, we can infer that the dismissal of genre texts as 'trivial,' and therefore unworthy of translation, was at least partially motivated by moral judgements concerning the appropriateness of the material. Clair Wills argues that the main problem with imported cultural forms in 1930s Ireland (jazz being the pre-eminent example) was that their appearance coincided with a perceived decline in Irish traditional culture, as signalled by the establishment of the Irish Folklore Commission 'to try to preserve the music and oral tradition associated with the Gaelic way of life' (30). One notable expression of this fear, building upon the paranoia of the texts outlined above, is Seosamh Ó Torna's 'Duinneall' [from *duine*, 'person,' and *inneall*, 'engine'], published in 1938, in which the possibly insane narrator tries to warn the reader of the transformation of everyday Irish citizens into ruthless, machine-like drones bent on the destruction of traditional life:

They are trying to bring about Maximum Efficiency. To that end, it is necessary to increase the Big and exterminate the Small. To destroy the small merchant and the individual craftsman, and to establish monopolies and mass-production in their place. To devastate the small towns and to widen the great city ... To force a mechanical arrangement on people that will make every mother's son of them into a cog in a massive engine. (74)[2]

During World War II, known in Ireland by the infamous official epithet 'The Emergency', efforts to maintain an appearance of neutrality meant that the press, radio broadcasting and cinema were heavily censored (Wills 163). Radio production was limited to sports coverage, traditional music, religious topics and educational programmes, while the few radio dramas produced suffered from a lack of development and funding (188–90). Local film production was largely limited to documentaries, thanks to official determinations that realist film was 'in the national and cultural interests of the people' (300–301). Despite these efforts to avoid cultural production that overtly signalled support for either side, some works did appear in which Gothic and horrific imagery was deployed to illustrate the evils of fascism, such as Mairéad Ní Ghráda's *Manannán* (1940), an otherwise standard boys' adventure story involving a summer-holiday mission to the titular planet (named after the pre-Christian god of the sea) which includes an eerie description of a gas attack that leaves its victims' bodies standing, 'like statues without soul or breath' (stalcaí gan anam gan anáil) (170–71). From 1943 to the early 1980s, author Cathal Ó Sándair would similarly pepper his chapbooks for younger readers with haunted ruins, secret societies and sinister mystics in hooded robes, particularly in his series featuring the detective Réics Carló. Other non-supernatural Gothic material from the same time included 'Agus Bás ar Leabaidh!' (And Death in Bed!) by 'Micil' (1944), in which an elderly woman is buried alive by accident and falls into 'a wild madness without a glimmer of thought' (geilt bán gan léas meabhrach) as she desperately tries to escape her grave (5).

Through the late 1940s and 1950s, an increasing number of Irish-language stories appeared in which the supernatural elements were taken seriously. The stories published during and after this point rely less on storytellers as narrators and instead position the narrators as eyewitnesses. Piaras Béaslaí's 1938 short story 'Deimhniú an Sgéil' (Verifying the Story) concerns a former IRA commander turned successful businessman who is asked to vouch for another man's volunteer status during the War of Independence, to allow him to claim a military pension from the Free State. However, the former commander never saw combat outside of Dublin, and no evidence or eyewitness testimony exists to confirm the alleged volunteer's account of a pitched battle against the Black and

Tans – until none other than the ghost of that unit's commanding officer shows up to validate it. Muiris Ó Súilleabháin's 'An Sean-Mairnealach agus an Taidhbhse a Chonnaic Sé'(The Old Sailor and the Ghost That He Saw), published in the *Irish Press* in March 1947, concerns a treacherous sea captain who is haunted at close proximity by the ghost of the mariner whom he murdered, until he eventually goes mad from lack of sleep and drowns himself. Risteard Ó Donnabháin's 'An Scréach!' (The Scream!), published in 1950, starts off like an older tale of a *seanchaí* and a prankster taking revenge on a sceptical loudmouth, with the narrator lying in wait in a graveyard, dressed as a ghost, in order to give said loudmouth a scare on his way home; when the moment arrives, however, a scream erupts from the prankster's own mouth and he blacks out, remembering nothing of how he got home – the implication being that he was momentarily possessed by a very real spirit. In 'Scéal Mná' (A Woman's Story) (1950) by P. Mac Coiligh, meanwhile, the narrator suspects that her husband is having an affair, but is not prepared for the revelation that the other woman is a ghost.

As well as print, a number of eerie tales were written in Irish for radio, either as scripted dramas or as narrated short stories, and popular pieces were often re-broadcast multiple times in the same year. Liam Mag Reachtain specialised in the latter and alternated back and forth between comedy and 'thrillers', which were normally around fifteen minutes long, with titles such as 'An Lóchrann' (The Lantern), 'Báthadh' (Drowning), 'Eagla' (Fear) and 'Dolacha' (Snares). One notable example of a scripted drama from the same time is Eamonn Ó Faoláin's *Uafás Ó'n Alltar* (Horror from the Far Country), based (like Maturin's *Melmoth the Wanderer* [1820]) on the myth of the Wandering Jew, which won the Radio Éireann Irish drama competition in 1951. The popularity and recognition of works such as these indicates that there was an appreciative audience for them. Despite this encouraging state of affairs, however, Irish-language literature continued to be perceived as dour, quotidian and resistant to experimentation.

Remixes and Resurrections

The perception of Irish as an anachronistic or dead language continued to bedevil it through the later twentieth century, as reflected in widespread attitudes to modern Irish-language literature. In 1981, Alan Titley complained of the lack of critical attention given to Irish-language works outside of a very narrow band of 'blasketite books' and similar texts, whose worth was judged according to their vocabular and philological qualities rather than their literary merit, blaming 'grammarians, linguists and dialectologists' for the belief 'that modern literature [in Irish] has to be based on the themes and signia of other centuries, or that the writer must acquaint himself with early Irish literature, or base his work upon folk forms and pieties, or stick to social realism and the delineation of the ordinarily dull' (59). Titley's own second novel, *Stiall Fhial Feola* (A Generous Cut of Meat) (1980), seems like a statement of intent in this context, delving into the abnormal psyches of several average-seeming characters whose lives are impacted by the actions of a cannibalistic serial killer. Cannibalism also features in Mícheál Ó Brolacháin's grim dystopian novella *Pax Dei* (1985), in which the majority of Earth's population live in crumbling tower-blocks, lorded over by gangsters and terrorised by ravenous rats, while distant mega-corporations decide all their fates: a ghoulish, satirical reimagining of 1980s Dublin, and the socially disadvantaged Ballymun Flats in particular. An increasing number of macabre genre works in Irish emerged over the following decades, seemingly in answer to Titley's rallying cry.

Mícheál Ó Ruairc's short story 'Séadna' (1994) obviously invokes Ua Laoghaire's novel, in a story about an employee of an international corporation who is offered a promotion with eye-opening perks if he identifies four under-performing employees in his section. This Séadna names three people that he does not particularly care about, and then learns that the fourth is a good friend of his. To claim the promotion and all its attendant rewards, he has to get rid of these people himself (67). Séadna accepts the offer and does not seem bothered by his conscience afterwards. Séadna's boss is not as flamboyant as the antagonist of the 1898/1904 novel, except for the name 'Feardorcha Ó Laoghaire' (from *fear dorcha*, sometimes used as a translation of 'Frederick' but literally meaning 'dark man') and 'the greed and the naked evil' ('an tsaint agus an olc nochtaithe') in his eyes (66). Ó Ruairc's collection *Daoine a Itheann Daoine* (People Who Eat People), including the titular cannibalistic satire, would later win the 2009 Oireachtas na Gaeilge award for original short story collections.

Experimentation with genre and subject matter would only become more pronounced. Robert Welch's *Tearmann* (1997) follows two investigators from the Department of Art and Culture as they are sent to the city of Tearmann (Sanctuary) to investigate the disappearance of a local Department inspector. Beginning as a vaguely futuristic noir thriller, the story changes tone with the revelation that the antagonists are a cult known as 'The Five', who can control the weather and vanish from sight at will (68–70), thanks to their allegiance to Satan; these villains later torture one of the investigators to death in an S&M dungeon (98–103). Along the way, an angel reveals to the main protagonist that Tearmann is the site of a struggle between the forces of good and evil (75–83), but this is thrown into doubt by the revelation that everything he has experienced is an illusion made possible by advanced technology (109). Unreliable narration and insanity are also central to Tomás Mac Síomóin's 2003 novel *Ag Altóir an Diabhail* (At the Altar of the Devil), in which the narrator's apparent confession to a terrorist attack, dictated from his cell in an institute for the criminally insane, is nested within a larger frame in which the entire narrative has been assembled from scraps of paper discovered at the base of a cliff known for suicides; we are told that the Garda Síochána are attempting to identify the still-missing author.

While English-language texts continue to dominate the print media, film has proved to be another fruitful avenue for Irish-language Gothic storytelling. The atmospheric animated short *An Fiach Dubh* (The Raven) by Declan de Barra (2003) follows the inner monologue of a deceased man who has returned from the dead as a raven, in an attempt to give his bereaved wife some closure before fully passing on. The visual design of the piece is unmistakably Gothic in an aesthetic sense: everything is in stark, high-contrast black and white, which renders the rotoscoped actors' faces in a 'goth' style, with black eyes and lips; the rotoscoped performers are juxtaposed with fully-animated figures, such as the titular raven and the skeletal spectre of Death himself, and the score is made up of overlapping droned notes, at once threatening and melancholy. Tom Cosgrove's 2005 short *Rógairí* (literally 'Rogues,' but historically applied to libertine aristocrats) is set in 1763 and tells the story of a callous landlord who commits murder to ensure his inheritance, only for a witch to transform him into a pig-headed creature as punishment for his crimes; in a gruesome touch, the local peasantry prepare to eat him at the end, apparently not at all put out by the fact that he still has the body and clothing of a fancy gentleman. The 2010 TV series *Na Cloigne* (The Heads) is a serial killer story inflected with the supernatural, incorporating spirits, clairvoyance and small-town conspiracy into the hunt for a murderer who decapitates his victims, while the 2014 short film *Dorchadas* (Darkness) is a serial killer's monologue, delivered to his latest victim after she has turned the tables on him and restrained him with his own chains. *An Gadhar Dubh* (The Black Dog), meanwhile, is a stop-motion animated tale set in rural Connemara in 1910, in which a man and his senile father are tormented by a monstrous black dog and other horrifying creatures (2021).

Conclusion

In the first half of the twentieth century, Gothic storytelling occurred in the specific contexts of language revival and nation-building – contexts which infuse the material with political significance. Translation and adaptation were charged issues and the translation of works such as *Dracula* or *Strange Case of Dr. Jekyll and Mr. Hyde* (translated into Irish by An Gúm), were liable to provoke angry responses from purist cultural nationalists. Original Irish-language Gothic material largely reflected the political tenor of the time in which it was written: we can see, for example, a dominant trend of the 'explained supernatural' during the 1930s and 1940s, in which ghostly tropes were rationalised or ridiculed, while depictions of nefarious cults and secret societies proliferated – reflecting the country's self-conscious attempts to straddle the division between tradition and modernity, while dealing with anxieties of infiltration and re-conquest. From the 1950s onwards, however, Irish-language Gothic stories proliferated in newspapers, chapbooks and short story collections, gradually outgrowing political orthodoxy, and it appears that the number of Irish-language genre texts is increasing steadily at the present moment.

With any analysis or overview of Irish-language texts in genres with transnational appeal, it is important to remember that there is no such thing as a monolingual *Gaeilgeoir*: be they a native speaker or one who acquired it as a second language, every Irish-speaker is also fluent in (at least) English. Thus, original works in Irish are open to the influence of genre trends from wider Western popular culture, but the reverse is not true. Another important consideration is that the Irish-language publishing sector is a fraction of the size of its English-language counterpart in Ireland, receiving far less coverage in the national press and garnering far less recognition internationally. Thus, the decision to create fiction in Irish is not an uncomplicated one: at the present moment, in choosing to write in Irish, the writer sacrifices a potentially wider audience to accomplish a specific goal, which often has to do with expanding or demonstrating the possibilities of the language overall. Thus, Irish genre fiction is very often intertextual and openly experiments with cultural references that the reader is expected to recognise. In other words, Gothic fiction *as Gaeilge* is particularly pitched at readers who are already somewhat well-versed in Anglo-American Gothic material and, perhaps to a lesser extent, at readers who are fairly familiar with prior Irish-language texts. This is an interesting reversal of the anachronism (or atavism) attributed to Irish in the nineteenth century: rather than occasionally being appropriated by the Gothic as a kind of linguistic set-dressing, it has become a language in which transnational genres are appropriated and made local.

Irish-language literature also has to contend with a legacy of official decisions that created an adversarial relationship between language learners and the language itself. Irish remains a compulsory subject in primary and secondary schools and until the 1990s it was preferentially weighted in state exams, while those who failed their Irish exams were automatically given failing grades across the board, regardless of how well they did in those other subjects. Combined with the corporal punishment that was endemic in the education system for much of the twentieth century, it was no surprise that 'Generations of children came to see it not as a gift but as a threat' (O'Leary, *Prose Literature* 265). Native speakers, meanwhile, are often marginalised within the same system on account of the differences between their own dialect and the government-approved standard form; as Tadhg Ó hIfearnáin points out, 'The decline of the dialects is not simply a coincidence, but in part a consequence of the promotion of the standard as a prestige form' (124–25). This means that genre fiction in Irish also serves a 'reparative' function, for lack of a less provocative term: as the amount and visibility of this material increases, the more obvious it becomes that the language's capabilities are not limited by the demands of the curriculum or government bureaucracy.

Litríocht Gotach may yet outgrow its overt 'sampling' phase and develop into its own variant, incorporating local and international influences into something new that fully engages with its recurring concerns (paranoia, mental illness and isolation, for example); if not, though, experimentation with international tropes and trends will still yield results that are never less than interesting.

Notes

1. Bhí an oiread sin rúpála aici leis an almóir gur dúisigh sí Máirdhia. Díreach nuair a bhí beagnach éirighthe leí d'osgail doras an almóra uaid féin. Céard bhí ina sheasamh istigh ann ach corp mná agus a cosa agus a lámha ceangailte do táirní. Chuir Tríona béic aisti féin agus dhúin an doras ar an toirt.
2. Táthar ad iarraidh Bárr na hÉifeachta a bhaint amach. Chuige sin ní fuláir Mór a mhéadughadh agus Beag a dhíotughadh. An ceannaidhe beag agus an ceárdaidhe aonair a scrios agus aoincheannaidheacht agus olldéantús a bhunughadh 'na n-ionad. Na bailte beaga a bhánughadh agus an ollchathair a leathnughadh … Eagar meicneach a chur ar dhaoinibh a dhéanfaidh máinle mór-inill de gach mac máthar aca.

Works Cited

Bairéad, Tomás. 'An Tríomhadh Bean.' 1930. *Cruithneacht agus Ceannabháin*. Comhlucht Oideachas na hÉireann, undated edition, pp. 83–92.

Béaslaí, Piaras. 'Deimhniú an Sgéil.' In Various Authors ('Iol-Ughdair'), *As na Ceithre hÁirdibh*. Oifig an tSoláthair, 1938, pp. 7–17.

Brown, Terence. *Ireland: A Social and Cultural History 1922–1985*. 1981. Fontana Press, 1990.

Cosgrove, Tom, director. *Rógairí*. TG4 and Igloo Films, 2005.

de Barra, Declan, director. *An Fiach Dubh*. TG4 and Lasair, 2003.

de Brún, Sorcha. '"In a Sea of Wonders": Eastern Europe and Transylvania in the Irish-Language Translation of *Dracula*.' *Acta Universitatis Sapientiae, Philologica*, vol. 21, no.1, 2020), pp. 70–83.

Doyle, Aidan. *A History of the Irish Language: From the Norman Invasion to Independence*. Oxford University Press, 2015.

Edgeworth, Maria, *Castle Rackrent*, edited by George Watson, 'Introduction' by Kathryn J. Kirkpatrick. 1800. Oxford University Press, 1995.

Fagan, Pádraig, director. *An Gadhar Dubh*. Matchbox Mountain Productions, 2021.

Fennell, Jack. *Irish Science Fiction*. Liverpool University Press, 2014.

———. *Rough Beasts: The Monstrous in Irish Fiction, 1800–2000*. Liverpool University Press, 2019.

Gibbons, Luke. *Gaelic Gothic: Race, Colonization and Irish Culture*. Arlen House, 2004.

Höglund, Panu Petteri. *An Leabhar Nimhe: scéalta agus aistriúchán*. Evertype, 2012.

Kiberd, Declan. *Inventing Ireland: The Literature of a Modern Nation*. Vintage, 1996.

———. *Irish Classics*. 2000. Granta Books, 2001.

Kilfeather, Siobhán Marie. 'Terrific Register: The Gothicization of Atrocity in Irish Romanticism.' *boundary 2*, vol. 31, no.1, Spring 2004, pp. 49–71.

Killeen, Jarlath. *The Emergence of Irish Gothic Fiction: History, Origins, Theories*. Edinburgh University Press, 2013.

Kirkpatrick, Kathryn J. 'Introduction.' In Maria Edgeworth (1800), *Castle Rackrent*. Oxford University Press, 1995. vii–xxxvi.

Mac Coiligh, P. 'Scéal Mná.' *Comhar*, June 1950.

Mac Liammóir, Mícheál. 'Aonghus Ó Cruadhlaoich.' *Fáinne an Lae* December (Nodlag) 15, 1923, pp. 8–10.

Mac Síomóin, Tomás, *Ag Altóir an Diabhail*. Dublin, Coiscéim, 2003.

Malone, Noel Anthony. *Dorchadas*. Alonze Productions, 2014.

Markey, Anne. 'The Gothicization of Irish Folklore.' *Irish Gothics: Genres, Forms, Modes and Traditions, 1760–1890*, edited by Christina Morin and Niall Gillespie. Palgrave Macmillan, 2014, pp. 94–112.

'Micil' [pseud.]. 'Agus Bás ar Leabaidh!' *Comhar*, October 1944.

Morin, Christina. *The Gothic Novel in Ireland, c.1760–1829*. Manchester University Press, 2018.

Ní Fhlannagáin, M. I. 'Taidhbhse Dhún Aonghusa.' *Irish Press*, 15 July 1946, p. 2.

Ní Ghráda, Máiréad. *Manannán*. Dublin: Oifig an tSoláthair, 1940.
Ní Mhunghaile, Lesa. 'Gaelic Literature in Transition, 1780–1830.' *Irish Literature in Transition, 1780–1830*, edited by Claire Connolly. Cambridge University Press, 2020, pp. 37–51.
Ó Bríain, P. 'Taibhse sa Comhrann.' *Irish Press*, 10 January 1947, p. 2.
Ó Brolachain, Mícheál. *Pax Dei*. Taibhse, 1985.
Ó Cadhain, Máirtín. *Cré na Cille*. Sáirséal agus Dill, 1945.
Ó Cuirrín, Seán. 'Beirt Dheiseach', in Ó Cuirrín, *Beirt Dheiseach*. Cuallacht Oideachas na hÉireann, 1922, pp. 1–33.
Ó Donnabháin, Risteárd. 'An Scréach!' *Feasta* June 1950.
Ó Guilín, Peadar. *The Call*. David Fickling Books/Scholastic Inc., 2016.
Ó hUallacháin, Colmán. *The Irish and Irish: A Sociolinguistic Analysis of the Relationship between a People and Their Language*. Irish Franciscan Provincial Office, 1994.
Ó hIfearnáin, Tadhg. 'Endangering Language Vitality through Institutional Development: Ideology, Authority, and Official Standard Irish in the Gaeltacht.' *Sustaining Liguistic Diversity: Endangered and Minority Languages and Language Varieties*, edited by Natalie Schilling-Estes, et al. Georgetown University Press, 2008, pp. 113–28.
Ó Laoghaire, Peadar. *Séadna*. 1898; 1904. 2 vols (continuous pagination). Brún agus Ó Nualláin, Teóranta, undated.
O'Leary, Philip. *The Prose Literature of the Gaelic Revival, 1881–1921: Ideology and Innovation*. Pennsylvania State University Press, 1994.
———. *Gaelic Prose in the Irish Free State, 1922–1939*. Pennsylvania State University Press, 2004.
Ó Nualláin, Gearóid. 'An Sprid.' *Sean agus Nua*. Brún agus Ó Nualláin, 1923.
Ó Ruairc, Mícheál. 'Séadna.' *Comhar*, vol. 53, no. 4, '30 Gearrscéal', April 1994, pp. 65–7.
Ó Súilleabháin, Muiris. 'An Sean-Mairneálach agus an Taidhbhse a Chonaic Sé.' *Irish Press*, 3 March, 1947, p. 2.
Ó Torna, Seosamh. 'Duinneall.' *Bonaventura*, Spring 1938, pp. 70–75.
Quinn, Robert, director. *Na Cloigne*. 3 episodes. TG4 and ROSG, 2010.
'Tadhg Tostach' [pseud.]. 'Taibhse an Caisleán.' *Irish Press*, 15 September 1950 and 16 September, 1950, pp. 2, 2.
Titley, Alan. *Stiall Fhial Feola*. Cló Iar-Chonnachta, 1980.
———. 'Contemporary Irish Literature.' *The Crane Bag*, vol. 5. No. 2, 1981, pp. 59–65.
Ua Laoghaire, Peadar. *Séadna*, edited by Liam Mac Mathúna, Carbad, 1995.
Welch, Robert. *Tearmann*. Coiscéim, 1997.
Wills, Clair. *That Neutral Island: A Cultural History of Ireland During the Second World War*. Faber and Faber, 2007.

Part III

Irish Gothic, Theology, and Confessional Identities

Chapter 8

Protestant Gothic
Alison Milbank

Chris Baldick was one of the first critics in the revival of Gothic criticism to attempt some definition of the genre and quickly noted its religious allegiances: 'it is no accident at all that Gothic fiction first emerged and established itself within the British and Anglo-Irish middle class, in a society which had through generations of warfare, political scares and popular martyrology persuaded itself that its hard-won liberties could at any moment be snatched from it by papal tyranny and the ruthless wiles of the Spanish Inquisition' (xiv). In this scenario, Gothic fiction is viewed as the product of a specifically Protestant culture. This is a persuasive argument, given that the classic eighteenth-century Gothic novel was a genre specific to the British Isles, with no exact equivalent in continental fantastic fiction, even though it was so influential in Europe. This evaluation chimes with the historian Linda Colley's emphasis on the importance of Protestantism in the construction and maintenance of British identity in the eighteenth century and beyond (19–54). An even earlier study than Baldick's, Victor Sage's *Horror Fiction in the Protestant Tradition*, situated Gothic horror historically in relation to the post 1688 Williamite settlement and culturally in tropes of Protestant self-examination and the mortuary tradition. Sage extended his analysis to Ireland, especially in the writing of Sheridan Le Fanu, but naturally emphasised, like Colley, the anti-Catholicism inherent in the identity of the Protestant Anglo-Irish. In a survey of writers broadly in this tradition, the following chapter while not denying this suspicion and the Gothicising of Catholicism, will discern in authors from Charles Maturin to Elizabeth Bowen a converse proto-ecumenism, which can make a space for their own faith within a broader Irish culture in a manner not unlike the Irish national romances of Maria Edgeworth and Lady Morgan.

Gothicising the Reformation

From its inception, the Gothic novel made overt reference to the Protestant Reformation, with Horace Walpole parodying Henry VIII's divorce attempts in his protagonist's desire to put away his wife and inventing the device of a lost manuscript in a recusant family archive, while the narrative structure of Ann Radcliffe's 'female' Gothic replays the Protestant Reformation with plots of escape from an often-Catholic corrupt institution. Such Gothicising historiography goes back to reformer, John Wycliffe, who preached the need for religious liberation from the oppression of the 'great cloisters of Caym's Castles', by which he meant the monastic system, with four major orders united in the acronym (the Carmelites, the Augustinians, the Jacobites or Dominicans and the Minorites or Franciscans), 'Caym', standing for Cain, the biblical fratricide and traditional father of monsters, as in *Beowulf* (Mellinkoff 143). Naming monasteries 'castles' stressed their usurpation of political power (221). Henry VIII's Dissolution programme left 'Caym's Castles' as heaps of ruins as visible witnesses to the overturning of papal authority over his realms. In a similar way, the heroine in a Gothic novel of the Romantic period seeks emancipation both from incarceration in a physical structure and from long-established tyrannical authority, with the Catholic convent or abbey uniting these temporal and spatial dimensions of power.

Whereas the Reformation eventually succeeded in England, the Irish situation was more complex, since most of the inhabitants of that island resisted and did not abandon Catholicism. Brendan Bradshaw reports that more monastic houses were destroyed in England between 1535 and 1542 than in Ireland in the seventy years between 1536 and 1606 (5–6). The Act of Supremacy transferring ecclesiastical power from the Pope to Henry VIII was duly passed by the Irish Parliament and took force in 1537 but there was no urban elite clamouring for reform, no printing press to disseminate Bibles, and no university to foster dissent until the foundation of Trinity College Dublin in 1592 as a bulwark of reform. Henry Jeffries has argued that the cause of the failure of the Reformation in Ireland was that there was an absence of indigenous support, active Catholic resistance and a renewed identity post the Council of Trent for Catholicism as a 'people's church'.

Scottish Presbyterianism was more successful in Ulster, but the reformed Church of Ireland only ever covered a minority of the population, numbering by 1871 only 667,900 out of a population of 5,412,000, and their adherents tended to be the Anglo-Irish settlers, either from the

Norman or Cromwellian plantations (McDowell 6). Thus, a situation grew up in which those who in economic terms dominated land ownership and the professions saw themselves as a beleaguered minority in religious terms, in a land in which the Reformation was still *reformanda*, in the process of reforming, not fully escaping from Catholic 'superstition'. Indeed, the fact of the need for further reform proved, all the more, the legitimacy of Protestant faith and conversion.

As the example from Wycliffe demonstrates, tropes of monstrosity are very much part of Protestant rhetoric. Sixteenth-century historiographers such as John Foxe drew deeply on the colourful imagery of Revelation, its many-headed beasts, and blood-drinking whore of Babylon to describe the Catholic authorities (Milbank 23–24). Jarlath Killeen has noted the same tendency in Sir John Temple's response to the conflicts of 1641 in Ireland, in which the Irish rebels are portrayed as perverted monsters in this apocalyptic idiom (*Gothic Ireland* 147), and Alan Ford has described the importance of Anti-Christ language employed by the British side ('Apocalyptic Ireland' 146–48). Such discourse is at the heart of Maturin's hectic portrayal of the Spanish Inquisition and Catholic monastic system in *Melmoth the Wanderer* (1820) as well as of the ambiguous figure of John Melmoth, who bears some resemblance to the Anti-Christ in his attempt to lead Immalee from Christianity, as well as in his inversion of Christ's redemptive taking on of the sins of others, which becomes an attempt to make his victims exchange places and assume his damned but immortal state. In Spain he is even accused of inverting the transubstantiation of the host (*Melmoth* 35). There are traces of this same apocalypticism in Bram Stoker's *Dracula* (1897), with the Count as the Anti-Christ, while Mina Harker's scorched forehead caused by the eucharistic host evokes the 'mark of the beast' from Revelation 13: 16–18. While in much English Gothic writing such lurid anti-Catholic language is transferred to foreign settings and continental monastic tyrants, and apocalyptic drops largely from English theological writing in the eighteenth century, in Ireland it remains a live Protestant discourse, employed as late as the Troubles of the 1970s by Ian Paisley, a free church minister and politician.

The Church of Ireland not only accepted the Thirty-Nine Articles of the Anglican settlement but added its own set at a convocation under Archbishop James Ussher in 1615, which included the explicit naming of the pope as Anti-Christ and the Calvinist doctrine of double predestination. This made the Irish Church much more overtly anti-Catholic and reformed than the Church of England, a pattern repeated in nineteenth-century legislation, which outlawed ritual and ceremonial practices already commonplace in the English Church.

Archbishop Ussher also wrote an important study of Irish ecclesiastical history, *A Discourse of the Religion Anciently Professed by the Irish and British* (1623/31). There he sought to argue for the original proto-Protestant character of the Irish Church as founded by St Patrick, claiming it enjoyed an independence only challenged as late as 1152 at the Council of Cashel, where the pope wrested control over the liturgy and appointment of bishops (117–18). For Ussher the Celtic Church was highly biblical, suspicious of images and more democratic. The reformed church was, therefore, no new religion but a return to the true faith of the early Christian centuries. It was Catholicism which played the role of colonial interloper.

Thomas Leland's *Longsword* and the Double Gesture

Understood in terms of the Protestant narratology of the Gothic novel, these patterns of liberation and recovery become manifest in the tropes by which the heroine escapes from tyrannical or Catholic imprisonment and is subsequently revealed as the true heir of the domains of her clerical or aristocratic usurper. This double gesture can be seen at work in Anglican Ann Radcliffe's *Romance of the Forest* (1792) but occurs earlier in the Church of Ireland cleric, Thomas Leland's *Longsword Earl of Salisbury: An Historical Romance* (1762), often considered the earliest Gothic novel. The tropes of incarcerated victim and true heir are split between wife and husband so that Ela is held at the mercy of the lecherous Raymond, who seeks control of Salisbury's castle and lands, while Salisbury returns incognito from pilgrimage and the wars, to find his very name usurped as well as his patrimony and wife. One specifically Gothic feature of this novel is the role of the monk Reginhald, who has used his habit to conceal his crimes and ambition, and who aids his brother in seeking to destroy Salisbury and prevent his claim. Salisbury is eventually acknowledged as the true Earl and his rights are restored, while his wife is liberated from Raymond's power. In that sense the Reformation narrative is replayed, with the monk's attempts to assist his brother in denying Salisbury his entitlements paralleling the papal incursion on royal power in Ussher's account of medieval history. It is noteworthy here that Salisbury is of royal blood: being the natural son of Henry II.

Jarlath Killeen has, however, persuasively argued that the anti-Catholicism in *Longsword* is muted and the murderous Reginhald an outlier, who is handed over to justice by his own monastic community. He also notes the eirenic role of a Cistercian abbot in the French scenes of the novel and attributes this positive portrayal to Leland's friendship with Catholics such as fellow historian Charles O'Conor and Leland's proven religious even-handedness. His historical fairmindedness was exhibited in a 1771 sermon about the errors of attributing blame for the 1641 rebellion exclusively to Catholics, an event which was still marked in the Church of Ireland calendar with annual prayers and sermon. Killeen describes Leland's criticism of the oppression of Catholics under the penal laws as 'political ecumenism' (*Gothic Ireland* 170).

Ecumenical Gestures

Several of the major contributors to what might be called Protestant Gothic in Ireland share Leland's ecumenical impulse, although I would agree with Killeen that 'the Irish Gothic tradition constantly tied itself into narrative knots trying to reconcile anti-Catholic prejudice and tolerant inclusivity' (*Emergence* 200). While later authors are not necessarily soaked in apocalyptic anti-Catholicism, their Protestantism is truly Gothic in embodying the double gesture of repudiation and the parallel desire to recover a true link to the religious past.

It would be a mistake to view this strain of Gothic writing as merely reactive to the political and ecclesiastical situation of its day, though it is necessarily shaped by contemporary concerns. Rather, for the often deeply religious writers of Protestant Gothic, the employment of tropes of terror can be a way of doing creative theological work. Gothic in their hands becomes a heuristic tool by which to imagine beyond the aporias of their social situation, and it can become a religious hermeneutic. The ecumenism, as with Leland, is often bound up with the island of Ireland, its representation and development, as in the national tales of Maria Edgeworth and Sydney Owenson, but in contrast to these and the Scottish nation-building novels (with the exception of Walter Scott's *The Monastery* [1820]), the Irish Protestant Gothic versions are porous to the mysterious and the supernatural.

Perhaps the most unlikely ecumenist among Irish Protestant Gothicists is Charles Maturin, descendent of a persecuted Huguenot minister and curate of St Peter's Church on Aungier Street in Dublin, where he preached a series of violently anti-Catholic sermons in 1824. He gave these fiery addresses during the period of Archbishop Magee's Second Reformation, when a campaign of evangelism to the Catholic population was inaugurated through Bible distribution and educational outreach, provoking strong Catholic reaction and, indeed, renewal (Bowen 88–95). Maturin's early fiction is inclusive, in the tradition of the national tale, with sympathetic portrayals of Catholic characters, such as Connal, representative of the displaced Catholic aristocracy in *The Milesian Chief* (1812), although as in Sir Walter Scott's Jacobite fiction, such a figure belongs to an irrecoverable past. Anglican clerics, by contrast, are the mediators and enablers in these novels, sympathetic to the doomed Catholic protagonists, but unable to save them, like St Austin in his faithful care of Connal, in *The Milesian Chief*. Even at the period of the anti-Catholic sermons, Maturin's last fiction, *The Albigenses* (1824), still preserves a strong ecumenical impetus, with a friendship between a proto-Calvinist minister and a Catholic priest central to the narrative. There is even some evidence of sympathy for Catholics in the *Five Sermons*, especially the 'amiable and excellent' Catholic laymen of Maturin's acquaintance, who, he claims, often reject the more authoritarian teachings of their own Church (*Sermons* 28–29). For Maturin there is, indeed, no 'true church' institutionally, but only the body of Christians of all faiths (*Sermons* 31).

In Maturin's most torrid Gothic novel, *Melmoth the Wanderer*, however, the Spanish Inquisition is presented as the most powerful emblem of religious cruelty and oppression in traditional Protestant style, but Maturin has a particular critique to make, which is that it encourages the splitting of natural ties and the betrayal of one's family, neighbours and fellow citizens. It is in this aspect that it mirrors the Irish situation, addressing the 1798 uprising and Emmett's rebellion of 1803, which Maturin's narrator references when a mob tears apart an executive of the inquisition. His death is compared to that of Lord Kilwarden, whose body was nailed to a door and to Dr Hamilton, who was reduced to a heap of mud during these revolts (*Melmoth* 256–7). Paradoxically, the reason for the mob's rage here is the fact that the Spaniard committed parricide: he broke the most holy of bonds and the appalling violence to his bodily integrity has a Dantesque poetic justice. In the same way in Monçada's story, the focus is on the way the Catholic system denies the holiness of familial bonds. Clerics demand his separation from his parents and brother through being conveyed against his will into a monastery to act as scapegoat for his parents' fornication. Catholicism is but the most prominent of a series of labyrinthine narrative threads, which reveal the monstrosity of situations that place mothers against daughters, turn brothers into Cains and lovers into cannibals.

The Protestant plot motif of escape from Catholic enclosure is foregrounded, and dealt with at greatest length, but it is not so much Catholic belief and practices that are critiqued as the power relations within the monastery and the religious authoritarianism that characterises much of monastic life. To the contrary, Monçada takes refuge from his oppressors in devotion to his crucifix, an object prohibited explicitly in nineteenth-century Church of Ireland legislation, and not permitted on the altar in church until 1964 (Gray-Stack).

> It was like a talisman to touch the crucifix, and I said as I felt for it, "My God is with me in the darkness of my dungeon; he is a God who has suffered, and can pity me. My extremest point of wretchedness can be nothing to what this symbol of divine humiliation for the sins of man, has undergone for mine!" and I kissed the sacred image. (*Melmoth* 146)

Monçada's veneration of a holy image is specifically Catholic, while the reference to Christ's suffering 'for the sins of man' has an evangelical emphasis. Maturin thus unites Catholic religious practice with Protestant theology of the atonement. Jonathan Harker in *Dracula* will similarly find comfort and protection in the crucifix he at first rejects as an object of Catholic superstition.

Another aspect of the anti-Catholicism of Maturin's novel lies in its critique of sacrificial language applied to Christians rather than Christ himself, denying the finality of Christ's atonement. Behind this lies an attempt to deconstruct Catholic prayers to the saints and for the departed as an attempt to avoid personal responsibility before God (*Sermons* 99). Characters in *Melmoth* frequently sacrifice others for their own spiritual benefit, in contrast to the offering of one's own heart. Catholics, for their part, would consider such prayer as an expression of the mutual communion of the body of Christ. And Maturin, too, so orchestrates the effect of Melmoth's offer of sacrificial substitution, as to reconstruct ecumenical communion among those who have resisted this temptation and kept faith with personal responsibility. This little 'church' allows Catholic style solidarity and reciprocity, represented by the Protestant John Melmoth the younger, who rescues the Spanish Catholic, Monçada, from shipwreck and by Monçada himself, who acts with equal courage in diving in to save John Melmoth. The two men are united across the denominational divide by this mutual self-giving. The novel concludes with their exchange of 'looks of silent and unutterable horror' after which they return slowly 'home' (*Melmoth* 542), united by their terrible understanding of Melmoth's end and finding a common home together.

This positive recuperation of friendship across the religious divide has parallels in Maturin's other fiction, but can also be detected in other Gothic novels, such as Regina Maria Roche's, *The Children of the Abbey* (1796), which includes several scenes among a community of Irish nuns, who have built a new convent amid the ruins of a pre-Reformation monastic structure. Several sisters are portrayed sympathetically, not only in their exercise of practical charity and handiwork but also in their worship, which raises the thoughts of the Protestant visitor, Amanda Fitzalan, heavenwards (Roche 129). St Catherine's Convent functions as a place of female succour for the Anglican heroine, as occasionally in Ann Radcliffe (and again, later for Jonathan Harker, after his escape from Dracula's castle) but here convent life is treated more realistically, and comically, as if from Roche's own observation from her childhood in Waterford. Amanda is also found praying to her dead father and mother in a manner more often associated with Catholic piety (Roche 172). Roche unites this cross-denominational practice with Killeen's 'political ecumenism' by making her protagonists the inheritors of Welsh and Scottish blood, while much of the novel takes place in Ireland. The radicalism of her attitude contrasts strongly with an earlier Gothic novel by an Anglo-Irish Protestant, Anne Fuller's *The Convent* (1786), where the heroine is incarcerated in a French convent with all the persecutions and sadism of Diderot and Maturin, and where even the sympathetic Sister Agatha is out to convert her.

A later Gothic writer sympathetic to Catholic piety is Charlotte Riddell, née Cowan, who was the author of several novels featuring the supernatural and a number of ghost stories, such as the collection, *Weird Stories* of 1882. Born in Carrickfergus in 1832, the daughter of the High Sheriff of County Antrim, she wrote consciously as an Irish Protestant but as one alert to the complexities of that religious position. This is particularly clear in *The Nun's Curse* (1888), which derives a curse on the Anglo-Irish Conway family from an incident in the Reformation when a Donegal community of nuns were 'smoked out like bees' from their convent by the Protestant authorities and were forced to jump into the sea to avoid the pikes urging them forward (Riddell 47). Ecumenical charity enters first through the hospitality of a Conway lady who succours a fleeing nun, only for her husband to discover the fugitive and expel her. As she goes to her death, the nun curses every future owner of Calgarry.

The story is mainly set in the Victorian present and is evidently indebted to study of James Tuke's *Irish Distress and its Remedies: The Land Question* (1880), which discusses Donegal, where the story is set, Riddell having a close interest in economic questions. Detailed discussions of farming practices are interwoven with a Gothic plot of usurpation, seduction and murder, and the main viewpoints are carried by representatives of different faith traditions, with a strong intervention for justice from the fiery Presbyterian minister and more moderately by the Anglican priest. The inheritor of the entail has a strong sense of Calvinist predestination, only exacerbated by the sense of the 'nun's mark' upon him and this, allied to his own weakness, leads to him squandering money and failing to act up to his responsibilities to his tenants. As a result of seduction and forced marriage he produces an heir whose peasant grandfather removes him abroad. The novel ends with the heir's return in the form of a Catholic priest in Calgarry parish but one who brings 'no gospel of peace, but one of vengeance, bitterness and all uncharitableness ... faint mutterings of a storm which will one day burst in all its fury over doomed Calgarry, and very possibly uproot the Conways from their native soil' (Riddell 407).

Whereas the earlier state of Ireland novels ended eirenically with marriage and accommodation, *The Nun's Curse*, like Maturin's *Milesian Chief*, is a tragedy but not for the Catholic Irish. Conway's son becomes the true heir of the Radcliffean Gothic but in a reversal of the Protestant narrative, in which the Protestant heroine finds herself inheriting the Catholic structure. Rather, young Conway escapes his Anglo-Irish Protestant paternity to take the Ascendancy Great House into the Catholic future. All the chances for ecumenical accommodation – or, indeed, agricultural improvement – are lost.

Bram Stoker is the writer who takes this ecumenism founded in a shared experience of Gothic horror furthest, beginning in *The Snake's Pass* (1890), a Young Ireland-style attempt to establish a renewed Irish identity on acts of mutual self-sacrifice across denominational divides, and culminating in his most famous novel, *Dracula*, of 1897. The figure of the vampire has already been identified as the Anti-Christ, but this bears no subliminal association with Catholicism, as Christopher Herbert has suggested. For Dracula is an aristocrat who comes from the eastern terrain of Romanian Orthodoxy rather than the west of working-class Irish immigration, and he is specifically threatened by Catholic sacramentals. Dracula is defined as an inversion of Christ and his vampirism as a blasphemous inversion of the biblical injunction against taking blood. Dracula's follower Renfield repeats the phrase, 'the blood is the life' (Leviticus 17:14), referring to a creature's lifeblood being offered sacrificially to God as he is the source of its existence. Dracula's blood-drinking therefore is an inversion of Jewish law and a parody of Christ's self-giving of his blood in the Eucharist. It is a close imitation of the dichotomy in Maturin between the sacrificing of others and the self-giving of Christ, evidenced in *Melmoth* by the scapegoating of Monçada, and by characters such as the Guzman children, who sell their hair and blood to save their family from starvation. Similarly, in *Dracula,* four men who care for Lucy Westenra give her blood transfusions to offset the depredations of the vampiric bite, while Mina Harker offers her psychic vulnerability to Dracula, caused through a blood baptism and a parodic Holy Communion, as a means of tracking him down.

Stoker may have been influenced, through his friendship with Tennyson, by the liberal Anglican theology of F. D. Maurice, for whom the Church is embodied in the family and the nation as much as in ecclesiastical structure. In Maurice's eirenic ecclesiology, every denomination in the Christian family has some particular charisma or insight lacking in the others, although he thought the Anglican Church more catholic and inclusive than others (Milbank 231–33). Stoker's group of vampire hunters and their bonding through self-giving has some analogies also with freemasonry. Stoker's brother was a senior Mason in Ireland and Stoker himself a member of English Lodge 1150 from 1883–89, keeping up close ties afterwards, as David Harrison has demonstrated (Harrison 132–33). It is therefore not surprising that like some ideal Masonic Lodge *Dracula* unites different nationalities and Christian denominations in its Gothic 'church' of vampire hunters, Freemasonry being an eirenic attempt to unite those of different backgrounds in the craft and worship of the 'Great Architect'. Although Stoker's story is set in England and Transylvania, Lucy Westenra suggests an Anglo-Irish Church of Ireland surname, associated with the Rossmore family, while Mina Murray's surname is indicative of Scots-Ulster Presbyterianism. In contrast to Irish Freemasonry, however, which was defined in specifically anti-Catholic fashion after the 1826 papal condemnation, this ecumenical 'lodge' is led by a Dutch Catholic physician, who employs Catholic sacramentals to contain the vampire, including somewhat improbably the eucharistic Host to prevent a vampire's passage in and out of its tomb.

The novel's ecumenism is demonstrated in the extensive, if somewhat instrumental use of Catholic devotional objects such as rosaries, crucifixes and the Host, which are, however, treated as effective holy objects. To defeat the vampiric threat, Catholic sacramentals must be united with the Protestant emphasis on the Word of God and scriptural authority. The Protestant characters notably seek to track Dracula by the use of documents that act in biblical fashion as forms of testimony. Entire biblical scenes, such as the finding of the empty tomb by Mary Magdalene and the doubting of the resurrection by Thomas from John 20, are parodied (Stoker 196–202), with Dr John Seward playing the evangelist's role. Yet while St John's gospel ends by an awareness that 'the world itself could not contain the books that should be written' about Christ (John 21:25), a statement of the excess of life and meaning in his story, the testimonials to Dracula's presence become nugatory – 'a mass of typewriting' (Stoker 378) – since his is a reverse resurrection, in which natural death ensues and there is nothing left of him except an empty coffin.

Dracula's deeper heuristic engagements are with mediation between the bodily and sexual and the metaphysical or transcendent, which is at the heart, I would argue, of the gothic mode, precisely because of its Protestant genesis and allegiances. The double gesture of rejection of a Catholic past and a simultaneous desire to connect with an even more 'authentic' Christian history renders historical movement forward problematic, just as Protestant denial of the prayers of the saints and sacramental realism leaves adherents bereft of modes of religious mediation.

As nineteenth-century English Anglicanism began to self-identify as a *via media* between Protestant and Catholic extremes, it offered a Romantic pan-sacramentality much needed in an Ireland in which, after the Famine, Catholic reconstruction had become more ascetic and puritan under Archbishop Cullen, and much more rigorous in its rejection of traditional folk practices. Yet although there were Tractarian adherents in Ireland, such as Maturin's own son, the Evangelical Revival was in the ascendent in the mid to late nineteenth century, and such moves to a more sacramental form of worship and doctrine were far from mainstream. The vampire carries this lack, being an image of a failed sacramentality in which the sign no longer signifies a spiritual meaning: the metaphor does not carry meaning across, so that the vampire is trapped in a circular economy of materiality. Only therefore, when vampiric Lucy Westenra is staked and restored to 'God's true dead, whose soul is with him' can her body be returned to signification:

> True that there was there, as we had seen them in life, the traces of care and pain and waste; but these were all dear to us, for they marked her truth to what we knew. One and all we felt that the holy calm that lay like sunshine over the wasted face and form was only an earthly token and symbol of the calm that was to reign for ever. (Stoker 217)

The narrator's reference to token and symbol parallels the language of the Anglican catechism, in which a sacrament is 'the outward and visible sign of an inward and spiritual grace' (*Book of Common Prayer* 294). Notably, not only does death allow Lucy's body to reveal her soul but freed from the vampiric state, time and change can now leave their mark. For to be a vampire is to lose not only the freedom of the soul but equally the freedom of the body to change; it is an extreme instance of Gothic entrapment. This same insight is at the heart of

Sheridan Le Fanu's vampire story, 'Carmilla' (1871–1872), in which the vampiric bite of the female vampire entraps her girl victim in an eternal adolescence.

Supernatural Realism in Sheridan Le Fanu and Elizabeth Bowen

The last two writers in this Protestant Gothic tradition are separated by a century but share this concern about mediation between physical and spiritual worlds. In contrast, however, to the encroaching materialism of the vampire, their supernatural is confident and utterly real. Like Maturin, Le Fanu was of Huguenot descent, through Charles de Cresseron who was brought to Ireland by William of Orange, and he was anxious to maintain the connection, using the ancestral name in his fiction. One of his earliest stories, 'Spalatro' (1843), owes much to Maturin, most notably its portrayal of an atheist monk, modelled on Fra Paolo in *Melmoth*, who seeks to unsettle Monçada's faith by inventing a miracle. Spalatro unites Fra Paolo's Enlightenment scepticism with Melmoth's temptation, as he seeks to make the protagonist kill himself and thus be damned, which is a popular Calvinist trope. Spalatro's method is to hypnotise the man so that he imitates his every action in a kind of mimetic contagion and this too is a trope imitated from *Melmoth*, when the terrified Monçada finds himself forced to copy the expressions and gestures of the mob outside his window.

Like the Maturins, for generations Le Fanus had been Church of Ireland clergy, with Le Fanu's father chaplain of the Military School just outside Dublin in Chapelizod and later Dean of Emly, resident in Abington, County Limerick (McCormack 14–15). W. J. McCormack stresses how precarious life at Abington became during the period of the Tithe Wars, both economically and in terms of physical security (McCormack 43–45) and Le Fanu, whose financial situation as editor of the *Dublin University Magazine* grew increasingly unstable, is a good candidate for the argument that Protestant Gothic evolves from a specifically Irish Protestant anxiety about loss of social status and significance. Although full of wonderful atmosphere and menace, Le Fanu's novels struggle to develop and only *Uncle Silas* (1864) manages to escape the corpse-like fixity of much of his longer fiction which, moreover, imitates 'Spalatro' in its obsessive mimesis, frequently rehearsing older plots and names of characters.

There are, however, muted ecumenical gestures in Le Fanu's work. The first is in his early stories, eventually collected in *The Purcell*

Papers (1880), which purport to be the collection of an eighteenth-century Catholic priest, Father Purcell of Drumcoolagh in the south of the country, through whom traditional supernatural and folkloric tales can be mediated to the present. Purcell is presented as a man of cultivation and reason, who seeks to find natural explanations for the events described (*Ghost Stories* 192), even though the material prevents this. It is noticeable that in the earliest of these tales. 'The Ghost and the Bone-setter' (1838) the squire who returns from the dead to get his leg reset is named 'Phelim' and his tenant's surname (derived presumably from the place and thus shared) is 'Neil', implying that the ghost is a descendent of Phelim O'Neill, one of the leaders of the 1641 rebellion, who was executed for his role. This event lies buried now in a folktale involving the belief of the Catholic peasantry that the last person interred in a churchyard must carry water to the other inhabitants, until another corpse arrives to take his place. Buried also here is that same substitutionary narrative that shaped Maturin's novel, *Melmoth*, with an echo of the comic leg-pulling scene from Christopher Marlowe's play, *Doctor Faustus* (1604), on which Melmoth's original bargain with the Devil is based. Again, as in Maturin's *Melmoth*, Catholicism is associated with substitutionary forms of mediation, albeit in a comic mode, whereas story-telling, and especially preserving and passing-on the tales of an older culture, is a purer mode of mediation and a more Protestant one, not only because it is of the word, but because it pushes the tale back into the past and engenders a sense of forward historical movement. This pattern is evident in *The Purcell Papers*, where an intermediary stands between the reader and Father Purcell's account and in a later sequence of supernatural Irish tales, narrated by Protestant ladies, who keep a William III anniversary cup on their dresser. The Williamite nostalgia of the women is gently ironised and they are distanced from the reader by a Catholic narrator of their story, who is also of another century as if to consign the opposed sides in the Battle of the Boyne to a 'single party' in the manner of T. S. Eliot with the English Civil War parties, now 'united in the strife which divided them' (*Ghost Stories* 220).

William Le Fanu reported that his brother was 'a man who thought deeply, especially on religious subjects' (140), but unlike churchwarden William, Le Fanu's interests were more mystical and esoteric, though certainly ecumenical, in his espousal of Swedenborgian metaphysics for his ghost stories and novel *Uncle Silas* (1864). The historian Roy Foster had no hesitation in attributing such hermeticism, in which Yeats and Stoker also had a strong interest (Stoker being a Freemason and *possibly*, like Yeats, a member of the Order of the

Golden Dawn) to Irish Protestant displacement and loss of political and social power. Foster writes that 'an interest in the occult might be seen on one level as a strategy for coping with contemporary threats (Catholicism plays a strong part in all their fantasies), and on another as a search for psychic control' (50). In the case of Stoker, it is much more likely to be an interest in spiritual friendship, aligned to his masonic adherence, as well as a source of mediatory spiritual practices outside Catholicism. A. E. Waite and other leaders of the Order of the Golden Dawn were devout members of the Church of England, offering a mystical theurgy and sacramental practice tailored in its moral elevation to Protestant piety.

In Le Fanu's case, hermeticism in the guise of Swedenborgian Platonism, in which the world of spirits is primary and our world the reflection, first, provides a vivid imaginary of animal forms, like the demonic monkey who confronts the Revd Mr Jennings on the omnibus in 'Green Tea' (1871), and secondly, restores the supernatural to its orthodox 'naturalness' and realism in a period when ghosts were becoming vestigial whisps of white and in which explanations for phenomena were scientific and the spiritual basis of reality increasingly not acknowledged. Where English Anglicans like Charles Kingsley and George MacDonald were turning to the Purgatorial visions of the poet Dante for a mediation between the absolutes of heaven and hell, in ultra-Protestant Ireland, Le Fanu reached for the Swedish Protestant visionary Swedenborg and his mediatory world of spirits, where after death souls reveal their ruling love for good or ill in an intermediate state.

This provides comfort in the story, 'The Familiar' (1847/72) in which a ghostly nemesis haunts the footsteps of a naval captain in the Dublin streets and sends letters through the post. The persecution sends the erstwhile 'infidel', Captain Barton, for clerical advice:

> "I am sure – I *know* ... that there is a God – a dreadful God – and that retribution follows guilt, in ways the most mysterious and stupendous – by agencies the most inexplicable and terrific; – there is a spiritual system ... malignant, and implacable, and omnipotent, under whose persecutions I am, and have been, suffering the torments of the damned! – yes, sir – yes – the fires and frenzy of hell!' (*Ghost Stories* 60)

The deity described here has some similarity to the unknowable God of Calvinism and the 'unsearchable depth of divine judgement' (Calvin 3.21.1). In the doctrine of double predestination, God's judgement on the reprobate has an inexorable logic in its operation, although their punishment is caused by their own sin, as in this case. In this systematic damnation there seems no room whatsoever for mediation. Barton sees himself cut off from prayer and the possibility of redemption in a manner again akin to Marlowe's Doctor Faustus, with the priest, Dr Malkin, who first believes him mentally disturbed and then urges prayer, takes the role of the devout scholars in the final act:

> SECOND SCHOLAR: Yet, Faustus, look up to heaven; remember God's mercies are infinite.
> FAUSTUS: But Faustus' offence can ne'er be pardoned: the
> Serpent that tempted Eve may be saved, but not Faustus ... (Marlowe 386)

Marlowe's protagonist never gives up on his rigid fatalism about damnation, the failure to pray being evidence to him of his reprobation. Yet although Captain Barton is frightened to death by his avenging spirit, there is hope for him after death. After swooning at the sight of his persecutor, he awakens in the arms of a young girl 'and she was singing a song, that told, I know not how ... of all my life – all that is past and all that is to come' (*Ghost Stories* 237). This is the girl whom Barton wronged, and he understands that he has been forgiven in the moment that his tears flow at her song.

In 'The Familiar' Le Fanu has melded Calvinist dualist anthropology to a Swedenborgian afterlife, which is more physically vivid than its earthly reflection and invades the earthly realm through gunshot, the postal service and demonic birds. The Familiar is locked even in the afterlife into this cycle of revenge – he has become his obsessive hatred – but his daughter, despite her sad ending has not, and she, ruled by love, is able to offer the 'vicarious supplication by the intercession of the good' that Barton craved and which resembles the desire of the prayers of a saint requested by a Catholic devotee (*Ghost Stories* 64).

This Swedenborgian interpretation is borne out by the framing of the tale, which like others in the *In a Glass Darkly* collection, purports to be the casebook of a Doctor Hesselius, who unites the viewpoint of a medical doctor with that of a Swedenborgian, for whom the natural world is dependent on that of the spiritual. The New Church then offers a way to understand the relation between these orders of reality, although it is noticeable how powerless Hesselius is to cure his patients, and how his explanations are more rationalist than the circumstances allow. This forces the reader to imagine beyond the facts of the case and to allow for the deep mysteries of our spiritual existence in a way Hesselius refuses to do.

In Le Fanu's greatest Gothic novel, *Uncle Silas*, the father and the uncle of Maud Ruthyn, the endangered protagonist, share an interest in Swedenborgian mysticism, and the heroine is aided by one of that faith's ministers. The novel culminates, moreover, in an assertion of Swedenborgian belief:

> This world is a parable – the habitation of symbols – the phantoms of spiritual things immortal shown in material shape. May the blessed second-sight be mine – to recognise under these beautiful forms of earth the ANGELS who wear them; for I am sure we may walk with them if we will, and hear them speak! (*Uncle Silas* 480)

Maud is referring to the women who were faithful to her and aided her escape from death, and suggests that angelic spirits have worked through them, as is attested in Swedenborg's writings. It is a sacramental perception of reality in which all our acts have a divine correspondence.

There is no evidence that Le Fanu was a Swedenborgian *tout court* and his personal journal and correspondence reveals a devout Protestant, even if one who increasingly withdrew from public worship. He worries about his wife's lack of assurance of salvation in her last illness but shows no doubt of religion itself, although he dramatises enlightenment infidelity in some stories, including 'The Familiar' and, most notably, 'The Mysterious Lodger', where crippling doubt strikes the narrator's wife as it appears to have done his own (McCormack 127–33). In a letter to his mother after the death of his wife in 1858, Le Fanu intercedes for her: 'I prayed to God for Christ's sake to accept her' (McCormack 128), showing clearly the impetus in his work towards a need for mediation and even 'vicarious substitution'. It is interesting that Susanna died in 1858 at the time of the evangelical revival in Ireland, where assurance was plentiful and instant, in contrast to a Calvinist unclear sense of election.

In an essay collection for Roy Foster, Hermione Lee applies his diagnosis of control and doubt to a twentieth-century Anglo-Irish writer, Elizabeth Bowen, who wrote a perceptive introduction to *Uncle Silas* in 1947, comparing it to *Wuthering Heights* (1846) in its 'pressure, volume and spiritual urgency (Le Fanu, *Uncle Silas* 8). Moreover, Bowen identified elements that are specifically Irish in this story set in England: 'the hermetic solitude and the autocracy of the great country house, the demonic power of the family myth, fatalism, feudalism and the "ascendancy outlook"' (ibid. 8). Bowen would acknowledge these same features in her own Anglo-Irish family history, centred on Bowen's Court in County Clare. Lee detects a theme of 'breaking or losing faith' which is 'bound up with the haunting eeriness of Bowen's work ... Dubious, marginal, and strange beliefs creep in where traditional religion or securely based spirituality have been eroded – by war, by the crash of civilizations, by exile or dispossession' (125).

Lee is quite accurate in her observation of 'dubious, marginal beliefs' and that they are presented as an effect of secularisation, but she misses the element of critique of these phenomena from a religious perspective. Bowen was a devout member of the Church of Ireland, who in later life wrote a nativity play, which was performed, unusually, by a cast of mixed Protestant and Catholic actors (Glendinning 233–4). One of Bowen's earliest Irish stories, 'The Back Drawing-Room' (1926), frames its tale of second sight amid the aftermath of the Irish Civil War with the affectations of a theosophical salon, viewed highly satirically. Bowen's tale ironises the advanced circle's certainty about the spiritual and their ability to turn the subjective into objective reality: 'because you remember a thing ... or even imagine it, or from loving it very much really know it, it *exists* apart from itself and you, even though you don't remember it, imagine it, or know it any more?' (*Collected Stories* 202). This language suggests the reality of the supernatural lies in the powers of the human subject but this viewpoint is questioned by the unnamed 'little man' who describes an actual haunting.

On a visit to cousins in Ireland, he is forced to knock on the door of an Anglo-Irish Great House to get help mending a bicycle puncture and finds himself witnessing the deep distress of a woman crying in the intimacy of a fusty, lace-curtained back drawing-room. Terrified by embarrassment and fear of intrusion, he leaves quickly and walks all the way back to his friends' house. He learns, of course, that the house he can minutely describe was burnt down by the Republicans two years before, so that there is no way in which his own memories could have become objectively manifest as Mrs Henneker and the girl Lois had stated. Nor, moreover, is the memory of Kilbarran's inhabitants active within the thoughts of his Anglo-Irish hostess, to the narrator's surprise:

> 'I couldn't help saying she seemed to have lost interest in her old friends, and she looked at me (quite strangely for such a practical woman) and said, "Well, how can one feel they're alive? How can they be, any more than plants one's pulled up? They've nothing to grow in, or hold on to."' (Bowen, *Collected Stories* 210)

The synergy between person and ancestral house assumed here is akin to that described by Bowen in relation to her own family: 'the land outside Bowen's Court left prints on my ancestors' eyes that looked out: perhaps their eyes left, also, prints on the scene' (*Bowen's Court* 451).

We learn little about the 'little man' who saw this distressed spectre but the nature of his gift here is one much more associated with Scotland, and current also among some Scots-Irish, which is second-sight. Identified as long ago as the seventeenth century by Robert Kirk, an episcopalian minister in Aberfoyle, who wrote of it as 'double-walking', it is a faculty of seeing a simulacrum of someone when they are elsewhere and often presages their death. This duality speaks in the Presbyterian context also of Calvinist anthropology, in which one is never sure whether one is elect or not, opening a fissure in the subject, most vividly realised in James Hogg's *Memoirs and Confessions of a Justified Sinner* (1824). Here the woman is fissured from her house like an uprooted plant, and her weeping is appropriately described by the narrator as drowning: she barely exists. The word 'drowning' is supplied by Mrs Henniker, the leader of the salon, who moves from disdain to recognition after listening to this story. She goes on to identify the woman's fear as that of 'the quenching of a world in horror and destruction that happens with a violent death' (*Collected Stories* 208). Now the weeping woman is not dead, except to the memories of her former neighbours, and she had no violent death. Neil Corcoran suggests that Mrs Henniker is thinking back to World War I but there is a more relevant context, and that is her occluded Irish background (34–35). Henniker is the family name of the baronry of Henniker of Stratford-upon-Slaney in County Wicklow. This suggests that she, too, unmoored from her home in Ireland, is drowning, which takes the form of entertaining those dubious pseudo-philosophies of which Hermione Lee writes. Mrs Henniker too has nothing 'to hold on to'.

I am suggesting that Bowen offers her own version of Protestant Gothic here, which explains Mrs Henniker's uncharacteristic silence after the narrator's words about the disturbed plants. She elides the dispossessed Anglo-Irish and the spiritually lost. While in *Bowen's Court* (1951) she exhibits an alert awareness of Ascendancy oppression and economic injustice among her forebears, what interests her is that period of their loss of social and political significance, a period of burnt houses and lost memories. Without metaphysical and relational ties, her characters become prey to the pull of a malevolent supernatural, just like Le Fanu's Mr Barton. Indeed, Bowen often imitates Le Fanu's effects, such as the letter from a dead man sent through the post in 'The Familiar'. Mrs Drover in the wartime story, 'The Demon Lover', discovers a letter in her shut-up London house, which comes from a former fiancé, missing presumed killed in the First World War. Just as the overbearing man had drained agency from her in their lovemaking, so now, amid 'the desuetude of her former bedroom, her married London home's whole air of being a cracked cup from which memory, with its reassuring power, had either evaporated or leaked away, made a crisis' (*Collected Stories* 664). Like Le Fanu's haunted Mr Jennings, Mrs Drover's veil between natural and supernatural is breached and she is prey to this former lover, who comes to claim her, trapping her into the locked interior of a black cab, by which he carries her away, as in the traditional folk tale, much imitated by Gothic writers, including Le Fanu, in 'Schalken the Painter,' in which Death himself carries his bride to the grave.

For Bowen and Le Fanu alike, it is the material which bears the scandalous power of the supernatural: a feather boa in 'Green Holly' (1944), the smell of musty wallpaper in 'The Back Drawing-Room', the box of memorabilia in 'The Happy Autumn Fields' (1944). For both writers there is an exercise of divine justice in some cases, especially evident in Bowen's reworking of Le Fanu's 'Authentic Narrative of the Ghost of a Hand' from *The House by the Church-yard* (1863): 'Hand in Glove' (1952). Two sisters, seemingly from the same garrison town milieu of Le Fanu's novel keep their strange old aunt locked up while they predate her wardrobe to keep them in respectable attire for husband-hunting. Concealing her aunt's death, Ethel steals her keys to locate white gloves. In Le Fanu, a ghostly hand has murderous intentions: 'protruding through the aperture of the press, and shrouded in the shade of the valance, they plainly saw the white fat hand, palm downwards, presented towards the head of the child' (*House* 62). Similarly in Bowen a hand fills itself out inside the coveted white glove and proceeds to strangle Ethel and 'so great was the swell of the force ... the seams of the glove split' (*Collected Stories* 775). This uncanny sense of a pressing physicality in a spectre is worthy of Le Fanu and is of a piece with the personification and enlivening of objects throughout Bowen's writing, including the land making prints on her ancestors' eyes in *Bowen's Court*. Charles Taylor has pointed out how in the premodern era 'objects were loci of spiritual power, which is why they had to be treated with care, and if abused could wreak terrible damage' (33–34). In a secular age, such imminent force in objects appears uncanny and is for the unwary dangerous. For Le Fanu and Bowen alike, however, such re-enchanted phenomena, even in malevolent action, are a way to witness to the metaphysical depths of the physical world. The red hand of Ulster is a symbol of contestation within Ireland but the white hand of Protestant Gothic speaks ultimately of the divine, evoking the stony right hand of God carved on ancient Irish crosses and reaching out through tropes of shared terror a hand of tentative friendship across denominational divides.

Works Cited

Baldick, Chris (ed). *The Oxford Book of Gothic Tales*. Oxford University Press, 1992.
Book of Common Prayer. Cambridge University Press, n.d.

Bowen, Desmond. *The Protestant Crusade in Ireland, 1800–1870: A Study of Protestant-Catholic Relations Between the Act of Union and Disestablishment.* Dublin, Gill and MacMillan, 1978.
Bowen, Elizabeth. *The Collected Stories of Elizabeth Bowen*, introduction by Angus Wilson. Penguin, 1980.
———. *Bowen's Court.* Longmans, Green and Co., 1942.
Bradshaw, Brendan. *The Dissolution of the Religious Orders in Ireland under Henry VIII.* Cambridge University Press, 1974.
Calvin, John. *Institutes of the Christian Religion*, edited by John T. McNeill and translated by Ford Lewis Battles, 2 vols. Westminster John Knox Press, 1960.
Colley, Linda. *Britons: Forging the Nation 1707–1837.* Revised Edition. Yale University Press, 2009.
Corcoran, Neil. *Elizabeth Bowen: The Enforced Return.* Oxford University Press, 2008.
Eliot, T. S. *Collected Poems, 1909–1962.* Faber, 1974.
Ford, Alan. 'Apocalyptic Ireland.' *Irish Theological Quarterly*, vol. 78, no. 2, 2013, pp. 125–48.
———. The *Protestant Reformation in Ireland, 1590–1641.* Peter Lang, 1985.
Foster, Roy. *W. B. Yeats: A Life*, Volume 1: *The Apprentice Mage, 1865–1914.* Oxford University Press, 1997.
Glendinning, Victoria. *Elizabeth Bowen: Portrait of a Writer.* 1977. Faber, 2012.
Gray-Stack, Charles. 'The Church of Ireland Synod 1964', *The Furrow*, vol. no. 15: 7, 1964, pp. 466–73.
Harrison, David. 'Bram Stoker, Freemasonry and the Byronic Hero.' *Gnosis*, vol. 7, no. 7, 2021, pp. 13–32.
Jefferies, Henry A. 'Why the Reformation Failed in Ireland.' *Irish Historical Studies*, vol. 40, no. 158, 2016, pp. 151–70.
Killeen, Jarlath. *Gothic Ireland: Horror and the Anglican Imagination in the Long Eighteenth Century.* Dublin, Four Courts Press, 2005.
———. The *Emergence of Irish Gothic Fiction: History, Origins, Theories.* Edinburgh University Press, 2014.
Lee, Hermione. 'Breaking Faith: Elizabeth Bowen and Disloyalties.' *Uncertain Futures: Essays about the Irish Past for Roy Foster*, edited by Senia Paseta. Oxford University Press, 2016, pp. 123–32.
Le Fanu, J. S. *Uncle Silas: A Tale of Bartram-Haugh*, introduction by Elizabeth Bowen. Cresset Press, 1947.
———. *Ghost Stories and Mysteries*, edited by E. F. Bleier. Dover, 1975.
———. *The House by the Church-yard.* New edition. Richard Bentley and Son, 1897.
———. *In a Glass Darkly*, edited by Robert Tracy. Oxford University Press, 1993.
Le Fanu, William. *Seventy Years of Irish Life: Anecdotes and Reminiscences.* E. Arnold, 1893.
Leland, Thomas. *Longsword Earl of Salisbury: An Historical Romance.* 2 vols. William Johnston, 1762.
Marlowe, Christopher. *The Tragical History of Doctor Faustus. Complete Plays*, edited by J. B. Steane, Penguin, 1986.

Maturin, Charles. *Melmoth the Wanderer.* Edited by Chris Baldick. Oxford University Press, 1998.

———. *Five Sermons on the Errors of the Catholic Church.* 2nd edition. William Curry; Hamilton, Adams and Co, 1826.

McCormack, W. J. *Sheridan Le Fanu and Victorian Ireland.* Clarendon Press, 1980.

McDowell, R. B. *The Church of Ireland 1869–1969.* Studies in Irish History. Routledge and Kegan Paul, 1975.

Mellinkoff, Ruth. 'Cain's Monstrous Progeny in *Beowulf*: part I, the Noachim Tradition.' *Anglo-Saxon England*, vol. 8, 1979, pp. 143–62.

Milbank, Alison. *God and the Gothic: Religion, Romance and Reality in the English Literary Tradition.* Oxford University Press, 2018.

Riddell, Charlotte. *The Nun's Curse.* 3 vols. Ward and Downey, 1888.

Roche, Regina Maria. *The Children of the Abbey: A Tale.* 1796. 3 vols. J. and B. Williams, 1828.

Stoker, Bram. *Dracula*, edited by Maud Ellman. Oxford University Press, 1996.

Taylor, Charles. *A Secular Age.* Belknap Press, 2007.

Ussher, James. *A Discourse of the Religion Anciently Professed by the Irish and British.* J. Y. for Partners of the Irish Stocke, 1631.

Wycliffe, John. *Tracts and Treatises and Translations from his Manuscripts*, edited by Robert Vaughan. Blackburn and Pardon, 1845.

Chapter 9

Bram Stoker, *Dracula* and the Irish Dimension
Jarlath Killeen

When Radu Florescu and Raymond T. McNally went *In Search of Dracula* (1972), those two intrepid adventurers (somewhat unsurprisingly) chased the Count to Transylvania, but not to Dublin, Sligo, Monaghan or Derry. One of the things that everyone 'knows' about the titular character of Bram Stoker's 1897 novel is that he was based on Vlad Țepeș (or 'Vlad the Impaler'), the fifteenth century Wallachian Voivode – even though the extent of the connection between them is an extremely contested one in scholarship on the text. In her rip-roaring treatment of what she calls 'sense and nonsense' in Dracula Studies, Elizabeth Miller complains: 'Count Dracula and Vlad the Impaler. Never has so much been written by so many about so little' (149).

Romania has had an ambivalent relationship with Count Dracula for decades. While it makes good economic sense to draw attention to the country's link to one of the most famous literary characters ever created and entice a steady stream of tourists down the trail to Bran Castle, the 'original' Castle Dracula (Huebner), the pop culture transformation of a national hero into a bloodthirsty, Satanic vampire has understandably been the cause of some resentment as well. That there was a direct line from Vlad to Dracula was a critical assumption for a long time, though the revelation that the most famous vampire name of them all was a relatively late addition to his plans has rather undermined the notion that Stoker was inspired by the historical figure. Stoker appended the name 'Dracula' to his creation only after he consulted William Wilkinson's *An Account of the Principalities of Wallachia and Moldavia* (1820) in the public library in Whitby while on holiday there in 1890, and after much of the plot had already been sketched out (Frayling). Even though Wilkinson's account actually contains very little on the historical Dracula, one eye-catching note glossed the meaning of that memorable patronymic, which Stoker then copied into his Notebook: 'DRACULA in Wallachian language means DEVIL' (*Bram Stoker's*

Notes, 245; Wilkinson 19n.). Prior to this find, Stoker appears to have given his villain the equally catchy, but rather less impressive moniker 'Count Wampyr' — the substitution is surely one of the most fortuitous in literary history, as it seems unlikely that a modern myth and a minor cultural industry could have been built on the back of a monster with such a silly name.

By the time Stoker was at work in Whitby public library, he had already decided to move the location of Castle Dracula from Styria (where he had originally placed it)[1] to Transylvania. The use of a name famous in Romanian history fixed the connection between Central and Eastern Europe and Dracula in the cultural imagination. The Count himself stresses his geographical specificity in one of the few scenes in the novel where he actually speaks, setting out in fascinating if hard-to-follow detail the intertwining of his family's exploits with centuries of European territorial dispute (Stoker, *Dracula* 69–70). In his speech on Dracula family history to Jonathan Harker, the Count directly mentions or alludes to an incredible range of locations, including Iceland, Asia, Africa, Turkey, Bulgaria, Hungary, Wallachia, Lombardy, and stresses the ways in which his family and his 'tribe' played important roles in the medieval and early modern period.[2] One place that is *not* mentioned, however, is Stoker's own birthplace, Ireland, and his monster makes no excursions to the Irish coast for reasons of either sightseeing or blood satiation during the course of the novel itself.[3] Whatever Count Dracula's ultimate mission to London actually involves, and there may well be a political and even imperial dimension to his plans (Coundouriotis), Ireland does not appear to play a role in it.

Recent scholarship has challenged the claim that Wilkinson's *Account* was the first time Stoker had encountered the iconic name 'Dracula'. Jason McElligott, the Director of Marsh's Library in Dublin, has demonstrated that, as a teenager, Stoker visited the library seven times in 1866 and 1867, and called for an eclectic variety of very specific items (3–5). Lurking in one volume Stoker consulted, Peter Heylyn's *Cosmographie* (1652),[4] is a reference to 'Dracala', and the 'battel of Cassova' (1448), cited in the Count's speech to Jonathan Harker as one of the key events in his family's history (Heylyn 172). As McElligott points out, 'With Heylyn's *Cosmographie*, it is possible to point to a book with an explicit reference to the historical figure of Dracula consulted by Stoker almost a quarter of a century before he is commonly acknowledged to have stumbled across him in William Wilkinson's *Account*', though he stresses that 'it is ... extremely unlikely that in the 1860s Stoker picked out the same passages in these books which interest scholars in the light of his famous 1897 novel' (71).[5]

Perhaps browsing through Heylyn's *Cosmographie* may have stirred up memories of another, and surely more significant reference to the historical Dracula, this time in John Foxe's polemical treatment of the martyrdom of Protestants by vengeful and sanguinary Catholics, *Acts and Monuments* (first edition 1563), which was still a cherished text in many Irish Anglican households in the nineteenth century.[6] While Foxe focuses on the martyrdom of English and Scottish Protestants, in a section of the 1570 edition, he devotes space to what he calls 'The Historye and Tyrannye of the Turks', in which considerable attention is paid to fifteenth-century Wallachia. For Foxe, Wallachia witnessed a struggle between the forces of darkness, represented by the Turkish army, and those of light, chief among which is 'Dracula the Prince', who, 'although he had no greate power of souldiours, yet he so enclosed and enuironed the Turke, that he had almost lost hys whole armye, of whom a great parte notwithstandyng was destroyed and manye of hys ensignes taken' (Book 6, 903).[7] In Foxe's account, Dracula is on the side of the angels and a participant in an age-old cosmic confrontation with 'Satan, the Old Dragon' (Book 5, 514).

If, for Foxe, Central and Eastern Europe was one important battleground in this conflict, according to the seventeenth-century sectarian pamphlets Stoker called up in Marsh's, Ireland was an analogous warzone. In pamphlets like *A Full and Impartial Account* (1689), a polemical history of the 'SECRET CONSULTS, Negotiations, Stratagems, and Intriegues OF THE Romish Party IN IRELAND, From 1660', the Catholic Church is represented as an instrument of evil, and Catholic plots to extirpate Protestantism a significant cause of Ireland's social and political difficulties.[8] The author of the pamphlet insists that, in the fullness of time, God will bring the 'hidden things of darkness to light', including the 'private Cabals, secret Machinations', 'barbarous and Inhumane Massacres' and 'hellish inventions' of the 'conclave at Rome' (49, Preface, 2, 16). As McElligott stresses, 'the Manichean dichotomy of the sectarian pamphlets (good versus evil, light against dark, and Christ against Anti-Christ) was reflected' in many of the texts Stoker called up in the library, with Transylvania and Ireland acting as strategic locations in a struggle for dominion over the earth between God and his Satanic nemesis (72).

Direct comparisons between Transylvania and Ireland were also available to Stoker as well. Lady Wilde, in *Ancient Legends, Mystic Charms and Superstitions of Ireland* (1887), insists that some Transylvanian legends are 'identical with the Irish' (127).[9] Stoker's biographer, Paul Murray, argues that 'as a close friend, Stoker would have read Lady Wilde's work', and points out that the publication of her volumes on

Irish legend and belief coincide with the beginnings of Stoker's research for what would eventually become *Dracula* (195). To Lady Wilde, Transylvania and Ireland are parallel places in which 'the ancient mysteries ... [can] still be traced in the popular superstitions and usages of the people', and extravagant claims like this — as well as a reference to Emily Gerard's 1885 essay on 'Transylvanian Superstitions', from which Stoker quotes in his Notebooks — may have contributed to the creation of the novel (127–28; *Bram Stoker's Notes* 120–23).

Such geographical and historical correspondences have been insufficient, though, for some of the most energetic enthusiasts of an 'Irish Dracula'. In one popular introduction to Romania and Dracula, Kurt Brokaw asks: 'What other land calls up such mystical visions of shrouded, misty forests; of driverless coaches pounding up treacherous, uncharted trails to hidden castles; of black-cloaked figures stalking across moonlit cemeteries in the chill of night?' (12; also Light 32). The obvious answer to this question is Ireland, of course. So far I have been discussing critical work that is circumspect in its situating of the 'origins' of *Dracula* in Stoker's Dublin reading habits. However, this exercise of scholarly restraint is considered unnecessary by some Irish Gothic aficionados who have been busy repatriating the Count, and for whom Dracula's Transylvanian identity is not even skin deep. For example, Bob Curran, author of an extraordinary number of books on Irish legends and supernatural figures, has insisted that, as far as he is concerned, 'Dracula is Irish', a claim he makes (according to the journalist who interviewed him) 'without a trace of doubt in his voice' (Sheerin).

For Curran, the Count is really a legendary Irish character that Stoker mysteriously disguised as a Transylvanian Prince. He links Dracula to a fifth century chieftain, the Abhartach, whose tyrannical control of an area of north Derry apparently included demands for regular supplies of human blood, and who was rumoured to have had a creepy habit of prowling about the neighbourhood in the dead of night. Notorious for his cruelty towards his subjects, the Abhartach proved difficult to dispatch and returned repeatedly from the dead, until finally being laid to rest by being buried upside down (Curran 12–15).[10] If the Abhartach seems too much of a stretch as a model for the Count, why not Brian Boru, the eleventh-century High King of Ireland? Or the undead, bloodsucking residents of Kerry's MacGillycuddy's Reeks (McIntyre 24, 32)? Or even Charles Stewart Parnell, the nationalist leader of the Irish Home Rule movement (Moses)? Other characters in the novel, too, might have Irish roots. Having asked 'Why [Lucy] Westenra?', historian Mark Pinkerton finds the answer in a memorial to Lady Rossmore, the first wife of Warner William Westenra, Baron

Rossmore, in St Patrick's Church of Ireland in Monaghan town. The memorial depicts one man being restrained by another while standing over the deathbed of a woman, which has a visual resemblance to the scene in *Dracula* where Lucy Westenra is staked: 'Is it possible that [Stoker] might have seen this striking memorial and been influenced by it?' (45). What about Mina Murray? Irish too, it seems since, 'in a coincidence too pointed to discount' her surname 'filiates her with native Celts of the name O'Muireadhaigh, which was anglicised to Murray sometime during the colonial occupation' (Valente 66). Enthusiasm, at times, seems on the verge of becoming zeal, though, with extravagant claims that eliminate Central Europe from the novel entirely, since 'Transylvania is really part of Ireland, just as … Whitby is Clontarf' (McIntyre 24). Indeed, according to an endlessly repeated, but nonetheless extremely unlikely claim, Stoker didn't derive his villain's name from a historical figure at all, or from reading William Wilkinson's dry history of Wallachia and Moldavia, but instead took it from 'droch fhola', an expression in the Irish language meaning 'bad blood' (Valente 61).[11]

Other Irish Studies scholars have considered whether the novel could be read as being 'about' Irish issues,[12] and deciphered the coded colonial (or potentially postcolonial) politics of *Dracula* in terms of the text's possible implication in Irish historical debates. Influential critics such as Terry Eagleton and Seamus Deane contend that the novel can be understood as a critique of British rule in Ireland and an attack on absentee Protestant landlords – represented by the Count – as vampiric parasites on their Catholic tenants (Eagleton 215; Deane 89–94). Dracula is opposed by a rag-tag group who describe their mission to destroy the Count as a 'plan of campaign' (Stoker, *Dracula* 367). This expression conveniently (or coincidentally?) echoes the title given to a strategy adopted by a group of Irish nationalist agrarian agitators in 1886 in response to the failure of the Home Rule Bill (Valente 136–37). In these readings, Stoker is represented as an Irish nationalist (and he did, importantly, describe himself as a 'philosophical Home Ruler' [Stoker *Reminiscences*, 1: 26–31; 2: 343–44]), and his best novel an exercise in analogical Irish politics. Other critics, including Chris Morash and Bruce Stewart, query the extent to which the novel is genuinely on the side of the supposedly oppressed in Irish history, and suggest instead an alignment with the Anglican establishment to which Stoker belonged. For the *Dracula* 'revisionists',[13] the Count analogises the Catholic rebels of the late nineteenth century (rather than their landlords), a depiction in line with representations of nationalists and Home Rulers in the British press as vampiric monsters.

Figure 5 'The Irish "Vampire"', *Punch*, 24 October 1885, 199. Courtesy of the British Library.

Analogies, suggestive connections, ambiguous hints, absolute identifications ... all for a novel in which Ireland is never mentioned. If it was once fashionable to uncover an Irish Dracula, though, scepticism is now the order of the day. William Hughes has warned against what he describes as the 'colonising' tendencies of Irish Studies as a discipline, and argued that Irish readings of *Dracula* are 'as much part of modern political polemic as they are associated with literary criticism'. He insists instead on a continued focus on Central and Eastern Europe rather than Ireland as a source for the political and symbolic power of the text (99–100). Darryl Jones, too, has argued that while *Dracula* is 'certainly' an 'Irish novel', it is not a novel 'about Ireland' ('which it might be but only if we accept the hypothesis that all works of literature by Irish writers are necessarily about the matter of Ireland') (19).

It is notable that the recently published *Cambridge Companion to Dracula* (2018) contains chapters on *Dracula* and race, and women, on screen, but none on *Dracula* and Ireland. In an aside, the editor, Roger Luckhurst claims that only 'Lack of space has squeezed out a particular focus on Stoker's place in the Anglo-Irish Gothic, although there is lots of work available elsewhere on this' (8). Luckhurst's clumsy use of the anachronistic term 'Anglo-Irish Gothic' is particularly telling here. W. J. McCormack has laboured hard to banish the spectre of the Anglo-Irish from analyses of Irish literature and culture. Though long in use as a shorthand description of Irish literature written in English (one which blithely homogenised diverse traditions, cultures, communities and practices), 'Anglo-Irish' is a term more accurately applied restrictively to describe the landed, Anglican, English-speaking descendants of families who (mostly) came to Ireland following the Williamite Wars of the late seventeenth century (McCormack, *Dissolute Characters* 181). It bears repeating that Stoker came from a solidly middle-class family of civil servants and professionals and was *not* Anglo-Irish.[14] Even more surprising, perhaps, is that in directing the interested reader to the 'lots of work available elsewhere', Luckhurst references the scholarship of Raymond T. McNally, who, as I pointed out at the start of this chapter, is best-known for his interest in Vlad III, and is not one of the leading exponents or critics of an Irish Dracula.

It is important to distinguish between what might be considered source study – whereby scholars identify an Irish 'origin' of some of the elements of *Dracula* – and an Irish 'reading' of the text which interprets it as a novel concerned with Irish politics and/or history. There is a difference, for example, between arguing that the name 'Westenra' might be derived from an Anglo-Irish Monaghan family, and insisting that this means that Lucy should be read as an 'Irish character', or as an allegory of Ireland itself. The probable source of Lucy's name is certainly suggestive, but suggestive of what exactly is a rather different matter. The local disagreement about how to read *Dracula* touches on the current debate in literary criticism between approaches that, in Rita

Felski's terms, account for 'what is in plain view' in a text, and those which go beyond, behind or through a text to the context, subtext or allegory, a debate elsewhere described as one between 'surface' and 'symptomatic' or 'suspicious' reading (Felski 31; also Marcus and Best). In a Gothic Studies context, these discussions resonate with Tzvetan Todorov's complaint that critics tend to interpret supernatural references in fantasy as meaning anything but their otherworldly 'literal meaning' (73). Many of the criticisms of Irish historicist readings of *Dracula* are generated by the sense that such readings are too strategic, too shaped by the contemporary politics of Irish Studies as a discipline, and too insensitive to specifically *Victorian* issues or the 'literal meaning' of the text itself.[15]

In a significant intervention into this debate, Victorianist Juliet John maintains that much of the interpretive disagreement in literary studies is conducted as if it is a zero sum game, and encourages an 'acceptance of multiplicity and complexity' (11). Certainly, Irish readings of *Dracula* have become something of a bellwether for much larger ideological disputes in Irish Studies, and the existence of many unrestrained interpretations (step forward 'droch fhola') has not helped. John Kucich defends historicist readings as predicated on 'a situated understanding of a text's cultural difference' (73), and I certainly think an alertness to national histories, including in Stoker's case the histories of the country where he lived much of his life, can make a substantial contribution to such a situated understanding as well as constraining tendencies to push interpretation so far as to become unloosed from empirical reality. Given the multiple ways in which Gothic images and tropes circulate in culture, it is, though, potentially misleading to stabilise even the surface meaning of a shapeshifting monster like Dracula. Indeed, given that he was writing about vampires in a period in which, among other things, Irish nationalists, absentee landlords, Charles Stewart Parnell, and the British Empire were all explicitly represented as vampiric, it seems more unlikely than not that Stoker would have been unaware of the Irish political resonances of his authorial choices.

Dracula himself indicates that it is impossible to understand *him*, without understanding also the history that produced him and in which his present self is inextricably intertwined, and the same can be argued for the text in which he makes his first appearance. Emma Mason has advocated moving beyond 'suspicion' and 'surface' to an 'amicable reading practice' that is fully alert to both similarities and differences between 'now' (when we are reading) and 'then' (when the text was written) (343). This chapter is not an attempt to uncover an Irish 'original' for the Count, or to reveal an Irish 'subtext' or allegory at work in

Stoker's novel that would dissolve its supernatural forces into something sexual, or political, or ideological. Rather, I want to argue that there are important reasons why this kind of novel was written by an Irish novelist at the end of the nineteenth century. The textual 'surface' – this is a Gothic adventure novel about a struggle with a supernatural menace – is central to this argument.

As Jason McElligott has stressed, the teenage Stoker was fascinated by historical material in which an apocalyptic battle between the powers of darkness and light take place; this war is still being waged in *Dracula* – but by this stage, the late nineteenth century, the stakes[16] could not be higher. In their struggle with the Count, the Crew of Light are pitted against a monster who may indeed have a political mission to take control of the British Empire, but even this ambitious goal is only a staging post in a war for the takeover of Christendom itself. One of the reasons why Dracula is initially successful on English soil is that he invades the country in a period of profound epistemological crisis when the status of the supernatural had been seriously challenged. Even when confronted with a straightforwardly preternatural threat, rationalist believers in the 'nineteenth century up-to-date' (Stoker, *Dracula* 77) are more likely to reach for the manuals of secular psychiatry and epidemiology than theology and demonology.

The Victorian period was punctuated by theories of, if not the death of God then at least what J. Hillis Miller calls his 'disappearance'. Many writers, intellectuals and commentators felt that whereas previous centuries were God-filled, when God seemed close to human affairs, the Victorian one was at times consumed by an anxiety that God was absent, even if the deity had not actually been read the last rites. Famously, in 1882, Frederich Nietzsche's madman in the marketplace declared that we had killed God. More, though, felt that God had abandoned us, leaving us all alone in a pitiless universe. This feeling of abandonment by God did not often lead to atheism or even agnosticism,[17] but more a profound crisis of confidence in the ability of orthodox Christianity to fully account for the universe in which we all live. While in perhaps the greater number of cases a deeper and more reflective faith was arrived at through facing and overcoming these challenges (see Larsen), others experienced an intense psychological anxiety that, even if God continued to exist, he had disappeared from view, 'slipped away from the places he used to be', and had left us all stragglers on a shore where the 'tide of faith' was on the ebb (Miller 2).[18] This cultural anxiety made a huge mark in the literature of the period. As scholars such as Laura Peters and David Floyd have pointed out, Victorian literature is packed with orphans (like Oliver Twist, Jane Eyre, Heathcliff, David Copperfield,

Little Nell, Esther Summerson, Eppie, Jude Frawley),[19] and very many of them are menaced by malevolent father figures who are inverted or perverted versions of God the Father Almighty.

In the absence of the Great Father, characters look for supreme authority elsewhere and become vulnerable prey to malevolent impersonations of the deity. The late-Victorian Satanic revival does not involve an outpouring of literature deeply invested in the worship of the Prince of Darkness, but refers to texts in which Satanic figures offer themselves as authoritative alternatives to characters who feel abandoned and orphaned, an orphanhood that is both literal (in that their parents are usually dead), and metaphysical (they feel forsaken by God).[20]

Dracula has more than its fair share of orphans, like Jonathan, Mina, John and Quincey, the absence of qualified guardians leaving the characters in desperate need of moral guidance as they face a threat from a monstrous patriarch trying to take over the country. Moreover, benevolent parents and parent-figures expire through the course of the plot, including Lucy's mother and Jonathan's employer Mr Hawkins. These plot parricides are merely rehearsals for the (symbolic) death of God Himself. Arthur's father, Lord Godalming (or, Lord God-almighty) (Bowles 249; Milbank '"Powers Old and New"') who is ailing at the start of the novel, dies half-way through, as the orphans are being menaced by a serpentine fiend. Dracula is represented as a version of the Anti-Christ from the Book of Revelations, or, indeed, possibly even Satan Himself, as suggested when he adopts the title, the Count de Ville, on his way back to Transylvania (Stoker *Dracula*, 317).

Indeed, the Count's mysterious decision to enter England through Whitby, even though London is his actual goal, can be explained by the fact that this quiet seaside town is perhaps most famous for a synod in 664 AD in which the dating of Easter for the Celtic Christian church was finally settled (Dailey). Dracula's passage through Whitby reminds the reader that he, like Christ, possesses a resurrected body, though in the Count's case it is a blasphemous and depraved one. Mina's grotesque breastfeeding from the Count is a monstrous parody of the traditional image of Christ as a pelican cutting open its breast to feed its young, an image that, as Patrick O'Malley points out, was added to the stained glass of Christ Church in Dublin during the 1870 restoration (159). Dracula's blood exchange is a Black Mass, and he is on a religious mission as much as a political one – he aims to be a new kind of Pope, who combines theological and political powers in one person, like an unambiguously satanic version of Ultramontanist Catholicism.[21] Dr Seward's patient Renfield is a powerful example of what happens when you transfer loyalty and belief in the Christian God to His occult alternative. Renfield, after all, is not just a believer in Dracula's alternative religion, but a fanatic who has swapped discipleship for servitude. 'I am here to do Your bidding, Master. I am Your slave, and You will reward me', he declares, rather mistaking the generosity of the new deity (Stoker, *Dracula* 146).

While a great deal of scholarship has spilt ink in decoding the sexual anxieties of this novel, in fact *Dracula* is far more interested in theology than psychosexuality and is an extraordinarily religious text.[22] Christopher Herbert has argued that we are dealing here with 'very likely the most religiously saturated popular novel of its time' (101).[23] Herbert's analysis makes clear how basic religious language is to the novel's prose, but also how the plot is structured as a cosmological battle between ultimate evil and the forces of goodness. The significantly named Abraham Van Helsing (a new patriarch for a new age, a modern father of faith armed with Eucharistic putty, papal indulgences and an M.Litt. from Oxford) insists that Dracula is not just an unnatural menace but 'an arrow in the side of Him who died for man', and he later explains that the Crew of Light are 'ministers of God's own wish; that the world, and men for whom His Son die, will not be given over to monsters, whose very existence would defame Him' (Stoker, *Dracula* 363).[24] He is aided in his battle against the dragon by 'the only son of Lord Godalming', phrasing which is highly suggestive of the Nicene Creed's declaration of belief in the 'one Lord Jesus Christ, the only-begotten Son of God' (ibid. 116). Although it is true that Lord Godalming dies, he is then immediately 'resurrected' in his son, Arthur (a name which invokes the once and future king of England Himself). These Victorian crusaders are in a battle to defeat the Evil One, combatants in an ancient war between Good and Evil, the kind that Bram Stoker was reading about in Marsh's Library when a teenager, that age-old 'Manichean dichotomy' (McElligott 72), and the novel alerts the late Victorian public of the dangers of any indulgence in God's (discursive) death and the need to bring Him back to life.

The possible limits of God's power and the extent of evil in the world were major subjects of popular discussion in the Victorian period, and Stoker's novel is not unusual in addressing these concerns. A growing awareness of the human suffering caused by natural disasters like pandemics and famines contributed much to the so-called 'crisis of faith'. Recent historians of religion have pointed out that while theodicy, the attempt to reconcile the existence of moral and natural evil in the world with the goodness of an omnipotent God, has been a persistent issue in Christianity, the Victorian period was a particularly fruitful time for the production of multiple responses to the problem.[25] Writers of fiction, too, often directly tackled the theological questions that were troubling their readers and themselves, particularly after the vexing decade of the 1840s in which the sheer extent of human suffering and natural evil was made clear to British readers in very powerful ways.

The 'providential aesthetic' that was prevalent in the fiction of the early nineteenth century, which communicated a sense that everything would eventually work out for the best, was challenged by an increasing knowledge of the sheer magnitude of the anguish caused particularly by natural disasters (Vargish 18, 33). For an Irish author, writing about human distress in the second half of the nineteenth century, one specific example of natural evil would surely have been foremost in mind. As Boyd Hilton points out, the extraordinary suffering of the victims of the Irish Famine, and the widespread discussion of this distress in the contemporary print media brought 'views about the Almighty' prominently into public debate (114), especially given that some commentators insisted that God Himself had sent this disaster on the Irish as a punishment for their sins.[26]

Born in 1847, Stoker entered a country living through one of the most catastrophic experiences of the nineteenth century, and the circumstances of his birth and first years must have had an enormous influence on his thinking about such matters. Stoker was extremely ill and physically weak as a child, so ill indeed that he claimed he had spent a large amount of time laid up in bed (*Reminiscences*, 1: 31). As biographers point out, Stoker never went through the normal childhood experiences of learning to walk through crawling and toddling and was instead carried everywhere by others, living on sofas and beds (Belford 17–20). His early years, then, were those of an invalid, although exactly what was wrong with him is unknown. David Skal argues that the much-discussed illness should be understood in terms of an Ireland still in the grip of the Great Famine. Skal points out that Charlotte Stoker was pregnant with Bram when a series of epidemics (dysentery, typhus, cholera) was sweeping the country, and contends that reading daily reports about Ireland as a gigantic miasma may have made the whole family paranoid about the dangers of infection and hyper-vigilant about the health of the new-born son, especially given that their house in Clontarf faced the sea (21). For Robert Smart and Michael Hutchinson, Stoker's childhood illness in a country in which disease and death were so prevalent 'must surely have provided him with vivid images of the death and dying victims of the invisible blights and fevers of the Famine' (112). During Charlotte's pregnancy the Stoker family would have been hearing daily about the fact that starving and evicted tenant farmers were being forced into Dublin city in their hundreds and thousands in a search for food and relief, many of them carrying highly contagious diseases into already overcrowded slums and workhouses.

The Famine reports in the newspapers would have reminded Charlotte Stoker of her own experiences and memories of the dreadful 1832 cholera epidemic in the Sligo of her youth, and it might have looked as if history was repeating itself:

> In the days of my early youth so long ago [...] the world was shaken with the dread of the new and terrible plague which was desolating all lands as it passed through them, and so regular was its march that men could tell where it next would appear and almost the day when it might be expected. It was the cholera, which for the first time appeared in Western Europe. Its bitter strange kiss, and man's want of experience or knowledge of its nature, or how best to resist its attacks, added, if anything could, to its horrors. (C. Stoker 412–13)

In her vivid description of the Sligo cholera, Charlotte Stoker invokes theological explanations and provides a profoundly providential account of the reasons why Sligo suffered so much (and, she suggests, so disproportionately). She recalls how 'A poor traveller was taken ill on the roadside some miles from the town, and how did those samaritans [the locals] tend him? They dug a pit and with long poles pushed him living into it, and covered him up quick, alive. Severely, like Sodom, did our city pay for such crimes' (ibid. 413). Her family eventually fled the town to escape infection, and 'live in peace till the plague had abated and we could return to Sligo'. When they did return they 'found the streets grass-grown and five-eighths of the population dead. We had great reason to thank God who had spared us' (ibid. 418). God had not, though, spared a great many others.

This biographical context of Bram Stoker growing up in an Ireland recovering from the after-effects not just of starvation but also disease and illness, a terror impressed on him most likely by his mother, and connected by her to memories of the Sligo epidemic, helps to explain why that evil, serpentine Anti-Christ Count Dracula is often represented in the novel as a kind of disease, as a walking miasma, a virus-carrying super-spreader, contact with which brings the victim into a state of rapid infection and death. Many critics have examined the ways in which the novel uses the language of disease and plague to describe the Count and his invasion, with Stoker employing the terminology of the two conflicting contemporary theories of disease, contagionism and miasmatism. That Dracula is an embodiment of plague and pandemic, however, does not, as Todorov feared, translate supernatural monstrosity into natural disaster or theology into epidemiology: for a Victorian writer, particularly one coming from a country in which the providentialist treatment of cholera and famine fever had been so important through the century, stark divisions between the natural and the supernatural would have sounded naïve. As the historian Alan Gilbert emphasises, epidemics and pandemics were understood as caused by an interventionist God – they were warnings from the Creator as well as manifestations of supernatural evil, and had important revivalist consequences (197). In *Dracula*, vampiric epidemiology is thoroughly inflected with the theodicean providentialism basic to treatments of supposedly 'natural disasters' in Romantic and Victorian Ireland.[27]

Dracula Himself, and vampirism more generally, then, are embodiments of disease, though not the equivalent of the cholera his mother encountered and survived in 1830s Sligo,[28] and to which Ireland succumbed during the Famine years. Dracula is a manifestation of an even more terrifying and insidious mutation or strain, since he 'can flourish in the midst of diseases that kill off whole peoples' (Stoker, *Dracula* 364). Like the Victorian epidemics he calls to mind, Dracula seems to challenge the sovereignty of God. As an insidious Monster buys up fifty properties to thoroughly infect Victorian London, the modern world is placed on the verge of an abyss of meaninglessness and ontological chaos, and the characters face their own theological and soteriological obliteration. If they fail to win their fight with Dracula, all is lost: 'Life is nothings ... [and] we henceforward become foul things of the night like him, without heart or conscience, preying on the bodies and the souls of those we love best. To us forever are the gates of heaven shut' (ibid. 281). This wider context of a threatened loss of meaning and existential security, in which debates about theodicy, natural disaster and providentialism shaped the public understanding of the crisis of faith, helps to clarify the ways in which Stoker's Irish life contributes to the novel.

In his pugnacious response to Irish readings of *Dracula*, Bruce Stewart posed the following question: 'How far is Bram Stoker's *Dracula* (1897) an Irish novel?' (238). As I have indicated, to this question Irish Studies scholars have supplied fascinating and dramatic answers. While I am not contesting the power of even some of the riskier Irish readings, I think that situating the novel in a general British reaction to events such as the cholera pandemics and the Irish Famine, where commentators attempted to understand such catastrophes theologically, places less strain on the critical conversation, while still drawing out potential Irish dimensions of *Dracula*. The cosmological battle between good and evil in Transylvania and London in *Dracula* echoes that fought in

Derry and Wallachia in the texts Stoker read in Marsh's Library as a young man, and between Protestants and Catholics in Foxe's *Book of Martyrs* with which he was probably familiar from childhood, and the providentialist interpretations of natural disaster reverberating in the post-Famine Ireland of his youth. This is a battle whose lessons were first learned by Charlotte Stoker in the west of Ireland in the 1830s, which her son then confronts again in one of the most important novels of the 1890s.

Notes

1. Possibly influenced by his reading of 'Carmilla' (1871–1872), the vampire novella by fellow Dubliner, Joseph Sheridan Le Fanu.
2. For a recent attempt to provide coherent annotation, see Stoker, *Dracula: The Postcolonial Edition* 56–63.
3. Unlike, for example, Mary Shelley's *Frankenstein* (1818), which does have an Irish episode in volume 2, chapter 3.
4. Heylyn was prominent 17th century controversialist. Marsh's has two editions of *Cosmographie*, from 1657 and 1682. Stoker consulted the 1682 edition.
5. The scholar interested in possible Irish links to *Dracula* should note that Heylyn expresses a dim view of the native Irish and describes them as blood-drinking cannibals: the natives are 'said by Strabo to be man-eaters; accustomed (as Solinus telleth us) to drink the blood of those whom they slew in fight' (290).
6. For the Victorian re-emergence of the *Book of Martyrs*, see Penny; Wolffe; Wickins.
7. Paul Murray helpfully directed me to Foxe as a potential source. Interestingly, Stoker called up the first volume of a 1684 edition of Foxe's text on 30 March 1867 while in Marsh's Library – though this volume does not contain the account of the historical Dracula. See McElligott 52–53.
8. Requested by Stoker, 6 July 1866.
9. Though, Lady Wilde also makes direct comparisons between the Irish and the Greeks, the Canadians, the Persians and the Egyptians.
10. In *Boys from County Hell* (dir. Chris Baugh; 2020), an enjoyable horror comedy set in the north of Ireland, the Abhartach legend is playfully explored, and the claim that Stoker once stayed in the area and drew on the legends when writing his vampire novel repeated.
11. Valente asserts that 'several critics' make the connection, but only references one, Lloyd, who (in an endnote) refers the reader to an article by Titley which links Dracula to 'nasty nicknames' for landlords, such as 'Ramsey na Drochfhola', though providing no evidence that this is where Stoker took the title. See Lloyd 119; Titley 136.
12. This critical attention came after some scholars, especially McCormack, 'Irish Gothic', and Foster, established that there existed a 'tradition' of

Irish Protestant Gothic writers (the most prominent being Charles Robert Maturin, Joseph Sheridan Le Fanu, Oscar Wilde, W. B. Yeats, and Stoker).
13. I use this controversial term with my tongue in cheek.
14. On the Stoker family's social position, see Murray 18–20.
15. Though the Manifesto of the V21 Collective of 2015, which called for a 'strategic presentism' in Victorian Studies, criticised historicist readings for not being political enough, for not bringing contemporary political concerns sufficiently into the analysis of Victorian texts. v21collective.org/manifesto-of-the-v21-collective-ten-theses/.
16. Pun intended.
17. It is important to stress that the nineteenth century witnessed a dramatic increase in neither intellectual nor sociological secularism. For an arresting reassessment of British religious history see Brown, who argues that secularisation did not become a major force until the 1960s.
18. The echoes of Matthew Arnold are deliberate.
19. As Auerbach has argued, 'Although we are now "all orphans", alone and free and dispossessed of our past, we yearn for origins, for cultural continuity' (416).
20. For this 'Satanic revival' see White. One of the bestselling novels of this period was Marie Corelli's *The Sorrows of Satan* (1895).
21. A reminder that, for many Protestant thinkers, Ultramontanist Catholicism was Satanic anyway. For versions of anti-Catholic Satanic panic, see Paz.
22. For critics who take religion in the novel seriously, see Beal; Montague-Étienne Rarignac; Bowles; Milbank, '*Dracula* and the *Via Media*'; Sage.
23. I would, however, qualify this claim somewhat. Many of the bestselling novels of the period are extremely interested in religion.
24. For Herbert's interesting discussion of these moments, see, 100–3.
25. My awareness of the importance of theodicy to the Victorians has been greatly enhanced by the work of my former doctoral student, Paula Keatley, who also helped guide me through the literature on the subject. See also, Shramm.
26. For Providentialism during the Famine, see Gray.
27. For examinations of the ways in which disease is represented in *Dracula*, see Willis; Forman; Mighall 108–24.
28. In other words, and *pace* McGarry, Dracula does not 'equal' cholera, but Draculean vampirism is 'like' cholera.

Works Cited

Anonymous. *A Full and impartial account of all the secret consults, negotiations, stratagems, and intriegues of the Romish party in Ireland, from 1660, to this present year 1689, for the settlement of popery in that kingdom.* London: Printed for Richard Chiswell, 1689.

Auerbach, Nina. 'Incarnations of the Orphan'. *English Literary History*, vol. 42, no. 3, 1975, pp. 395–419.

Beal, Timothy K. '"The Blood Is the Life"'. *Religion and Its Monsters*. Routledge, 2002, pp. 123–46.

Belford, Barbara. *Bram Stoker and the Man Who Was Dracula*. Da Capo Press, 1996.
Bowles, Noelle. 'Crucifix, Communion, and Convent: The Real Presence of Anglican Ritualism in Bram Stoker's *Dracula*'. *Christianity and Literature*, vol. 62, no. 2, 2013, pp. 243–58.
Brokaw, Kurt. *A Night in Transylvania: The Dracula Scrapbook*. Grosser and Dunlop, 1976.
Brown, Callum. *The Death of Christian Britain: Understanding Secularisation, 1800–2000*. Routledge, 2009.
Coundouriotis, Eleni. '*Dracula* and the Idea of Europe'. *Connotations*, vol. 9, no. 2, 1999/2000, pp. 144–59.
Craft, Christopher. '"Kiss Me With Those Red Lips": Gender and Inversion in Bram Stoker's *Dracula*'. *Representations*, vol. 8, 1984, pp. 107–33.
Curran, Bob. 'Was Dracula an Irishman?'. *History Ireland*, vol. 8, no. 2, 2000, pp. 12–15.
Dailey, E. T. 'To Choose One Easter from Three: Oswiu's Decision and the Northumbrian Synod of AD664'. *Peritia*, vol. 26, 2015, pp. 47–64.
Deane, Seamus. 'Landlord and Soil: *Dracula*'. *Strange Country: Modernity and Nationhood in Irish Writing Since 1790*. Clarendon, 1997, pp. 89–94.
Eagleton, Terry. *Heathcliff and the Great Hunger*. Verso, 1995.
Felski, Rita. 'After Suspicion'. *Profession*, vol. 8, 2009, pp. 28–35.
Floyd, David. *Street Urchins, Sociopaths and Degenerates: Orphans of Late-Victorian and Edwardian Fiction*. University of Wales Press, 2014.
Forman, Ross G. 'A Parasite for Sore Eyes: Rereading Infection Metaphors in Bram Stoker's *Dracula*'. *Victorian Literature and Culture*, vol. 44, no. 4, 2016, pp. 925–47.
Foster, R. F. 'Protestant Magic: W. B Yeats and the Spell of Irish History'. *Paddy and Mr. Punch: Connections in Irish and English History*. Penguin, 1995, pp. 212–232.
Foxe, John. *The Unabridged Acts and Monuments Online* or *TAMO* (1570 edition), Book 6, 903 (The Digital Humanities Institute, Sheffield, 2011). www.dhi.ac.uk/foxe. Accessed 9 April 2021.
Frayling, Christopher. 'Mr Stoker's Holiday'. *Bram Stoker: Centenary Essays*, edited by Jarlath Killeen, Dublin, Four Courts Press, 2013, pp.179–200.
Gilbert, Alan. *Religion and Society in Industrial England: Church, Chapel and Social Change, 1740–1914*. Longman, 1976.
Gray, Peter. *Famine, Land and Politics: British Government and Irish Society 1843–50*. Irish Academic Press, 1999.
Herbert, Christopher. 'Vampire Religion'. *Representations*, vol. 79, 2002, pp. 100–21.
Heylyn, Peter. *Cosmographie in foure Books Contayning the Chorographie & Historie of the whole World*. 6th Edition. London: Printed for T. Pabenger, B. Tooke, and T. Sawbridge, 1682.
Hilton, Boyd. *The Age of Atonement: The Influence of Evangelicalism on Social and Economic Thought, 1795–1865*. Clarendon Press, 1988.
Huebner, Anna. 'Who came first – Dracula or the Tourist? New Perspectives on Dracula Tourism at Bran Castle'. *European Journal of Tourism Research*, vol. 4, no. 1, 2011, pp. 55–65.
Hughes, William. *Bram Stoker's* Dracula. Continuum, 2009.

John, Juliet. 'Introduction: Literary Culture and the Victorians'. *The Oxford Handbook of Victorian Literary Culture*, edited by Juliet John, Oxford University Press, 2016, pp. 1–21.

Jones, Darryl. 'Dracula Goes to London'. *Ireland and Popular Culture*, edited by Sylvie Mikowski, Peter Lang, 2013, pp. 19–38.

Keatley, Paula. *'Some explanation of this hard, real life': the problem of evil in mid-Victorian literature and culture.* 2015. Trinity College Dublin. D.Phil. thesis.

Kucich, John. 'The Unfinished Historicist Project: In Praise of Suspicion'. *Victoriographies*, vol. 1, no. 1, 2011, pp. 58–78.

Larsen, Timothy. *Crisis of Doubt: Honest Faith in Nineteenth-Century England.* Oxford University Press, 2009.

Lloyd, David. *Anomalous States: Irish Writing and the Post-Colonial Moment.* Duke University Press, 1993.

Luckhurst, Roger. 'Introduction'. *The Cambridge Companion to Dracula*, edited by Roger Luckhurst, Cambridge University Press, 2018, pp. 1–8.

Manifesto of the V21 Collective of 2015. v21collective.org/manifesto-of-the-v21-collective-ten-theses/. Accessed 9 April 2021.

Marcus, Sharon and Stephen Best. 'Surface Reading: An Introduction'. *Representations*, vol. 1, no. 108, 2009, pp. 1–21.

Mason, Emma. 'Religion, the Bible, and Literature in the Victorian Age'. *The Oxford Handbook of Victorian Literary Culture*, edited by Juliet John, Oxford University Press, 2016, pp. 331–49.

McCormack, W. J. *Ascendancy and Tradition in Anglo-Irish Literary History from 1789 to 1939.* Clarendon, 1985.

———. 'Irish Gothic and After (1820–1945)'. *The Field Day Anthology of Irish Writing*, edited by Seamus Deane, vol. 2, Field Day, 1991, pp. 831–949.

———. *Dissolute Characters: Irish Literary History through Balzac, Sheridan Le Fanu, Yeats and Bowen.* Manchester University Press, 1993.

McElligott, Jason. *Bram Stoker and the Haunting of Marsh's Library.* Marsh's Library 2019.

McGarry, Marion. 'Cholera = Dracula', Bodies of Data: Intersecting Medical and Digital Humanities, Irish Humanities Alliance conference, 22–23 November 2018. soundcloud.com/ucd-digital-culture/marion-mcgarry-dracula-cholera?in=ucd-digital-culture/sets/bodies-of-data-intersecting-medical-and-digital-humanities. Accessed 9 April 2021.

McIntyre, Dennis. *Bram Stoker and the Irishness of Dracula.* The Shara Press, 2013.

Mighall, Robert. '"A Pestilence which walketh in darkness": Diagnosing the Victorian Vampire'. *Spectral Readings: Towards a Gothic Geography*, edited by Glennis Byron and David Punter, Macmillan, 1999, pp. 108–24.

Milbank, Alison. '*Dracula* and the *Via Media*: Bram Stoker's Ecumenical Ecclesiology'. *International Journal for the Study of the Christian Church*, vol. 12, nos. 3–4, 2012, pp. 293–308.

———. 'Powers Old and New: Stoker's Alliances with Anglo-Irish Gothic'. *Bram Stoker: History, Psychoanalysis and the Gothic*, edited by William Hughes and Andrew Smith, Macmillan, 1998, pp. 12–28.

Miller, Elizabeth. '*Coitus Interruptus*: Sex, Bram Stoker, and *Dracula*'. *Romanticism on the Net, The Gothic: From Ann Radcliffe to Anne Rice* 44 (2006). www.erudit.org/en/journals/ron/2006-n44-ron1433/014002ar/. Accessed 9 April 2021.

———. *Dracula: Sense and Nonsense*. Southend-on-Sea, Essex: Desert Island Books, 2006 edition.

Miller, J. Hillis. *The Disappearance of God: Five Nineteenth Century Writers*. Belknap Press, 1963.

Montague-Étienne Rarignac, Noel. *The Theology of Dracula: Reading the Book of Stoker as Sacred Text*. McFarland, 2012.

Morash, Chris. '"Ever under Some Unnatural Condition": Bram Stoker and the Colonial Fantastic'. *Literature and the Supernatural: Essays for the Maynooth Bicentenary*, edited by Brian Cosgrove, Columba, 1995, pp. 95–119.

Moses, Michael Valdez. 'The Irish Vampire: *Dracula*, Parnell, and the Troubled Dreams of Nationhood', *Journal x* vol. 2, no. 1, 1997, pp. 66–111.

Murray, Paul. *From the Shadow of Dracula: A Life of Bram Stoker*. Jonathan Cape, 2004.

O'Malley, Patrick. *Catholicism, Sexual Deviance, and Victorian Gothic Culture*. Cambridge University Press, 2006.

Paz, D. G. *Popular Anti-Catholicism in Mid-Victorian England*. Stanford University Press. 1992.

Penny, Andrew. 'John Foxe's Victorian Reception'. *The Historical Journal*, vol. 40, no. 1, 1997, pp. 111–42.

Peters, Laura. *Orphan Texts: Victorian Orphans, Culture and Empire*. Manchester University Press, 2000.

Pinkerton, Mark. 'Why Westenra?'. *Dracula: Celebrating 100 Years*, edited by Leslie Shepard and Albert Power. Mentor Press, 1997, pp. 12–16.

Reijnders, Stijn. 'Stalking the Count: Dracula, Fandom and Tourism'. *Annals of Tourism Research*, vol. 38, no. 1, 2011, pp. 231–48.

Sage, Victor. *Horror Fiction in the Protestant Tradition*. Macmillan, 1988.

Sheerin, Robin. 'Never mind Transylvania, Dracula was Irish', BBC News, 17 January 2020. www.bbc.com › uk-northern-ireland-51053870. Accessed 9 April 2021.

Shelley, Mary. *Frankenstein*, edited by Maurice Hindle. Penguin, 2003.

Shramm, Jan-Melissa. *Atonement and Self-Sacrifice in Nineteenth-Century Narrative*. Cambridge University Press, 2012.

Skal, David J. *Something in the Blood: The Untold Story of the Man Who Wrote Dracula*. Liveright, 2016.

Smart, Robert A. and Michael Hutchinson. '"Negative History" and Irish Gothic Literature: Persistence and Politics'. *Anglophonia: French Journal of English Studies*, vol. 15, 2004, pp. 105–18.

Stewart, Bruce. 'Bram Stoker's *Dracula*: Possessed by the Spirit of the Nation?' *Irish University Review*, vol. 29, no. 2, 1999, pp. 238–55.

Stoker, Bram. *Dracula*, edited by William Hughes and Diane Mason. Artsworks Books, 2007.

———. *Dracula: The Postcolonial Edition*, edited by Cristina Artenie and Dragos Moraru. Universitas Press, 2016.

———. *Personal Reminiscences of Henry Irving*. Heinemann, 1906, 2 vols.

———. *Bram Stoker's Notes for Dracula: A Facsimile Edition*, annotated and transcribed by Robert Eighteen-Bisang and Elizabeth Miller. McFarland and Co., 2008.

Stoker, Charlotte. 'Charlotte Stoker's Account of "The Cholera Horror" in a Letter to Bram Stoker (c.1875), Appendix II, Bram Stoker, *Dracula*, edited by Maurice Hindle, preface by Christopher Frayling. Penguin, 2003, pp. 412–3.

Titley, Alan. 'The City of Words'. *Dublin and Dubliners*, edited by James Kelly and Uáitéar MacGearailt, Grehan Print Limited, 1990, pp. 52–72.

Todorov, Tzvetan. *The Fantastic: A Structural Approach to a Literary Genre*. Translated by Richard Howard, Cornell University Press, 1975.

Valente, Joseph. *Dracula's Crypt: Bram Stoker, Irishness, and the Question of Blood*. University of Illinois Press, 2002.

Vargish, Thomas. *The Providential Aesthetic in Victorian Fiction*. University Press of Virginia, 1985.

White, Lizzie. 'Representations of the Devil in *Fin-de-Siécle* Literature'. *Literature Compass*, vols. 5/6, 2008, pp. 1170–78.

Wickins, Peter. *Victorian Protestantism and Bloody Mary: The Legacy of Religious Persecution in Tudor England*. Arena Books, 2012.

Wilde, Lady. *Ancient Legends, Mystic Charms and Superstitions of Ireland*. Ward and Downey, 1888.

Wilkinson, William. *An Account of the Principalities of Wallachia and Moldavia*. Longmans, 1820.

Willis, Martin. '"The Invisible Giant". *Dracula*, and Disease', *Studies in the Novel*, vol. 39, no. 3, 2007, pp. 301–35.

Wolffe, John. *The Protestant Crusade in Great Britain 1829–1860*. Clarendon Press, 1991.

Chapter 10

Irish Catholic Writers and the Gothic: Situating Thomas Furlong's *The Doom of Derenzie* (1829)
Sinéad Sturgeon

On Tuesday, 6 March 1827, during a lengthy and fractious Commons' debate, Sir John Singleton Copley (the Master of the Rolls), vociferously opposed Sir Francis Burdett's motion for Catholic relief. During his long speech – Copley had to take several breaks 'from the effect of exhaustion' – he complained that the Catholics of Ireland, under 'the most marvellous and extraordinary' sway of the incendiary (as he clearly viewed it) Catholic Association, were demanding equality before the law as though they were entitled to it:

> Those who came forward to seek the boon did not condescend to ask it as a favour; they demanded it as a right. To use the figurative language of one of their orators, 'Ireland, gigantic Suppliant, thunders at the gates of the Constitution'.[1]

Copley's rhetoric regarding Ireland and Irish Catholics carries a distinctly supernatural charge – 'marvelous', 'extraordinary', and 'gigantic' – which echoes the Gothic overtones of his earlier warning that a revivified Spanish Inquisition, 'that hated engine of misery and tortures, that instrument of cruelty and revenge, was again established in all its original power and deformity in Spain and in Italy' (HC Deb, col. 917). Copley's discourse draws on longstanding English perceptions of Ireland as an Othered place of strangeness and irredeemable difference, an intrinsic part of which was its stubborn adherence to the Catholic Church; Ireland had for centuries been suspiciously viewed from Westminster as a conspirator with Catholic Europe in a pincer-plot to bring down British Protestant liberty. Two years before Burdett's motion, a Parliamentary Select Committee on the state of Ireland had focused particularly on Catholicism, and the practice of confession, which appeared to many as the furtive facilitator and fomentor of rebellion. As Willa Murphy remarks, the subsequent report 'tells us more about certain Protestant Gothic fantasies about Catholic ritual than the actual Irish practice of confession' (80). Copley's 1827 speech plays on these enduring prejudices: should they be admitted, he implies, the Catholic-Irish barbarians at the gate would, much like the Gothic tribes that sought sanctuary in Roman territory in the fourth century, destroy the empire from within. 'Faith, to tell you the truth, Paddy's origin is real Gothic', a writer for the pro-emancipation journal *The Dublin and London Magazine* joked in 1826, in a burlesque parody of the supposedly 'martial blood' and 'pugnacity' of the Irish. What was an absurd caricature to one side was to the other a credible and urgent threat of atavistic collapse; according to at least one contemporary source, Copley's speech against Catholic relief was rewarded the following year with elevation to the peerage as Baron Lyndhurst of Lyndhurst.[2] This uncertainty of identity – are Irish Catholics unjustly disenfranchised or a monstrous threat to law and order? Are Irish Protestants oppressors or oppressed? – manifests itself in 1820s Irish writing in an obsessive turn to states of existential and historical crisis, often with strongly Gothic inflections.

A substantial amount of this literature was produced by Irish Catholic writers, and it has not, until quite recently, been considered within the remit of the Gothic literary tradition as it was developing in the nineteenth century.[3] There is reason for this; these writers did not produce Gothic texts in the conventional scholarly sense of the genre. Questions of terminology and taxonomy, widely discussed in Gothic studies generally, have generated much debate in the Irish context. In contradistinction to the critical orthodoxy of Irish Gothic as a Protestant tradition, first established (rather hesitantly) by W. J. McCormack in 1991, Seamus Deane first proposed, on the basis of James Clarence Mangan's *Autobiography*, the existence of 'a new genre – what we may call Catholic, or Catholic-Nationalist Gothic' (Deane 126). Richard Haslam has since pointed out that Mangan's '*Autobiography* does not "introduce" something "new" so much as alert us to something that was already there, but overlooked: the presence of characteristically Gothic motifs and devices in the fiction of earlier nineteenth-century Irish Catholic writers' (Haslam 2006, 218). From the 1820s, Irish Catholic writers began in numbers to draw on the Gothic across a diverse range of genres: regional and historical novels of a purportedly realist and often ethnographical flavour, as well as autobiography, poetry, translation, short stories and supernatural fiction. While the Gothic novel in its purist sense – in its bones a Protestant form and fiercely anti-Catholic – presented obvious obstacles to often devoutly religious Irish Catholic writers, nevertheless, key inflections of the genre proved irresistibly appealing: dramatic landscapes; Byronic male antiheros; taboo sexual relationships; Faustian pacts; the return of the unburiable past to disturb and torment the present. In the course of the ongoing critical revaluation of what 'Irish Gothic' denotes, a small cohort of Catholic writers has emerged who can be classed as Gothic (or Gothic-adjacent): Thomas Moore, William Carleton (who converted to Protestantism in the early 1820s), John Banim and his younger brother Michael, James Clarence Mangan, and Gerald Griffin. All made significant use of Gothic motifs, to varying extents and for differing purposes: from the avowedly realistic representation of Irish life to the more idiosyncratic reaches of romantic imagination.[4]

It is within this context that the work of another, largely overlooked Catholic writer, Thomas Furlong (1794–1827), and his posthumously published long poem, *The Doom of Derenzie* (1829), offers an opportunity to continue the closely argued critical reappraisal of Irish Gothic that has now been underway for more than two decades. Furlong's complex text exemplifies the disparate and innovative ways Irish Catholic writers engaged with the Gothic in the 1820s, both adapting existing modalities of the genre and resituating elements of Irish folklore and superstition in a distinctively Gothic mode. While there seems now to be something of a critical consensus in the need to revise and expand our understanding of what Irish Gothic writing might look like, it remains important to emphasise the kind of oblique and refracted nature of the Gothic that this critical recuperation tends to uncover; if W. J. McCormack was loath to describe Protestant Irish Gothic as a tradition, Irish Catholic Gothic is yet more discontinuous and fugitive. Nor is this to imply that we are dealing with separate traditions, but rather a living stream of cross-cultural exchange and inter-influence that was developing in lockstep with the formidably difficult historical conditions of the Irish nineteenth century. Taken together, moreover, a more stable and durable trajectory of influence emerges. As Morin observes, the perceived gap in the lineage of Irish Gothic between the publication of *Melmoth the Wanderer* (1820) and *Uncle Silas* (1864) is in fact illusory when the work of writers such as the Banims, Furlong, Carleton, Griffin, and Mangan are taken into account: post-1820, 'the Gothic remains a central point of return for Irish writers as they negotiate, among other things, national politics, class relations and the effects of migration, emigration, famine and persistent social upheaval' (367). Catholic Irish Gothic is just one aspect of an Irish Gothic increasingly understood as extending beyond questions of political and colonial history to encompass issues of gender, famine, the environment, and produced in forms beyond the novel (poetry, drama, autobiography and short fiction). It is also instructive to bear in mind the larger trends of the Gothic. In and around the 1820s, it is generally agreed, the Gothic tradition changed.

From a distinctive type of fiction that deployed horrid plots in stylised historical settings in order to terrify and delight its readers, it migrated so widely across cultural forms as to become ubiquitous. Scholars have frequently discussed the Gothic's development from its inaugural 'classic' period (generally dated from around 1764–1820, or, to put it another way, from Horace Walpole's *The Castle of Otranto* to Charles Robert Maturin's *Melmoth the Wanderer*), to its subsequent, diasporic diffusion in British and Irish writing. Post-*Melmoth*, Jarlath Killeen remarks, the Gothic 'fragmented and took up ghostly habitations elsewhere, indeed everywhere, in nineteenth-century culture' (*Gothic Literature* 3). The ways in which Irish Catholic writers are using the Gothic in the 1820s – fusing modalities of the genre with regional and historical fiction of a purportedly more realist style – is part of a much wider transformative trend of dispersal and fragmentation.

Still, it is worth noting the historical conditions of Ireland in the 1820s. The generation of Catholic writers then coming of age emerged from a small and fragile middle class that had been fostered by the Catholic Relief Acts of the late eighteenth century, and were among the earliest to exercise a native command of the English language. They were, almost to a man (Carleton being the notorious exception), committed advocates of the contentious campaign for Catholic emancipation; Furlong was the most active in this respect. In general, these writers were concerned less with the doings of the big house than they were with the life of the Irish cabin, precariously set in a rural landscape marked by extreme, one might even say indescribable, levels of violence, poverty and suffering. Not yet wholly recovered from the catastrophic risings of 1798 and 1803, Ireland was undergoing a prolonged and serious period of agrarian unrest in the Rockite disturbances of 1821–1824. Tadgh O'Sullivan remarks that 'this rural insurrection was the most serious outbreak of violence since the summer of 1798, and was represented in those terms by many contemporary commentators' (74). During the first quarter of the nineteenth century, Ireland was frequently under martial law, the 'state of exception' that Giorgio Agamben has analysed as the means to a totalitarian state: 'a legal civil war that allows for the physical elimination not only of political adversaries but of entire categories of citizens who for some reason cannot be integrated into the political system' (2). Between the 'outrages' of agrarian secret societies and the recriminatory (and often calculatedly prohibitive) cruelties inflicted by a punitive state, Ireland was afflicted by an excess of horror. If the English public perceived in this unrest only a barbaric and historically characteristic lawlessness, Irish Catholic writers were more attuned to the contextual complexities of the often shocking violence of rural agrarian factions, which they frequently depicted in their fiction alongside the rich folklore and tradition of the Gaelic world that they were attempting to bring into literary being. As is often observed, however, representing the everyday realities of Irish life in the available literary forms of the day was a challenging if not impossible task. 'From 1798 to 1848 the terrain of Irish fiction – and of Irish autobiography – is littered with corpses', writes Siobhán Kilfeather, 'intact and dismembered, before interment and disinterred, sometimes piled so deep one can hardly scramble over them to discover plot or understand characters' ('Ireland and Europe' 39).

Irish Catholic writers did experiment with the Gothic proper, notably in the more forgiving environs of romantic poetry: for H. P. Lovecraft, it is the wildly popular Gothic balladry of Gottfried August Bürger (*Lenore*, 1774, and *The Wild Huntsman,* 1786) 'which echoes so shiveringly' in Moore's little-read poem 'The Ring' (1801) (26). And amongst Mangan's juvenilia is a slight but evocative puzzle poem, published in *Grant's Almanack* of 1822, which features a Celtic-hued vampire. More commonly, however, aspects of the Gothic crept into Irish Catholic writers' historical and regional fiction, and in two especially marked areas of representation: the agrarian secret societies, and the superstitions and folklore of the peasantry. The midnight meetings, horrific violence, and intrinsic subversiveness of the agrarian factions lent themselves to strongly Gothic overtones, as in Moore's *Memoirs of Captain Rock* (1824); the Banims' 'Crohoore of the Bill Hook' and 'John Doe' (*Tales of the O'Hara Family*, 1825); and William Carleton's 'Confessions of a Reformed Ribbonman' (1830), better known by its later title, 'Wildgoose Lodge'. Irish superstitions and folklore similarly proved a rich seam for Gothic effect: John Banim's 'The Fetches' (1825) and 'The Ace of Clubs' (1838); William Carleton's 'The Lianhan Shee' (1830); Gerald Griffin's *Holland-Tide* (1827) and 'The Barber of Bantry' (1838).[5] James Clarence Mangan is a notable exception to these two arterial routes of Irish Catholic Gothic writing, even as he is also a founding figure of singular import in any discussion of Irish Catholic Gothic. Ardently attached to the archetype of the romantic transgressor, devoted disciple of Maturin, Byron and Goethe – Mangan, it is fair to say, did not so much practice as inhabit a Gothic aesthetic. With his cape and pointy hat, wig and eccentric glasses, Mangan comes down to us through literary history in Gothic shades. He was also devoutly Catholic; Mangan's faith becomes pressingly relevant, in an unusually direct and even doctrinal way, to some of his more sustained forays into the genre. While much of his poetry is replete with Gothic imagery and themes (moonlit ruins, spectral revenants, a bloody and unsettled past), elsewhere a more combative and subversive engagement with the genre emerges. In his prose pieces 'The

Man in the Cloak' (1838) and 'Chapters on Ghostcraft' (1842), Mangan mounts an adroit defence of Catholic doctrine and dignity via Gothic parody and satire; an attack on the anti-Catholicism integral to the genre that was also a biting of the thumb at the Protestant gate-keepers of nineteenth-century Irish politics and culture.[6]

In keeping with these contemporaries, Furlong draws on both the violence of Irish subaltern secret societies and the superstitions and traditions of popular culture for his long Gothic poem, *The Doom of Derenzie*. As both writer and poem have been largely forgotten, some contextualization may be helpful here in framing the analysis to follow. While Furlong's talent was praised by such leading literary lights as Moore, Maturin, Sydney Owenson, and Sir Walter Scott, he was quickly forgotten after his early death in July 1827 at the age of 33. 'I would not wish from life to go / 'Midst nameless ghosts enlisted', begins 'The Last Wish' (1826), one of Furlong's final poems, but posterity has not been kind (Mythen 246). Furlong's oeuvre consists of three long poems (*The Misanthrope*, 1819; *The Plagues of Ireland: An Epistle*, 1824; *The Doom of Derenzie*, 1829); numerous poetical and satirical poetical and prose pieces, often in strong support of Catholic Emancipation, published in a variety of journals (including the *Monthly Magazine*, *Morning Register*, *London and Dublin Magazine*); and numerous translations from Turlough Carolan, included in James Hardiman's collection *Irish Minstrelsy* (1831).[7] Furlong's life and career evidences that while Irish history is fraught with sectarian strife, inter-denominational relations 'on the ground' were far from clear cut. The son of a County Wexford Catholic farmer and carman, Furlong was educated at a hedge school and apprenticed to a Dublin grocer in 1809. His early publications secured him the patronage of the Protestant John Jameson, the well-known distiller, who was grief-stricken at the poet's early death. Furlong seems to have been a popular figure: Whitty's preface to *The Doom of Derenzie* notes that Furlong's funeral was followed by 'Above one hundred mourning coaches', and funds were raised for a handsome headstone, on which was memorialised his 'Superior Poetical Genius' (vii–viii).[8] Eulogies were published by his friend and fellow Wexford man Whitty (in *The Literary Gazette*) and Hardiman, the dedicatee of *The Doom of Derenzie*, wrote a 'Memoir of Thomas Furlong' for *Irish Minstrelsy*. Thereafter, Furlong fell quickly into obscurity; not until the end of the twentieth century did sustained critical interest revive. Sean Mythen's volume, *Thomas Furlong: The Forgotten Wexford Poet* (1998), rescues Furlong from 'the throng / Who rot, no tidings giving' (to return to 'The Last Wish'); this comprehensive and meticulous study valuably clarifies the poet's biography and career, and collects the poet's many occasional poems alongside *The Misanthrope*, *The Plagues of Ireland* and *The Doom of Derenzie*.

Furlong did not live to see his most ambitious work into print: 'one sheet only', the Preface informs us, 'had the advantage of the author's corrections: it had scarcely passed through his hands when the grave prematurely closed upon him' (vii). Like Griffin's *The Collegians* (and published the same year), *The Doom of Derenzie* attempts to capture in its 117 pages Irish society *in toto*, embedding the story in a richly textured world registered variously in romantic, naturalist, ethnographical, psychological and melodramatic tones. The predominant mood of the text is Gothic. The narrative, again like *The Collegians*, concerns a young Irish woman of lower social class murdered by her lover, a member of the local gentry; both writers seem to have had in mind the 1819 murder of County Limerick-born Ellie Hanley, nicknamed 'the Colleen Bawn' (an anglicisation of the Irish *Cailín Bán*, meaning literally 'white girl'; 'white' connoting innocence and beauty). Formally, the text is composite and changeable, shifting from full, regular rhyme schemes in couplets or quatrains, to passages of what Gregory A. Schirmer has described as 'remarkably supple blank verse [...] shot through with Gothic effects' (88). While Furlong does not quite manage to pull off his challenging aesthetic aims in narrative, plot, and technical form, the poem still makes for an absorbing read, due in large part to the powerfully wrought character of Wrue. There are also rich evocations of the County Wexford landscape as well as, perhaps less predictably, striking passages on the 'dark wild waste of blood' of the Napoleonic Wars in France, Flanders, and Germany (42). As is so often the case with Irish writing of this period, *The Doom of Derenzie* is all the more fascinating for its formal 'failures', which throw light on a society existing so long in crisis that its realities are more recognisable when couched in the supposedly far-fetched terms of romance or Gothic (shocking violence, horrifying images, corpses, dismembered bodies, skeletons), than the tempered urbanity of literary realism.

The Doom of Derenzie is concerned with two crimes, both committed many years earlier. The first is well-known to the community at large and echoes the infamous burning in 1816 of Wildgoose Lodge that also inspired Carleton: the murder-by-arson of an English farmer and his family by the Whiteboys, described in retrospect as Wrue walks the site of the atrocity.[9]

> Fearful and gloomy was the night when near
> That quiet cottage came the heartless crew;
> When their wild cry burst on the victim's ear,

That cry which many a startled sufferer knew;
When the thick death-shot swept the dwelling through,
And, o'er the roof, sprung wide the wasting flame;
And foes, all arm'd, to close each passage, flew. (33)

The second crime in *The Doom of Derenzie* is the murder of Wrue's beloved niece, Margaret, though this is a secret history for years known solely to Wrue (through his occult powers, he claims), and is publicly revealed only on the final page of the text. The two crimes – the one political and horrifyingly dispassionate, the other personal and terrifyingly intimate – are gruesomely inscribed onto the rural landscape. Wrue walks past the remains of Wilson's cottage, 'a dark heap of walls, all burn'd and bare, / A mournful wreck – the remnant of a cot' (32), and he later uncovers the skeletal remains of Margaret: a skull, scattered bones, 'the poor worn remnant of an arm' (116). These Gothic remnants are insistently linked in the text, not only via the figure of Wrue but also the younger Derenzie, who has, we are told, spent much time 'Where, yet half-warm, around him spread / The reeking remnants of the dead' (47). The Gothic morselisation of bodies is a recurrent feature of nineteenth-century Irish Gothic, as Kilfeather observes ('The Gothic Novel' 88); in Furlong's text it also embodies a psychological atomisation that contrasts with an underlying quest for a proof of universal spiritual harmony, a catholic code by which horrific and seemingly unjust events may be ciphered. Derenzie is guilty of seducing and murdering Margaret, but he is arrested and hung for the fatal arson attack on Wilson's home, a crime of which he is innocent. Furlong seems to have intended this plot twist as a proof of providential design – 'Awful and wondrous are thy ways, O Lord, [...] thy all-righteous hand / Hath struck me in its justice', the older Derenzie exclaims in the final lines of the text (117) – but the effect is closer to something much more darkly anarchic, 'chaotic', as Bruce Stewart has described the work in its entirety.[10] The revelation of Derenzie's murderous past comes too late to denude of their harrowing import the scenes of his execution for a crime he did not commit, the 'laying out' of his corpse, and the grief of a father over his 'murder'd child' (105); the reader is left in the uncomfortable and disorienting position of sympathising with a man who murdered his young and pregnant lover. The conclusion of the text seems to bring about confusion rather than resolution, provoking more questions than it answers. Did Wrue falsely inform on Derenzie to bring about his execution? Is the authority of the colonial state fatally undermined by its execution of a man for a crime of which he is innocent, or is it ultimately upheld and even validated as the instrument of divine will? Most problematic of all: how could the younger Derenzie, presented in Part Second as a compassionate and principled witness of the carnage of the Napoleonic Wars, also murder Margaret?

What appears to be an insurmountable flaw in characterisation is on closer inspection only the most visceral example of a pattern integral to the structure and obsessive preoccupation of the text: a prevalent uncertainty of identity, frequently overlaid with supernatural and Gothic charge. Echoing the doubled discourse relating to Irish identities in the run-up to emancipation, the young Derenzie and Wrue at different times take on different roles: they are both hero and villain, victim and victimiser, protagonist and antagonist. This ambiguity of identity extends to the formal structuring of the plot: the supposedly leading role of Derenzie is wholly eclipsed by the character of Wrue, the principal focus for the text's Gothic energies.[11] In creating Wrue, Furlong draws on both local folklore as well as the literary Gothic tradition. In his childhood Furlong had become acquainted with a local 'fairy-man' (a figure credited with mystical powers of healing and prophecy), who formed the basis for the character.[12] Wrue also clearly bears the influence of Maturin and his iconic creation, Melmoth. Maturin was a close friend of Furlong's and advised on early drafts of the poem (see Preface, x) which begins with a darkly evocative quotation from the older writer's successful play *Bertram; or, the Castle of Aldobrand* (1816): 'Of some shadowy thing / Crossing the traveller on his path of fear'. Wrue is repeatedly described as a 'wizard', a 'mysterious wanderer' with dark mantle and hazel staff, who is believed to possess supernatural powers and a connection to the Celtic Otherworld. The closing lines of Part First are suggestive also of a nuanced historical positioning:

> And such was he, who, at this dim hour,
> Went forth by Ferns's tottering tower;
> Such was the strange one, who stalk'd on
> Beneath its black and broken wall,
> Like some grim guest of the times long gone,
> Who came to wait, and weep its fall;
> Or, as one of the old baronial train,
> Whom the yawning earth had upwards cast,
> As if to yield to the world again,
> One gloomy image of the past. (28)

Wrue is aligned here with a pre-conquest, native Irish gentry (Ferns Cathedral was founded by Diarmait Mac Murchada in the twelfth century), as opposed to the much later Anglo-Irish landed class emblematised by the Derenzies; Furlong named the titular family after the local gentry family who in the early 1820s were completing the construction of their family seat, Clobemon Hall, an imposing Georgian manor that still stands on the banks of the Slaney.[13] In the passage cited above Wrue appears as a revenant, a literal embodiment of how history stalks the present, with all the predatory quality that this verb implies; Wrue both mourns the wrongs of the deep historical past (fulfilling the phonetic double of his name, *rue*), and awaits his opportunity to avenge it. This gloomy, history-infused tenor might lead one to expect Wrue to be the supernatural villain of the piece and Derenzie his long-suffering victim, with a predictable overlaying of respective national allegiances, but the story's outcome precisely reverses such expectation: Wrue is closer to the figure of the outcast Byronic hero, while Derenzie's son is the villain who has seduced and murdered Margaret. Yet as the narrative progresses it works to undercut the differences between Wrue and the older Derenzie. Both are bereft by the loss of beloved children, and as Wrue becomes the arbitrator of justice (usually the prerogative of the landlord), so too does Derenzie take on the qualities of the wizard. By Part Third, the prosperous and pragmatic landowner Derenzie has become a kind of double of Wrue. He takes 'lonely walks' and holds apparently supernatural communication 'With visitants whose voice no vulgar ear / Distinguish'd, and whose shape no common eye / Did ever rest upon' (73). Like Wrue, and indeed some of Sheridan Le Fanu's most memorable protagonists (such as the Rev Mr Jennings in 'Green Tea'), the older Derenzie has had his eyes opened to a deeply discomfiting spiritual vision.

> His breath was still – his wither'd lips lay open,
> And every vein, that rang'd his aged forehead,
> Stood crowded and collected. So he sat,
> Mute, motionless, and wild, as tho' high Heaven
> Had, in that moment, from his sight withdrawn
> Some earthborn film, and to his glance disclos'd
> All the dread secrets of the unseen world. (73–4)

If the character of Wrue bears the hallmark of Melmoth, so, too, does the younger Derenzie, who is repeatedly described as 'the wanderer', having travelled Europe and especially the battlefields of the Napoleonic Wars, spending much time, as noted above, among 'the reeking remnants of the dead' (47). Standing upon the 'mangled victims of the day' provokes Derenzie, much like Melmoth, to offer some acidic commentary on European realpolitik:

> Their little all of life they gave;
> They claim'd – but got not yet a grave:

> In the damp dews of even they slept
> Unnam'd – unheeded – and unwept –
> Even by that weak and worthless one
> For whom they battled, and bled and died.
> Their worth was o'er, they hour gone by,
> Their place – fresh ideots [sic] would supply. (48)[14]

The dream-vision of Agnes concerning her beloved's final doom also bears striking similarity to the fate of Melmoth, as recounted in the 'Wanderer's Dream'. In a pacy, compelling passage, Agnes recounts how Margaret drags the young Derenzie to his doom.

> She wrung, she forc'd, nay, tore away
> This hand that would have held thee fast;
> I struggled, sunk, and there I lay,
> Quite reckless of what pass'd.
> And yet, methought, I saw thee led,
> O'er the black cliffs uneven head;
> Methought, she hurried thee along,
> With death-like grasp, confirm'd and strong;
> And wanting time for penance given,
> And wanting thought to look on Heaven;
> Down from the dark and rugged height,
> Swift as the swiftest flash of light,
> She bore thee, screaming, from my sight –
> This was my dream of yesternight. (85)

The principal female characters, Margaret and Agnes, are also shaped and linked by this motif of shifting, doubled identities. Indeed, at the narrative's close, they appear less as individuated characters than alternating aspects of the archetypal victimised Gothic heroine. Margaret's role is doubled: in Part First she is an 'angel', 'bright, beautiful, and innocent' (12); in Part Third, she is a vengeful spectre, appearing in 'lurid light ... as threatening evil' (77–78) and possessing 'The cold wan colouring of the tomb, / The earthy paleness of the dead' (84). She is symbolically and structurally linked to Agnes via the legend of how Wrue gained his occult powers: drinking the milk of a lamb impregnated by a mystical snowy ram. While Agnes's name is derived from the Latin *agnus*, meaning lamb, the legend also parallels the seduction and abandonment of Margaret, as Brian Earls has argued (116).[15] Both women are destroyed by the younger Derenzie, transformed, in another echo of the Colleen Bawn, into literal 'white girls'. Agnes, by the end of the story, has the same 'pallid' (Furlong 103) complexion as the spectral Margaret (a name which itself denotes 'pearl'), having gone insane following Derenzie's execution. Furlong's dual aspects of the Gothic heroine – one seduced, impregnated and murdered, the other psychologically tormented into madness – constitute a female Gothic layered with shades of Irish language, folklore and history. Moreover, in a text preoccupied with the integrity of bodies, both physical and psychological, the incidence of Margaret's pregnancy is especially intriguing. 'Although all Gothic women are threatened, no woman is in greater peril in the world of the Gothic than is the mother', argues Ruth Bienstock Anolik (25), and it is presumably the 'fearful secret' of Margaret's pregnancy, which her 'alter'd shape' (Furlong 13) can no longer conceal, that brings about her murder at the hands of her lover. While Margaret's pregnancy signifies the breaking of class and religious taboos – although sexual relationships between the landed gentry and the peasantry were common enough, particularly in the history of the De Renzy family (Mythen 31) – it also represents a literal splitting of the self that, in a text obsessed with existential instability, simply cannot be borne. The murder of the pregnant Margaret can consequently be read as an example of abjection, made clear by Wrue's horrified reaction to unearthing her 'loathsome' skull (Furlong 115). In its violent contrast to the cross-cultural love-match central to the national tale pioneered by Sydney Owenson and Maria Edgeworth, Margaret's decomposed and dismembered pregnant body constitutes a dark Gothicisation of the national romance plot, and an unremittingly bleak commentary on the political project of Union instituted nearly thirty years earlier. The spectral Margaret, pregnant at the time of her murder, is both a doubled and double haunting, signifying not only the colonial sins of the past, but also the aborted future of post-Union Ireland.

Closely allied to the theme of uncertainty and doubling of identities is the paradoxical treatment of the supernatural; at different times, the text both rejects the possibility of the supernatural, and endorses the genuine power of the occult. In Part First, Wrue's mysterious powers are presented as deceitful and duplicitous, successful in large part because they are exercised on a 'credulous race' (7):

> And still, to dupe the undiscerning crowd,
> That round his path in trembling reverence bow'd
> To catch conceit, or lull credulity,
> Full many a smooth and specious turn had he –
> In truth he knew, or seemed to know, a part
> Of every strange and every occult art – (15)

Furlong seems to play here to popular stereotypes of the Irish as a superstitious and backward race, yet the traditionally inspired legend of how

Wrue gained his powers is recounted straight-faced and endowed with psychological depth. Earls argues that Furlong's 'elaborate notation' of Wrue's state of mind during this episode 'represents a new privileging of the subjective and a corresponding break with the epic pattern. What results might almost be seen as an interiorisation of the legend genre' (116). The narrative ultimately bears out as valid Wrue's claims to prophetic and preternatural gifts: this is evidenced most obviously in the 'superhuman impulse' that leads him to discover Margaret's grave, a site that combines the secret Gothic history of her murder with the underground fairy forts of Irish folklore.

> And I did fancy, that upon the spot
> Thus lonely and weed-cover'd, some strange hand
> Of mystic might detain'd me; and it seem'd
> As tho that earth, o'er which I went in stillness,
> Was fram'd of fairy echoes, for it rung
> All hollowly beneath me.
>   Low I knelt
> Upon the spell-mark'd place, and tore away,
> Half-heedlessly, the black and noxious growth
> That spread there in luxuriance. (114–15)

In the end, the supernatural is not explained away in *The Doom of Derenzie*, and superstitious belief is shared by both upper-class, educated Irish Protestants (both Derenzies, and the 'curate's daughter' Agnes Vere), as well as lower-class Irish Catholics. The cumulative effect of this theme of abiding ambiguity – concerning knowledge of oneself as well as what one believes – is to leave the reader in a state of profound epistemological uncertainty, a kind of existential crisis deeply related to the transitional, turbulent state of Ireland in the 1820s.

The Doom of Derenzie offers an unusual perspective on a central image and structure of Irish Gothic: the big house in its terminal and self-induced dissolution. We see little of the big house itself, however; the narrative is located firmly outside the walls of the demesne, amidst the rural landscape of County Wexford and the daily life and popular culture of its people. Despite Furlong's occasional moments of overcompensation for his Catholic and nationalist background – such as the swipe at Rosary beads which measure prayer 'not by the kind, but the quantity' (101) – the text is damning in its linking of Anglo-Irish decline to its callous, casual exploitation of a vulnerable tenantry. Furlong did not live to see the Emancipation he had worked so assiduously toward; *The Doom of Derenzie*, though published in the same year that Parliament finally passed the Catholic Relief Act, offers little in the way of optimism that the competing claims of Irish Catholic nationhood and British citizenship could be reconciled. The narrative ends in chaotic confusion and grief, rather than hopeful reconciliation. In a portentous exchange, Wrue gives Derenzie 'the ominous weapon' used to murder Margaret:

> To thee and thine, old man, I do bequeath
> The blood-mark'd legacy – that blade shall be
> Unto thy kindred, thro' the years to come,
> As a recover'd trophy. (117)

Even by 1824 – when the writing of *The Doom of Derenzie* was already completed – Furlong was clearly anticipating a more wholesale constitutional and indeed violent revolt. The first two decades of the nineteenth century 'has revealed to them [the Irish people] the dangerous secret of their strength', he writes in his biting poetical satire *The Plagues of Ireland* (1824), in many ways a kind of political companion-piece to *The Doom of Derenzie*: 'If those who govern still betray their trust, / And will not act – a tortur'd people must' (Mythen 81). For Furlong, as for other Irish Catholic writers of the period, the Gothic was an indispensable and increasingly inevitable means to explore the intimate interworkings of political and psychological precarity, making visible the complex predicament of Catholic Ireland and the yet more difficult, delicate work of bringing gigantic Ireland into (or out of?) the unwilling arms of the British Constitution.

Notes

1. 'That this House is deeply impressed with the necessity of taking into immediate consideration the Laws imposing Civil Disabilities on His Majesty's Roman Catholic Subjects, with a view to their relief' (HC Deb 6 March 1827, col. 920, 916, 918). I have been unable to trace Copley's quotation from one of the Catholic Association's 'orators'.
2. In the anti-emancipation tract, *A solemn appeal to the common sense of England, against the principles of Mr Canning. By a lay Protestant* (London 1827), the writer claims that 'It is well known that he [Copley] is indebted for his elevation partly to his late admirable speech in opposition to the Catholic Claims' (60).
3. I focus here on English-language texts, but it should be noted that elements and forms of the Gothic are also frequently to be found in Irish-language texts, by writers such as Eibhlín Dhubh Ní Choinaill, Seán Ó Coileán, and Aomhlaith Ó Súileabháin. See Kilfeather, 'The Gothic Novel'.
4. While the period under view here is the 1820s, it should be noted that this list can be expanded well beyond this delimited timeframe and has escalated exponentially since the political and socioeconomic upheavals

of the twentieth and twenty-first centuries: Jarlath Killeen writes that 'the Gothic permeates much of the long and short fiction of post-independence Catholic writers' ('Irish Gothic Fiction', 59). A critical figure in this transition is the long-neglected Dorothy Macardle (1889–1958), particularly the supernatural stories of *Earth-Bound* (1924) and her reworking of the Big House Gothic novel, *The Uninvited* (1942), which mounts a fierce feminist challenge to the suffocating consequences of Catholic Mariology beneath the cloak of its male (and distinctly masculinist) narrator.

5. For more on how these Irish Catholic writers use the Gothic, see: Haslam, 'Maturin's Catholic Heirs'; Kilfeather, 'The Gothic Novel'; Killeen, 'Irish Gothic Fiction'; and Morin, 'The Gothic in Nineteenth-Century Ireland'.
6. In 'The Man in the Cloak' Mangan reverses the anti-Catholic fervour of Maturin's *Melmoth the Wanderer*; in his influential analysis, Haslam describes the story as a 'Gothic Trojan horse' in the conservative and anti-Catholic pages of the *Dublin University Magazine*. Andrew Cusack makes a similar case for 'Chapters on Ghostcraft'; see 'Intercultural Transfer in the *Dublin University Magazine*', p. 96.
7. Furlong's posthumous reputation was not helped by Samuel Ferguson's notorious review of *Irish Minstrelsy* (published in the *Dublin University Magazine*, 1834) which singled out Furlong's translations for especially marked excoriation. Mythen robustly defends Furlong who, as a prominent member of the Catholic Association particularly attracted Ferguson's wrath in the context of a contemporary culture war 'for the ownership of the Celtic past' (Mythen 38).
8. All quotations from *The Doom of Derenzie*, including Whitty's Preface, refer to the 1829 edition.
9. *The Doom of Derenzie* was published a year before the Carleton story now best known as 'Wildgoose Lodge' first appeared: 'Confessions of a Reformed Ribbonman' appeared in the *Dublin Literary Gazette*, 1830. Furlong's Wrue, 'a prophet and seer of skill' (19) might be argued as an influence on Carleton's depiction of 'prophecy man' Donnel Dhu, in *The Black Prophet* (1847).
10. See Stewart's Foreword in Mythen, *Thomas Furlong*.
11. Mythen argues that 'there is no evidence that Furlong ever used the title *The Doom of Derenzie* and it is probable that this was the idea of M. J. Whitty' (29). Furlong's drafts of the text were titled *The Old Man of Clone*, and later *Tale of Superstition*.
12. Amongst Furlong's surviving papers is a memoir on 'Old Wrue', in which he recalls 'having, when very young, been sent many miles to bring the wizard to a relative, who was supposed to have been fairy struck' (quoted in *The Doom of Derenzie*, p. 127). In his explanatory endnotes to *The Doom of Derenzie*, Whitty claims that Furlong is the first writer to create 'a full length portrait of an Irish fairyman' (129).
13. The German-born Sir Matthew De Renzy (1577–1634) emigrated in the early seventeenth century to Ireland where he settled as a planter and strongly supported the English government's policy of conquest via plantation. He is often cited in the context of his staunch opposition to Irish culture and particularly the Irish language (in which he made himself accomplished); he advocated its complete eradication on the grounds that

'For as long as that is currant amongst them, they will ever be shrewder and more suttler than the English that comes out of England'. See McCuarta 41. See also MacCuarta's entry for De Renzy and his son in the *Dictionary of Irish Biography* ('De Renzy, Sir Matthew'). By Furlong's time, the family spelled their name Derinzey.
14. Compare especially to Melmoth's explanation of war to Immalee, in vol. 3, ch. XVII in *Melmoth the Wanderer* (1820).
15. Brian Earls notes that this legend of the white ram was common in Ireland and was especially associated with the seventeenth-century poet Cearbhall O Dálaigh (115). Furlong's 'unquestionably daring' use of this legend, Earls contends, 'provides an impressive climax to the opening section of the poem' (115).

Works Cited

A solemn appeal to the common sense of England, against the principles of Mr Canning. By a lay Protestant. John Stephens, 1827.

Bienstock Anolik, Ruth. 'The Missing Mother: The Meanings of Maternal Absence in the Gothic Mode'. *Modern Language Studies*, vol. 33, no. 1/2, 2003, pp. 24–43.

Cusack, Andrew. 'Intercultural Transfer in the *Dublin University Magazine*: James Clarence Mangan and the German Gothic'. *Popular Revenants: The German Gothic and its International Reception, 1800–2000*, edited by Andrew Cusack and Barry Murnane, Camden House, 2012, pp. 87–104.

Deane, Seamus. *Strange Country*. Oxford University Press, 1997.

Earls, Brian. 'Supernatural Legends in Nineteenth-Century Irish Writing'. *Béaloideas*, vol. 60/61, 1992/3, pp. 93–144.

Furlong, Thomas. *The Doom of Derenzie*. Joseph Robins, 1829.

Haslam, Richard. '"Broad Farce and Thrilling Tragedy": Mangan's Fiction and Irish Gothic'. *Éire-Ireland*, vol. 41, no. 3, 2006, pp. 215–44.

———. 'Irish Gothic'. *The Routledge Companion to Gothic*, edited by Catherine Spooner and Emma McEvoy, Routledge, 2007, pp. 83–94.

———. 'Maturin's Catholic Heirs: Expanding the Limits of Irish Gothic'. *Irish Gothics: Genres, Forms, Modes, and Traditions, 1760–1890*, edited by Christina Morin and Niall Gillespie, Palgrave Macmillan, 2014, pp. 113–29.

HC Deb (6 March 1827). Vol. 16. Available at hansard.parliament.uk/ Commons/1827-03-06/debates/672586f4-0b00-4b85-b5d8-c4e9dcbc8bd7/ RomanCatholicClaims%E2%80%94AdjournedDebate#main-content. Accessed 23 November 2021.

Kelly, James. 'Gothic and the Celtic Fringe, 1750–1850'. *The Gothic World*, edited by Glennis Byron and Dale Townshend, Routledge, 2014, pp. 38–50.

Kilfeather, Siobhán. 'Ireland and Europe in 1825: Situating the Banims'. *Ireland and Europe in the Nineteenth Century*, edited by Leon Litvack and Colin Graham, Dublin, Four Courts Press, 2006, pp. 29–50.

———. 'The Gothic Novel'. *The Cambridge Companion to the Irish Novel*, edited by John Wilson Foster, Cambridge University Press, 2006, pp. 78–96.

Killeen, Jarlath. *Gothic Literature 1825–1914*. University of Wales Press, 2009.

———. 'Irish Gothic Fiction'. *The Oxford Handbook of Modern Irish Fiction*, Edited by Liam Harte, Oxford University Press, 2020, pp. 49–65.

———. 'How Celtic Tiger's death led to a Gothic revival'. *The Irish Times*, April 28, 2017. www.irishtimes.com/culture/books/how-celtic-tiger-s-death-led-to-a-gothic-revival-1.3065069. Accessed 13 January 2022.

Lovecraft, H. P. *The Annotated Supernatural Horror in Literature*, edited by S. T. Joshi, Hippocampus Press, 2012.

McCormack, W. J. 'Introduction to Irish Gothic and after, 1820–1945'. *The Field Day Anthology of Irish Writing*, edited by Seamus Deane, Field Day Publications, 1991, vol. II, pp. 831–53.

McCuarta, Brian. 'Matthew De Renzy's Letters on Irish Affairs'. *Analecta Hibernica*, vol. 34, 1987, pp. 107, 109–82.

———. 'De Renzy, Sir Matthew'. *Dictionary of Irish Biography*. Cambridge University Press, 2009. Available online at www.dib.ie/biography/de-renzy-sir-matthew-a2468. Accessed 1 December 2021.

Morin, Christina. 'The Gothic in Nineteenth-Century Ireland'. *The Cambridge History of the Gothic*, edited by Dale Townshend and Angela Wright, vol. 2, Cambridge University Press, 2020, pp. 359–75.

Murphy, Willa. 'Confessing Ireland: Gerald Griffin and the Secret of Emancipation'. *Éire-Ireland*, vol. 48, no. 3, 2013, pp. 79–102.

Mythen, Sean. *Thomas Furlong: The Forgotten Wexford Poet*. Clone Publications, 1998.

O'Sullivan, Tadhg, '"The Violence of a Servile War": Three Narratives of Irish Rural Insurgency Post-1798'. *Rebellion and Remembrance in Modern Ireland*, edited by Laurence M. Geary, Four Courts Press, 2000, pp. 73–92.

Schirmer, Gregory A. *Out of What Began: A History of Irish Poetry in English*. Cornell University Press, 1998.

Part IV

Irish Gothic Writers: Gender and Sexuality

Chapter 11

Irish Women Writers and the Supernatural
Melissa Edmundson

Women have long been associated with the supernatural, and this connection is especially true in Ireland. Ideas of 'Mother Ireland' and 'Dark Rosaleen' permeate Irish identity and culture. The mythic figure of Kathleen Ní Houlihan symbolises Irish nationalism and is found throughout the country's art and literature. The banshee, a wailing woman who roams the countryside, foretells doom and death to any who hear her plaintive cries. The Morrígan, a goddess from Irish mythology who is also known as the 'Phantom Queen', represents war and strife. The Hag of Beara is the ancient goddess of winter who has power over life and death. Historical Irish landmarks are also the provinces of female spirits. The Red Lady of Leap Castle holds a dagger and searches for those who wronged her and her child. Máire Rua O'Brien (Red Mary) was, according to legend, sealed inside a hollow tree for practicing witchcraft and haunts her former home of Leamaneh Castle, while the mysterious White Lady of Malahide Castle emerges from her painting in the Great Hall. And the popular ballad reminds us that the ghost of Molly Malone still drives her wheelbarrow through the streets of Dublin.[1]

Yet as longstanding as these legends are, critical discussions of Irish women's literary history are relatively new. In *Irish Women Writers: An Uncharted Tradition* (1990), Ann Owens Weekes remarks that 'the student who searches the shelves for works on Irish women's fiction … feels very much as Virginia Woolf did when she searched the British Museum for work on women by women. The most determined researcher detects only a few slim volumes' (1). Nonetheless, 'Despite centuries of oppressive conditions, Irish women have written, initially in Gaelic and English and latterly chiefly in English, and judging by what survives of their writing, they have written well' (ibid. 2). A decade later, in her introduction to *Border Crossings: Irish Women Writers and National Identities* (2000), Kathryn Kirkpatrick stresses the need to reclaim such a history, claiming that 'Irish women's literary history remains largely unexplored', despite the fact that literature is 'a dialogue in which women have always spoken, though their voices have not often been heard' (6).[2] Nationalist images of Ireland that abounded in the work of Yeats, Joyce and Heaney – writers who depicted the country as a passive, wronged voiceless woman – also did little to foster a distinctive female voice in Irish writing. In fact, the idea of 'nation' in Irish writing tended to work against the canonisation of women writers. As Heather Ingman and Clíona Ó Gallchoir state:

> Demands for women's rights have often been seen as either in competition with, or even incompatible with, the imperative of national self-determination that dominated Irish political and intellectual life from the late 1800s, and the privileging of the national was reflected in the construction of a 'literary tradition' that could not encompass voices that either challenged the national narrative, or whose primary focus simply lay elsewhere. (3–4)

More recently, studies of Irish women's writing have focused on the often-neglected period of the later nineteenth century, attempting to fill the gaps between earlier writers such as Maria Edgeworth and Sydney Owenson and later twentieth-century authors such as Elizabeth Bowen, Mary Lavin and Edna O'Brien.[3] Anna Pilz and Whitney Standlee, in *Irish Women's Writing, 1878–1922* (2016), trace women's involvement in the Irish literary tradition post-Famine by considering the effects of emigration and increased educational opportunities. They claim, 'The preoccupations of Irish women writers of the late nineteenth century reflect the changes they witnessed, experienced, and confronted' (Pilz and Standlee 10). Yet seeking out opportunities continued to be an uphill battle as 'Irish women, regardless of class, often found their ambitions and options curtailed' (ibid.). Literacy rates for women in Ireland increased steadily throughout the nineteenth century, which gave them more opportunities to become professional writers. This newfound 'female literary agency', according to Pilz and Standlee, led to 'a tendency for women to use their texts as a means of blurring the spheres of the public and private, the political and the cultural' (ibid. 11). Heidi Hansson, in her study of nineteenth-century Irish women's prose, has likewise sought to reclaim the value of the private sphere and how it shapes literary texts, remarking, 'Women writers have been censured as being uncommitted to the important questions of the day, while in fact they were engaged with creating a different literary-political scene that included women's private experiences' (4).

In thinking about a specific female attitude in Irish writing then, we must consider how Irish women functioned in Irish society, often being seen as inferior or subservient to Irish men and thus confined to the domestic sphere. Yet, women have consistently turned this neglect to their literary advantage. As Jennifer Uglow suggests, 'Women bring to their writing the qualities of their particular experience, their history of living on the margins' (ix). In this sense, Irish women have much in common with their American and British compatriots in that their writing has been dismissed as too 'domestic' and relying too much on romance and sensation. This attitude has, in turn, led critics to ignore important social critiques embedded in such popular literature. As challenging as scholars have found uncovering and establishing an Irish women's literary tradition, it is even more difficult to recognise a tradition of Gothic and supernatural writing by Irish women. If we factor in the longstanding (at least, until recently) view that Gothic literature is light, popular reading, devoid of any social or cultural importance, combined with the neglect of Irish writing and the dismissal of women's writing in general (and particularly within the Gothic genre), then we begin to see how Irish women writers of the supernatural are triply damned. Siobhán Kilfeather's 1994 article 'Origins of the Irish Female Gothic' attempts to remedy this imbalance as she focuses on how early novelists such as Regina Maria Roche, Maria Edgeworth and Sydney Owenson used the Gothic mode to comment on women's anxieties regarding silence and consent and women's place within the home and nation. Traditionally, however, studies of Irish Gothic fiction have been dominated by discussions of male authors such as Charles Maturin, Bram Stoker and Sheridan Le Fanu. Peter Denman traces a distinct Irish ghost story tradition to the 1820s with Thomas Crofton Croker's *Fairy Legends and Traditions of the South of Ireland* (1825–1828) and John Banim's novel *The Fetches* (1825). Denman claims that in the work of more well-known Irish writers, most notably Le Fanu, 'there are no real grounds on which to argue for a specifically Irish supernatural fiction; there are only Irish writers of supernatural fiction' (70). While there are exceptions, this statement is generally not true for Irish women's supernatural fiction. Their emphasis on landscape and Irish history, culture and legend is directly impacted by geographic place and the experience of being Irish. Such experiences foreground remote, isolated settings, issues of domestic instability and abuse, poverty, famine, emigration and displacement, the importance of family and community, inheritance, the detrimental effects of colonialism, ideas of nationhood and political unrest.[4]

During the Victorian period, a time which saw the continuing development of the ghost story, Irish women used gender concerns from earlier Gothic texts to incorporate social themes in their short fiction. Throughout the second half of the nineteenth century and into the first half of the twentieth century, women responded to rapid social and political changes by creating literary ghosts that reflected contemporary concerns about female autonomy, marriage, domestic abuse, haunted houses, money and property, colonialism, poverty and war. This chapter discusses how these themes evolved from the Victorian period into the twentieth century and how Irish women writers described the changing role of women and the continuing struggles of the Irish through the lens of the supernatural. The authors surveyed cover a broad range of Gothic writing, including folk horror, the macabre, comic Gothic and more traditional ghost stories. By examining these distinct and rich female voices within the larger field of Irish Gothic and recognising a tradition of Irish women's supernatural fiction, we can begin to appreciate how integral women were to both Irish literature and the Irish ghost story.[5]

Otherworldly Women: Irish Myths and Legends

Irish myths, legends and superstitions are recorded in women's fiction and nonfiction and are used to connect Ireland to an ancient and powerful past.[6] The importance of storytelling and a continuing oral tradition passed down from one generation to the next are also central to these narratives, which feature witches, banshees and merwomen, among other such figures. Rosa Mulholland's 'Not to Be Taken at Bed-Time' (1865), originally published as part of the series 'Doctor Marigold's Prescriptions' in the Christmas Number of Charles Dickens's *All the Year Round*, incorporates witchcraft and folk magic as it relates the story of Coll Dhu (Black-Coll), whose family lost their land and who lives in a remote house in the Connemara mountains called the Devil's Inn. Coll Dhu shuns everyone's company until he saves the life of Colonel Blake, a sworn enemy who Coll Dhu blames for his father's destitution and eventual suicide. When Coll Dhu falls in love with Blake's daughter Evleen, she spurns him. He then overhears that a witch named Pexie na Pishrogie could provide a love spell. In her initial description of Pexie, Mulholland utilises traditional notions of witches:

> In a hovel on a brown desolate heath, with scared-looking hills flying off into the distance on every side, he found Pexie: a yellow-faced hag, dressed in a dark-red blanket, with elflocks of coarse black hair protruding from under an orange kerchief swathed round her wrinkled jaws. She was bending over a pot upon her fire, where herbs were simmering, and she looked up with an evil glance when Coll Dhu darkened her door. ('Not to Be Taken at Bed-Time' 52)

The tragic ending to the story reinforces its emphasis on hatred, vengeance, isolation and fate – all set within a folk horror tradition that uses local folklore, legends and superstitions for its overall effect.[7]

In Charlotte Riddell's 'Hertford O'Donnell's Warning', also known as 'The Banshee's Warning', which was published in her collection *Frank Sinclair's Wife and Other Stories* (1874), the title character is an up-and-coming surgeon at Guy's Hospital in London. From the story's beginning, Riddell portrays O'Donnell as a foreigner among his English colleagues: 'He was Irish – not merely by the accident of birth, ... but by every other accident and design which is objectionable to the orthodox and respectable and representative English mind' (252). O'Donnell tries to separate himself from his Irish upbringing and has cut ties with his family, but, through the call of the banshee, Riddell makes it clear to her readers that he cannot completely leave Ireland behind. The wailing cry leads him to anticipate that he is needed at Guy's. When O'Donnell arrives, he sees, 'An old woman with streaming grey hair, with attenuated arms, with head bowed forward, with scanty clothing, with bare feet; who never looked up at their approach, but sat unnoticing, shaking her head and wringing her hands in an extremity of grief' (ibid. 284). Because of his Irishness, and because the banshee's call is connected to the imminent death of one of his family members, O'Donnell sees the woman when others cannot. Yet there is one exception. The only other person who can see the woman is a young boy who has sustained mortal injuries after a building collapse. By the story's end, the connection between the two becomes apparent, and O'Donnell's backstory of tragic love 'divided by old animosities and by difference of religion' is revealed as Riddell critiques the societal prejudices that result in the death of the individual as well as of the family unit (ibid. 291). The presence of the banshee thus represents the consequences of intolerance and cultural displacement as her cry speaks the suffering of the living woman who has lost her home and her son.

The legends of Ireland's coastal areas become a main focus in Katharine Tynan's 'The Sea's Dead', published in *An Isle in the Water* (1896). The story opens with a bleak description of how the sea impacts life (and death) on Achill Island, as lines between the natural and supernatural are blurred:

> There was a grief and trouble on all the Island. Scarce a cabin in the queer straggling villages but had desolation sitting by its hearth. It was only a few weeks ago that the hooker had capsized crossing to Westport, and the famine that is always stalking ghost-like in Achill was forgotten in the contemplation of new graves. The Island was full of widows and orphans and bereaved old

people; there was scarce a window sill in Achill by which the banshee had not cried. (Tynan, 'The Sea's Dead' 113)

Tynan tells the story of Moya Lavelle, who loses her husband Patrick to the sea. There is something otherworldly about Moya and when a giant wave carries her body away during her wake, the island's inhabitants claim that she was a mermaid as they 'remembered a thousand unearthly ways in her' (ibid. 120). Tynan's use of the supernatural in the story provides an effective way to foreground Moya's isolation, while also describing how the sea both gives and takes: how it causes loss and grief but also represents a freedom that finally carries Moya away from the community that cannot fully understand her.

Tynan's supernatural tales often utilise Irish traditions and reimagine those traditions through the lens of folk horror and pagan ritual practices that are at odds with Catholic doctrine. 'The Death Spancel', also published in *An Isle in the Water*, concerns Mauryeen Holian's use of a death spancel to bind Sir Robert Molyneaux to her. At the beginning of the story, Tynan portrays Molyneaux as a destructive force in the community. As a member of the landed aristocracy, he drinks, gambles and takes advantage of the local women, one of whom must emigrate to America 'with her unborn child' where she is destined 'to perish miserably, body and soul, in the streets of New York' ('The Death Spancel' 139). Yet as one working-class woman is Sir Robert's victim, another is his undoing. 'Dark Mauryeen', a servant in a local great house, uses the death spancel, 'the strip of skin unbroken from head to heel' and taken from a 'new grave', to place a love spell on Sir Robert (ibid. 138). Though Sir Robert continues to abuse his tenants 'and rack-rented his people far worse than in the old days' (ibid. 145–46), Mauryeen is able, through her 'devil's charm' (ibid. 137), to keep other local women from becoming the victims of his sexual advances. Tynan melds pagan and Christian belief by the story's end, as the death spancel hangs in the rafters of Aughagree Chapel. However, though it becomes a symbol of sin, it loses none of its power and meaning. It is a lesson to those in the church of the future awaiting the unrepentant, but it carries a less convenient meaning as well. The death spancel, for the abused Irish tenants that frequently suffered under Sir Robert's control – particularly the working-class women on whom he preyed – represents a form of folk magic, an ancestral knowledge and a form of power for an otherwise powerless community.

Political and Cultural Anxieties: The National and the Domestic

Within many Gothic stories, sickness and disease become catalysts for supernatural events and provide women important opportunities to critique social inequalities in Ireland during the nineteenth century. This emphasis often reflects the poor conditions under which the working-class Irish lived, including the effects of famine and malnourishment in rural areas as well as sicknesses arising from crowded, unhealthy living conditions in cities and towns. In Mulholland's macabre story 'The Hungry Death', first published in *All the Year Round* in July 1880 and later included in *The Haunted Organist of Hurly Burly and Other Stories* (1891), the starving inhabitants on the remote island of Innisbofin are described in spectral, Gothic ways. As Brigid Lavelle, herself described alternatively as a 'ghost' and a 'spectre of herself', walks among the people, they are described as skeletons reaching out for food (Mulholland, 'The Hungry Death' 123, 116). Katharine Tynan's 'The Body-Snatching', published in the 15 January 1902 issue of *The Sketch*, opens with a description of Dublin during an outbreak of smallpox. The narrator has spent time in Newgate Prison for fighting against the British and returns to Ireland to find that his ancestral property – and his beloved Eleanora – has been confiscated by them. As the title suggests, there is an encounter between the narrator and the surgeon Ned Brady, who plans to steal a body from a local city cemetery. The story ultimately has a happy ending, but the many hardships and desperate situations Tynan includes in her brief tale illustrate how the supernatural, with its fantastic descriptions, provides an effective and memorable way to describe real world conditions. In 'Samhain' (1924), set during The Great Hunger, Dorothy Macardle draws on her lifelong interest in Celtic myths and legends. Father Patrick O'Rahilly, a parish priest in a small West Kerry fishing village, nurses the local population when 'the spectre of famine' comes one summer (Macardle, *Earth-Bound* 14). When Father Patrick is stricken with typhoid and cannot pray for the dead on Samhain night (the ancient Gaelic festival marking the start of winter), the dead come to him instead. The narrator hears 'a multitude of voices at prayer … but not in Latin – it was Irish – I knew the soft, rich sounds' (ibid. 19).

Concerns with lost property, wealth and inheritance are recurring themes in Irish women's supernatural literature and represent anxieties over ownership and autonomy that were a direct result of Anglo-Irish relations throughout the nineteenth and early twentieth centuries.

Frances Power Cobbe's 'A Spectral Rout', originally published in the December 1865 issue of *The Shilling Magazine*, concerns reclaimed inheritance. In the story, the presence of a ghost ultimately saves two sisters from poverty and ensures their future comfort. Instead of squandering the fortune as their relatives did, the sisters choose to give a substantial portion of their money to the establishment of a children's charity home in the ancestral house, thus ending the family curse through good deeds. Similarly, in Rosa Mulholland's 'The Lady Tantivy', originally published in the January 1898 issue of *Temple Bar*, a ghost's part in finding a lost will secures the present-day heir's claim to the house; yet the ghostly presence reminds readers that one's (dis)connection to a past home is often layered with feelings of sorrow and dispossession. Mulholland's 'The Ghost at the Rath', included in *The Haunted Organist of Hurly Burly* (1891), also concerns a stolen inheritance while incorporating traditional Gothic plot-devices such as a *femme fatale*, secret rooms and poisoning.

During the Victorian period, Irish women benefitted from the growing appeal of popular literature. The bestselling author L. T. Meade found success both as a novelist and as a writer of short fiction. According to Gerardine Meaney, Mary O'Dowd and Bernadette Whelan, writers such as Meade 'had been extremely successful internationally in the nineteenth century in popular genres such as mystery, ghost stories and children's fiction, as well as in domestic and romantic narratives' and marketed themselves as distinctly 'Irish women writers' (185, 6). Meade also took advantage of '[t]he association of Irishness with access to a world of storytelling, natural and supernatural' (ibid. 186). Like many of her contemporaries, Meade marketed her work for the public taste.[8] She is best known today for her books for young girls and for the occult detective Diana Marburg, whose stories were collected in *The Oracle of Maddox Street* (1904). Meade's story 'Eyes of Terror', published in *The Strand* in December 1903, blends the mystery and ghost story genres while incorporating other sensational elements such as nefarious cousins, stolen wills, hereditary insanity and secret chambers. 'The Woman with the Hood' (1897), published in the *Weekly Scotsman*, emphasises the importance of storytelling and the transmission of knowledge from one woman to another. In this way, women gain control over their own narrative, a narrative that was silenced by more dominant powers in Ireland – most significantly through the frameworks of British colonialism and the Catholic Church, and the unequal gender dynamics these institutions relied upon in order to keep Irish women in subservient positions within the home and within society at large – that historically sought to erase women's experience from history and literature. The uncovering of secrets functions as an analogy for women's writing itself and how these stories reveal lost voices, shared experiences and struggles.

Communities of women feature in several stories, although the descriptions of domesticity that readers find in these narratives differ widely between writers. Often, the supernatural is used to show how women support other women in times of trial, but there are also portrayals of jealousy and mistrust between women, often of the same class but between women of differing classes as well. In Katharine Tynan's 'The First Wife', collected in *An Isle in the Water* (1896), the titular deceased woman returns to her home, and her presence disrupts the jealous second wife's efforts to erase/exorcise the woman from both the husband's memory and from the household. Despite these efforts, however, the first wife roams through the house and eventually saves everyone (including the home) from a fire. Tynan remains ambiguous about whether it is the first wife's desire to return to her former home or if she must do penance before moving on to the afterlife. In either case, the ghost allows Tynan to interrogate notions of memory, loyalty and the connection we have to place and home. In women's ghost stories, the domestic roles forced upon many women are frequently challenged. These stories provide women a way to voice the instabilities that existed behind the doors of the private home. As such, these stories provide a vital link between the private and public world of Irish women.

Clotilde Graves's 'The Compleat Housewife', published in *Under the Hermés and Other Stories* (1917), concerns a domestic situation where an American heiress named Lydia arrives at her new ancestral home in England to find the ghost of Lady Deborah, a supernatural version of Mrs Beeton, whose soul is attached to the cookbook that gives the story its title. In a twist on the usual ghost story, in which the ghost's presence instils fear, the young, isolated bride hopes to find a companion in Lady Deborah. After remarking on the uncouth modern sensibilities of the new mistress of the house, Lady Deborah convinces Lydia to turn housewife and cook a battalia pie from the book, which, in turn, will set the ghost free. Yet, by the story's end, it is evident that such a devotion to domestic duty and to being the 'perfect wife' could prove harmful. Graves, who wrote under the pseudonym 'Richard Dehan', excelled at the comic ghost story, and 'The Compleat Housewife' is one of her best in how it effectively combines social commentary with humour.[9] As Lady Deborah prepares to leave, she reassures Lydia that she has arranged for other ghosts to take her place because 'a family residence without a ghost' would be disreputable:

> Sir Umphrey ... has arranged to haunt the inhabited wings as well as the shut-up portion. You have also a third share in a banshee brought into the family by one of the Desmonds ... and there is a hugely impressive death-watch in the wainscotting of your room. (Graves, 'The Compleat Housewife' 64)

Other ghost stories by Graves, such as 'A Vanished Hand' and 'How the Mistress Came Home', both published in *The Cost of Wings* (1914), are more sombre and feature women who, like the title character in Tynan's 'The First Wife', return from the grave in an attempt to connect (or reconnect) to physical places and lives that are no longer available to them.

Dora Sigerson Shorter's *The Father Confessor: Stories of Death and Danger* (1900), as the subtitle to the collection suggests, contains several stories delving into the Gothic, macabre and supernatural, while also foregrounding women's experience. 'All Souls' Eve' is about a grieving young woman who waits for the return of her dead lover who has died at sea. Yet when he comes to her, she is terrified and misses her chance to be reunited with him. 'The Strange Voice' tells of two lovers, and the story once again ends in tragedy for the living woman. It is concerned with emigration, as the group talks of the young man's journey to make his fortune and anticipates his return for his beloved Eileen Murphy. In America, Eileen will be 'a grand lady', but Sigerson Shorter's narrative takes a darker turn ('The Strange Voice' 206). Eileen leaves the safety of her home to follow a voice that says, 'Follow me, Eileen'. The voice leads her farther away from her family, and the natural environment seemingly tries to warn her of the dangerous journey. Eileen continues to follow the voice until she enters a bog and dies there. Sigerson Shorter suggests that leaving home and family for an unknown future – Eileen's journey through the dark woods serves as a metaphor for emigration – is dangerous and potentially life-threatening. And even if one survived to make it to America or Dublin, many Irish families never saw their loved ones again. This permanent separation is like a death. Other stories in *The Father Confessor* enter nightmarish territories. 'Transmigration' is a story of a doppelgänger, told from a criminal's point of view, while 'The Mother' is a bleak stream-of-consciousness narrative in which a woman laments her empty life with an abusive husband. Separated from her family and friends and full of regret for giving up her own chances at a fulfilling life in favour of her husband's career, the woman, who is dying from tuberculosis, wrestles with the idea of killing her son in order to save him from future abuse and neglect. The story is a searing indictment of the prevalence of domestic abuse and the lack of choices faced by so many Irish women. It likewise points to how women's use of domestic settings in their macabre fiction draws attention to the damaging effects of religious and social structures that consistently placed women as inferior beings and thus justified such abuse at the hands of men. Additionally, if we consider how Celtic mother-goddess traditions elevated women in ancient society before the advent of Christianity, stories such as 'The Mother' provided a way for women writers to reclaim an empowered voice that speaks the experience of women. Through their writing, Irish women gained autonomy in the professional world while at the same time raising awareness of domestic issues that otherwise would remain behind closed doors.[10]

The supernatural is also used to critique Ireland's ongoing fight for independence from Britain and thus complicates notions that women did not usually incorporate political messages in their writing. The stories in Dorothy Macardle's *Earth-Bound* (1924) were written while she was a prisoner in Mountjoy and Kilmainham Gaols due to her support for the Irish republican cause, and it is no surprise that many of the stories in the collection are set during the Irish Civil War. In the title story, two republicans are pursued by Black and Tans after the men escape from prison and flee to the Wicklow Hills, a place Donal, one of the escapees, says is haunted 'by the old Chieftains and Kings' (Macardle, 'Earth-Bound' 5). His friend and fellow escapee notes that Donal himself looks like 'The King of Ireland's son' with 'the crown of his red-gold hair' before observing more ominously that '[h]e is the sort England always kills' (ibid. 5). Trapped in the bitter cold with the troops closing in, the two men are saved by the spirit of Red Hugh O'Donnell, a sixteenth-century nobleman who himself fought against English rule.

In Macardle's 'The Prisoner', the O'Carrolls are visited by Liam Daly, who appears unexpectedly from a thirty-eight-day prison hunger strike, 'a thin, laughing shadow of the boy we had known at home' (31). While in a solitary 'punishment cell' in Kilmainham, Daly encounters what he calls the evil spirit of a former inmate which causes Liam to fear that if he died insane, the ghost would 'take possession of me and I'd get lost in Hell' (ibid. 32–33). Indeed, even before his encounter with this supernatural presence, Daly is becoming a ghost himself. He is so isolated from others in the living world that he loses his sense of time, recalling, 'I used to think that time went past outside like a stream, moving on, but in prison you were in a kind of whirlpool – time going round and round with you, so that you'd never come to anything, even death, only back again to yesterday and round to today and back to yesterday again' (ibid. 32). While in his cell, Daly also sees the apparition of a young boy whose 'whole torment was the need to speak, to tell something' (ibid. 34). The boy relates how he was accused of informing on his master to the 'red-coats' during the Irish Rebellion of 1798. When Daly asks his name, the boy says he cannot remember. Yet Daly ensures that the boy's story is told and that he and his loyalty to Ireland are not forgotten by history. In the story, Macardle draws direct parallels between two Irish rebellions against British rule, separated by over a hundred years but with similar causes. Though the fight for Irish independence remains largely the same, she highlights the bravery of individuals who, because of a supernatural occurrence, come together for a brief but meaningful moment through shared experience and suffering. The act of speaking that is symbolised by the boy's account is Macardle's attempt to assert a woman's voice within the larger narrative of the nationalist movement. Her own firsthand experience as a political prisoner brings attention to the role women played during the fight for Irish independence in the beginning decades of the twentieth century. As such, the supernatural stories in *Earth-Bound* represent both a literary and political commentary on the time and a testament to the sacrifices made for the future nation. Like the nameless boy, Macardle's ghosts represent so many other 'nameless' members of Irish society who fought and died, but whose names were forgotten by history.

In 'Escape', published in *Sinn Féin* in December 1924, Macardle continues to show how the conflict between the Irish and the British destroyed families. Nora Fahy's brother Shawn has already been dragged from his home and killed by the Black and Tans and her brother Festy is in prison. While in a delirious fever, Nora begs for Festy to visit her on Christmas Eve and Father Kiernan goes to beg for clemency. When the Governor of the jail refuses to help unless Festy informs on his friends, he attempts an escape and is fatally shot. Yet Nora claims that Festy did visit her, telling her that he 'escaped' and 'would be safe from them now: he will be in a place where they can't find him ever' (Macardle, 'Escape' 92). Macardle plays with the double meaning of 'escape' in this supernatural tale, as Festy's failed attempt to escape from prison leads to his only true avenue for escape: death. In the afterlife, he gains his freedom, but is also permanently separated from his family.

In other historical ghost stories by Irish women, the figure of the ghost represents the return of the past onto the present and the haunted aspects of individual and cultural memory. As Jarlath Killeen notes, '[T]he Irish Gothic ruptures the present by the re-entry of elements of the past that the present wants to forget' (113). This idea is a central preoccupation in Elizabeth Bowen's supernatural fiction. The decaying Anglo-Irish 'Big House', which itself represents the diminishing status of the Anglo-Irish aristocracy, looms over several of her stories concerned with the relentless pull of the past. In the Postscript to *The Demon Lover and Other Stories* (1945), Bowen describes the inspiration for her writing as a kind of re-opening of the past: 'Each time I sat down to write a story I opened a door; and the pressure against the other side of that door must have been very great, for things – ideas, images, emotions – came through with force and rapidity, sometimes violence' (94–95). In the time-slip story 'The Happy Autumn Fields', from *The Demon Lover*, Bowen combines two settings: a manor house and surrounding countryside in Victorian-era County Cork and a home in World War II-era London during the Blitz.[11] The past and present become one as Mary in London connects with the spirit of Sarah in Ireland. The two time periods disrupt one another until the final tragedy is revealed at the story's conclusion. These women both experience a mental disruption to their normal lives and attempt to reclaim a past and an identity that is forever altered by the people and events around them in the present as well as from the past and future. An overwhelming sense of loss pervades each era, and both Sarah and Mary are left longing for something that is unattainable, whether it be a genuine human connection or a need to reconnect with a simpler and more contented past: a homeland that is forever out of reach.

Irish Women's Gothic: The Ghost Who Speaks

In the introduction to *Irish Gothics* (2014), Christina Morin and Niall Gillespie call for a wider consideration of the Irish Gothic, one that takes into account its 'multi-generic, cross-sectarian nature' and 'foregrounds the complexity of Irish gothic literature' (6, 10). Because of their contributions to supernatural fiction, Irish women writers deserve a place in this critical reassessment of the Irish Gothic. Their writing represents a sustained involvement with the social issues that existed within Ireland itself, as well as the experiences of Irish women during the second half of the nineteenth century and the beginning decades of the twentieth. This was a formative time for women's rights in Ireland and a period that saw the expansion of Irish women's education, a development that led directly to women's pursuit of professional writing careers and their emergence as published authors.[12]

For Irish women writers, the inability of the ghost to speak or to fulfil unfinished business – the incomplete life that causes the act of haunting itself – is analogous to the struggles of women in Ireland to find their own voices within the Irish nation and to become autonomous beings within that nation and its history. For so long, the Irish woman was herself socially, politically and legally invisible. As Vanessa D. Dickerson has asserted, women's ghost stories represented a way to be seen. She says that women's supernatural fiction 'constituted both expression and exploration of their own spirituality and their ambiguous status as the "other" living in a state of in-betweenness: between the walls of the house, between animal and man, between angel and demon' (8). These stories provided women agency and a way 'of making her position as well as her self legible, visible, readable, so that she who had been legally, financially, even intellectually absent in the broad light of day could assert in her supernatural writings the truth of her spiritual and cultural being' (ibid.). As the ghost comes back to enact its suffering or to relay its message, these authors could indirectly comment on the nebulous existence of women who were also liminal, on the margins of society. The disruption caused by the supernatural entity and its demand to be seen and heard symbolises the struggles of women during Ireland's growth from a British colony to an independent country. Their ghosts tell us that the dark secrets of the past must be exorcised in order to move on to a better future.

Throughout much of the nineteenth century (and indeed well into the twentieth), women were relegated to the home and assumed the role of caregiver: sisters, daughters, wives and mothers. They were expected to run the household and support male members of the family and care for children, all while remaining the symbols of Christian virtue, an existence that was dominated by the Catholic Church. In her discussion of Eamon de Valera's ideal Irish republican woman, Maryann Gialanella Valiulis states:

> She has no work of her own to do but rather fulfills the wishes of her sons or husband or brothers. She performs her role in public, not with an agenda of her own but rather as a living vessel through which the dead may speak. All of this bespeaks an air of self-effacement, of meekness, of indirectness. What it lacks is passion, vitality, independence, and assertiveness. What it does not incorporate is a public identity for women. (118)

The use of the supernatural in Irish women's writing provides an important reimagining of how women have historically been a 'vessel through which the dead may speak'. Irish women's ghost stories challenge official narratives that for many decades sought to erase women's experience from history. Through their literary ghosts, these women found their own individual voices as they turned to the Gothic, macabre and supernatural to describe the experience of being Irish, particularly of being an Irish woman. Thus, their writings give us an important alternative to the ghost stories written by Irish men, whose work has dominated discussions of Irish Gothic fiction. These women did not shy away from the horrors of everyday life. Rather, they chose to document it in their fiction. In so doing, they gave a voice to people's struggles and sorrows through war, plague, famine and emigration. Yet what also emerges in these stories is strength and resolve. Like their characters, these women persevered and made a name for themselves, both during their own times and within the tradition of Irish Gothic writing.

Notes

1. For more on the connections between Irish women and the supernatural, see Patricia Lysaght's *The Banshee: The Irish Supernatural Death-Messenger* (1985) and Rosalind E. Clark's doctoral thesis, *Goddess, Fairy Mistress, and Sovereignty: Women of the Irish Supernatural* (1985). For more on how Ireland has been historically represented as female, see C. L. Innes, *Women and Nation in Irish Literature and Society, 1880–1935* (1993).
2. It should be noted that *The Field Day Anthology of Irish Writing Volumes IV and V: Irish Women's Writing and Traditions* (2002), along with these important critical studies of Irish women's contributions to literature, was also instrumental in helping to define and expand the tradition of Irish women's writing.
3. Other important studies that focus on this period include Tina O'Toole's *The Irish New Woman* (2013), Whitney Standlee's *'Power to Observe': Irish Women Novelists in Britain, 1890–1916* (2015), and Kathryn Laing and Sinéad Mooney's *Irish Women Writers at the Turn of the Twentieth Century: Alternative Histories, New Narratives* (2019).
4. The concept of 'Irishness' in literature has been a contested subject, even amongst Irish writers themselves, and women have been at the forefront of the debate. Rosa Mulholland, in 'Wanted an Irish Novelist', published in *The Irish Monthly* in February 1891, and Katharine Tynan in 'The Neglect of Irish Writers', published in *The Catholic World* in April 1908, both commented on the problems faced by Irish writers in the nineteenth and early twentieth centuries, their place within the British publishing world, and the struggles to maintain a distinct Irish identity within one's published work. For more on women and Irish identity, see Elizabeth Cullingford's *Ireland's Others: Ethnicity and Gender in Irish Literature and Popular Culture* (2001) and D. A. J. MacPherson's *Women and the Irish Nation: Gender, Culture and Irish Identity, 1890–1914* (2012).
5. In *Re-Reading the Short Story* (1989), Clare Hanson notes the subversive qualities of the short story form, qualities which have served Irish writers well. She claims that the 'short story is a vehicle for various *kinds* of knowledge, knowledge which may be at odds with the "story" of dominant culture' (6, emphasis in original). For Hanson, the defining qualities of the short story, 'disjunction, inconclusiveness, obliquity', represent 'its

ideological marginality'. This marginality, in turn, allows the story 'to express something suppressed/repressed in mainstream literature' (ibid.).
6. Irish women have been instrumental in the collection of the nation's folklore, especially Lady Wilde's *Ancient Legends, Mystic Charms, and Superstitions of Ireland* (1887) and Lady Gregory's *Visions and Beliefs in the West of Ireland* (1920).
7. Rosa Mulholland would later describe her interest in local ghost stories and legends in her essay 'About Ghosts', published in *The Irish Monthly* in July 1892.
8. For more on L. T. Meade's success as a short story writer for popular magazines, see Chan. Chan notes that Meade's short stories often tested the magazine's 'market-tested formulae' by including 'proto-feminist plots and subtexts' (61).
9. Like her predecessor Charlotte Riddell (who published under the pseudonym 'F. G. Trafford' and then 'Mrs J. H. Riddell'), Graves's decision to adopt a male pseudonym for the publication of her Boer War novel *The Dop Doctor* (1910) had to do with issues of reception and the contemporary notion that women could not write about non-domestic issues. Yet the name 'Richard Dehan' had even more significance for Graves who used it as an alternative persona that allowed her the freedom to write on a wide variety of topics (despite the fact that it was widely known that 'Richard Dehan' was Clotilde Graves). She continued to use the name for the rest of her publishing career and even signed her letters 'Richard Dehan/Clotilde Graves'.
10. Like many other cultures, Irish women have been victimised by both the church and state. The Catholic Church has historically sought to control women's reproductive rights, and it was not until 1996 and the Fifteenth Amendment to the Constitution of Ireland (which passed by only a narrow margin) that Irish women could seek a divorce based on instances of domestic abuse.
11. In the Preface to *A Day in the Dark* (1965), Bowen states, 'the locale of the Victorian family in "The Happy Autumn Fields" is, though not stated, to me unshakably County Cork' (9).
12. The establishment of women's ghost stories as a distinct part of the Irish literary landscape developed alongside watershed moments in Irish women's history, from the food protests of the Great Famine years to the increasing access to education after the Intermediate Education Act of 1878. Women achieved more protection under the law with The Infant Custody Act of 1873, The Matrimonial Causes Act of 1878, and The Married Women's Property Act of 1882. The Poor Law Guardians (Ireland) (Women) Act of 1896 gave women the right to act as poor law guardians. During this time, women also left their homes and took advantage of employment opportunities in cottage industries, domestic service and factories. The second half of the nineteenth century saw the formation of societies dedicated to women's suffrage. The founding of the Dublin Women's Suffrage Association in 1876 (which eventually became the Irish Women's Suffrage and Local Government Association) and The Irish Women's Franchise League in 1908 were both instrumental in establishing organised communities for women in Ireland and providing a voice for women in national politics.

Works Cited

Bowen, Elizabeth. 'The Happy Autumn Fields'. *The Collected Stories of Elizabeth Bowen*. Vintage, 1982. pp. 671–85.
———. 'Postscript to *The Demon Lover*'. *The Mulberry Tree: Writings of Elizabeth Bowen*, edited by Hermione Lee, Virago, 1986, pp. 94–99.
———. 'Preface'. *A Day in the Dark and Other Stories*. Jonathan Cape, 1965.
Chan, Winnie. 'The Linked Excitements of L. T. Meade and… in the *Strand Magazine*'. *Scribbling Women and the Short Story Form: Approaches by American and British Women Writers*, edited by Ellen Burton Harrington, Peter Lang, 2008, pp. 60–73.
Denman, Peter. 'Ghosts in Anglo-Irish Literature'. *Irish Writers and Religion*, edited by Robert Welch, Colin Smythe, 1992, pp. 62–74.
Dickerson, Vanessa D. *Victorian Ghosts in the Noontide: Women Writers and the Supernatural*. University of Missouri Press, 1996.
Graves, Clotilde [Richard Dehan]. 'The Compleat Housewife'. *Under the Hermés and Other Stories*, Dodd, Mead and Company, 1917, pp. 44–67.
———. 'How the Mistress Came Home'. *The Cost of Wings*, William Heinemann, 1914, pp. 188–200.
———. 'A Vanished Hand'. *The Cost of Wings*, William Heinemann, 1914, pp. 154–68.
Hanson, Clare. 'Introduction'. *Re-Reading the Short Story*, edited by Clare Hanson, Palgrave Macmillan, 1989, pp. 1–9.
Hansson, Heidi. 'Introduction: Out of Context'. *New Contexts: Re-Framing Nineteenth-Century Irish Women's Prose*, edited by Heidi Hansson, Cork University Press, 2008, pp. 1–16.
Ingman, Heather, and Clíona Ó Gallchoir. 'Introduction'. *A History of Modern Irish Women's Literature*, edited by Heather Ingman and Clíona Ó Gallchoir, Cambridge University Press, 2018, pp. 1–17.
Kilfeather, Siobhán. 'Origins of the Irish Female Gothic'. *Bullán*, vol. 1, no. 2, 1994, pp. 35–45.
Killeen, Jarlath. *History of the Gothic: Gothic Literature 1825–1914*. University of Wales Press, 2009.
Kirkpatrick, Kathryn. 'Introduction'. *Border Crossings: Irish Women Writers and National Identities*. The University of Alabama Press, 2000, pp. 1–12.
Macardle, Dorothy. 'Earth-Bound'. *Earth-Bound and Other Supernatural Tales*. Dublin, The Swan River Press, 2020, pp. 1–10.
———. 'Escape'. *Earth-Bound and Other Supernatural Tales*. Dublin, The Swan River Press, 2020, pp. 85–93.
———. 'The Prisoner'. *Earth-Bound and Other Supernatural Tales*. Dublin, The Swan River Press, 2020, pp. 31–38.
———. 'Samhain'. *Earth-Bound and Other Supernatural Tales*. Dublin, The Swan River Press, 2020, pp. 11–21.
Meade, L. T. 'Eyes of Terror'. *The Strand*, vol. 26, December 1903, pp. 698–710.
———. 'The Woman with the Hood'. *Bending to Earth: Strange Stories by Irish Women*, edited by Maria Giakaniki and Brian J. Showers, Dublin, The Swan River Press, 2019, pp. 34–52.

Meaney, Gerardine, Mary O'Dowd and Bernadette Whelan. *Reading the Irish Woman: Studies in Cultural Encounter and Exchange, 1714–1960*. Liverpool University Press, 2013.

Morin, Christina, and Niall Gillespie. 'Introduction: De-Limiting the Irish Gothic'. *Irish Gothics: Genres, Forms, Modes, and Traditions, 1760–1890*, edited by Christina Morin and Niall Gillespie, Palgrave Macmillan, 2014, pp. 1–12.

Mulholland, Rosa. 'About Ghosts'. *Irish Monthly*, no. 20, July 1892, pp. 337–41.

———. 'The Ghost at the Rath'. *The Haunted Organist of Hurly Burly and Other Stories*. Hutchinson, 1891, pp. 22–51.

———. 'The Hungry Death'. *The Haunted Organist of Hurly Burly and Other Stories*. Hutchinson, 1891, pp. 90–125.

———. 'The Lady Tantivy'. *Temple Bar*, vol. 113, January 1898, pp. 119–27.

———. 'Not to Be Taken at Bed-Time'. *Dr. Marigold's Prescriptions. The Christmas Numbers of All the Year Round*. Chapman and Hall, 1865, pp. 39–63.

———. 'Wanted an Irish Novelist'. *The Irish Monthly*, no. 19, February 1891, pp. 368–73.

Pilz, Anna, and Whitney Standlee. 'Introduction'. *Irish Women's Writing, 1878–1922: Advancing the Cause of Liberty*, edited by Anna Pilz and Whitney Standlee. Manchester University Press, 2016, pp. 1–16.

Power Cobbe, Frances. 'The Spectral Rout'. *A Suggestion of Ghosts: Supernatural Fiction by Women, 1854–1900*, edited by J. A. Mains, Black Shuck Books, 2017, pp. 29–53.

Riddell, Charlotte [Mrs Riddell]. 'Hertford O'Donnell's Warning'. *Frank Sinclair's Wife and Other Stories*, vol. 3, Tinsley Brothers, 1874, pp. 247–93.

Sigerson Shorter, Dora. 'All Souls' Eve'. *The Father Confessor: Stories of Death and Danger*, Ward, Lock and Company, 1900, pp. 305–11.

———. 'The Mother'. *The Father Confessor: Stories of Death and Danger*, Ward, Lock and Company, 1900, pp. 357–68.

———. 'The Strange Voice'. *The Father Confessor: Stories of Death and Danger*, Ward, Lock and Company, 1900, pp. 203–12.

———. 'Transmigration'. *The Father Confessor: Stories of Death and Danger*, Ward, Lock and Company, 1900, pp. 101–27.

Tynan, Katharine. 'The Body-Snatching'. *The Sketch*, no. 36, 15 January 1902, pp. 506–8.

———. 'The Death Spancel'. *An Isle in the Water*, Adam & Charles Black, 1896, pp. 136–47.

———. 'The First Wife', *An Isle in the Water*, Adam & Charles Black, 1896, pp. 1–11.

———. 'The Neglect of Irish Writers'. *The Catholic World*, no. 87, April 1908, pp. 83–92.

———. 'The Sea's Dead'. *An Isle in the Water*, Adam & Charles Black, 1896, pp. 112–21.

Uglow, Jennifer. 'Introduction'. *The Virago Book of Ghost Stories: The Twentieth Century*, edited by Richard Dalby, Virago, 1990, pp. ix–xvi.

Valiulis, Maryann Gialanella. 'Power, Gender and Identity in the Irish Free State'. *Journal of Women's History*, vol. 6, no. 4; vol. 7, no. 1, Winter/Spring 1995, pp. 117–36.

Weekes, Ann Owens. *Irish Women Writers: An Uncharted Tradition*. 1990. The University Press of Kentucky, 2009.

Chapter 12

Reflection, Anxiety and the Feminised Body: Contemporary Irish Gothic
Ellen Scheible

Gothic trauma in recent Irish fiction is often performed on, and sometimes produced, repressed and reclaimed by a female body, a reminder of the inevitability of newness, development and mortality during periods filled with struggle, reconciliation, cultural prosperity and, finally, the anxiety provoked by economic collapse. Recent work on trauma and conflict sees this kind of anxiety as part of a larger discussion of the modern Gothic from the nineteenth century onwards and its connection to physiology and the economy. In *Tense Future*, Paul Saint-Amour points out, in a discussion of Virginia Woolf's Gothic writing on war, that the technique of 'perpetual suspension', or a suspense that never ends, perhaps producing its own sense of repetitive trauma, is one way that Woolf re-enacts wartime experience in her fiction (96). Saint-Amour connects this technique to a 'bourgeois' Gothic that 'fus[es] trauma with the quotidian' and argues that Woolf developed a 'critique of ... gendered metaphysics' that led her to see 'the male soldier and the female civilian not as opposed by nature and law but as intimately connected through social webs, structures of feeling, and their shared legitimation by a reproductive view of a national future' (98). Woolf's reproductive view of the future, as Saint-Amour describes it, is contingent on an image of the female body that is both fertile and generative: she has the potential to reproduce while remaining vulnerable to eradication through conflict. Similarly, in contemporary Irish fiction, the 'grotesque rather than romanticized' gendered body, as Kathleen Costello-Sullivan describes Veronica Hegarty from Anne Enright's *The Gathering* (2007), has the power to 'subversively [recuperate] the traumatized body' (30). Veronica's body, regardless of its grotesqueness, still might have the power to produce the future, as Enright hints at a potential pregnancy at the end of the novel. Even in texts like *The Gathering* that interrogate the complexities of articulating trauma and memory, reproduction offers one possible path toward the recuperation of the body that might mediate a history of trauma and abuse.

In his essay 'Contemporary Gothic: Why We Need It' from the 2002 *Cambridge Companion to Gothic Fiction*, Steven Bruhm identifies the work of Sigmund Freud and the emergence of psychoanalysis as pivotal catalysts for the shift from past notions of the Gothic to what he sees as contemporary Gothic: 'The contemporary Gothic, in other words, reveals the domestic scene in a world after Freud and the degree to which that domestic scene is predicated on loss' (264). Even in the early years of the twenty-first century, critics read the Gothic fears associated with technological and economic change as articulations of a universal threat to the family, a consistent site for the disruption and anxiety underlying modern trauma, where rupture and loss become regular characteristics of human consciousness during and after a century of mechanised warfare. While the success of Freudian theory, or psychoanalysis in general, to provide useful frameworks for understanding the Gothic might leave us, as Steven Jay Schneider suggests, with an 'open question' of critical value and debate, psychoanalysis is still an effective tool that offers 'insight into many of the figures of horror – not so much into what they metaphorically *mean* as into what they literally *say*, or at least suggest, in terms taken from the languages of Gothic fantasy' (8–9). Such language of fantasy and horror is fundamental to how we understand the connection between Freudian anxiety and trauma. Bruhm insists, 'it is finally through trauma that we can best understand the contemporary Gothic and why we crave it' (268). We seek ways of understanding the dissolution of the unified self and the exposure of fragmented identity that emerges in modern and contemporary life. The Gothic offers us a literary home for those trauma narratives, sometimes accessible and other times jarring, broken, and resistant to the very act of reading.

Contemporary Irish Gothic, as employed by current Irish women's fiction, also negotiates a traumatic history from which a fear of domestic failure from both nation and family exposes immediate dangers, and does so through the lens of the feminised body, suggesting specific concerns with reproduction and sexuality. The Irish woman's body becomes the canvas for cultural change in a national literature haunted by the economic rise and fall of Ireland's Celtic Tiger, suggesting a loss inherent to present-day life that is no longer associated with colonial violence or the trenches of war but, instead, with financial decline and disaster. As Anne Fogarty explains, 'the enforced jettisoning of nostalgic images of traditional Irish society as inherently communitarian and caring has also involved the shattering of apparently sacrosanct notions of a benign and nurturing femininity' (64). Bruhm's insistence on Freud as the generator of a contemporary Gothic framework that demarcates bifurcated identity as the precursor to modern trauma positions the split self and, eventually, the female body, as the ultimate threat to the family and to individual identity. For Freud, particularly in his ground-breaking essay, 'The Uncanny' (1919), the modern self is both familiar and unfamiliar because it is constantly searching for a home to which it can never return, a home that may not have existed in the first place, a home that originates in the female body. As early as the Irish literary renaissance, sometimes known as the Celtic Revival, if not before, Irish fiction has imagined a national landscape that simply did not exist before the push to nationalism in the nineteenth century. As Declan Kiberd notes in *Inventing Ireland*, the Irish searched 'for a Messianic hero through the nineteenth century, from O'Connell to Parnell' only to unearth 'a catalogue of revivalist icons made and then broken' (180). The Gothic has been and still is a genre through which we can express the impossibility of fully reviving an imagined Irish past that 'after the famines and emigrations of the 1840s ... had almost ceased to exist', leaving 'a terrifyingly open space, in places and in persons' (ibid.) For Kiberd, open landscapes as well as absent figures constitute the leftover imagination of the nation in the nineteenth century, a place traumatised by loss, terrifying in its physical and bodily vacuity.

Freud's *The Uncanny* is oddly preoccupied with the roles that Gothic confrontation and the body, particularly the female body, play in the relationship between self and other that proves foundational to our contemporary understanding of trauma. At the end of Section II of *The Uncanny*, Freud leaves us, almost nonchalantly, with an image of 'neurotic' men as figures for whom the act and unconscious memory of birth is conjured each time they glimpse female genitalia, presumably during a sexual encounter:

> It often happens that neurotic men state that to them there is something uncanny about the female genitals. But what they find uncanny ['unhomely'] is actually the entrance to man's old 'home', the place where everyone once lived. A jocular saying has it that 'love is a longing for home', and if someone dreams of a certain place or a certain landscape and, while dreaming, thinks to himself, 'I know this place, I've been here before', this place can be interpreted as representing his mother's genitals or her womb. (151)

Such a man sees the vagina as an 'old home' and the uncanny resurrection of unheimlich leaves him only with the trauma of that repeated image and an inability to separate a woman's genitals from the memory of his mother. While fantastical and given to readers as a kind of aside,

Freud's reference to the vagina's ability to reveal neuroticism in men is awarded a powerful textual location, at the very end of the second section where Freud lays out the basic definitions of the uncanny and right before the final section where he discusses the way that myth and language can use the uncanny to produce meaning. The vagina is the gateway from Freud's diagnosis of male neuroticism to his belief that narrative, and eventually talk therapy, can harness the uncanny to expose the trauma beneath repetition compulsion. In other words, the female body, specifically the part that makes reproduction manifest, works as a decoder for the most troubled men, the neurotic beings for whom sexual desire will always provoke thoughts of home and possibly of incest. In Freud's narrative, the female body can cause perversion in men and, more importantly, serves as a reflective device on which the entirety of Freud's argument depends because it is identified as the first and original place of home in a text where 'unhomely' or the unfamiliarity of home is one of the closest definitions for the uncanny.

One of the strongest defining features of the Irish Gothic is its intertwined relationship with the national tale and its use of the female body as a template for cultural tension, change, and anxiety, similar to Freud's use of the body as a home for the recognition of trauma.[1] The contemporary novels by Emma Donoghue and Tana French that I discuss in this chapter infuse the complex relationship between Gothic fiction and the national tale with an organic and sometimes humanistic expression of the many fears surrounding reproduction (human, mechanical, scientific, artistic) that haunts modern consciousness and fuels contemporary concerns about social anxiety and self-destruction. The female sexuality that underlies and haunts both the Gothic and the uncanny is often a marker of gender disparity and sexual bias in contemporary writing. It is also a site from which modern and contemporary Gothic novels depart to either solve the crime or tell the story of assault, loss or death. Not the woman herself, but her body is that marker. She is usually already dead before the novel begins, launching the plot into a journey of self-as-other discovery, as in Cassie Maddox's undercover portrayal of a dead college student in *The Likeness* (2008), Tana French's second novel in her Dublin Murder Squad series.

In his introduction to *The Oxford Book of Gothic Tales*, Chris Baldick maps out a careful timeline for the development of a cultural Gothic rooted in a history of patriarchal subjugation. From the clash of the Roman Empire with the Goths in the fifth century to the British and Irish middle class of the eighteenth century, and finally to the twentieth-century Gothic of writers such as Jorge Luis Borges, Angela Carter and Joyce Carol Oates, Baldick explores the emergence of social and economic anxiety. He traces Gothic fear specifically to a Protestant anxiety of losing property and economic status to Catholic greed: 'Gothic fiction first emerged and established itself within the British and Anglo-Irish middle class, in a society which had, through generations of warfare, political scares, and popular martyrology persuaded itself that its hard-won liberties could at any moment be snatched from it by Papal tyranny' (xiv). In the contemporary Irish Gothic that I discuss in this chapter, the fear that Celtic Tiger wealth might have been a misleading illusion replaces the Protestant concern with property theft. For instance, in *The Likeness* French critiques property ownership as part of a failed system, rather than the loss of property itself, when the main character is unable to escape her co-ownership of an Anglo-Irish Big House and remain alive.

Beyond his introduction to the texts in the collection, Baldick provides a crucial breakdown of how Gothic fiction depends on and critiques anxiety, particularly the anxiety associated with modern traumas derived from the fear of economic and historical regression:

> while the existential fears of Gothic may concern our inability to escape our decaying bodies, its historical fears derive from our inability finally to convince ourselves that we have really escaped from the tyrannies of the past … Gothic fiction is a way of exercising such anxieties, but also of allaying them by imagining the worst before it can happen, and giving it at least a safely recognizable form. (ibid. xxii)

In the present, 'imagining the worst before it can happen' is how modern life defines cultural trauma as the template for an everyday, recognisable existence produced and replicated by mechanical reproduction, international warfare, and economic instability. Yet, Baldick sees 'the traditional sphere of the domestic interior' as represented by female writers of the Gothic, to be the original site for the formation of Gothic anxiety (ibid.). Female-provoked anxiety generates the earliest understanding of Gothic sensibility because 'the imprisoning house of Gothic fiction has from the very beginning been that of patriarchy, in both its earlier and its expanded feminist senses' (ibid). While Freud sees the vagina as the first home, Baldick relocates the metaphor onto the patriarchal world that glimpses its own neuroticism in the female body that birthed it, turning any idea of home into a prison. Anne Williams refers to such metaphors as 'lines' and 'boundaries' that 'may be real – the cold, hard stone of the castle and the cathedral – or the almost equally adamant principles of the elaborate cultural system Lacan called "the Law of the Father"' (12). The transgression of lines and boundaries in Gothic fiction can lead to imprisonment in 'the attics, dungeons, or secret chambers of the family or the state' (ibid.), and after the failure of Celtic Tiger capitalism, such prisons might masquerade as ghost estates or other financial excesses where entrapment takes the form of financial suffocation and exploitation.

According to Jason Buchanan in his 2017 article 'Ruined Futures: Gentrification as Famine in Post-Celtic Tiger Irish Literature', the height of the Celtic Tiger was often characterised as 'the era when Ireland could finally shrug off the history of colonialism and embrace a new vision of itself as a nation with wealth and global influence' (51). From the mid-1990s to roughly 2008, the Tiger flourished as a great wave of cultural and economic capital, positioning Ireland as one of the leading western economies and, to some, fulfilling Robert Emmet's final wishes that Ireland take her place among the 'nations of the world' (938). Mark Quigley describes the Tiger as 'the product of an intense modernization drive … culminating in the late 1990s with Ireland posting GDP growth that outpaced most of Europe', leading Ireland to follow 'in the wake of the Asian "tiger" economies of the early 1990s such as Singapore, Taiwan, and South Korea to become – at least briefly – an important site for high-tech and pharmaceutical design and manufacturing' (174–75). The economic success of the Tiger 'brought huge social and cultural change' resulting in 'a shift from a sense of originality or discrete difference to a reveling in interchangeability' (ibid. 175). However, the 2008 crash that destroyed some of the major national economies of the western world also had catastrophic effects on the Irish economy, leaving the nation, while globally interchangeable, frozen in developmental chaos. Buchanan argues that the economic success of the Tiger was never dependable and may not have fully emerged in the way proponents of the period boasted. This lack of stability became a mainstay of contemporary Irish experience: 'if the Tiger was not a stable moment of national, cultural, and economic transformation, the boom now comes to represent how globalization incorporates risk and speculation as a part of everyday life' (51).

While Irish Gothic fiction at the end of the twentieth-century was thriving before and during the Celtic Tiger, the period that Joe Cleary refers to as economic modernity's 'dramatic recovery' in Ireland (14), there was a resurgence of another Gothic moment for contemporary Irish writing in the post-Tiger era. In the 1990s, writers like Patrick McCabe and Martin McDonagh launched their own neo-Gothic movements that exposed the uncanny danger that a romanticised vision of rural and traditional Ireland presents to the evolution of Irish identity during and after political violence and trauma. Literary criticism often labels this era as 'Bog Gothic', referencing the rural Irish landscape and provincialism that underscores much of the Gothic tension in such texts. However, according to Derek Gladwin, the term 'Bog Gothic' is a complicated and potentially discriminatory term, as it 'appropriates older forms of colonial racism and discrimination toward the rural Irish who live on or near bogs, and whose families depended upon them for fuel to survive' (215). The 1990s resuscitation of the Gothic mode may have critiqued what it feared to be a dangerous Irish provincialism during a time of great economic change, but attention to the gender or racial disparities inherent to the development of Irish identity in the late twentieth century often maintained a complicated relationship with narratives of economic difference. Now, decades later, more recent writers, particularly female writers, are engaging the genre again in an attempt to reconsider both the economic and sexual repercussions of the Tiger. Such writers diagnose how the Tiger's death continues to haunt Ireland's national development in intersectional ways. As Jarlath Killeen explained in a 2017 *Irish Times* piece, 'The Celtic Tiger turned out to be all shine and no substance, and beneath the surface glamour dark and mysterious forces continued to operate' ('How Celtic Tiger's Death').

One of the overlapping metaphors of Gothic fiction from the 1990s and today's Irish Gothic is the employment of the female or feminised body as a trope, or a home, for the many articulations of national traumatic fear, one version of those 'mysterious forces' that Killeen reads as elements of Gothic repression. For example, we can trace the repetitive surfacing of Gothic anxiety from figures like the hybridised transgender body of McCabe's *Breakfast on Pluto* (1998) that challenges and exposes the complications of partition, or the dead maternal body that forecasts Ireland's necessary maintenance of a national past to move into a more economically productive future in McDonagh's *The Beauty Queen of Leenane* (1996), to Eimear McBride's sexually abused girl body in *A Girl is a Half-formed Thing* (2013), Emma Donoghue's starving child body in *The Wonder* (2016), and Tana French's many dead female bodies in her Dublin Murder Squad series (2007–16). Finally, Sally Rooney's presentation of an adolescent female body that enacts the effects of domestic violence and abuse through sexual perversion in *Normal People* (2018) offers one of the more recent approaches to historical trauma. Further, Northern Irish literature also uses a Gothic impulse to deal with the Troubles, particularly in works like Eoin McNamee's *The Blue Tango* (2001) and *The Ultras* (2004), as well as some of Glenn Patterson's works like *Burning Your Own* (1988). Ireland's status as a land that is both alien and familiar in all of these texts underscores the uncanny way that the Celtic Tiger transformed Irish national consciousness while often murdering, disfiguring or erasing its national past. Women writers employ the contemporary Irish Gothic to represent the global threat of domestic erasure to both nation and family as a revelation of the ironic expectations placed on the female body to reproduce the nation while simultaneously repressing an innately dangerous sexuality.

While the land itself can signify danger and bifurcation in Gothic fiction, as in the final scene of 'The Fall of the House of Usher' (1839) when the ground opens up to swallow Usher's family home in one giant moment of erasure, contemporary Irish Gothic also connects the history of the land, bog or otherwise, to the danger of the home through the figure of the female body. This is especially true in Emma Donoghue's novels, where women's bodies become sites of trauma that mirror Ireland's national history of rape (*Room*, 2010), starvation (*The Wonder*, 2016), and dead or dying mothers and children (*The Pull of the Stars*, 2020). One important contemporary metaphor in this framework is the Irish ghost estate, a relic from the Celtic Tiger, where the haunted space in question is an unfinished residence rather than an ancient Gothic castle.[2] Ghost estates earn bit parts in many contemporary Irish works, especially in French's Murder Squad series where she devotes an entire novel, *Broken Harbour* (2012), to the concept. Again, Rooney pens one of the more recent and memorable ghost estate scenes in *Normal People* where the dirty, broken space of a ghost estate with a soiled mattress[3] conjures Marianne's desire for a sex act that does not happen:

> The front door of number 23 was unlocked. It was quieter in the house, and darker. The place was filthy. With the toe of her shoe Marianne prodded at an empty cider bottle. There were cigarette butts all over the floor and someone had dragged a mattress into the otherwise bare living room. The mattress was stained badly with damp and what looked like blood. (33)

When Marianne asks Connell if he will have sex with her in that space, the text resists notions of sexiness or erotica and replaces them with clichéd naïveté: 'She closed her fingers around his school tie. It was the first time in her life she could say shocking things and use bad language, so she did it a lot. If I wanted you to fuck me here, she said, would you do it?' (ibid. 35). Rooney suggests that we might be right to be afraid for Marianne when we sense that her request mirrors her own self-perception and then wonder what trauma underlies her desires. Rooney's overlapping of the never-inhabited domestic space built by economic boom and bust with Marianne's adolescent, abused and sexualised body suggests that the historic trauma of broken female sexuality haunts the fragmented leftovers of an Irish cultural landscape that produced an empty shell of a future.

While unpredictable bedfellows in criticism of Gothic literature, Eve Sedgwick and Edmund Burke help to underscore the way that contemporary Gothic novels use dead, broken or othered female bodies to reflect gazes constantly back to their onlookers, challenging the heteronormative and capitalistic structures that are under scrutiny in these novels and returning to a common Gothic motif present in Irish political and philosophical discourse. Burke's famous eighteenth-century argument about the organic nature of the sublime hinges on confrontations with objectified female bodies. Perhaps the most remarkable confrontation in Burke's text occurs when Burke uses the image of a headless female torso to define the power of the beautiful:

> Observe that part of a beautiful woman where she is perhaps the most beautiful, about the neck and breasts; the smoothness; the softness; the easy and insensible swell; the variety of the surface, which is never for the smallest space the same; the deceitful maze, through which the unsteady eye slides giddily, without knowing where to fix, or whither it is carried. Is not this a demonstration of that change of surface continual and yet hardly perceptible at any point which forms one of the great constituents of beauty? (115)

This passage is discussed often in literary criticism, especially work that seeks to show the tension between the beautiful and the sublime in Burke's *A Philosophical Enquiry into the Origin of Our Ideas of the Sublime and the Beautiful* (1757).[4] Beyond Burke, though, critics regularly underscore the connection between an immobilised female body and aesthetic interpretations of beauty. Elisabeth Bronfen articulates such curiosity in the preface to her seminal text, *Over her Dead Body: Death, Femininity, and the Aesthetic*: 'because the feminine body is culturally constructed as the superlative site of alterity, culture uses art to dream the deaths of beautiful women ... this representation lets the repressed return, albeit in a disguised manner' (xi). Similar to Freud's neurotic vagina gazer who sees a home instead of a woman, a repression instead of a reality, the male viewer in the *Enquiry* recognises something about the experience of the sublime, rather than the beautiful, in his gaze. Beauty dissolves into erratic voyeurism and a maze-like, sublime agitation emerges. Burke's description in this segment is of a fundamental Gothic separation between self and other, where the female body is fragmented, disempowered and repackaged as a canvas for a philosophical male experience. This kind of confrontation is both a cornerstone of Gothic fiction and essential to the contemporary Irish Gothic where female bodies sometimes betray, not always willingly, their reproductive potential, leaving them maternally vacant, in search of something to fill the void that is left behind but resistant to traditional solutions even if they must give in to them in the end. Cassie Maddox, Tana French's detective-heroine in *The Likeness*, unapologetically chooses abortion in a novel that viciously critiques the dependency of capitalism on reproduction, but she also chooses to get engaged to her male partner in the end, suggesting a future of status-quo heteronormativity. Burke's torso illustrates this contradiction in its expression of beauty as an unavoidable sublime experience for the male gazer: Burke's female body is both beautiful and impossible.

In *The Coherence of Gothic Conventions*, Eve Sedgwick offers a useful explanation that better clarifies what happens to Burke's male subject when he sees the female torso. Sedgwick argues that a Gothic 'spacialization' of the self occurs when

> the self and whatever it is that is outside have a proper, natural, necessary connection to each other, but one that the self is suddenly incapable of making. The inside life and the outside life have to continue separately, becoming counterparts rather than partners, the relationship between them one of parallels and correspondences rather than communication. This, though it may happen in an instant, is a fundamental reorganization creating a doubleness where singleness should be. (13)

The confrontations in Burke mirror Sedgwick's idea of self-spacialisation in the creation of a double between a male subject and a female other, reflecting an unrecognisable image back to the gazing male subject, and creating an other where only an imaginary self used to be. Instead of welcoming the male gaze, the female body subverts and redirects penetrative attempts to aesthetically trap or limit female signification. For Burke and Irish colonial history, as well as for Sedgwick and the Gothic canon that followed her, the embodiment and subsequent recognition of otherness, female or otherwise, happens in a sudden instant, a momentary act of confrontation, or a Freudian glimpse of an inaccessible home.

Edmund Burke might not be the obvious departure point for a conversation about the contemporary Irish Gothic, but his controversial writings on the sublime articulate an organic subjectivity that is only formed through bifurcation, separation and distance. The contemporary Irish Gothic wrestles with those very same notions, reimagining Irish bodies, landscapes and domestic interiors as complicatedly, and sometimes necessarily, partitioned. With a major revolution just decades away and an emerging understanding of eighteenth-century subjectivity that depended on pain, physical identity and public execution, Burke understood the way that a philosophical category like the sublime evoked the spacialisation of the self for an Irish thinker. Burke's sublime famously fails; Kant emerges as the interlocutor for beauty and the canonical voice for sublime power, even if that sublimity is sacrificed for beauty's superiority. Burke's sublime is historically discarded because it is organic and physical, because it depends on the body.[5]

The contemporary Irish Gothic might be the phoenix rising from Burke's eighteenth-century ashes. The feminised body is sublime for Burke because the form is not representable as fully other to the male subject; she is a text that reflects the repressed and often unspoken anxiety of the gazer and of the eighteenth-century colonial project. For Irish writers like Donoghue and French, the female body is a similar Gothic necessity, exposing the power of the duplicitous, tortured, starved and sometimes dead female self to challenge structures of inequality, expose sexual abuse and, in the case of French, solve the crime. Anna O'Donnell's half-starved child-body in *The Wonder* exposes the exploitation of both women and children by a Catholicism that seeks all possible forms of financial support in its post-Famine quest to articulate the Irish nation, both as an ideological concept and as a literal geographical location. Buchanan points out that the Celtic Tiger's numerous 'physical changes to the Irish landscape are a famine of gentrification that makes land unable to sustain, both materially and culturally, an Irish community' (53). For contemporary Gothic writers, the same famine metaphor is aligned with the trope of the female body as a landscape of unsustainable and threatened Irish cultural history. The moments of resolution (if there are any) in such writing tellingly provide a critique of, but not a solution for, Celtic Tiger capitalism, compulsory heteronormativity and tenuous notions of Irish history and trauma.

While they differ in time period, setting, and plot, Tana French's 2008 novel *The Likeness* and Emma Donoghue's *The Wonder* (2016), both rely on the recognisable Gothic themes of repressed female sexuality and oppressive domestic space, suggesting a shared, contemporary critique of the place of women in modern Ireland. *The Likeness* features a contemporary Dublin suburb where a group of college students take up residence while *The Wonder* is set in the nineteenth-century rural Irish midlands and follows the lives of a young, starving girl and her nurse. In both novels, the maternal body is a site of loss and a detriment to, rather than an incubator for, reproduction, signaling both Donoghue and French's concerns with how women's reproduction underscores the compulsive heterosexuality of capitalistic development and growth, yet cannot thrive when forced to conform to that compulsion. Adrienne Rich breaks down this concern in her pivotal 1980 article 'Compulsory Heterosexuality and Lesbian Existence', where she argues that compulsory heterosexuality and the exploitation of the female body as an object for male dominance is linked to economics and xenophobia: 'the failure to examine heterosexuality as an institution is like failing to admit that the economic system called capitalism or the caste system of racism is maintained by a variety of forces, including both physical violence and false consciousness' (648). The success of the Celtic Tiger capitalism of the early 2000s invoked a metaphorical paradox that is both a classic Gothic trope and a patriarchal tool of oppression: reproduction by, and then destruction of, the female body as a cliché, but unavoidable representation of global and national development.

The Likeness is cross-over fiction, where crime noir meets Gothic when a woman is found dead before the story begins, a technique French employs in a few of her Dublin Murder Squad books, most memorably in *In the Woods* (2007), the first instalment in the series and still the most popular. This time there's a twist: the main character, Detective Cassie Maddox, is both the dead body and the living protagonist, one a real human being and the other an alias, Lexi Madison, invented for her by the murder squad to solve a previous crime. At different moments in the story, we learn that both women were once pregnant but did not carry their pregnancies to term. Cassie chooses to go to England to have an abortion and Lexi's baby dies in her womb after she's stabbed to death in a famine cottage on the property of an Anglo-Irish Big House, or ancestral mansion, that she co-owns with her four other roommates. The pregnancy is the ultimate cause of Lexi's murder by another housemate: she's planning to sell her portion of the house so she can move away with her new baby, but the property would then be co-owned by an outsider to the communal, idealistic utopian group around which the plot centres. She also cannot have a baby in the confines of French's story because the capitalistic fantasy that excludes marriage but comprises the group's friendships and romantic engagements is clearly not a sustainable or reproductive model for future development. Instead, it breeds jealousy, incest-like behaviour and violence. This is part of the basic history of capitalism in Ireland, as Margot Backus reminds us when she explains that 'the emergence of the capitalistic family cell sexualized familial relations regardless of whether children were literally sexually violated within the family' (44). While the family unit in this novel suggests a progressive, new approach to domestic life in an educated Ireland, it still produces a familiar historical trauma: intra-familial sex and violence resulting in the punishment-by-death of an unmarried, pregnant female character. Further, French shows how even though co-ownership or shared equity was one route to obtaining a mortgage that was encouraged at the height of the Tiger, it ultimately led to a similar, if not worse, failure as that endured by individual property ownership.[6]

Cassie, too, is unmarried throughout the story, but her decision to end her pregnancy and engage a life of chosen singleness, property rental and abortion stands in stark contrast to Lexi's murder, where no choices outside of communal ownership are possible. The Big House in *The Likeness* is not quite a ghost estate, but it carries a similar haunting legacy where modifying, or improving, what seems to be the repressive structure of a domestic history of economic oppression and disenfranchisement does not produce an actual future of change; instead, it kills the one version of the future conceived within it: a fetus that might one day be a child. The inhabitants of the Big House in *The Likeness* work hard to keep the property from falling into the hands of investors who would tear it down and build a series of potential ghost estates, thinking that their way of managing property ownership bypasses the darkness of capitalism in Ireland. Instead, French shows that ghost estates and Big Houses are part of the same root problem; in fact, ghost estates are built on the back of Big House histories. Nicholas Allen points out the potential danger of both ghost estates and Big Houses when he argues that for many Irish modernist writers 'the fall of the Big House is part of a wider process of global realignment', because the 'Big House is in no way representative of any national identity, but its interiors frame one history of Ireland's global past' (451). Global wealth that does not originate in or properly partner with the domestic interior of the nation threatens to undermine the future of the nation itself. As Joe Cleary emphasises in his introduction to *The Cambridge Companion to Modern Irish Culture*, both tradition and modernity are integral to a thriving future Ireland. Modernisation for the purposes of gentrified wealth without the incorporation of Irish history and memory (a 'no pasts' rule of law enforced by the novel's patriarch and original property owner, Daniel March)[7] will only result in the return of the repressed: a Gothic domestic space that does not just kill its inhabitants, but prevents anyone from living in it to begin with.

French acknowledges that her interest in Irish ghost estates informed many of the narrative decisions she made in her novels. Her descriptions suggest that she is particularly interested in the ghost estate's ability to emphasise the spatialisation of the self that Sedgwick marks as the defining feature of the Gothic. In a 2012 interview in *The Guardian*, Alison Flood asked French specifically about her portrayal of ghost estates in her writing and French described the economic collapse that led to the abandoned houses as 'haunting and terrible … something that never should have happened' ('Tana French'). French identifies the home as a vulnerable space where a 'dislocation between inner and outer reality' added to the feeling that domestic space was 'under attack' and produced a 'sensation of dislocation' that 'might have swelled to the sense that it can't be controlled' (ibid). It is specifically this image of an invaded or threatened home that led French to focus on ghost estates in her writing, particularly in *The Likeness* and *Broken Harbour*. In the latter text, she sees the estate itself as a kind of double for the protagonist and his struggle with social expectations, where an attack on the home after the Tiger's fall exposes its false representation as 'sacrosanct and solid and uninvadable' (ibid.). The 'uninvadability' or resistance to invasion that is characteristic of a nation that is no longer a colony is easily undermined in a future Gothic Ireland where the idea of home comes 'under attack, either from something in the wall or for the walls themselves from outside, and then all life feels as if it is made of tissue paper instead of solid brick. It coalesced into the idea of someone for whom all the rules he's followed start to let him down' (ibid.). Ireland may have followed all the rules of nationhood, but nation-building and even nation-thriving cannot protect an economy from the ebbs and flows of global capitalism, where nothing more than a 'tissue paper' life can develop.

Emma Donoghue's *The Wonder* (2016) flirts with Gothic mystery and guilt in a more overt way than *The Likeness* by invoking the possibility of the supernatural and waiting until the end to offer a more realistic explanation for the actions taken by the main character. Just as the supernatural presence in the text is an illusion, the novel's main proposition rests on a red herring that even the most careful readers have swallowed, hook, line and sinker. In her 2016 *Los Angeles Review of Books* piece, 'Maternal Ecstasies in Emma Donoghue's "The Wonder"', Meghan O'Gieblyn suggests, '*The Wonder* stands as an unmistakable conversion narrative. It is the story of a woman denying, resisting, and ultimately accepting the call to nurture. Even within the context of Donoghue's previous work, *The Wonder* is especially insistent – at times even polemical – on the nourishing effects of childbearing' ('Maternal Ecstasies'). Donoghue's novel tells the nineteenth-century Gothic story of two parallel female characters, Anna, a starving girl who suffers a horrific sexual trauma and must be convinced to live through spiritual rebirth, and Lib, a young nurse who lost a child and remains married only to her scientific calling until she, too, is figuratively reborn. O'Gieblyn insists that the text is a call to motherhood, a manifesto of 'familial love', an argument that 'childlessness is a kind of starvation, a willful spiritual emptiness' (ibid.), even though it details the actual death and near-death experiences of every child mentioned in the narrative. If childbearing is the sustenance needed to overcome modern and historical trauma in Donoghue's novel, then no one recovers and trauma is absolute because neither female character successfully births a child in the span of the text. (Lib's loss of a child before the story begins haunts the lack of reproduction that is actually present in the narrative). In fact, *The Wonder* follows a similar formula to some of Donoghue's earlier novels where family is redefined as more than a series of blood relationships. Just as we are left with a group of unrelated characters, living together and trying to cope after the death of a loved one in *Hood* (1995), *The Wonder*, too, ends with a new version of family where all members are connected through survival and compassion but not through blood.

More important than motherhood in this narrative, is the power of the female body to reflect and expose both the dangerous effects of intra-familial sexual assault and rape and the willingness of the church to ignore, commodify and weaponise sexual fear and trauma. Both nurse and patient, as unrelated mother and child, experience variations of physical trauma where their bodies turn against them: Lib loses an infant to starvation because she cannot nurse and Anna is raped by her brother, leading her to starve herself after his death in an attempt to eradicate the 'sin' of that sexual experience. The female bodies of our two main characters are the front and centre metaphors of British Victorian sensibility and Irish colonial history, respectively. Donoghue is careful to make neither character totally likeable as they personify the detrimental aspects of their cultural referents: British skepticism keeps Lib ignorant and judgmental of the Irish while Irish Catholicism pushes Anna to naively interpret the church's theology literally, leaving her no choice but to starve out the indiscretion that she believes has trapped her brother's soul in purgatory for an interminable amount of time.

While Anna struggles to understand the incestuous assault she experiences at the hands of her brother, the leaders of the church in *The Wonder*, mostly priests, are driven to determine if Anna is, in fact, a walking miracle because of her ability to survive without food:[8]

> 'I don't want to prejudice you in any way,' he went on, 'but what I may say is that it's a most unusual case. Anna O'Donnell claims – or, rather, her parents claim – that she hasn't taken food since her eleventh birthday.'
> ...
> 'How long has it been since her birthday?' she asked.
> McBrearty plucked at his whiskers. 'April, this was. Four months ago today!' (12–13)

They hire a British nurse and an Irish nun to investigate Anna's survival as a potential miracle and enjoy the economic profits of Anna's home-turned-tourist-trap where visitors from all over the world come to donate to the cause and see the wonder child who can live without food. What the church leaders do not do and what must be done for Anna's redemption and survival is figure out why the girl's religious piety is connected to her hunger strike or her life without food. As Molly Ferguson explains, 'The story Anna was telling through her body – that she no longer wished to sustain it with food – was the story to which her caregivers and community needed to listen. If young women's only vehicle for speech is their bodies, the novel further suggests that a girl's fasting in the Midlands of Ireland of 1859 is not so very different from practices in contemporary Western cultures that fetishize women as symbols' (108).

The church elders as well as her family members ignore her confessions of a pseudo-marriage and sex with her adolescent brother who dies before the narrative begins; they forgive her sins and move quickly past the crime, burying it in family history and focusing instead on the possibility of an actual miracle that could rejuvenate everyone's faith in the church after several years of famine and struggle. When Anna's naïveté emerges as the force that keeps her alive – she believes she is fed on 'manna from heaven' delivered to her by her mother each night before bed, during a goodnight kiss that is eerily reminiscent of the incest and rape that originally induced the starvation (ibid. 90) – she must discard that sustenance, leading her body to truly deteriorate as she gets closer and closer to physical collapse. Anna's starving body, as the product of rape and incest, reflects the church's chosen ignorance of her sexual assault that perpetuates her self-destruction. She erases herself and her body to make way for forgiveness and redemption, not only for herself but also, allegorically, for a Catholic Ireland that privileges superstition, family and money over fact. Donoghue shows us how this is a dangerous exchange when the narrative parallels Lib's experience of missing meals with Anna's starvation. In a fatalistic way, Lib, too, must function without food in this novel until she finds a way to save Anna. Donoghue's emphasis on the female body and the physical wasting away of both characters without successful reproduction demands a reconsideration of the role of the family in Irish economic development.

At the end of *The Likeness* and *The Wonder* we see representations of new family dynamics that are both heteronormative and nontraditional. The new family structures are forecasted in both instances by the burning down of the domestic spaces central to the narratives:

> I could feel the map of Whitethorn House branded on my bones: the shape of the newel post printed in my palm, the curves of Lexie's bedstead down my spine, the slants and turns of the staircase in my feet, my body turned into

a shimmering treasure map for a lost island. What Lexie had started, I had finished for her. Between the two of us, we had razed Whitethorn House to rubble and smoking ash. (French, *The Likeness* 438)

But would the whole room go up in flames? This was their one slim chance of getting away with fraud. Was the thatch dry enough after three days of sunshine? Lib glared at the low ceiling. The old beams looked too sturdy, the thick walls too strong. Nothing else to be done; the lamp swung in her hand, and she hurled it into the rafters.
 Rain of glass and fire. (Donoghue, *The Wonder* 278)

In effect, the past versions of family on which both of the novels' critiques focus (a communal group of students in *The Likeness* and a traditional Catholic family in *The Wonder*) are destroyed and new constructions replace them. Both Cassie's engagement to her detective partner, Sam, at the end of *The Likeness* and Lib's marriage to the journalist, Byrne, and their subsequent adoption of Anna in *The Wonder* present us with alternative family units that still participate in traditional narratives. While both novels use the Gothic to challenge the systemic oppression inflicted by systems of power (capitalism and Catholicism), they do not offer a break from the system entirely.

While not a Gothic text in the same vein as French and Donoghue's novels, Rooney's *Normal People* engages Gothic devices, such as a focus on dangerous domestic interiors and threats of economic disempowerment, to position the female body as the central metaphor for the trauma of global capitalism after the Celtic Tiger. But the end of the novel is a glaring departure from *The Likeness* and *The Wonder* in that the two main characters immersed in the novel's romance plot do not end up together. Instead, in this version of the nation-as-female-body, the female protagonist, Marianne, cannot leave Ireland because it is through her body, bleeding and broken by the end, that we see the domestic violence generated from economic excess in the wake of the Celtic Tiger.

Donoghue, French and the contemporary Irish Gothic underscore how the commodification of sexuality has always been essential to the formation of Irish national identity. However, in novels like *Normal People*, money, not religion, is exposed as the root cause of sexual and domestic violence and exploitation. Marianne and Connell attend a contemporary and secular version of church when they visit the ghost estate, testifying to the vindication of female desire by a global capitalism that equally and paradoxically depends on a destructive history of sexual repression and oppression. In a moment of reckoning, Rooney puts Marianne in the position to tell Connell that she will do anything for him, while they are surrounded by an abandoned and broken Irish suburban landscape, and, at that same moment, Marianne becomes the pathway through which Connell can leave Ireland. She encourages him to go to Trinity, to major in English, to write and ultimately to leave. Ireland and the Celtic Tiger made it possible for Marianne to stay in Dublin, granting her domestic mobility akin to cosmopolitanism, but masculinity cannot cohabitate that space without violence. The contemporary Irish Gothic demands that we look the traumatic past that produced that violence in the face and recognise the familiar reflection that stares back at us.

Notes

1. See Morin, and Killeen, *The Emergence of Irish Gothic Fiction*.
2. In 'Risk and Refuge: Contemplating Precarity in Contemporary Irish Fiction', Malcolm Sen explains the literary significance of the Irish ghost estate: 'Space during the Celtic Tiger became transfigured … without any intrinsic communal value. … It was only after the financial meltdown of 2008, when the spectacle of the Celtic Tiger gave way to the spectre of ghost estates, that the literary boom was forcefully set in motion. It should not come as a surprise then that housing and real estate, homeliness and dwelling, provide the vocabulary of literary speculation and recovery in contemporary Irish literature' (24–25).
3. See also the ghost estate in *Pure Mule: The Last Weekend* (2009), which may be an influence here.
4. See Gibbons for a detailed reading of this passage.
5. Burke's *Enquiry* provides the basis for Immanuel Kant's theories on aesthetics in his late eighteenth-century manifesto, *The Critique of Judgment*. Kant purports that Beauty is understood as the superior aesthetic principle precisely because it transcends organic and/or physical experiences. Burke, instead, relies on the corporal system of the body to support his theories, and by the end of the eighteenth century, this is seen as a dated system of aesthetic philosophy.
6. In an *Irish Times* piece from 3 March 2021, Jennifer Bray details Sinn Fein's current resistance to the Irish government's scheme to support shared equity in the contemporary housing market because it could trigger a 'price spiral' reminiscent of Celtic Tiger property costs.
7. 'Daniel glanced up from his book. "No pasts," he said. The fall of it, the finality, told me it was something he had said before. … There was a long, not-quite-comfortable silence … For some reason, the past—any of our pasts—was solidly off-limits' (French, *The Likeness* 184).
8. In her depiction of Anna as a potential saint who can live without food, Donoghue invokes twentieth-century work on religion and hunger, such as *Holy Anorexia* by Rudolph Bell and *Holy Feast and Holy Fast* by Caroline Walker Bynum.

Works Cited

Allen, Nicholas. 'Modernism and the Big House'. *A History of the Modernist Novel*, edited by Gregory Castle, Cambridge University Press, 2015, pp. 449–63.

Backus, Margot Gayle. *The Gothic Family Romance: Heterosexuality, Child Sacrifice, and the Anglo-Irish Colonial Order*. Duke University Press, 1999.

Baldick, Chris. 'Introduction'. *The Oxford Book of Gothic Tales*, edited by Chris Baldick, Oxford University Press, 2009.

Bray, Jennifer. '"Dead as a Dodo": Scrap Shared Equity Home Loan Scheme, says SF TD'. *The Irish Times*, 3 March 2021.

Bronfen, Elisabeth. *Over her Dead Body: Death, Femininity and the Aesthetic*. Manchester University Press, 1992.

Bruhm, Steven. 'The Contemporary Gothic: Why we Need it'. *The Cambridge Companion to Gothic Fiction*, edited by Jerrold E. Hogle, Cambridge University Press, 2002, pp. 259–76.

Buchanan, Jason. 'Ruined Futures: Gentrification as Famine in Post-Celtic Tiger Irish Fiction'. *Modern Fiction Studies*, vol. 63, no. 1, 2017, pp. 50–72.

Burke, Edmund. *A Philosophical Enquiry into the Origin of our Ideas of the Sublime and the Beautiful*, edited by James T. Boulton, University of Notre Dame Press, 1958.

Cleary, Joe. 'Introduction'. *The Cambridge Companion to Modern Irish Culture*, edited by Joe Cleary and Claire Connolly, Cambridge University Press, 2005, pp. 1–22.

Costello-Sullivan, Kathleen. *Trauma and Recovery in the Twenty-First-Century Irish Novel*. Syracuse University Press, 2018.

Donoghue, Emma. *The Wonder*. Little, Brown, and Co., 2016.

Emmet, Robert. 'Speech from the Dock, 1803'. *The Field Day Anthology of Irish Writing*, edited by Seamus Deane et al., volume 1, Field Day, 1991, p. 938.

Ferguson, Molly. '"To Say No and No Again": Fasting Girls, Shame, and Storytelling in Emma Donoghue's *The Wonder*'. *New Hibernia Review*, vol. 22, no. 2, Summer 2018, pp.93–108.

Flood, Alison. 'Tana French: I'm Haunted by Ireland's Ghost Estates'. *The Guardian*, 27 July 2012.

Fogarty, Anne. 'Uncanny Families: Neo-Gothic Motifs and the Theme of Social Change in Contemporary Irish Women's Fiction'. *Irish University Review*, vol. 30, no. 1, Special Issue: Contemporary Irish Fiction, spring-summer 2000, pp. 59–81.

French, Tana. *Broken Harbour*. Penguin, 2012.

———. *The Likeness*. Penguin, 2008.

Freud, Sigmund. *The Uncanny*. Penguin Classics, 2003.

Gibbons, Luke. *Edmund Burke and Ireland: Aesthetics, Politics, and the Colonial Sublime*. Cambridge University Press, 2003.

Gladwin, Derek. *Contentious Terrains: Boglands, Ireland, Postcolonial Gothic*. Cork University Press, 2016.

Hogle, Jerrold E., ed. *The Cambridge Companion to the Modern Gothic*. Cambridge University Press, 2014.

Horner, Avril and Sue Zlosnik. 'Gothic Configurations of Gender'. Hogle, pp. 55–70.

Kiberd, Declan. *Inventing Ireland*. Harvard University Press, 1996.

Killeen, Jarlath. *The Emergence of Irish Gothic Fiction: History, Origins, Theories*. Edinburgh University Press, 2014.

———. 'How Celtic Tiger's Death Led to a Gothic Revival'. *The Irish Times*, 28 April 2017.

Morin, Christina. *Charles Robert Maturin and the Haunting of Irish Romantic Fiction*. Manchester University Press, 2011.

O'Gieblyn, Meghan. 'Maternal Ecstasies in Emma Donoghue's *The Wonder*'. *Los Angeles Review of Books*, 18 September 2016.

Quigley, Mark. *Empire's Wake: Postcolonial Irish Writing and the Politics of Modern Literary Form*. Fordham University Press, 2013.

Rich, Adrienne. 'Compulsory Heterosexuality and Lesbian Existence'. *Signs*, vol. 5, no. 4, 1980, pp. 631–660. JSTOR, www.jstor.org/stable/3173834. Accessed 16 February 2020.

Rooney, Sally. *Normal People*. Faber, 2018.

Saint-Amour, Paul. *Tense Future: Modernism, Total War, Encyclopedic Form*. Oxford University Press, 2015.

Schneider, Steven Jay. 'Introduction'. *Horror Film and Psychoanalysis: Freud's Worst Nightmare*, edited by Steven Jay Schneider, Cambridge University Press, 2004, pp. 1–16.

Sedgwick, Eve Kosofsky. *The Conherence of Gothic Conventions*. Methuen, 1986.

Sen, Malcolm. 'Risk and Refuge: Contemplating Precarity in Contemporary Irish Fiction'. *Irish University Review*, vol. 49, no. 1, 2019, pp. 13–31.

Williams, Anne. *Art of Darkness: A Poetics of Gothic*. University of Chicago Press, 1995.

Chapter 13

Foreign Bodies, Irish Voices: Gothic Masculinities in Irish Literature, Film and Radio Drama
Sorcha de Brún

In P. J. Dillon's seminal Irish language short film, *An Ranger* (*The Ranger*; 2013), the closing and opening shots of the film reveal a lone horseman silhouetted left of screen against a dramatic setting sun in the West of Ireland. In a scene awash with the muted grey and blue colours of a Connemara evening in the late nineteenth century, the male character and his horse appear framed in a conflation of light and shadow, of animal and human. Both horse and man appear not merely to merge as one into the approaching blackness, but into each other. What is striking in this classic short of Irish language film is the absence of sound and voice, the solitary pose of the equestrian, and the complete stillness of the scene. The medium shot is sufficiently distant to prevent the viewer from observing the rider's face. Reminiscent of German Romantic art and, in particular, Caspar David Friedrich's painting *Der Wanderer uber dem Nebelmeer* (*Wanderer Above the Sea of Fog*; c.1818), all meaning is vested in the sense of existing *le faobhar na hoíche*: on the blade edge of the night. The symbolic imagery of a moment in time on the edge of something belies a murderous intent that reveals itself presently in the journey the protagonist takes shortly afterwards towards violence and revenge. The sense of man merging with animal, the suspension of voice and sound, and the face turned from the camera resonate with David Punter's comment on 'the dehumanizing force in gothic generally' (11).

The proliferation of the Gothic in modern Irish language literature and film has received scant critical attention, but it is one of the most consistent features of contemporary modern Irish language narrative since 1980. Works of fiction that rely heavily on Gothic modes include Joe Steve Ó Neachtain's *Lámh Láidir* (*A Strong Hand*, 2005), Liam Mac Cóil's *I dTír Strainséartha* (*In a Foreign Land*, 2014), Anna Heusaff's *Bás Tobann* (*Sudden Death*, 2005), and Colm Ó Ceallaigh's *Éiric Fola* (*Blood Retribution*, 1999), to name but a few. Feature films such as *An Leabhar* (*The Book*, dir. Robert Quinn; 2004) and *Arracht* (*Spectre*, dir.

Tomás Ó Súilleabháin; 2019) depend largely on Gothic modes to depict the aggression and violence that frequently accompanied the cultural transition from English to Irish. Yet despite this recent turn towards a more modern form of Gothic in Irish language narrative, the theme of terror is rooted in the oral tradition of the Irish language. Anne Markey notes, for example, how 'critics have repeatedly argued that folklore is a significant source for gothic tropes and themes' (94). Perhaps the two most significant events in the move from terror to Gothic in modern Irish literature was marked by the publication of *Séadna* by Peadar Ó Laoghaire in 1901, followed by the translation of *Dracula* (1897) in 1933. Alan Titley comments that Ó Laoghaire would not have had to depend on Gothic literature in English to find inspiration for *Séadna*: 'níor ghá dó dul chucu sin chun uafás na linne a nochtadh' (he would not have had to depend on them to explore contemporary terror) ('Séadna', 19, 20). However, *Séadna*, a 1901 Irish language novel of the literary revival, uses conventions very similar to those in Gothic literature. The translation of *Dracula* was a seminal moment in the creation of an Irish language Gothic. It succeeded in creating a Gothic mode at once faithful to Stoker's original, yet it is brimming with cultural references to terror specific to the Irish language literary and oral tradition (de Brún, '"In a Sea of Wonders"', 81). What is perhaps most noteworthy about Irish language Gothic is its emphasis on the representation of masculinities. *An Ranger* is just one text that illustrates the emerging features of twenty-first century Irish Gothic. In this more recent variant of Irish Gothic, in addition to its more conventional use, terror can be suggestive of what Gabor Maté refers to as the 'hungry ghost realm' (1). Used by Maté as a metaphor to describe addiction and the psychological 'aching emptiness' that drives it, the 'hungry ghost realm' has origins in the *mandala*, or wheel of life in Eastern philosophy, where the ghost is characterised not by passion but by a hunger exacerbated by past trauma and marked by 'emotional pain' (203).

Unusually perhaps in Gothic literature, then, the ghosts in the texts explored in this essay are rarely visible or perceived externally. Furthermore, the classic Gothic convention of the big house is not their natural home. On the contrary, it is frequently through the skilful manipulation of sound and voice that the darker side of humanity reveals itself. For this reason, as will be shown in this essay, voice is of particular importance, when the true voice of the individual male finds itself silenced and marginalised, literally and linguistically. I argue that sound design and use of voice comprise an emerging feature of Gothic in twenty-first century literature in Irish and English where the manipulation (and absence) of voice and sound serves as a distinctive Gothic mode. In this essay, I explore that nexus between masculinities and Gothic literature, comparing six texts in English and Irish. I look at how the ghost reveals itself in hegemonic masculinity in Aodh Ó Domhnaill's *An Duairceán (The Gloom)* (2016); in female masculinity in Paul Lynch's *Grace* (2017); in disembodied masculinity in *Black '47* (dir. Lance Daly; 2018); through emasculation and colonised masculinity in *Lámh Láidir*; in the affective, anxious masculinity of John Morton's *100 Everyday Menaces* (2014); and of violent masculinity in *An Ranger*. Through analysing these narratives, I show how the depiction of traumatised masculinities, all inhabitants in different ways of a world akin to Maté's 'realm of the hungry ghosts', is achieved primarily through use of techniques more commonly seen in stage drama and visual art, rather than through classic character development or plot. Each of these works comprises a particular expression of masculinity where that depends on a number of Gothic conventions to achieve its aim.

If the 'aching emptiness' (203) that Maté refers to reflects an aspect of the Gothic in the texts under discussion here, the radio drama could be said to be a perfect medium with which to explore loss and absence. While studies of Gothic literature traditionally confined themselves to fiction, and later to film, horror in radio drama has a long and illustrious history. Indeed, Martin Grams Jr. notes that horror had become a staple of the genre by the late 1940s (34). English language radio drama has overwhelmingly used Gothic modes, and recent developments in sound design and effects, as well as in the realm of podcasting, have brought radio drama to a new and contemporary audience, highlighting the suitability of the medium to the Gothic mode. Since the 1980s, for example, the use of the 'foley artist' (Willems 234), enabled the director to create additional sounds post-production and to add aurality to the narrative that was not possible in the early days of radio drama. In a complex interplay between diegetic and non-diegetic techniques in both radio drama and film, sound and voice function as a central funnel for the Gothic in the narration of the text. Diegetic aurality is used to extraordinary effect in *An Ranger*, where dialogue is minimal. The change in tempo as the main character rides his horse ever faster towards his nemesis's home is matched by a crescendo that succeeds in building fear only to be stopped abruptly when the horse and rider pause at the brow of the hill. In a similar way, a central aspect of the Gothic in *An Duairceán* is the ambiguity created between diegetic and non-diegetic aurality. It is unclear, for example, whether the birds' screams are also experienced by the characters; or whether have they been added post-production as a narrative device with which to create Gothic tension for the listening audience. In addition, through a subtle and imaginative use of the natural environment to portray landscapes and settings, the big house of Irish Gothic, a staple of Irish Gothic as noted by W. J. McCormack (832), is subverted and challenged by its opposite: the humble cottage, the lowly cabin, the majestic, untamed mountain. Furthermore, by replacing physical terror with psychological and existential terror, a significant number of Gothic texts since 2010 succeed in what Christina Morin and Niall Gillespie describe as the 'delimiting' of the Gothic (1). At the heart of this existential terror, it is noteworthy how the protagonists are predominantly men, and how politics itself becomes the source of the existential terror. If the implications of national politics and the failings of the colonised state resulting in famine, war and forced migration are used as thematic material in the following texts, I argue that inadequate attempts to deal with historical and political legacies form the basis for much of the anxiety represented in the narratives explored in this essay.

If the sonic aspect of the Gothic and the creation of night fears, terrors and sounds are central to the Irish Gothic, it could be argued that radio drama is one of the best, yet least examined, means through which to create the Gothic. In his seminal work on radio drama in Ireland and on the work of the BBC in influencing the development of radio drama in English, Dermot Rattigan describes the form as 'aural performance literature' (2). The contribution of radio drama to the gothic since the Golden Age of radio in the 1930s and 1940s has been, simply put, astonishing, and yet under-estimated. The culture of radio drama that produced Gothic horrors such as Orson Welles' *War of the Worlds* (1938) as well as the 'wireless zombie' podcasts of the twenty-first century (Challis, D'Arcy, et al.) show both medium and practice that harness new technologies while harking back to an age where story-telling was of the utmost importance. Dylan Thomas's *Under Milk Wood*, first produced for the BBC in 1954, for example, used the medium of radio to chronicle the 'aspirations and assignations, dreams and drudgeries, lives and loves' of the Welsh fishing village of Llareggub (Rattigan 80). The versatility of radio drama for many different genres was perhaps nowhere more evident than in Irish-born Giles Cooper's *Under the Loofah Tree* first broadcast on the BBC in 1958 and an absurdist parody of domestic masculinity.

In her analysis of Gothic art and its connections with folklore, Tracy Fahey (153) notes how Irish folklore had a significant impact on Irish art and was 'a precursor of an influence on the later Gothic tradition'. *An Duairceán* by Aodh Ó Domhnaill is one such Irish language Gothic radio drama that combines themes of folklore and technology, in both subject matter and form, to weave a Gothic story of highly original proportions. First broadcast on RTÉ *Drama on One* in 2016, it tells of two radio producers who are recording an Irish language radio programme on the disappearance of a Father Harrington after climbing a local mountain – called an Duaircéan. It transpires that, according to local folklore, this mountain has always been a place that inspires fear and terror in the local population: Father Harrington, Úna tells us, was found decapitated, a notion that her colleague Seán scoffs at. Seán's scoffing at the decapitation story is consistent with Ó Domhnaill's portrayal of the contrast between those, like Úna, who believe in 'piseoga' (superstitions) and who suspend their disbelief, to Seán's trust in 'réalachas' (reality) and 'ciall' (sense). As the story progresses, the technology used by the couple gradually begins to fail them, the batteries die and – in classic Gothic mode – a storm breaks on the mountain. The drama concludes with a solitary voice telling us that Seán and Úna, in line with many others before them, have disappeared and that there is no trace of their whereabouts.

In the first instance, much of the terror that the protagonists of *An Duaircéan* record on their devices in Ó Domhnaill's radio drama achieves its power in its portrayal of Seán's hegemonic masculinity (Connell and Messerschmidt 839), and in his relationship with and attitude towards Úna. Their trip to the mountain where they meet their end – a conclusion the audience have been prepared for by the narrator from the beginning of the play – is a portrayal not merely of their demise in the face of unseen horrors, but also a depiction of a relationship that is doomed. Indeed, Ó Domhnaill's play shows how the failure in the relationship between Seán and Úna is the primary cause of their deaths. The radio recording of the disintegration of that relationship, and Seán's misogyny in relation to Úna's terror, expressed through his derision, explores the sense of impending doom that is highlighted by Seán's cavalier attitude to the signs of danger. In addition, Úna's dependence on Seán as her only companion on the lonely mountain examines what Lucie Armitt describes as the fragility of the human body as a central trope in Gothic literature (150). Ó Domhnaill's drama goes further, however, in the manner in which the relationship between the rational and the irrational, the emotional and the superstitious, and the power struggle therein, mirrors the juxtaposition of the elemental forces of nature and the supernatural against the power of technology. This uncomfortable alliance succeeds in highlighting the intrinsic fragility of technology and the advance of rational modernity against the force of an Duaircéan. Its name contains allusions to darkness (*duairc*) in the literal and figurative sense, and the gradual realisation that an Duaircéan is a haunted place is only secondary to Úna's horror that Seán does not believe any of her warnings. A central theme running throughout Ó Domhnaill's narrative is the power of listening, whether to others (as in the case of Seán not listening to Úna) or to the signs of impending tragedy. *An Duaircéan* is a portrayal, therefore, of the repercussions in ignoring the significance of what is heard, as opposed to what is visible.

The narrative contains extended passages where Seán mocks Úna, using a high-pitched feminine voice to imitate her superstition and fear. The mountain is a place without defined borders, because when the mists descend and the maps no longer serve their purpose, the characters of *An Duaircéan* have stepped into a world where order and clarity break down. Sound effects include the howling of the wind, and the birds of the mountain appear to scream in human-like voices in the skies above them. Comprising what Porter Abbott describes as a framing narrative in the style of much Irish language Gothic fiction (25), the drama is constructed around an ostensibly real-time telling of events as they unfold in the present tense. Ó Domhnaill's portrayal of the mountain expands the Gothic mode, in showing how the mountain and its craggy summit resembles a large castle, or house – so that the classic big house trope of Irish Gothic appears like an enormous castle at the pinnacle of the world. However, this is an illusion. There is no such Gothic castle, and both the protagonists and the listener realise that this large edifice of a mountain and its caves that resemble rooms of a house, its large open spaces with deadly crevices that can consume Seán and Úna at any time, are not merely of the characters' imaginations, but also of the listeners'.

More than any other element of the drama, it is the soundscape of *An Duaircéan*, in particular the contrast of high-pitched and low-pitched frequencies, the use of far-off voices to indicate distance and perspective, and the use of intervals between speech which adds to the Gothic sense of foreboding. These auditory techniques in the radio narrative in turn function to highlight Seán's hegemonic masculinity. At particular points in the drama, when the protagonists listen back to their recordings, additional wails and screams are reflected back to them using echo sound effects. Ó Domhnaill's use of this auditory narrative device is significant and artful. On the one hand, it can be interpreted as flashbacks to an alternative account of what takes places on the mountain. However, it can also be understood as an example of where 'gothic literature typically places characters out of sync with time and induces historical time to lie heavily on the present' (de Brún, 'Temporality and Irish Revivalism' 18). In this instance, when the characters listen back to their recordings, and to the fate that has already befallen them in the past tense, we see an example of what Abbott describes as a 'kind of deranged narrative discourse' (30). This technique of sonic manipulation is further reflected in the laboured breathing of the characters to depict the terror that awaits them on the mountain and, ultimately, the essence of their being. As in the case of film, the use of diegetic techniques such as this contribute to the narrative of terror and tell their own story.

In this way, the main protagonists in *An Duairceán* become ghosts themselves, and we witness that transformation. Ó Domhnaill's radio drama is successful in conjuring terror, not through a narrative description of what can be 'seen' by the listener; but rather what can be imagined, and what, perhaps, has already happened. Of necessity, the eschewal of what is visible in favour of an allusion to what has taken place is an effective technique for radio drama (in that nothing can be portrayed visually), as well as harnessing the power of the listener's imagination. Furthermore, the projection of the possibility of terror, rather than the actual terror itself, is what adds to the Gothic sense of fear. For this reason, the terror in *An Duairceán* is never quite past: in Ó Domhnaill's drama, the Gothic is continuous, because the mountain as Gothic trope in the narrative is an eternal site of terror and an unbeatable foe. As in the case of *The Blair Witch Project* (dir. Daniel Myrick and Eduardo Sánchez; 1999), and other experimental Gothic narratives, the listener or viewer becomes part of the Gothic experience, and witness to the evil forces that are leading the main characters to their deaths. The drama finishes with the calm reasoned voice of the male narrator who appears to be the mountain itself, speaking slowly from the depths in a deep bass voice. However, the use of this pitch of voice is reflective of what Judith Butler describes as a 'corporeal style' in relation to the performance of masculinity (139). In this way, the narrator performs a version of masculinity, but due to its invisibility, Ó Domhnaill creates an ambiguity surrounding the gender of the speaker. Reeser (83) notes how a fundamental aspect of Butler's concept of the corporeal style entails that of change. Throughout *An Duairceán*, both the narrator's and Seán's voice change constantly in both pitch and timbre to reflect the Gothic narrative in purely acoustic and auditory terms. Ultimately, the implications of such constant change is a portrayal of masculinity as both 'fluid' and physically disembodied (Reeser 106). Framing the narrative of the radio drama at both outset and conclusion, the return of the narrator reveals, through the use of auditory techniques, that the mountain has functioned as the storyteller all along and is, in essence, controlling both the Gothic narrative and, through manipulation of Seán's high-pitched voice and the voice of the narrator, the performative masculinity of the characters. Furthermore, the mountain itself appears to be yielding up what is left of the radio documentary found after Seán and Úna's death, reflecting the central importance of the 'retrieved will, diary or fragment' so prevalent in Gothic literature (de Brún, 'Temporality and Irish Revivalism' 27). In this way, the idea of the unreliable narrator is forged

(Mullan 43); however, unlike the multiple narratives of *Dracula* (1897) multiple voices voice are employed to create uncertainty on the part of the listener:

> The use of multiple narratives, though somewhat unorthodox, is not entirely original: many of the Gothic novels of the nineteenth century, including Mary Shelley's *Frankenstein*, have several story-tellers and stories enframed within the main story. One of the reasons for using such a method, particularly in supernatural tales of terror, is to make an incredible story more credible by providing plenty of good witnesses to vouch for it. (Ellman xvii)

The wild and untamed landscape of the mountain in *An Duairceán* is replicated in other texts that explore gothic terror and, the breaking of societal conventions. The wild landscape as pathetic fallacy and as representing the untamed and uncontrolled can be seen in works from Thomas Mann's *Der Zauberberg* (1924), published in English in 1927 as *The Magic Mountain*; to Annie Proulx's *Brokeback Mountain* (1997) to the Carpathian Mountains of Stoker's *Dracula*, and the mountains that feature in M. K. Joseph's *A Soldier's Tale* (1976). Similarly, as Roger Robinson points out, the mountain as Gothic trope is one that has not been widely researched in Gothic studies, even though wild, isolated settings such as the mountain feature in many Gothic fictions in both Irish and English. The terror in *An Duairceán* is as much centred on the fear of abandonment by a fellow human in that wild place, as it is of the supernatural forces of the mountain.

Greg Whitehead has noted the suitability of the medium of radio for horror, where radio drama 'has created an uncanny world of the living dead' (145). Using the lens of the 'uncanny world' as a framework through which to explore the Gothic in *An Duairceán*, the mountain, while not appearing to be a foreign place, is alien to those who visit it. It is noteworthy how Ó Domhnaill shows in *An Duairceán* that the act of walking in unknown territory provides the perfect thematic material with which to explore the foreign, unknown parts of that which we think we know well, and those whom we think we know. In this case, the male protagonist Seán becomes a foreboding, threatening figure to his female companion. A uniquely original drama, *An Duairceán* is a showcase for multiple interpretations of Gothic masculinity in Irish language literature and culture. In this way, language itself, and dialogue between a male and a female protagonist, takes on darker undertones in this drama of Irish language surrealism.

Sonic design in *An Duairceán* portrays a hegemonic masculinity at war with the feminine in a Gothic landscape where the male voice – as opposed to the 'male gaze' as described by Mulvey (qtd. in Flood,

Gardiner et al. 376) – is the primary weapon. This can be contrasted with the short Irish language film *An Ranger*. Returning to a ruined Connemara in 1854 as a soldier in the British Army after twenty-one years, Myles is met with scenes of devastation and destruction, and learns how his mother was evicted and left to die on the side of the road during the Great Famine (1845–1849). Suspecting a local older man, Ignatius, as collaborator, he calls on him and learns that he has taken on the lease of the ruins of his family's cabin, which he is now using for his pigs. A tense stand-off ensues between the two men, Ignatius yielding a gun, and Myles bearing a long knife, where Myles describes the horrors, 'na huafáis', that he has witnessed in Bengal, the Crimea, Afghanistan and Connemara. Yet Myles notes that the difference between the violence and injustice that was visited on his mother was that Ignatius is not foreign; he contributed to the eviction of Myles's mother from her home in collaborating with the crown forces and did it to 'his own people'. Myles ultimately beheads Ignatius and replaces his head with that of a pig, in a possible cinematic homage to William Golding's *Lord of the Flies* (1954).

An Ranger depicts a Gothic masculinity that conveys a world of inner torment, isolation, and, ultimately revenge, where young men are shaped by the violence of war. Reflecting a Gothic 'terror', the once lived-in abode of Myles's childhood is now a veritable graveyard where men prepare to carry out violent acts that represent 'a new recreation of an older venue' and a place where 'secrets from the past … haunt the characters, psychologically, physically or otherwise' (Hogle 2). However, part of the disgust that Myles feels at the debasement of his mother is, in part, his self-hatred due to the part that he played himself as a soldier involved in the business of murder and death. From the outset of the film, the stark red of the soldier's army coat is in sharp relief to the dark colours of the Gothic setting of the Cong landscape and, later, Ignatius's blood. Myles spends his first night back in Connemara in the outdoors, discovering that he sleeps on the bones of his recently deceased ancestors, finding a set of human teeth barely concealed beneath the earth. This reflects what Hogle describes as an unresolved crime of conflict 'that can no longer be held from view' (2). As in *An Duairceán*, while there is no dialogue in the opening scenes of the film that tell the story of Myles's family, Dilllon contrasts that silence by foregrounding the call of the birds in the evening and the sound of rushing water. The red coat of the British soldier, and the bright red flames of the fire Myles has lit, reflect heightened emotion in close shots of Myles's face as he lifts his head to look towards Ignatius's cottage. In this way, they narrate both Myles's grief and his personal transformation from grieving soldier to revengeful son. Indeed, the symbolism of Myles's open-air fire is at once reminiscent of the importance of the hearth and, in the tales that were traditionally 'transmitted by the hearth', legend and folklore, of the passing on of narrative from one generation to the next (Fahey 166). For that reason, it is noteworthy that the dialogue between Ignatius and Myles takes place by the hearth: in the final domestic shot of the film, the camera sweeps in to show Ignatius sitting beheaded by the fire. In this way, their tales of mutual violence appear ready for transmission, using this central practice and theme of folklore, thereby replacing the traditional male storyteller dominant in Irish language culture, with that of a violent, off-camera act. However, the rivalry between Ignatius and Myles is not merely limited to what masculinities scholar Reeser describes as an aspect of social masculinity: the rivalry between the men, and Myles's ultimate act of violence is a feature of this socialised model of masculinity (56). In a sense, Myles's act of violence towards Ignatius is an exploration of how the violence that he has witnessed himself as a soldier on foreign soil and his castigation of Ignatius for his actions towards his mother, form part of Myles's development into a violent man. The masculinity that we see at play in *The Ranger* comprises a continuum of masculinity, ranging from, as R. W. Connell notes in relation to the stable categories of masculinity, the 'four patterns of masculinity in the current Western gender order', namely hegemonic masculinity, subordinated masculinity, complicit masculinity, and marginalised masculinity (77–81). *An Ranger* is a depiction of Myles as he passes through these different repertoires of masculinity, to arrive at a form of masculinity complicit in violence and destruction.

The military has long been associated with masculinity, as noted in Caroline Magennis's discussion of violence and masculinities in the Northern Irish works of Eoin McNamee and Glenn Patterson (122). Indeed, it could be argued that the categories of masculinity as outlined by Connell are descriptors in the context of social relations, rather than as an individual process. The importance of *An Ranger* is that the different categories of masculinity as described by Connell are evident in the lives of one individual character where the use of the Gothic mode functions not just in the external, outer world of the protagonist, but in his own, inner world. This short film, while dealing with the languages of both Irish and English, paradoxically relies on extended silence, close-up shots and minimal use of music to portray that violent, revengeful masculinity. Transformation, a staple feature of the Gothic, is portrayed as that which happens internally to the character. Relying as the film does on colour and visual imagery, the cinematography brings rocks and fallen stones into relief, emphasising decay and abandonment, where the only sound of anything living is in the wind moving through the grass. The ruins of this humble cabin are reflective of what David Punter considers of crucial importance to Irish and Scottish Gothic, where the ruin tells its own story about the after-effects of colonisation:

> Both of these notions, I believe, point us toward the 'uncanny', in that they speak always of history, but of a history that is constantly under the threat of erasure. They speak of history not as a living presence nor yet as an irrecoverable absence, but as inevitably involved in specific modes of ghostly persistence which may occur when, particularly in Scotland and Ireland, national aspirations are thwarted by conquest or by settlement, as they have been so often. I want to show how the Gothic is especially powerful in rendering the complex hauntings in such conflicted histories. (1)

In a significant number of Irish language Gothic texts, however, the 'hauntings' and 'conflicted histories' as described by Punter frequently originate with the protagonists themselves. Furthermore, the proliferation of hallucinations, terrors, and demons in a number of Gothic texts that explore masculinity is frequently based in narratives of addiction. Drugs, alcohol and other forms of addiction as an expression of the Gothic has received surprisingly little critical attention to date. Davison, for example, notes how 'Gothic pharmographies' are an 'unidentified and unexplored branch of the gothic' (69). Yet drug taking occurs in *Dracula* when one of the characters reaches for morphine by way of calling on the god Morpheus, in order to confront her terrors (Stoker 101). John Morton's *100 Everyday Menaces* is a highly charged radio drama that describes the return of a separated father, recovering alcoholic and occasional drug user to his home town, where there are 'Dangers everywhere'. But the dangers and terrors that surround Joe in the town of 'cracked pavements' comprise the simple things in life such as 'a betrayal, a hot cup of tea', reflecting as they do the fear of an everyday type of Gothic in the form of anxiety, addiction, and Joe's failed attempts as a friend and a father. *100 Everyday Menaces* makes full use of design and voice quality, where sound quality is described by John Laver as 'roughness, breathiness, creakiness, nasality and register' (qtd. in Rattigan 144). The radio drama commences with the sounds of sharp, repeated inhalations, and syncopated background voices, mirroring as they do not merely psychological duress but, as the drama unfolds, the physiological nature of drug use. Joe's multiple voices, all of which articulate his fears and demons, are designed for the listening audience through a contrast between a distance, lowered volume in the portrayal of his public voice of addiction recovery, and a crescendo as the drama relays his private voice of anxiety and dependency.

Roy Foster describes *Dracula* as epitomising 'a sense of displacement' (220), and the same can be said for Joe as he returns to the city of his youth. Expecting renewal and revival, he is disappointed. The drama draws on how his life is an eternal cycle of reflecting the classic Gothic modes of inescapable death and decay. 'Every phone call is not a dead person', Joe muses, where decay and death are due to the ravages of drug abuse. Throughout the drama, Morton depicts, as in much Gothic literature, the constant inner turmoil faced by Joe between 'chaos' and 'order'. The climax of the drama takes place in a 'neglected suburban house full of ugly old carpets', fulfilling Hogle's description of the Gothic as 'some new recreation of an older venue' (2). In this radio drama which explores affective masculinity where addiction leads to loss of control and to a reduced sense of masculinity, one of the characters, Jenny, urges Joe to 'man up' and to 'call your Ma'. Dale Townshend comments on the centrality of death and its paraphernalia in Gothic literature and on the manner in which 'death and its paraphernalia loom large ... tombs, graves, winding cloths, shrouds, churchyards, coffins and taper-lit funeral processions' (23). Joe and Gussy inhabit that 'paraphernalia' of death when they talk of how they used to 'haunt' the town together, and the way in which the local pub represented as 'where dreams go to die', depicting addiction and the ensuing psychosis as a Gothic experience. Not only do these characters consume themselves but their loved ones in the process. In this way, the act of injecting reflects Maud Ellman's discussion of the relationship between Gothic literature and the literature of invasion (ix), where drugs and acid have replaced Joe's life's blood. Addiction is what ultimately dooms Joe. 'Acid, that's what flows through his blood', he muses, as he parties with his old drinking friends, refusing 'a bag of gear' that comes his way. Joe's journey is finally complete when, in the penultimate scene of the drama, he meets the estranged son he has returned to be with, only to be deeply disappointed by the realisation that the boy, like the father, has developed his own form of OCD (Obsessive Compulsive Disorder) in his father's absence.

In her examination of extreme violence, Nancy Chodorow points out that military in 'all societies is by definition masculine' (252). Hegemonic masculinity in the guise of violence, and its portrayal between the military and the masculine is explored further in *Black '47*. However, although the film depicts the horrors of the Famine, the primary Gothic element in *Black '47* is the Irish language itself. Ruinous for those who speak her, the Irish language becomes a matter of life or death for the nearly all-male cast of characters. As in the case of *Lámh Láidir*, there are neither castles nor ruined abbeys in sight. Yet *Black '47* is a subversion of the Gothic in that it questions, in its very cinematic structure, how the Gothic trope of the ruin can be limited to the built environment and to buildings which carry what Catherine Spooner describes as 'the weight of history' (184). The film explores the ruined human lives of those who live in penury perhaps *because* of those who have claimed lands on which they build castles. *Black '47*, in its production and its thematic material appears to have achieved what Dudley Andrew described in 2006 as an island cinema with 'a local sensibility (habits, references, gestures and concerns) tied to struggles of social history that, despite the digitally cleansed appearance of movies everywhere, cannot and must not be forgotten and aestheticized' (28).

The reality of hunger and famine as a Gothic event and the horrors of the withering, decaying male body as a central part of those occurrences have long been a feature of Irish language literature since the years of the literary revival. In his discussion of Stoker's *Dracula*, Alan Titley describes how the Irish language novel has long been associated with horror, arguing that *Séadna*, for example, is a novel laced with such elements (*An tÚrscéal Gaeilge* [*The Irish Language Novel*] 67). While Titley does not go so far as to suggest that the early Irish language novels of the twentieth century such as *Séadna* are Gothic, I would argue that texts such as this comprise many Gothic conventions that have been consistently developed in twenty-first century Irish language Gothic. Famine and the impact of poverty and hunger on the male body has been explored in some detail by Seámus Mac Grianna, in 'Ar an Trá Fholamh' (On the Deserted Beach) (1929), by Pádraic Ó Conaire in 'Páidín Mháire' (1956), by Siobhán Ní Shúilleabháin in her novella *Eoghan* (1992), and by Pádraig Ua Duinnín in his 1901 revival drama *Creideamh agus Gorta* (*Faith and Famine*). In addition, it is noteworthy that English language works which deal with the question of hunger deal with it in a variety of ways, from the metaphorical hunger depicted in Patrick Kavanagh's *The Great Hunger* (1942) to the direct realism of Liam O'Flaherty's *Famine* (1937). However, they do not deal with questions of famine and male language.

It is for this reason that the publication of *Grace* by Paul Lynch in 2017 marked an important shift in the Gothic in English language literature in Ireland and in its exploration of female masculinity. Set during the Great Famine in Ireland, the novel begins with the young girl Grace being dressed by her mother as a young man, cutting her hair and divesting Grace of all symbols of traditional femininity by binding her breasts with cloth to make them appear smaller. Grace's journey through the

Irish countryside with her brother Colly for company is a journey into the transformative effects of hunger and famine, as well as allowing her a brutal vision of male adulthood. Her personal, forced transformation into female masculinity to defend her against the unwanted advances of her mother's partner Boggs, is one of the few depictions in Irish literature of what Jack Halberstam refers to as 'tomboyism', 'an extended childhood period of female masculinity' (5). In Lynch's novel, female masculinity is forced on Grace. At the conclusion of the novel, Grace undergoes another transformation, this time when she is given the name of Mary Ezekiel by a group of soupers (314), and when an entirely different name and religion is given her without her consent. Grace's passage to safety is a journey that is replete with dark and violent forces, and Lynch's novel emphasises how it is only through taking on a different identity that she manages to survive. The Irish language and its rites and customs dominate the formal aspects of the novel, in terms of structure, voice and dialogue. Lynch's novel achieves a sense of terror not least because much of the narrative is a representation in English of English as spoken by somebody whose first language is Irish, where the syntax is influenced by Irish. Grace, Colly and Bart (a friend they pick up along their journey of displacement through Limerick and Clare), find themselves in an abandoned farmhouse that holds the ghosts of the recently dead, and reminds them of the racist cartoons that depict the Irish as animalistic, a point not understood by the children in this dystopian description:

> They stand in the yard of an abandoned farmhouse that shapes its gloom over a barren garden, a feeling of emptiness like presence. She wonders why an elm has had its bark stripped to head height and sees another just like it. Colly says, this was a house of tree eaters, I told you this was going on. For a moment she can imagine them, strange creatures with long arms like that drawing one time passed around in school that showed a monkey-man wearing a stovepipe hat and a jacket and breeches that was supposed to be an Irishman talking to some Englishman, long teeth for nibbling. (260)

The use of the present tense in the novel is central to the creation of what Fionntán de Brún describes as the temporality of the Gothic, the narrative pulling the reader into the horror of the famine (13). While the novel begins with the Irish language festival of *Samhain* (November), the gradual loss of Grace's ability to speak runs parallel to her own displacement, to the loss of her identity as female, and to her removal from the customs and traditions with which she is familiar. Grace loses the ability to talk, and it is only through the ghosts of her mother, Colly, and Bart that she finally finds her voice. Yet, it is in the reclaiming of her womanhood and the birth of her first child that she finally finds her voice again, leaving behind the Gothic nightmare of a world destroyed by famine.

In his discussion of the Irish language translation of *Dracula*, Alan Titley posits that the Gothic is intimately connected to the 'stíl an uafáis' (horror style) frequently found in the Irish language novel (*An tÚrscéal Gaeilge* 67). Perhaps the most significant proponent of this Gothic style in the Irish language is Joe Steve Ó Neachtain whose novels explore a darker side of masculinity. In *Lámh Láidir*, Ó Neachtain explores a particular form of Gaeltacht Gothic, where the modern Irish language in the Gaeltacht is continually under threat from the colonised forces and the English language that have long since ceased to impact the rest of Ireland. Ó Neachtain's novel, as in *Black '47*, is based on the intertwining of language and masculinity, mirroring what Eve Patten describes as a 'haunted or traumatized Irish society' (259). The haunting in *Lámh Láidir*, however, is mainly linguistic in origin.

The novel centres on a long-running and ancient dispute between two families, the Seoighes and the Barretts, and their relationship with the local Protestant landowning ascendancy, the Bromleys. Lady Bromley is elderly and a resident of the 'teach mór' (the big house), which the locals call The Lodge but which they avoid, staying 'glan ar an áit' (away from the place) (68). Barrett, the agent, works for Lady Bromley and his insistence on using English to the Irish-speaking men he employs to work breaking stones as they build new roads around The Lodge is portrayed by Ó Neachtain as a form of linguistic colonisation and an attempt to remove the men's power. Indeed, Ó Neachtain represents this linguistic assault on the local men as one frozen in time, reflecting what Armitt refers to as the temporal and spatial remove of the Gothic (153). Although all characters in the novel are Irish, Ó Neachtain succeeds in describing masculinities that are categorised according to the languages they speak, that are desirable and undesirable according to those categories, and to exploring how the Irish language renders the men ghost-like and mute in the face of their English-speaking overseer. The muteness they experience mirrors what Luke Gibbons refers to in commenting that 'the Gothic picks up where the visibility of race leaves off' (745). One of the most powerful aspects of *Lámh Láidir* is Ó Neachtain's description of the working men's attire: their patched and re-patched clothes ('éadaí paisteáilte' and 'athphaisteáilte'), and the fact that they dress alike, reducing the individual men to a uniform appearance akin to a group of modern-day prisoners, 'ar aon fheisteas' (all dressed alike) (22). Central to the marginalisation and discrimination experienced by the men is the reduction of their adult status to that of boys:

Bhí scuaine fear thart timpeall an leoraí taobh istigh de chúpla nóiméad mar a bheidís ag éirí amach as taobh an tsléibhe. Fir a bhí chomh crua tanaí le slise-anna giúsaí. Cliamhrach seachtaine ag cur dreach deilgneach ar a n-éadan... 'How are ye, lads?' ar seisean, chomh réchúiseach is dá mbeadh aithne i gcaitheamh a shaoil aige orthu.

(There was a group of men gathered around the lorry within a few minutes as if they had just emerged from the mountain. Men that were as hard and as lean as timber. The week's work giving their faces a hard, thorny appearance. 'How are ye, lads?' he said, as easygoing as you please, as if he knew them all his life). (Ó Neachtain 22)

Central to the novel is The Lodge, or big house, a crumbling edifice that continues to impact the lives of those living in its vicinity. Ó Neachtain shows in his description of the big house how, in the words of Spooner, the Lodge comprises a ruin which is 'often peopled with the spectral remains of Catholic history' (20). The big house of *Lámh Láidir* encompasses what McCormack describes as 'the Irish concern for the Big House' in Irish Gothic (832). Yet of central importance to the Gothic in Ó Neachtain's novel is that the 'death of empire' (Armitt 153) is taking place in an Irish-speaking area in Ireland, where English and the big house trope are symbolic of a language in decline, stuck in the transition between colonisation and post-colonisation. Indeed, the ghost of Lord Bromley is known to frequent the Lodge, coming between Lady Bromley and her night's sleep: 'go raibh sé ráite go láidir go mbíodh taibhse shean-Choirnéal Bromley le feiceáil ina thimpeall' (69) (it was said locally that the ghost of Old Colonel Bromley was to be seen around the place).

In writing on the history of Irish masculinity and Gothic literature from 1760–1890, Jarlath Killeen notes that 'The Gothic genre has been concerned with masculinity since its inception' (168). And while the narratives explored in this essay draw heavily on conventional Gothic modes in their exploration of masculinity, perhaps what is most distinctive about them is that they express multiple masculinities. In her discussion of what she terms 'endangered masculinities' in Irish poetry, Sarah E. McKibben notes how the 'binary opposition between coloniser and colonised' appears repeatedly in Irish poetry of the period, and argues that this is 'superimposed on to an implicit gender polarity' (7). In the twenty-first century narratives examined in this essay, I have shown these multiple masculinities do not exhibit the same polarity, and that there are no easy binary oppositions. If one of the sources for Irish Gothic in the nineteenth and twentieth centuries was the 'myth of eternal return' (Kiberd 379), the texts examined in this essay offer no such comfortable resolution. On the contrary, perhaps the common theme that runs through these diverse texts is that the 'hungry ghosts' of these dramas, films and novels can never quite feel at home in either Irish or English. Irish but foreign, in the past, yet present, these narratives portray masculinities in flux in contemporary Irish literature, as well as containing new and exciting elements to Irish Gothic. In the final analysis, perhaps these texts show that there are as many similarities as differences between the two literatures, as writers of both Irish and English continue to draw together on the deep well of the Gothic.

Works Cited

Abbott, H. Porter. *The Cambridge Introduction to Narrative*. Cambridge University Press, 2002.

Althofer, Jayson and Brian Musgrove. '"A Ghost in Daylight": Drugs and the Horror of Modernity'. *Palgrave Communications*, vol. 4, no. 112, 2018. Available online at doi.org/10.1057/s41599-018-0162-0. Accessed 31 March 2022.

An Duaircéan, by Aodh Ó Domhnaill, first broadcast on RTÉ Radio One, 2016. Available online at www.rte.ie/radio/dramaonone/780830-an-duaircean-le-aodh-aodh-o-domhnaill. Accessed 14 December 2022.

Andrew, Dudley. 'Islands in the Sea of Cinema'. *National Cinemas and World Cinemas*, edited by Kevin Rockett and John Hill, Dublin, Four Courts Press, 2006, pp. 15–30.

An Leabhar. Directed by Robert Quinn, 2004.

An Ranger. Directed by P. J. Dillon, 2013.

Armitt, Lucie. 'Twentieth Century Gothic'. *Terror and Wonder: The Gothic Imagination*, edited by Dale Townshend, British Library, 2014, pp. 150–77.

Arracht. Directed by Tomás Ó Súilleabháin, 2019.

Black '47. Directed by Lance Daly, 2018.

Bottomley, Andrew J. 'Podcasting, Welcome to Night Vale, and the Revival of Radio Drama'. *Journal of Radio & Audio Media*, vol. 22, no. 2, 2015, pp. 179–89.

Butler, Judith. *Gender Trouble: Feminism and the Subversion of Identity*. Routledge, 1990.

Chadorow, Nancy J. 'The Enemy Outside: Thoughts on the Psychodynamics of Extreme Violence with Special Attention to Men and Masculinity'. *Masculinity Studies & Feminist Theory: New Directions*, edited by Judith Kegan Gardiner, Columbia University Press, 2002, pp. 235–60.

Challis, Ben, Geraint D'Arcy, Robert Dean, Richard Hand, Rob Smith and Mary Traynor. 'Wireless Zombies! A Re-creation of Golden Age Radio Drama for a Contemporary Audience'. *Studies in Theatre and Performance*, vol. 34, no. 3, 2014, pp. 252–59.

Connell, R. W. *Masculinities*. University of California Press, 1995.

Connell, R. W. and James W. Messerschmidt. 'Hegemonic Masculinity: Rethinking the Concept'. *Gender and Society*, vol. 19, no. 6, pp. 829–59.

Davison, Carol. '"Housing the Voluntary Bondage": Theorizing the Nineteenth-Century Gothic Pharmography'. *Gothic Studies,* vol. 12, no. 1, pp. 68–85.
de Brún, Fionntán. 'Temporality and Irish Revivalism: Past, Present and Becoming'. *New Hibernia Review/Iris Éireannach Nua,* vol. 17, no. 4, 2013, pp.17–47.
de Brún, Sorcha. '"In a Sea of Wonders": Eastern Europe and Transylvania in the Irish-language Translation of *Dracula*'. *Acta Universitatis Sapientiae, Philologica*, vol. 12, no. 1, 2020, pp. 70–83.
Ellman, Maud. 'Introduction.' *Dracula*, edited by Maud Ellman. Oxford University Press, 1996, pp. vi–xxviii.
Fahey, Tracey. 'A Dark Domesticity: Echoes of Folklore in Irish Contemporary Gothic'. *The Gothic and the Everyday*, edited by Lorna Piatti-Farnell and Maria Beville, Palgrave Macmillan, 2014, pp. 152–69.
Flood, Michael, Judith Kegan Gardiner, Bob Pease and Keith Pringle. *International Encyclopedia of Men and Masculinities*. Routledge, 2007.
Foster, Roy. *Paddy and Mr. Punch: Connections in Irish and English History*. Penguin, 1995.
Girard, Rene. 'The Plague in Literature and Myth'. *Texas Studies in Literature and Language*, vol. 15, no 5, 1974, pp. 833–50.
Gibbons, Luke. *Gaelic Gothic: Race, Colonization and Irish Culture*. Arlen House, 2004.
Golding, William. *Lord of the Flies*. Faber, 1954.
Grams, Jr., Martin. *Inner Sanctum Mysteries: Behind the Creaking Door*. OTR Publishing, 2002.
Halberstam, Jack. *Female Masculinity*. Duke University Press, 1998.
Heussaf, Anna. *Bas Tobann*. Cois Life, 2004.
Hogle, Jerrold E. 'Introduction: The Gothic in Western Culture'. *The Cambridge Companion to Gothic Fiction*, edited by Jerrold E. Hogle, Cambridge University Press, 2002, pp. 1–20.
Joseph, M. K. *A Soldier's Tale*. Harper Collins, 1976.
Kavanagh, Patrick. *The Great Hunger*. Penguin, 2018.
Kiberd, Declan. *Irish Classics*. Harvard University Press, 2001.
Killeen, Jarlath. 'Muscling Up: Bram Stoker and Irish Masculinity in *The Snake's Pass*'. *Irish Gothics: Genres, Forms, Modes and Traditions 1760–1890*, edited by Christina Morin and Niall Gillespie, Palgrave Macmillan, 2014, pp. 168–87.
Kinzel, Till. 'Narrativity and Sound in German Radio Play Adaptations of Paul Auster's The New York Trilogy'. *Partial Answers: Journal of Literature and the History of Ideas*, vol. 15, no. 1, 2017, pp. 151–65.
Laver, John. *The Gift of Speech: Papers in the Analysis of Speech and Voice*. Edinburgh University Press, 1991.
Lynch, Paul. *Grace*. Oneworld, 2019.
Mac Cóil, Liam. *I dTír Strainséartha*. Cló Iar-Chonnacht, 2014.
Mac Grianna, Séamus. *An grá agus an ghruaim*. Oifig an tSoláthair, 1929.
Magennis, Caroline. *Sons of Ulster: Masculinities in the Contemporary Northern Irish Novel*. Peter Lang, 2010.
Mann, Thomas. *Der Zauberberg*. S. Fischer Verlag, Alfred A. Knopf, 1924.
Mann, Thomas. *The Magic Mountain,* translated by Helen Tracy Lowe-Porter, Secker and Warberg, 1927.

Markey, Anne. 'The Gothicisation of Irish Folklore'. *Irish Gothics: Genres, Forms, Modes and Traditions 1760–1890*, edited by Christina Morin and Niall Gillespie, Palgrave Macmillan, 2014, pp. 94–112.

Maté, Gabriel. *In the Realm of Hungry Ghosts: Close Encounters with Addiction.* Ebury, 2018.

McCormack, W. J. 'Irish Gothic and After: 1820–1945', *The Field Day Anthology of Irish Writing*, edited by Séamus Deane, vol. 2. Derry, Field Day Publications, 1991, pp. 831–949.

McKibben, Sarah E. *Endangered Masculinities in Irish Poetry 1540–1780.* University College Dublin Press, 2010.

McLean, Tom. '"An Amateur Self-Deceiving Job": M. K. Joseph's *A Soldier's Tale* and the Gothic Tradition in New Zealand Literature'. *JNZL: Journal of New Zealand Literature*, vol. 35, no. 2, 2017, pp. 90–113.

Morin, Christina and Niall Gillespie. 'Introduction: De-Limiting the Irish Gothic'. *Irish Gothics: Genres, Forms, Modes, and Traditions, c.1760–1890*, edited by Christina Morin and Niall Gillespie, Palgrave Macmillan, 2014, pp. 1–12.

Morton, John. '100 Everyday Menaces'. *Drama on One* from RTÉ Radio One, 19 November 2017, www.rte.ie/radio/podcasts/21273049-100-everyday-menaces-by-john-morton/.

Mullan, John. *How Novels Work.* Oxford University Press, 2006.

Ní Shúilleabháin, Siobhán. *Eoghan.* Cló Iar-Chonnacht, 1992.

Ó Ceallaigh, Colm. *Éiric Fola.* Coiscéim, 1999.

Ó Conaire, Pádraic. *Scothscéalta.* Sairséal agus Dill, 1956.

O'Flaherty, Liam. *Famine.* Random House, 1937.

O'Leary, Peter. *Séadna.* Irish Book Company, 1904.

Ó Neachtain, Joe Steve. *Lámh Láidir.* Cló Iar-Chonnacht, 2005.

Patten, Eve. 'Contemporary Irish Fiction'. *The Cambridge Companion to the Irish Novel,* edited by John Wilson Foster. Cambridge University Press, 2007, pp. 259–275.

Piatti-Farrell, Lorna and Maria Beville, editors. *The Gothic and the Everyday: Living Gothic.* Palgrave Macmillan, 2014.

Proulx, Annie. *Brokeback Mountain.* Fourth Estate, 1998.

Punter, David, 'Scottish and Irish Gothic'. *The Cambridge Companion to Gothic Fiction,* edited by Jerrold E. Hogle, Cambridge University Press, 2002, pp. 105–23.

Rattigan, Dermot. *Theatre of Sound: Radio and the Dramatic Imagination.* Dublin, Carysfort Press, 2002.

Reeser, Todd. *Masculinities in Theory: An Introduction.* Wiley-Blackwell, 2010.

Robinson, Roger. 'Mountain Gothic and Other Variants: Samuel Butler and M. K. Joseph'. *JNZL: Journal of New Zealand Literature*, vol. 35, no. 2, 2017, pp. 151–72.

Schmid, Thomas H. 'Addiction and Isolation in *Frankenstein*: A Case of Terminal Uniqueness'. *Gothic Studies*, vol. 11, no. 2, 2009, pp. 19–29.

Singleton, Brian. *Masculinities and the Contemporary Irish Theatre.* Palgrave Macmillan, 2011.

Spooner, Catherine. 'Twenty-First Century Gothic'. *Terror and Wonder: the Gothic Imagination,* edited by Dale Townshend, British Library, 2014, pp. 180–205.

Stoker, Bram. *Dracula*. 1897. Oxford University Press, 1996.
Taken too Far. Directed by Paul Lynch, 2017.
The Blair Witch Project. Directed by Daniel Myrick and Eduardo Sánchez, 1999.
Titley, Alan. *An tÚrscéal Gaeilge*. An Clóchomhar, 1991.
Titley, Alan. 'Séadna'. *Úrscéalta na Gaeilge*, edited by Ronan Doherty, Brian Ó Conchubhair and Philip O'Leary, Cló Iar-Chonnacht, 2017.
Townshend, Dale. 'Terror and Wonder: the Gothic Imagination'. *Terror and Wonder: The Gothic Imagination*, edited by Dale Townshend, British Library, 2014, pp. 10–37.
Ua Duinnín, Pádraig. *Creideamh agus Gorta*. Ponsonby, 1901.
Under Milk Wood. Dylan Thomas, BBC, 1954.
Van Elferen, Isabella. *Gothic Music: The Sounds of the Uncanny*. University of Wales Press, 2012.
War of the Worlds. Directed by Orson Welles, 1938.
Willems, Gertjan. 'Radio Drama as Art and Industry: A Case study on the textual and institutional entanglements of the radio play The Slow Motion Film', *The Radio Journal International Studies in Broadcast and Audio Media*, vol. 18, no. 2, 2020, pp. 227–241.
Whitehead, Greg. 'Radio Art Le Momo: Gas Leaks, Shock Needles and Death Rattles', *Public*, vol. 4, no. 5, pp. 141–149, 1990.

Notes on Contributors

Sorcha de Brún lectures in Modern Irish in the University of Limerick, Ireland where she is also Director of European Studies. She has published extensively on twentieth- and twenty-first-century Irish language prose and literary translation. She has published poems and short stories in various anthologies, and a selection of her poetry and stories for children is on the *Séideán Sí* Primary Curriculum, published by An Gúm. A recipient of Duais Foras na Gaeilge (Foras na Gaeilge Award), Duais Ghearrscéalaíochta Mháirtín Uí Chadhain (Máirtín Ó Cadhain Short Story Award) and Oireachtas na Gaeilge literary awards, Sorcha has translated and published a selection of poems by nineteenth-, twentieth-, and twenty-first-century German poets to Irish as part of the *Dánnerstag* Irish-German poetry project, of which she is co-director. She is also a co-editor of *EuropeNow Campus* journal and a member of the Royal Irish Academy Committee on Irish language and Celtic Studies (Coiste Léann na Gaeilge agus an Léinn Cheiltigh). Sorcha is currently working on her monograph on masculinities in Irish language prose writing.

Melissa Edmundson is Senior Lecturer of English at Clemson University. She specialises in nineteenth- and early twentieth-century women's supernatural fiction. She is the author of *Women's Ghost Literature in Nineteenth-Century Britain* (2013) and *Women's Colonial Gothic Writing, 1850–1930: Haunted Empire* (2018). She has edited several critical editions, including *Women's Weird: Strange Stories by Women, 1890–1940* (2019). Her edition of Clotilde Graves's imaginative fiction, *A Vanished Hand*, was published in 2021 as part of the 'Strange Stories by Irish Women' series.

Jack Fennell is a writer and researcher who teaches at the University of Limerick, Ireland. He is the editor of two anthologies, *A Brilliant Void* (2018) and *It Rose Up* (2021), collecting lesser-known Irish science fiction and fantasy stories respectively, and the author of two academic studies, *Irish Science Fiction* (2014) and *Rough Beasts: Monstrosity in Irish Literature, 1800–2010* (2019).

Eóin Flannery is Associate Professor of English Literature in the Department of English Language and Literature at Mary Immaculate College, University of Limerick. He was the Peter O'Brien Visiting Scholar in Canadian Irish Studies at Concordia University, Montreal in 2022. He has published over 60 scholarly articles and book chapters, and is the author of five books: *Form, Affect and Debt in post-Celtic Tiger Fiction* (2022); *Ireland and Ecocriticism: Literature, History, and Environmental Justice* (2016); *Colum McCann and the Aesthetics of Redemption* (2011); *Ireland and Postcolonial Studies: Theory, Discourse, Utopia* (2009); and *Versions of Ireland: Empire, Modernity and Resistance in Irish Culture* (2006). He has edited special themed issues of journals such as the *Journal of Ecocriticism*, *Postcolonial Text* and *Irish Studies Review*. His current research projects include a study of the career and work of Eugene McCabe, a book entitled, *Sounding the Contemporary in Irish Poetry*, and, with Eugene O'Brien, a co-edited volume of *Études Irlandaises* on contemporary Irish poetics.

Michael Patrick Gillespie is Professor of English at Florida International University and the Director of the Center for the Humanities in an Urban Environment. He has written eleven books and numerous articles on the works of James Joyce, Oscar Wilde, William Kennedy, Chaos Theory and Irish Film. His many publications include: *Oscar Wilde and the Poetics of Ambiguity* (1996), *Branding Oscar Wilde* (2019), *The Aesthetics of Chaos: Nonlinear Thinking and Contemporary Literary Criticism* (2003), *Reading the Book Himself: Narrative Strategies in the Works of James Joyce* (1989), *James Joyce and the Exilic Imagination* (2015) and *The Myth of Irish Cinema* (2008).

Jarlath Killeen is a lecturer in Victorian literature in the School of English, Trinity College Dublin. He has published extensively on Irish Gothic fiction, including *Gothic Ireland* (2005) and *The Emergence of Irish Gothic Fiction* (Edinburgh University Press, 2013). His most recent monograph is *Imagining the Irish Child: Discourses of Childhood in Irish Anglican Writing of the Seventeenth and Eighteenth Centuries* (2023).

Anne Markey, former president of the Irish Society for the Study of Children's Literature, is a Literature Tutor and Monitor in Dublin City

University. Her research has focused on early Irish fiction, intersections between Gaelic traditions and Irish writing in English, and the representation of childhood in a variety of texts from the seventeenth century to the present day. She is editor of *Patrick Pearse: Short Stories* (2009), *Children's Fiction 1765–1808* (2011); co-editor of *Vertue Rewarded; or, The Irish Princess* (2010) and *Irish Tales* (2010); and author of *Oscar Wilde's Fairy Tales: Origins and Contexts* (2011).

Alison Milbank is Associate Professor of Literature and Theology at the University of Nottingham. She was John Rylands Research Fellow at the University of Manchester and, after a temporary position at Cambridge, taught for five years at the University of Virginia. She has taught at Nottingham since 2004, and is also Priest Vicar and Canon Theologian at Southwell Minster. She has published widely on the Gothic, and also publishes on Anglican ecclesiology and theology. Her publications include *Daughters of the House: Modes of the Gothic in Victorian Fiction* (1992); *Dante and the Victorians* (1998); and most recently *God and the Gothic: Religion, Romance, & Reality in the English Literary Tradition* (2018).

Christopher Morash is the Seamus Heaney Professor of Irish Writing at Trinity College Dublin, where he previously served as Vice-Provost. His most recent books include *Yeats on Theatre* (2021), and *Dublin: A Writer's City* (2023); he has published widely on Irish literature and culture, having written histories of Irish theatre, Irish media and Irish Famine writing. He is a Member of the Royal Irish Academy, and chairs the judging panel for the Dublin Literary Award.

Christina Morin is Senior Lecturer in English and Assistant Dean of Research in the Faculty of Arts, Humanities and Social Sciences at the University of Limerick. She is the author of *The Gothic Novel in Ireland, c.1760–1829* (2018) and *Charles Robert Maturin and the Haunting of Irish Romantic Fiction* (2011), and co-editor of *Traveling Irishness in the Long Nineteenth Century* (with Marguérite Corporaal, 2017) and *Irish Gothics: Genres, Forms, Modes and Traditions* (with Niall Gillespie, 2014). She is currently editing, with Ellen Scheible, a special issue of the *Irish University Review* on 'Irish Gothic Studies Today'.

Ellen Scheible is Professor of English and coordinator of Irish Studies at Bridgewater State University. Her current projects include *Body Politics*, a monograph on contemporary Irish women's fiction; The Dark: *A Critical Edition*, co-edited with Anna Teekell; *Teaching James Joyce in* *the 21st Century* and *Sally Rooney: Perspectives and Approaches*, both co-edited with Barry Devine. She has published in various journals, including *New Hibernia Review*, *James Joyce Quarterly*, and *Tulsa Studies in Women's Literature*. She has forthcoming an essay on the Irish Bildungsroman and a special issue on Gothic studies for the *Irish University Review*, co-edited with Christina Morin. She is co-editor, with Claire Culleton, of *Rethinking Joyce's Dubliners* (2017).

Sinéad Sturgeon is a Lecturer in Irish Writing at Queen's University Belfast. She has published widely on nineteenth-century writing and culture; her most recent publications have focused on the work of James Clarence Mangan and Elizabeth Bowen. She is currently working on late nineteenth-century Irish women's writers, particularly May Laffan.

Julia M. Wright, FRSC, is Professor and George Munro Chair of Literature and Rhetoric at Dalhousie University, Canada. She is the author of four monographs, including *Representing the National Landscape in Irish Romanticism* (2014) and *Men with Stakes: Masculinity and the Gothic in US Television* (2016). She has edited two novels by Lady Morgan, *The Missionary* (2002) and *The O'Briens and the O'Flahertys* (2013), *Irish Literature, 1750–1900: An Anthology* (2008), and the two-volume *Companion to Irish Literature* (2010), as well as co-edited a further seven volumes, including an edition, with appendices, of Ian Fleming's *Casino Royale* (2020).

Index

1641 Rebellion, 67, 155, 157, 165

A Full and Impartial Account, 176
A Ghost Story for Christmas, 10
Abbey Theatre, 65, 72, 73, 80n1
Abhartach, 177, 188n10
Act of Supremacy, 154
Aeschylus, 77–8
   Eumenides, 77–8
Agamben, Giorgio, 197
Allingham, William, 53
Altman, Robert, 88
   Images, 88
Anglicanism, 67, 75, 153–73, 176–88, 194–6, 199, 236, 266
Anglo-Irish Bank, 7
An Godhar Dubh ('The Black Dog'), 146
An Gúm, 142
   Translations of Gothic texts into Irish 142, 147
Annals of the Four Masters, 55
Anthologia Hibernica, 33
Aristotle, 74
   Physics, 74
Arnold, Matthew, 10, 189n18
Austen, Jane, 38, 43n9
   Emma, 38
   Northanger Abbey, 38–9

Bairéad, Tomás, 'An Tríomhadh Bean' ('The Third Woman'), 140–1
Banim, John
   'Ace of Clubs', 198
   'Chaunt of the Cholera', 51
   Damon and Pythias, 66
   'The Fetches', 198, 215
   Tales of the O'Hara Family, 198
Banim, Michael, *Tales of the O'Hara Family*, 198
Béaslaí, Piaras, 'Deimhniú an Sgéil' ('Verifying the Story'), 143–4
Beckett, Samuel, 66
   Breath, 79
   Not I, 79
   Waiting for Godot, 66
'Big House' fiction, 116, 123–9, 224–5, 267
The Blair Witch Project, 258
Borges, Jorge Luis, 235
Boru, Brian, 177
Bowen, Elizabeth, 19, 116, 124, 126–9, 153, 164, 168–71, 214, 224–5
   A Day in the Dark, 228n11
   'The Back Drawing-Room', 169, 171
   Bowen's Court, 169, 170, 171
   'The Demon Lover', 170–1
   The Demon Lover and Other Stories, 225
   'Green Holly', 171
   'The Happy Autumn Fields', 171, 225, 228n11
   'Hand in Glove', 171
   The Last September, 116, 124, 126–9
Breatnach, R. A., *Scéal Shéadna*, 107
Brice, Edward, 50
British Critic, 41–2
Brontë, Emily, *Wuthering Heights*, 142, 168

Browning, Robert
  'My Last Duchess', 47
  'Porphyria's Lover', 47
Burdett, Francis (Sir), 194
Bürger, Gottfried August
  Lenore, 53, 198
  The Wild Huntsman, 198
Burke, Edmund, 20, 50–1, 52, 56
  A Philosophical Enquiry Into the Origins of our Ideas of the Sublime and Beautiful, 20, 50–1, 52, 56, 240–2, 249n5
Burney, Frances, 34
Burrowes, Roberts, 49, 51
Byron, George Gordan (Lord), *Manfred*, 47

Callanan, J. J., 'Convict of Clonmel', 56
Carleton, William, 196, 197, 200, 208n9
  'The Lianhan Shee', 198
  'Wildgoose Lodge', 198, 200, 208n9
Carmilla (YouTube series), 2
Carolan, Turlough, 199
Carr, Marina, 18, 65–9, 71–4, 75–6, 77–8, 115
  By the Bog of Cats..., 18, 66–9, 71–4, 75–6, 77–8
  The Mai, 66
  Portia Coughlan, 66
Carter, Angela, 235
Cary, Lucius, 2nd Viscount Falkland, 36
Casey, Eamon (Archbishop), 8
Catholicism, 7–12, 15, 20, 22n20, 40, 46, 52, 59n2, 67, 86–7, 89, 96, 101, 105, 107, 109, 138, 153–69, 176–7, 178, 183, 188, 189n21, 194–209, 218, 220, 226, 228n10, 236, 242, 246, 247, 248, 267
Celtic Revival, 234
Celtic Tiger, 2, 4–8, 12–17, 20, 22n14, 96, 116, 129–32, 233, 236, 237–8, 241, 242–3, 245, 248–9, 249n2, 249n6
children's literature, 18–19, 98–111, 136
cholera, 20, 51, 185–8, 189n28

Cobbe, Frances Power, 'A Spectral Rout', 220
Coleridge, Samuel Taylor, 47, 137
  'Christabel', 47, 55
  'Rime of the Ancient Mariner', 47
Coll Dhu (Black-Coll), 216–17
Comfort, Lance, *Daughter of Darkness*, 86–7
Commissioners for National Education, 138
Connor, J., 30
Cooper, Giles, *Under the Loofah Tree*, 255
Coppola, Francis Ford, *Dementia 13*, 88, 89
Corkery, Margaret, *Eamon*, 94–6
Corman, Roger, *The Young Racers*, 88
Cosgrove, Tom, *Rógairí* ('Rogues'), 146
Cottingley Fairies, 15
Critical Review, 29, 34–5, 41, 42n1, 43n6
Croker, Thomas Crofton
  Fairy Legends and Traditions of the South of Ireland, 215
  Researches in the South of Ireland, 53
Cromwell, Oliver, 49, 155
Cronin, Lee, *The Hole in the Ground*, 12–13, 16–17, 90–1
Crutwell, R. 30
Cullen, Stephen, 32, 39–42
  The Castle of Inchvally: a tale – Alas! Too true, 39–41
  The Haunted Priory, 39–41

Dalton, Jane, 37–8
Daly, Lance, *Black '47*, 254, 263–4, 266
Daly, Rebecca, *The Other Side of Sleep*, 90
D'Arcy McGee, Thomas, 55
Dante, 14, 158, 166
'Dark Rosaleen', 213
Darwin, Charles, 10
Davis, Thomas, 51, 55, 58
  'My Grave', 51, 58
de Barra, Declan, *An Fiach Dubh* ('The Raven'), 146
de Cresseron, Charles, 164

Dermody, Thomas, 'Contemplative Verses', 48–9, 50, 51, 58
Dessen, Sarah, *Just Listen*, 109
Dickens, Charles, 10, 216
All the Year Round, 216, 219
Dillon, P. J., *An Ranger (The Ranger)*, 252, 253, 260–2
Donoghue, Emma, 20, 235, 238, 239, 242, 245–8, 249n8
The Pull of the Stars, 239
Room, 239
The Wonder, 238, 242, 245–8, 249n8
Dorchadas ('Darkness'), 146
Drennan, William, 48, 51, 52–3, 58
'Glendalloch', 51, 52–3
Dublin and London Magazine, 195
Dublin University Magazine, 164, 208n6, 208n7
Dunsany, Lord, 9, 12
My Ireland, 9
The Curse of the Wise Woman, 9

Echard, Laurence, 33
Edgeworth, Maria, 40, 48, 99, 100, 103, 106, 110n2, 135–6, 153, 157, 205, 214, 215
Castle Rackrent, 40, 135–6
The Parent's Assistant, 103
Practical Education, 100
Edwards, Hilton
From Time to Time, 87–8
Return to Glennascaul, 87
Eliot, George, 10
Eliot, T. S., 165
Emmet, Robert, 58, 158, 237
Enright, Anne, *The Gathering*, 232–3
Ethelred the Unready, 33
Euripides, *Medea*, 77
Evans, T. J., 30

Farrell, J. G., 19, 116
The Siege of Krishnapur, 124
The Singapore Grip, 124
Troubles, 116, 124–6
Fenianism, 55; see also Irish Republican Brotherhood
Finnegan, Lorcan, *Without Name*, 11, 12

Fisher, Jonathan, *Scenery of Ireland*, 52
folk horror, 8–17, 216–18
Foucault, Michel, 76
Foxe, John, 155, 176, 188
Acts and Monuments (Book of Martyrs), 176, 188, 188n7
French, Tana, 20, 238, 241
Broken Harbour, 239, 245
In the Woods, 2, 243
The Likeness, 235, 236, 341, 242, 243–5, 247–8, 249n7
Freud, Sigmund, 20, 95, 233–5, 236, 240, 241
'The Uncanny', 20, 234–5
Friedrich, Caspar David, *Der Wanderer uber dem Nebelmeer (Wanderer above the Sea of Fog)*, 252
Furlong, Thomas
The Doom of Derenzie, 20, 194–209
'The Last Wish', 199
The Misanthrope, 199, 200
The Plagues of Ireland, 199, 200, 207

Gaelic Journal, 106
Gaelic League, 106
Garner, Alan
The Owl Service, 10
The Weirdstone of Brisingamen, 10
Gavin, Liam, *A Dark Song*, 11
Gerard, Emily, 'Transylvanian Superstitions', 177
ghost estates, 6, 130–2, 237, 239, 244–5, 248, 249n2, 249n3
Gibbon, Edward, 39
Glorvina solution, the; see also national tale, 40, 43n10
Godwin, William, 31, 104
Goethe, Johann Wolfgang von, 198
Faust, 59n8
Golding, William, *Lord of the Flies*, 260
Goldsmith, Oliver
'Deserted Village', 50
History of Little Goody Two-Shoes, The, 99, 100, 110n3
Gothic
'bog', 237–8
first-wave, 31–2

historical, 32–6
Irish Catholic, 52, 194–209
medievalism, 55
trade, 31
see also terror fiction
Grattan, Henry, 51
Graves, Clotilde, 20
'The Compleat Housewife', 221–2
The Cost of Wings, 222
The Dop Doctor, 228n9
'How the Mistress Came Home', 222
Pseudonym, 'Rechard Dehan', 221, 228n9
Under the Hermés and Other Stories, 221
'A Vanished Hand', 222
Gray, Thomas
'Elegy Written in a Country Churchyard', 18, 47–52, 58
Plagiarism, accusations of, 48
Great Irish Famine, 20, 22n24, 51, 58, 115, 116–21, 123, 137–8, 163, 185–8, 214, 219, 228n12, 242, 260, 263, 264–5
Green, Sarah, 39
Gregory, Lady Augusta, *Visions and Beliefs in the West of Ireland*, 228n6
Griffin, Gerald, 196
'The Barber of Bantry', 198
The Collegians, 200
Holland-Tide, 198
Grotowski, Jerzy, 78–9
Guattari, Felix, *The Three Ecologies*, 114–15

'The Hag of Beara', 213
Haggard, Piers, *Blood on Satan's Claw*, 10
Halse, Laurie, *Wintergirls*, 109
Haly, J., 30
Hampden, John, 49
Hardiman, James, *Irish Minstrelsy*, 199
Hardy, Corin, *The Hallow*, 11, 15–16
Hardy, Robin, *The Wicker Man*, 10
Hastings, Warren, 36
Hazlitt, William, *The Romanticist and Novelists Library*, 41
Heaney, Seamus, 115, 214

Heidegger, Martin, *Being and Time*, 74
Hennessy, Claire, *Nothing Tastes as Good*, 19, 101, 108–10
Henry VIII, 154
Heusaff, Anna, *Bás Tobann*, 252
Heylyn, Peter, *Cosmographie*, 175–6, 188n4, 188n5
Hogg, James, *Memoirs and Confessions of a Justified Sinner*, 170
Höglund, Panu Petteri, *An Leabhar Nimhe* ('The Book of Poison/ The Poison Book'), 136
Hume, David, 33, 39

Irish Folklore Commission, 9, 136, 142
Irish Republican Brotherhood, 55; *see also* Fenianism, 55–6

James, M. R., 10, 15, 16
Jameson, John, 199
Jordan, Neil
The Butcher Boy, 89–90
Mistaken, 2
Joseph, M. K., *A Soldier's Tale*, 259
Joyce, James, 214

Kane, Sarah, *Cleansed*, 78
Kant, Immanuel, 241–2
The Critique of Judgment, 241–2, 249n5
Kavanagh, Ivar
The Canal, 91
Never Grow Old, 91
Tin Can Man, 92–3
Kavanagh, Patrick, *The Great Hunger*, 264
Keating, David, *Wake Wood*, 11, 13–15
Keats, John, 47, 55
'The Eve of St Agnes', 55
Kelly, Isabella, 43n8
Kilroy, Claire, *The Devil I Know*, 116, 129, 130–2
King, Margaret (Lady Mount Cashell), *Stories of Old Daniel*, 19, 101, 104–6, 110
King, Stephen, *Pet Sematary*, 14
Kingsborough, Lord and Lady, 101–2
Kingsley, Charles, 166

Kirk, Robert, 169–70
Knowles, James Sheridan, *Virginius*, 66
Kostova, Elizabeth, *The Historian*, 2

Landy, Derek, *Skulduggery Pleasant*, 108
Lane, William, 30, 42n2
Lang, Fritz, *Metropolis*, 85, 94
Lavin, Mary, 214
Le Fanu, Joseph Sheridan, 2, 3, 4, 15, 16–17, 19, 21n7, 21n8, 22n20, 31, 35, 48, 136, 153, 164–8, 170–1, 188n1, 188n12, 203, 215
   'Authentic Narrative of the Ghost of a Hand', 171
   Carmilla, 164, 188n1
   'The Child that Went with the Fairies', 15
   'Familiar, The', 166–7, 168, 170
   Ghost Stories of Chapelizod, 136
   'Green Tea', 35, 166, 170, 203
   The House by the Churchyard, 171
   In a Glass Darkly, 167
   'The Mysterious Lodger', 168
   The Purcell Papers, 16–17, 164–5
   'Schalken the Painter', 171
   'Spalatro', 164
   Uncle Silas, 48, 164, 165, 167–8
Le Fanu, Susanna, 168
Le Fanu, William, 165
Lebor Gabála Érenn (The Book of Invasions), 16
Lee, Sophia, *The Recess*, 33, 43n6
Leland, Thomas, 19, 32, 156–7
   Longsword, 32, 156–7
Leslie, John, *Killarney*, 52
Lewis, Matthew, 29, 31, 32, 37, 41
   The Monk, 41
Literary Gazette, 199, 208n8
Locke, John, *Some Thoughts Concerning Education*, 99, 100
Long, H., 30
Longchamp, Bishop of Ely, 35–6
Lovecraft, H. P., 53, 136, 198
   Cthulhu Mythos, 136
Lovering, Jeremy, *In Fear*, 7
Lyell, Charles, 10
Lynch, Paul, *Grace*, 254, 264–6

McBride, Eimear, *A Girl is a Half-Formed Thing*, 238
McCabe, Eugene, 115, 117, 119–21, 123, 129
   Tales from the Poorhouse, 119–21
McCabe, Patrick, 237
   Breakfast on Pluto, 238
   The Butcher Boy, 89
McCann, Donal, 89
Macardle, Dorothy
   Earth-Bound, 223–4
   'Escape', 224
   'The Prisoner', 223–4
   'Samhain', 219
McCardle, Tommy, *The Kinkisha*, 18, 88–9
Mac Cóil, Liam, *I dTír Stráinseartha*, 252
Mac Coiligh, P., 'Scéal Mna' ('A Woman's Story'), 144
McDonagh, Martin
   The Beauty Queen of Leenane, 238
   The Cripple of Inishmaan, 78
MacDonald, George, 166
McGuckian, Mary, *Words upon the Window Pane*, 18, 89
Mac Grianna, Seámus, 'Ar an Trá Fholamh' ('On the Deserted Beach'), 264
McKenna, Siobhán, 86
Mackenzie, Anna Maria, *Danish Massacre: an Historic Fact*, 32–3
MacLimmoir, Micheál
   'Aonghus Ó Cruadhlaoich', 141
   From Time to Time, 87–8
   Return to Glennascaul, 87
McMahon, Conor, *From the Dark*, 11
MacMurchada, Diarmait, 203
McNamee, Eoin, 261
   The Blue Tango, 238
   The Ultras, 238
McPherson, Conor, *The Weir*, 66
Macready, William Charles, 66
Mac Síomóin, Tomás, *Ag Altóir an Diabhail* ('At the Altar of the Devil'), 146
McTaggart, J. M. E., 74
Magee, William (Archbishop), 157

Mag Reachtain, Liam
  'Báthadh' ('Drowning'), 144
  'Dolacha' ('Snares'), 144
  'Eagla' ('Fear'), 144
  'An Lóchrann' ('The Lantern'), 144
Malone, Molly, 213
Mangan, James Clarence, 19, 21n7, 46, 52, 53, 56, 59n2, 115, 116–19, 123, 129, 195, 196, 198–9, 208n6
  Autobiography, 195
  'Chapters of Ghostcraft', 198–9
  'Kathaleen Ny-Houlahan', 56
  'The Man in the Cloak', 198–9, 208n6
  Siberia, 117–19
  'A Vision of Connaught in the Thirteenth Century', 55
Mann, Thomas, *Der Zauberberg* (*The Magic Mountain*), 259
Marlowe, Christopher, *Doctor Faustus*, 59n8, 165, 167
Marsh's Library, 4, 21n9, 175–6, 184, 188n4, 188n7
Maturin, Charles Robert, 2, 3, 18, 19, 21n7, 21n9, 31, 40, 48, 66–80, 144, 154, 155, 157–60, 161, 163, 164, 165, 189n1, 197, 198, 199, 202, 208n6, 215
  Bertram, 18, 66–80, 202
  The Albigenses, 158
  Melmoth the Wanderer, 3, 48, 144, 155, 158–60, 161, 165, 197, 202, 208n6
  The Milesian Chief, 158, 161
Maurice, F. D., 162
Meade, L. T., 106, 220
  'Eyes of Terror', 220
  The Oracle of Maddox Street, 220
  'The Woman with the Hood', 220
Meinhold, William, *Sidonia the Sorceress*, 53
Memento mori, 48
'Micil', 'Augus Bás ar Leabaid!' ('And Death in Bed!'), 143
Milliken, Anna
  Corfe Castle, 32–3, 36
  Eva; an Old Irish Story, 32–3
Milton, John, 49, 51
Mind, 74

Minerva Press, 30–1, 37–8, 39, 42n2, 43n9
Mitchelstown Castle, 101, 102, 103, 104
Monthly Magazine, 199
Moore, Stephen (Earl of Mount Cashel), 104
Moore, Thomas
  'By that Lake Whose Gloomy Shore', 52, 53
  Epistles, Odes, and Other Poems, 53
  Irish Melodies, 53, 58
  Memoirs of Captain Rock, 198
  'O Breathe Not His Name', 58
  Poetical Works of Thomas Little, 53
  'Reuben and Rose', 53
  'The Ring', 53, 198
  'Shall the Harp Then Be Silent', 51
  'Written on Passing Dead-Man's Island', 53
Morning Register, 199
'The Morrígan', 213
Morton, John, *100 Everyday Menaces*, 254, 262–3
Moss, Kate, 108
'Mother Ireland', 57, 213
Mulholland, Rosa
  'About Ghosts', 228n7
  'The Ghost at the Rath', 220
  The Haunted Organist of Hurly Burly and Other Stories, 219, 220
  'The Hungry Death', 219
  'The Lady Tantivy', 220
  'Not to be Taken at Bed-Time', 216–17
  'Wanted an Irish Novelist', 227n4
Munch, Edvard, 85
Murnau, F. W., *Nosferatu*, 85, 92
Museum of Literature Ireland, 4, 21n7

Na Cloigne (*The Heads*), 146
The Nation, 51, 55
national tale, 31, 43n10, 59n3, 157, 158, 205, 235
Newman, Kim, *Anno Dracula*, 2
Ní Choileáin, Orna, *Vampír*, 136
Ní Fhlannagáin, M. I., 'Taidhbhse Dhún Aonghusa' ('The Ghost of Dún Aengus'), 140

Nietzsche, Frederich, 182
Ní Ghráda, Máiréad, *Manannán*, 143
Ní Houlihan, Kathleen, 56–7, 213
Ní Shúilleabháin, Siobhán, *Eoghan*, 264

Oates, Joyce Carol, 235
Ó Bríain, P, 'Taibhse sa Comhrann' ('A Ghost in the Chest/Trunk'), 140
O'Brien, Edna, 214
Ó Brolacháin, Micheál, *Pax Dei*, 145
Ó Cadhain, Máirtín, *Cré na Cille (Graveyard Clay)*, 5
Ó Ceallaigh, Colm, *Éiric Fola*, 252
Ó Ciosáin, Seán, *Árda Wuthering*, 142
Ó Conaire, Pádraic, 'Páidín Mháire', 264
O'Connell, Daniel, 137, 234
O'Connell, Frederick William
  An Dr Jekyll agus Mr Hyde, 142
  Pen name, Conall Cearnach, 142
O'Connor, Frank, 115
O'Connor, Joseph, *Shadowplay*, 1–2, 21n1
O'Connor, Sinead, 90
O'Conor, Charles, 157
Ó Cuirrín, Seán
  'Beirt Dhéiseach' ('Two Waterford Men'), 140–1, 142
  Dracula, 142
Ó Domhnaill, Aodh, *An Duaircéan (The Gloomy One)*, 254, 255–9, 260
O'Donnell, Red Hugh, 223
O'Donoghue, John, *Anam Cara*, 12
Ó Donrabháin, Risteard, 'An Screách!' ('The Scream'), 144
Ó Faoláin, Eamonn, *Uafás Ó'n Alltar* ('Horror from the Far Country'), 144
O'Flaherty, Liam, *Famine*, 264
Ó Guilín, Peadar, *The Call*, 136
O'Leary, Peter, Fr (Peadar ÓLaoghaire / Peadar Ua Laoghaire), *Séadna*, 19, 101, 106–7, 110, 138–9, 145, 252, 264
O'Malley, Brian, *The Lodgers*, 2, 11
Ó Neachtain, Joe Steve, *Lámh Láidir*, 252, 254, 264, 266–7

Ó Nualláin, Gearóid, 'An Sprid' ('The Spirit'), 141
Order of the Golden Dawn, 165–6
Ordnance Survey, 53
Orr, James, 49
  'Elegy, Written in the Church-yard of Templecorran', 50
Ó Ruairc, Micheál
  Daoine a Itheann Daoine (People Who Eat People), 145
  'Séadna', 145
Ó Sándair, Cathal, 143
Ó Súilleabháin, Amhlaoibh, 137
Ó Súilleabháin, Muiris, 'An Sean-Mairneálach agus an Taidhbhse a Chonnaic Sé' ('The Old Sailor and the Ghost that he Saw'), 144
Ó Súilleabháin, Tomás, *Arracht*, 252–3
Ó Torna, Seosamh, 'Duinneall', 142–3
Owenson, Syndey (Lady Morgan), 40, 153, 157, 199, 205, 214, 215
  The O'Briens and the O'Flahertys, 48
  The Wild Irish Girl, 43n10

paganism, 8–16, 22n23, 218
Parker, Stewart, *Pentecost*, 66
Parnell, Charles Stewart, 177, 181, 234
Parnell, Thomas, 'A Night-Piece on Death', 48
Patrick, Mrs F. C.
  The Jesuit, 33–4, 36
  More Ghosts!, 29, 30, 39, 42
Patterson, Glenn, 261
  Burning your Own, 238
Pavlou, George, *Rawhead Rex*, 89
Pearse, Pádraig, 139, 142
Poe, Edgar Allan, 47
  'The Fall of the House of Usher', 239
  'The Raven', 47
Proulx, Annie, *Brokeback Mountain*, 259
Punch, 179

Quinn, Robert, *An Leabhar*, 253

Radcliffe, Ann, 29, 31, 32, 37, 43n8, 105, 140, 154, 160, 161
  The Romance of the Forest, 156

Rapin, Paul de, 33
'The Red Lady of Leap Castle', 213
Reeves, Michael, *Witchfinder General*, 10
The Reviews, 30, 37, 42n1, 43n7
Richard, I, of England (Richard the Lionheart / Richard Coeur-de-Lion), 34–6
Riddell, Charlotte, 17, 19, 20, 160, 228n9
  Frank Sinclair's Wife and Other Stories, 217
  'Hertford O'Donnell's Warning' (also 'The Banshee's Warning'), 217
  The Nun's Curse, 160
  Weird Stories, 160
Roche, Regina Maria, 19, 32, 37, 43n8, 215215
  The Castle Chapel; A Romantic Tale, 37
  The Children of the Abbey, 37–8, 42, 159–60
  Clermont, 29, 30, 37, 38
  The Maid of the Hamlet, 30
  The Tradition of the Castle: or, Scenes in the Emerald Isle, 37
Rockite disturbances, 197
romance, Gothic, 17, 29, 30, 32, 34, 36, 38, 39, 43n7
Rooney, Sally, 20
  Normal People, 238, 239, 248–9
Rose, Peter, *Snatch*, 78
Rossetti, Christina, 'Goblin Market', 47
Rousseau, Jean-Jacques, 38, 39
Rua O'Brien, Máire (Red Mary), 213

St Kevin, 52
St Patrick, 156
St Pierre, Bernardin, *Paul et Virginie*, 37–8
Scott, Walter (Sir), 158, 199
  The Monastery, 157
Second Reformation, 157
Shan, Darren, 108
  Cirque du Freak, 108
Shaw, Fiona, 90
Shelley, Mary, 31
  Frankenstein, 106, 188n3, 259
Shelley, Percy Bysshe, 47

Sheridan, Mark, *Crone Wood*, 11
Shiels, Richard Lalor, *The Apostate*, 66
Shyamalan, M. Night, *The Village*, 14
Sigerson Shorter, Dora
  'All Soul's Eve', 222
  The Father Confessor: Stories of Death and Danger, 222
  'Lady Kathleen', 56–7
  'Man's Discontent', 57
  'The Mother', 222–3
  'The Strange Voice', 222
  'Transmigration', 222
  Verses, 57
Singleton, John (Sir), 194
Society for the Preservation of the Irish Language, 138
Stevenson, Robert Louis, *Strange Case of Dr Jekyll and Mr Hyde*, 142, 147
Stoker, Bram, 161, 162, 165–6, 215
  Dracula, 142, 147, 161, 162–3, 174–93, 253, 259, 262, 264, 266
  The Snake's Pass, 161
  Under the Sunset, 106
Stoker, Charlotte, 185
Stoker, Dacre, *The Undead*, 2
sublime, 20, 50, 51, 57, 114, 115, 118, 240–2
Symbolism, 47, 117, 122, 261
Swinburne, A. G., 10, 47

'Tadhg Tostach', 'Taibhse an Chaisleán', 139
Temple, John (Sir), 255
Tennyson, Alfred (Lord), 162
  'Lady of Shalott', 54, 56
  Maud, 47
Terry, Ellen, 1, 2
Thomas, Dylan, *Under Milk Wood*, 255
Tithe Wars, 164
Titley, Alan, *Stiall Fhial Feola* ('A Generous Cut of Meat'), 145
Tractarianism, 163
Tuam babies controversy, 8
Tuke, James, *Irish Distress and its Remedies*, 160
Tully, Michael, *Don't Leave Home*, 11

Tynan, Katharine, 17, 20
  'The Body-Snatching', 219
  'The Death Spancel', 218
  'The First Wife, 221, 222
  An Isle in the Water, 218, 221
  'The Neglect of Irish Writers', 227n4
  'The Sea's Dead', 217–18

Ua Duinnín, Pádraig, *Creideamh agus Gorta (Faith and Famine)*, 264
Ussher, Archbishop, 155
  A Discourse of the Religion Anciently Professed by the Irish and British, 156

Vlad Tepes, 174
Voltaire, 39

Waite, A. E., 166
Walpole, Horace, 31, 105, 154
  The Castle of Otranto, 33, 34–6, 37, 41, 197
Walsh, Aisling, *The Daisy Chain*, 93
Welch, Robert, *Tearmann*, 145–6
Welles, Orson, 87
  War of the Worlds, 255
Westenra, Warner William (Baron Rosssmore), 177–8, 180
Wheatley, Ben
  A Field in England, 11
  In the Earth, 11
  Kill List, 11
  Sightseers, 11
White, James, 32
  The Adventures of John of Gaunt, 32
  The Adventures of King Richard Coeur-de-Lion, 32, 34–7
  Hints for a Specific Plan for an Abolition of the Slave Trade, and for Relief of the Negroes in the British West Indies, 36
'The White Lady of Malahide Castle', 213
Whyte, Samuel, 49, 51
  A Collection of Poems, on Various Subjects, 48

Wiene, Robert, *The Cabinet of Dr Caligari*, 84–5
Wilde, Lady Jane (Speranza), 46, 55
  Ancient Legends, Mystic Charms, and Superstitions of Ireland, 16, 176–7, 188n9, 228n6
  Driftwood from Scandinavia, 53–4
  Poems, 53
  'The Prisoners', 55–6
  'The Stricken Land', 51
  'Thekla, a Swedish Saga', 53–5, 57
Wilde, Oscar, 3, 21n7, 31, 46, 47, 189n12
  'The Ballad of Reading Gaol', 46, 57–8
  The Happy Prince and Other Tales, 106
  The Picture of Dorian Gray, 2,3, 54, 57
  'Requiescat', 57
Wilkinson, William, *An Account of the Principalities of Wallachia and Moldavia*, 174–5, 178
Wollstonecraft, Mary, 101–2, 204
  Original Stories from Real Life, 19, 101, 102–3, 106, 110
  Thoughts on the Education of Daughters, 101
  A Vindication of the Rights of Woman, 38
Woolf, Virginia, 213, 232
Wright, Jon, *Grabbers*, 11
Wycliffe, John, 154, 155

X case, 109

Yeats, W. B., 12, 46, 73, 89, 123, 166, 214
  On the Boiler, 67
  The Only Jealousy of Emer, 71
  Purgatory, 18, 65, 66, 67–8, 71–2, 76–7
  The Secret Rose, 9–10
  'The Stolen Child', 15, 116, 122–3
  'Swedenborg, Mediums and the Desolate Places', 71
  'Village Ghosts', 13
  A Vision, 71